Voices for African Liberation

Voices for African Liberation:
Conversations with the Review of African Political Economy

Edited by Leo Zeilig, Chinedu Chukwudinma, and Ben Radley

Ebb

First published 2024
© Copyright by the Review of African Political Economy

All rights reserved. No part of this book may be reproduced, stored in a retrieval system, or transmitted by any means, electronic, mechanical, photocopying, recording, or otherwise, without prior permission of the publisher.

Ebb Books, Unit 241, 266 Banbury Road, Oxford, OX2 7DL

PB ISBN: 9781739985202
EB ISBN: 9781739985295

British Library Cataloguing-in-Publication Data
A catalogue record for this book is available from the British library.

Typeset in Dante

roape.net
ebb-books.com

Front cover artwork by Malangatana Valente Ngwenya, 'Cry for Freedom' (1973), MoMA ©

Contents

Old and New Voices of Socialist Change – the Review of African Political Economy*'s Radical Agenda*   i

Part I: Lessons From the Past

    1. John Saul (2015), "Life in a Struggle that Continues!"   2
    2. Hakim Adi (2017), Pan-Africanism and Communism   26
    3. Victoria Brittain (2023), Lives Invisible to Power   37
    4. Jesse Benjamin (2020), A Life of Praxis with Walter Rodney   53
    5. Anne Braithwaite (2021), Walter Rodney and the Working People's Alliance   81
    6. Georges Nzongola-Ntalaja (2021), A People's Historian   100
    7. Reinhart Kössler (2016), Namibia, Genocide and Germany   118
    8. António Tomás (2023), Amílcar Cabral's Life, Legacy and Reluctant Nationalism   129
    9. Pascal Bianchini (2018), Senegal's Street Fighting Years   141
    10. Explo Nani-Kofi (2016), Rawlings and Radical Change in Ghana   146
    11. Mosa Phadi (2018), Understanding Steve Biko   160
    12. Tamás Szentes (2018), To Be Bravely Critical of Reality   169
    13. Frej Stambouli (2021), When I Was a Student of Fanon   180
    14. Jean Copans (2019), Radical Scepticism   188

Part II: Weapon of Theory

    15. Samir Amin (2017), Revolutionary Change in Africa   201
    16. Issa Shivji (2021), Let a Hundred Socialist Flowers Bloom   216
    17. Lena Anyuolo (2021), Politics, Poetry and Struggle   230
    18. Max Ajl (2021), A People's Green New Deal   237
    19. Ndongo Sylla (2022), Economics and Politics for Liberation   251

20. Tunde Zack-Williams (2021), Alternatives to Western Prescriptions	265
21. Lyn Ossome (2019), Talking Back	280
22. Hannah Cross (2021), Borders and Corporate Domination	290
23. Ray Bush (2022), Justice, Equality and Struggle	298
24. Yusuf Serunkuma (2021), Oil, Capitalists and the Wretched of Uganda	311
25. Nombuso Mathibela (2017), Protest, Racism and Gender in South Africa	317
26. David Seddon (2021), Riots, Protests and Global Adjustment	326

Part III: Militants at Work

27. Abioudun Olamosu (2017), Looking Back to Move Forward	347
28. Nnimmo Bassey (2021), Extraction-Driven Devastation	359
29. Bienvenu Matumo (2022), The Struggle for Change in the Congo	365
30. Trevor Ngwane (2016), South Africa's Fork in the Road	373
31. Antonater Tafadzwa Choto (2016), Resistance, Crisis and Workers in Zimbabwe	393
32. Yao Graham (2016), Pan-African Challenges	401
33. Guy Marius Sagna (2021), Decolonising a Neo-Colony	413
34. Esther Stanford-Xosei (2022), Afrika and Reparations Activism in the UK	424
35. Femi Aborisade (2019), The Roots of the Crisis in Nigeria	436
36. Irene Asuwa and Cidi Otieno (2022), Imperialism and GMOs in Kenya	452
37. Habib Ayeb (2018), Food Sovereignty and the Environment	466
38. Marjorie Mbilinyi (2017), Gender and Politics in Africa	487
Glossary of Acronyms	507
Index	511

Old and New Voices of Socialist Change – the Review of African Political Economy's Radical Agenda

In 1974, 50 years ago, the newly launched *Review of African Political Economy* (*ROAPE*) journal boldly announced its intentions in the first editorial, "Appropriate analysis and the devising of a strategy for Africa's revolution must be encouraged and we hope that the provision of this platform for discussion will assist that process". The question of what is to be done to change Africa's capitalist underdevelopment was also answered, "an anti-capitalist class struggle … as a reminder that liberation is still on the agenda for most of the African continent". The review was born in a period of great, radical hope. The continent, like the world, was being transformed not simply by the political and economic forces of capitalism, but by major social struggles. These counter-hegemonic movements were not only a challenge to this or that policy or discrimination – as great as these struggles were – but frequently to the entire social and political order.

The global 1968, as it is now described, played out in Africa as much as it did in Europe and North America. As South African-based writer Heike Becker told us in 2017, "students and workers in a range of African countries … contributed to the global uprising with their own interpretations, from Senegal and South Africa to the Congo, to mention just a few. Yet, those African revolts and protests have been forgotten in the global discourse of commemoration". There were movements from below that joined up with and were part of the same energy for transformation and revolution felt across the world – even if they were generated by distinct dynamics.

By 1974, progressive change on the continent, which since

independence had frequently come from above in the form of big state projects of change, had started to flounder. Even in Tanzania, once regarded as the Mecca of revolution, the project of *ujamaa* (cooperation, or familyhood) was beginning to spoil. To a generation who saw hope in Julius Nyerere's and the Tanganyika African National Union's (TANU) efforts to reverse a long, brutal history of colonial underdevelopment, cynicism had begun to emerge about the appearance of a new class of exploiters, a petty-bourgeoisie, or bureaucratic elite. Tanzania in 1974, where several founders of the review first cut their political teeth, was no longer the dynamic force it had once been.

Early state-led projects proclaiming socialism elsewhere on the continent had also started to fail or had been overturned. In Ghana, Kwame Nkrumah – the "father of African independence" and one of the main advocates of African socialism – had been overthrown in an American backed coup in 1966. In Guinea, Algeria, Egypt, and Congo-Brazzaville, left-leaning projects and the socialist politics of the first wave of independence were looking fragile, and often oppressive. Yet, independence was still being keenly fought for in large parts of the continent, and in these late independence movements, or second wave of liberation struggles, new and radical forces seemed to promise real independence, and a socialism grounded in each country's specificities.

The first issue in 1974 was enthusiastic about these possibilities, noting in the editorial there were "valuable lessons for the mobilisation of popular forces throughout the continent, but also a specific determination on the part of the liberation movements and the peoples, notably in Guinea, Angola and Mozambique, not to settle for token independence and continued economic domination". Or as Ruth First, one of the founders of the review, described in 1975 to her husband – Joe Slovo – after a visit to newly independent Mozambique, "I may say I'm thrilled to bits. Tanzania is one thing, but Mozambique! Wow". Two years later, she moved to Maputo to contribute to the transformation of the country.

Frantz Fanon – the greatest theorist of national liberation – had argued in his 1961 classic, *The Wretched of the Earth*, that only in armed struggle was real liberation a prospect. So, it was to these new, second phase liberation struggles – which had seen hard and long armed resistance to colonial occupation – that the hopes of socialism and transformation could be firmly pegged. Amílcar Cabral, the great leader of Guinea-Bissau's late independence, saw in the earlier wave of struggle the inherited state as the central failure: "It's the most important problem in liberation movements. The problem is perhaps the secret of the failure of African independence".

By the mid-1970s, the first issues were being written, copy-edited, typeset, then collated, folded, and put into hand-addressed envelopes and sent around Africa, to liberation movements, political prisoners – including smuggled to African National Congress (ANC) and South African Community Party (SACP) prisoners on Robben Island, wrapped in Christmas paper! – and to universities and activists around the world.

The journal – or the "new platform" as it was described in the first editorial – was enthralled by Guinea-Bissau's independence in 1974 along with Angola and Mozambique the following year in 1975, countries that seemed to promise real liberation and socialist transformation in the victory against Portuguese colonialism. *ROAPE* saw itself as a fraternal, broad, though Marxist platform, supporting these movements and helping, where possible, with the exceptionally difficult issues of socialist development. Yet this was not a scholarly activity, far from it. As the first editorial pointed out, "merely providing an alternative analysis could be ... emptily 'academic'. It is hoped therefore that our contributors will also address themselves to those issues concerned with the actions needed if Africa is to develop its potential".

Agency was vital, with a range of questions being asked about the subjective factors of liberation. Among the questions the review posed were what role was there for the state? Could it be wielded for radical change? What about the development and role of popular classes in political change? Who powered the new movements on the continent, and was there a viable socialist project in the renewed struggles for national liberation? What role did the working class play, were they the agents in the projects for socialist reconstruction or the recipients of reforms from above?

In these early days these questions were vital. They could be seen in the debate between Ruth First and [anthropologist] Archie Mafeje in *ROAPE*'s pages in 1978 about the meaning of the Soweto uprising in 1976 in South Africa, or in the discussions on the intervention of Cuban forces in Angola from 1975. The Cuban intervention was celebrated by some at the review while others remained sceptical. Were Cuban troops not in Angola to make sure the oil (and profits) from American owned rigs in Cabinda continued to flow? As part of this security detail, Cuban troops were required to repress striking workers. The contradictions abounded, and arguments raged on.

ROAPE was also clear about its role in providing a forum for the debates on the frailty of socialist projects from above, intended as direct interventions which could explain and assist the movements and new governments attempting to challenge the continent's underdevelopment. Many of its early members – John Saul, Peter Lawrence, Ruth First, Robin Cohen, Mejid Hussein, Duncan Innes, Mustafa Khogali, Katherine Levine, Jitendra Mohan, Gavin Williams – were militants in these new projects, in one way or another. Yet, in these years there was always a tension at the heart of the review's radical endeavour. A tug of war between state-led, top-down projects for socialist change, and class struggle – in the strikes and workers' occupations in Tanzania in 1973, the strikes of oil workers in Angola, or the uprisings across South Africa after 1976, for example – empowering change from below. This tension, from above or below, remains alive in *ROAPE* today.

In 2014, the Editors of *ROAPE* wanted to connect to a new generation of radicals on the continent and elsewhere, who were involved and interested in socialist politics and revolutionary change. The connection was a homecoming for the journal, where the Review's heart had always been, but to some extent we had become lost in the thicket of academia and publishing. Many barriers stood in our way: paywalls that locked down our content, academic grants, career advancement and research assessments, and the deadweight of post-structuralism. Yet much was with us. The spirit of the period contained prodigious revolutionary energy, in the celebrated and tragically defeated struggles in North Africa and the Middle East, but also in the almost entirely unreported revolutionary wave further south – most remarkably in Burkina Faso, Nigeria, and Senegal. Roape.net was launched in 2014. For a decade, roape.net has been a forum for radical commentary, analysis and debate on political economy and the vibrant protest movements and rebellions on the continent. One of the most exciting areas of the website has been our interviews. These interviews – perhaps more than any other part of the website – bring to life older voices of liberation, frequently hidden, or lost histories, and newer initiatives, projects and activists who are engaged in the contemporary struggles to reshape Africa: to make, win, and sustain a revolutionary transformation in our devastated world.

In the pages that follow, we present an edited selection featuring 38 of these interviews conducted between 2015 and 2023, organised into three parts. The first part, Lessons from the Past, focuses on historical movements, figures, and periods – from Walter Rodney, Amílcar Cabral, and Steve Biko to Ghana, Senegal, and Tanzania in the 1960s and 1970s, and beyond – as part of the vital process of learning from past defeats and victories to inform contemporary struggle.

The second part, Weapon of Theory, should not be mistaken for abstract theorising. On the contrary, the section features conversations with organic intellectuals and committed scholar-activists of national and international renown whose prime focus and concern is on developing theory from real-world observation to inform revolutionary struggle and transformative change. As

Amílcar Cabral said in his speech of the same title, delivered in 1966 to the first Tricontinental Conference of the Peoples of Asia, Africa and Latin America held in Havana, "every practice produces a theory, and [if] it is true that a revolution can fail even though it be based on perfectly conceived theories, nobody has yet made a successful revolution without a revolutionary theory".

The third and final part, Militants at Work, covers a range of contemporary anti-imperialist and anti-capitalist struggles, as told by those directly involved. It moves from Shell Oil in Nigeria, anti-imperialism in Senegal, and reparations activism in the United Kingdom, to food sovereignty in Kenya and North Africa, campaigning against patriarchal oppression in Tanzania, and crisis and resistance in Zimbabwe. The full archive of interviews, along with all other material on the site, can be found at www.roape.net.

www.roape.net

Part I: Lessons From the Past

1. John Saul (2015), "Life in a Struggle that Continues!"

John Saul was an author for and then an editor of *ROAPE* from its beginnings in 1974. He spent many years teaching, writing about and participating in attempts to realise profound social, political and economic change – liberation and socialism – in Tanzania, Mozambique and South Africa. In Canada, he was a long-time activist in the southern African anti-apartheid solidarity movement. Throughout his life, Saul remained committed to anti-imperialist and anti-capitalist work in Canada, Africa and elsewhere. Here, he speaks to David MacDonald, a professor at the University of Toronto, about his involvement in African liberation struggles of the 1960s and 1970s. He also reflects more broadly on the past 50 years of struggle on the continent, with a particular focus on South Africa, and provides an assessment of the potential for a pan-African anti-capitalist movement in the coming decades.[1]

***

You've been involved in liberation struggles in Southern Africa for a long time. When and why did you first get involved?

---

1   As John Saul (1938-2023) wrote about this interview: "The following interview, carried out expertly by my friend David MacDonald of Queen's University was, several years ago, to have appeared a part of a Festschrift then being prepared in my name. I'm happy to have the interview disinterred by Leo Zeilig here for the inaugural issue of roape.net and hope it may be of interest. In fact, it seems to me quite fitting since I was actually onboard as an author in the very first print issue of *ROAPE* in 1974. Indeed, with one brief hiccough, I've been an editor of one sort or another of *ROAPE* since the very beginning. I also think *ROAPE* has stuck pretty successfully to its mission as a radical voice in African Studies and I'm proud to have been a part of it over all these years, including as an active participant in this new venture [roape.net] that seeks to keep *ROAPE* even more on top of events and ever-present in the fight for humane and equitable outcomes both on the continent and more widely."

I first went to Africa to teach in Tanzania from 1965 to 1972. Those were exciting times, the years of the Arusha Declaration and of the heyday of Tanzanian socialism. I myself became involved, as did many others, in the struggles for change that then took place throughout the society – principally, in my case, in efforts to move the University too in a more socialist-relevant (in terms of pedagogy and academic practice) direction. True, as things transpired, I was soon to be fired for such activities by Canada's External Aid, my original employer, but I was then strongly encouraged to take up a local contract. This I did quite happily for a number of years (although, as the contradictions inside Tanzania deepened, I was eventually to find that contract terminated as well). But I had learned a great deal and written a lot (especially with Giovanni Arrighi and Lionel Cliffe) during my years in Dar es Salaam and had made many close friends, both Tanzanians and expatriates.

In addition, Dar es Salaam during those years was the key centre for the various liberation movements engaged in struggle in the white-ruled territories further south – and I got to know them all. This was especially true with respect to Mozambique's Frelimo for I was soon working with them on their English language publications – while learning a great deal more, as I went along, about what was happening in southern Africa more generally. Then, in 1972, and as I prepared to leave Dar, Samora Machel, Frelimo's President, came to see me and invited me to travel with a group of Mozambican guerillas deep into their country to see for myself the liberated areas there and to gauge the meaning of Frelimo's struggle. When I got back to Tanzania from this "long march" Machel then asked me to speak out, when I returned to Canada, about Frelimo's efforts and about what I had learned. Looking back, I can see that my life-long involvement in the struggle for liberation in southern Africa, and in encouraging Canadians to also take it seriously, was grounded both in this direct experience and in Samora's request.

In retrospect, the late 1960s and early 70s were particularly fertile years for progressive scholarship and activism in Africa. Were you aware, at the time, of how momentous this period was, and how did it shape the way you saw yourself as a scholar-activist?

You're right, it was a fertile moment indeed. In Tanzania, in Mozambique, in southern Africa more generally, you felt that you were swimming with the tide of history for a change, and not merely against it. There were people – I think in particular of Cabral, Eduardo Mondlane, Samora Machel – and movements – Frelimo certainly – in which you could ground both your hopes and your writing, as a comrade in revolutionary change as well as a careful scholar: a "scholar activist," as you say.

Of course, we were well aware of countertrends: Frantz Fanon's *Wretched of the Earth* became a particularly resonant point of reference in both my teaching and writing during these years, especially his powerful Chapter 3, "The Pitfalls of National Consciousness." We also knew – as I would discover at closer hand when I returned to Canada in 1972 – that western countries and global capitalism itself did not wish such revolutionary aspirations in southern Africa well: indeed Frelimo was to invite me, of all unlikely people, rather than the Canadian government, to come to Maputo on behalf of our now active Toronto Committee for the Liberation of Southern Africa in order to represent the Canadian people at Mozambique's independence day celebration in 1975 – precisely because Canada had been on the wrong side, the side of Portuguese colonialism, during their struggle!

In short, in a whole host of ways we did know that something momentous was afoot, part of a promising global shift towards socialism and genuine independence that was even more clearly exemplified by Vietnam's historic victory. And we basked in it and took inspiration from it – even though, momentous as it was, the moment of triumph also proved to be transitory. To be honest, we didn't quite grasp just how fleeting such victories would prove to be… Or just how strong the forces pulling southern Africa back into the orbit of recolonisation actually were.

Despite this, there's no doubting that these instances of genuine accomplishment – like the on-going struggles for freedom that, beyond 1975 and well into the 1990s, continued in Zimbabwe, in Namibia and in South Africa itself – shaped many of us profoundly. Cumulatively, living this history helped lock me personally firmly into the role of scholar-activist – ever more committed to an anti-capitalist/anti-imperialist politics, to a closely-linked intellectual practice as both teacher and writer, and to the genuine liberation of Africa. As I still am.

Can you expand a bit on the ups and downs of the past 50 years of struggle in the region: what would say have been the biggest successes (sustained or otherwise) and what have been the biggest disappointments?

The past 50 years have seen both successes and disappointments, the biggest success being, without question, the removal, by armed liberation movements and by dramatic popular mobilisation, of the parasitic – evil seems not too dramatic a word for it – grip of racist rule as defined by the dominance of whites in firmly institutionalised positions of power (apartheid and the like). Of course, things have not yet turned out quite as many of us had hoped they would in terms of the attendant realisation of class and gender equality and the establishment of genuine democratic control by the poorest of the poor in the region. Yet this, in political and cultural terms, was a great triumph – and one that, due to genuinely heroic efforts by the people of southern Africa, occurred rather against the odds.

One must hope that some memory of the accomplishments of the "thirty years war for southern African liberation" (1960-1990) survives, however, for it could be one resource useful to any attempt to spawn a next liberation struggle. And make no mistake: this is what is desperately needed presently in southern Africa. Indeed, to return to the question asked, the failure of the region's liberation struggles, once their leaders had come to power, to make any very dramatic difference, economically and in many other ways, to the lives of the vast mass of the population there constitutes the greatest single disappointment of recent years, both for residents of the region as well as for any committed outsider who would wish the peoples of southern Africa well. Put simply, in fact, the region has been recolonised by global capital in the wake of its ostensible liberation and the grim results – in terms both of continuing poverty and exploitation by capital, both global and local, and of an absence of any meaningful popular empowerment – are all too evident.

The neoliberal turn of the African National Congress in South Africa has been one of these disappointments. Mainstream analysts tell us that the ANC had no choice but to become market-friendly – given the collapse of the Soviet Union and the potential for white, reactionary revolt – and yet there seemed to be a period in the early 1990s where a more transformative politics seemed possible. What, if anything, do you think could have shifted the balance at that time?

The simplest answer would be that the ANC leadership had come, primarily, to represent aspirant black middle-class elements (a tendency never, from the outset, far from the surface of the movement in any case) who saw little advantage, to themselves, to lie in the pursuit of more egalitarian and socialist policies. The Soviet Union argument is a bit of a canard here because, although that country had been close to many in the ANC leadership, it exemplified no real socialist alternative anyway, entirely hostile to the kind of democratic empowerment of the mass of the South African population that could alone have dissuaded the ANC leadership from taking the line of least resistance towards global capitalism.

That said, it is obviously true that great pressure springing from the global capitalist system was also crucial. As were both white mining, financial and commercial capital players within the country itself and the full range of additional black aspirants, from within the state and private sectors (the Black Economic Empowerment set), to personal economic advancement. To deflect these various pressures would have required a great deal more commitment to popular mobilisation and continuing struggle to realise a broad-scale liberation than the ANC (including, I'm sorry to say, Mandela himself) was interested in.

For starters there was probably more room for active popular empowerment, egalitarian policies, and defiance of imperial dictate – in the honeymoon period of possibility that existed after first overcoming apartheid at any rate – than the ANC ever conceived of availing itself of. The questions then multiply: did the ANC elite become just too comfortable in their own novel power and privilege? Were they simply tired of struggle? Or perhaps too nervous about the risks involved in defying a generally hostile world? Or what?

For the fact is (as Rusty Bernstein has argued) that, either due to mere class opportunism or to failure of nerve, they turned their backs on genuine mass politics (running down rather than further enabling any independent and on-going UDF (United Democratic Front) initiative, for example) – and on real popular liberation. They thus settled comfortably for SA's becoming, in Neville Alexander's chilling characterisation of the country's post-apartheid landscape, "just another country," one marked by the acceptance, on the part of the ANC, of extreme inequality and of a very soft landing indeed for both global capital and the new African elite.

And what of the other members of the Alliance – COSATU (Congress of South African Trade Unions) and the SACP? What is your take on their acquiescence at that time?

On the COSATU side, with liberation the union made a fateful miscalculation – a failure, encouraged by the ANC, to cast its lot with various grass-roots organisations still struggling within civil society but instead to link itself ever more closely to the party in power. But this absorption – oh, so tempting, even for a movement that had been so crucial to the resistance to apartheid inside South Africa – into a (not terribly effective) proximity to power was also being reinforced by sociological and organisational trends. An increasingly high percentage of workers in South Africa were marginalised, semi-employed and/or informally employed and certainly not organised (within COSATU or any other union body). Increasingly, COSATU (and its leaders!) has found itself the organisation of a kind of labour aristocracy, incapable of reaching out to the vast mass of the unorganised and the marginalised in both the urban and rural areas in order to build the left force that the ANC has refused to become.

The SACP, for its part, was, historically, a pretty Stalinist outfit, important though its links to the Soviet Union had been in getting the ANC favoured status as a movement to be armed and otherwise assisted. Neither the Soviet Union nor the SACP directed the ANC of course, but the SACP did have an important role in shaping the ANC's form of radicalism, albeit one of a distinctly Stalinist, vanguardist and not particularly left character: much more rhetorical than real, as events would soon show. At the same time, the SACP was also imprisoning itself within a nationalist movement problematic – where it still finds itself. It has a certain radical base, and some of its members are now mildly left-wing Ministers (under Zuma). But the party is chiefly to be thought of as just one more agent of ANC power, wielded from above.

In short, both COSATU and the SACP remain players within post-apartheid South Africa, but players who have been primarily defined by their short-sighted opportunism: definitely, at the moment, part of the country's problem rather than part of its solution!

Where does this leave the struggle for more radical liberation in South Africa today? What are the potential rupture points, who can pry them open, and how might things be done?

Living now far from the frontline, I'll refrain from offering too precise a recipe as to the most effective and appropriate form of on-going struggle. Nonetheless, some facts are clear. There are vast numbers of people who are dissatisfied in South Africa and with good reason. This discontent can all too easily curdle, as we have seen, into crime, xenophobia, violence against women and the like in the absence of a convincing and resonant counter-hegemonic socio-economic imaginary and a movement that can give such an imaginary full expression. In other words, the challenge for the aggrieved is to craft increasingly effective long-term vehicles that give clearer and more sustained political voice to their grievances and through which they could press them ever more forcefully and appositely.

Of course, one has already seen many such positive expressions of protest, the apparent building blocks of a counter-hegemony so to speak. I felt, for example, that I saw something of this for myself as early as 2002 when I had the opportunity to join many thousands (20,000 plus) of demonstrators, representing the Anti-Privatisation Forum, the Landless People's Movement and the like, as we marched from impoverished Alexandra township to affluent Sandton to protest against the ANC (it was then hosting in Johannesburg a World Summit on Social Development) – although, unfortunately, at the time, such protest could not long sustain itself at that high level. But I also felt the same kind of oppositional energy to be close at hand when I was invited to speak, in Cape Town and under the banner of the Municipal Services Project, to a large and impressive workshop of activists from the townships and rural settlements in 2007. It was difficult, in fact, not to sense that the initiatives those comrades represented were the seeds of something much broader in the making.

Even more striking are the statistics of fledgling resistance to the present system's severe defaults – as expressed in short-falls in housing, electricity supply, water and sanitation, in the lack of availability of meaningful skill-training and of jobs, and in the massive inequality that is now twinned so dramatically to widespread corruption. "Service delivery protests," as they are termed, are rampant, said to be at a rate that is among the very highest in the world – and the level of very real anger is also marked. True, such anger has still not found its voice as a firm, coordinated and proto-hegemonic political force. Nonetheless it is around such issues, and with the further release of these palpable popular energies, that the dispiriting stalemate and profound sense of anti-climax that has come to define post-apartheid South Africa might really be beginning to be pried open.

As you note, much of this new resistance is being led by social movements and community groups, often in conflict with unions that are seen to be too cosy with the ANC. Some commentators see this as a healthy move away from restrictive class politics that open up a broader potential for counter-hegemonic action and dialogue, while others are concerned that it runs the risk of losing coherent analytical punch and practical force. What are your thoughts on this?

I think that, despite some small risk of a possible loss of focus and clout in the formula you first suggest, it is indeed time to get away from any too rigid a preoccupation with exclusively class-derived concepts of revolutionary agency – not least with regard to southern Africa. Of course, Marx had good reason to emphasise the role of the working class in divining potentially revolutionary contradictions within a capitalist mode of production: it was the most exploited (at least in the technical sense in which he deployed the word) and is also brought together as a potentially self-conscious class by the very capitalist dynamic of concentration and centralisation that has also defined its exploitation. It is not surprising that Marx's formulation has served as the staple of left thinking and action for generations.

Yet there is a vast multitude beyond the ranks of the organised working class (and their workplaces) who also live, in southern Africa, in teeming urban and peri-urban settings where social inequality is at its most extreme. There is a whole range of legitimate urban grievances – service delivery (health, housing, electricity, water, education and so much more) and unemployment, for starters – that are on the agenda and that people are seeking to deal with directly at the grassroots and on their home ground. And this is not even to begin to speak about the more desperate situation in many of the rural areas – from where people are teeming to the cities!

Here I'll throw in a favourite quotation of mine, if you'll permit me, one that is entirely apposite, I think. It's from a book by Ken Post and Phil Wright and it hits the mark directly:

> The working out of capitalism in parts of the periphery prepares not only the minority working class but peasants and other working people, women, youth and minorities for a socialist solution, even though the political manifestation of this may not initially take the form of a socialist movement. In the case of those who are not wage labourers (the classical class associated with that new order) capitalism has still so permeated the social relations which determine their existences... that to be liberated from it is their only salvation. The objective need for socialism of these elements can be no less than that of the worker imprisoned in the factory and disciplined by the whip of unemployment. The price [of capitalism] is paid in even the most "successful" of the underdeveloped countries, and others additionally experience mass destitution. Finding another path has ... become a desperate necessity if the alternative of continuing, if not increasing, barbarism is to be escaped.

Yes! But bear in mind too that the working class, even when so broadly and inclusively defined, is cut across by fissures and hierarchies and divisions (along lines of race, ethnicity and gender, to go no further afield) that can impede its self-consciousness and its collective practice. Moreover, self-evidently, such identities can also speak to grievances and demands that are entirely real in their own right and therefore cannot be glibly reduced and subordinated to the rigid terms of a slogan like class struggle.

Yet such identities and the grievances they give rise to cannot stand alone either. For they are best understood as festering most flagrantly within the selfish, unequal and individualistic ethos of a capitalist society. I'd say that the bearers of such identities – alongside feminists, environmentalists, anti-racists, activists around issues of sexual orientation and the like – must join into a broader community-in-the-making and within a universalising project of anti-capitalist transformation. That's what the best of militants in South Africa and beyond are beginning to do even as we speak.

Note, too, one other corollary of this kind of approach to movement building. For the inevitable tensions and differences of emphasis between the bearers of such diverse goals and purposes will not then simply disappear, even under the umbrella of a broadly shared socialist purpose. In short, no vanguardist edict can cancel out the necessity that such a project be a firmly democratic one. This enlarged definition of class struggle underscores the pressing need for more open methods of negotiation of both the means and the ends of revolutionary work than has characterised most past socialist undertakings. This will be true both in mobilising the forces to launch revolutionary change and in sustaining the process of socialist construction in the long run. Hard work plus genuine democracy then – but South Africans have a future to win.

How does one operationalise this democratic process/practice in South Africa, where there is a dominant party that claims left-wing credentials yet marginalises any radical thought and action, a union movement and communist party that shows few signs of progressive resistance, and a fragmented and under-resourced set of social movements, particularly in rural areas? When compared to Latin America, South Africa seems a long way from any sustained anti-capitalist realisation. What is your practical advice to people working on the ground?

A very tough question. You can see why I've chosen to become an historian in my old age, primarily seeking to trace the evolution of the Thirty Years War (1960-1990) for southern African liberation both in the region itself and, as a world-wide liberation support/anti-apartheid movement, more globally. In fact, I feel myself (as I said previously) to now be just too far from the nitty-gritty of struggles on the ground in southern Africa to any longer have a real right to speak on such pressing contemporary matters.

That said, I do feel the way you summarise the current situation is accurate, albeit quite bleakly phrased. But at the same time, it's a bit like the futility and disempowerment many of us, both in the region itself and beyond, felt some fifty years ago – after Sharpeville and the like. To argue that the Portuguese, the Rhodies and the Nats could all be defeated: now that really seemed fanciful. But, of course, it wasn't.

Moreover, it ain't over yet – that's what I would want to say to people on the ground (who don't really need me to tell them this, in any case). True, some would argue that there are too many on the left in South Africa who merely wallow in a sell-out narrative regarding the ANC and what has happened in the past 20 years in the country. But I'm not convinced that this is the truth. In fact, most of the sceptics (sceptical, to be clear, regarding the actual liberatory content of "liberation") whom I know well are largely correct in their negative evaluations of what has occurred in South Africa.

More importantly, most such sceptics are also, in fact, actively involved simultaneously in the kind of painstaking work – within civil society and the interstices of the system (from the Treatment Action Campaign to the Anti-Privatisation Forum) – that gives promise of real human betterment and substantive change. At minimum, such work is immensely helpful and healing – on very many fronts – to ordinary people in the present difficult moment. But one senses that it is also sowing the seeds of the kind of more general challenge to the status quo – radical reform, in the militant sense of that concept forged by Gorz and Kagarlitsky – that promises, cumulatively, to be substantively revolutionary. Here, in short, is the basis for the necessary next liberation struggle in

South/southern Africa that I have evoked in the title of a recent book of mine.

True, it is certainly the case that such instances of resistance as continue to manifest themselves in southern Africa haven't yet begun to add up into a forceful counter-hegemonic movement (as they apparently have begun to do in some parts of Latin America, for example). The ANC still lives, for popular consumption, off its liberation history and its struggle credentials. And, as I said earlier, COSATU and the SACP are far too comfortable with their insider status to help in overcoming the fragmentation of the left and in facilitating any efforts by others to wage, publicly and entirely confidently, full-fledged anti-capitalist struggle. And these are problems, to put it mildly.

But this is simply to say, trite but true, that the struggle continues. Myself, perhaps I'm just too Irish to quit. More generally, though, we must take hope from the fact that the numbers (made up of the vast and swelling ranks of the exploited and the marginalised) are, potentially, on our side, the revolutionary side, in southern Africa – and more globally as well! Here's the basis for what I once called, in South Africa, a possible small-a alliance of popular forces (as distinct from the big-A alliance of the ANC, the SACP and COSATU): a genuine and increasingly effective movement in the making, what the late Fatima Meer was no doubt anticipating when she spoke of the need for a South African Social Forum separate from and opposed to the wielders of established power. Of course, the other side (imperialism and its local henchmen) is trying too, but the stakes – in terms of human decency, equity and equality – are simply too high for us, here or there, to merely walk away from the table.

And what of other countries in the region, where social and class forces are very different and where many nations remain under the (sub)imperial thumb of a re-energised South Africa? Do you see similar potential for "small-a" alliances? If so, where, and what is the potential for a broader regional (or even pan-African) anti-capitalist movement in the next 10-20 years?

For the moment South Africa seems the most promising site for the genesis of a counter-hegemonic political project – and we've already discussed just how difficult it is to see anything transformative happening anytime soon even there. Elsewhere in the region the prospect for a renewed challenge to the debilitating stranglehold of global capital and its local puppets (a term I don't feel comfortable in using but, under the circumstances, it's difficult to think of an alternative) is even less immediately promising.

For example, I've recently felt forced to write extremely pessimistically of Mozambique in whose national left experiment I had once invested many of my own hopes. And Zimbabwe, so bedevilled by the horrors perpetrated by Mugabe and his cruel coterie of ZANU (Zimbabwe African National Union) followers (and by the support this gang receives from countries like South Africa, Mozambique ... and China), has seen the high hopes once placed in the more promising kind of opposition originally offered by the Movement for Democratic Change (MDC) there forced to wither. Angola, Namibia: not pretty pictures either, as other contributors to the volume of *AfricaFiles* I've just referred to soberly attest.

As for myself, I've also written both an article a year or two ago on what I called the strange death of liberated southern Africa and another on the far too narrow notion of liberation that we have been content to settle for – national and racial liberation (up to a point), but not also a parallel liberation in class, gender and other terms. In evaluating the liberation struggle in southern Africa in these broader terms, the results of the liberation struggle must thus be seen as having been very mixed – and I speak as one who devoted a great many years to liberation support and anti-apartheid work both in the region itself and also here in Canada.

But as I've already told you, I've now become a card-carrying historian and consequently have felt constrained to hand in my crystal ball and to return my prognosticator-of-the-future badge. That doesn't mean I no longer care about future outcomes and, in fact, the "next 10-20 years" that you mention does seem like a long time, with the situation – in terms of inequality and sheer penury, of disease (AIDS, for starters) and malnutrition, of environmental despoliation – just too drastic for us to easily imagine that people, especially in the global South, will passively accept their fate.

Dare to struggle, dare to win. I quite simply don't feel I/we have got any other choice, as trite as that cliché sounds and as bleak as things look right now. But I'll keep any of the dark thoughts about the future that occasionally assail me to myself, if you don't mind. Instead, I'll hope to continue to hear more hopeful ones both from engaged activists on the ground who are seeking to assist more positive things to happen there and also from other contributors to this volume who, more actively than I am now able to do, are taking the pulse of the theory and practice of the moment.

Let's return, then, to the 1970s, and your role in creating awareness about, and activism against, repression in Southern Africa from your home base in Canada. You were instrumental in the establishment and continuation of the Toronto Committee for the Liberation of Portugal's African Colonies (TCLPAC) (later the Toronto Committee for the Liberation of Southern Africa (TCLSAC)), and an editor of Southern Africa Report (from 1985-2000). What impact did these organisations and publications have on the anti-apartheid struggle in Canada and on Canada's official (or unofficial) policies towards oppressive regimes in the region?

I've actually written quite a bit on this (as have others), including in my own memoir, *Revolutionary Traveller*, and also in a long report I've recently done about the North American front of struggle for a research project, sponsored by the region's own Southern African Development Community, on the world-wide liberation support/anti-apartheid movement. It's very difficult to tell our precise impact on western policy, of course. What we can say at minimum, perhaps, is that our efforts and those of other like-minded militants across Canada communicated to and reinforced the confidence of the liberation movements in the region itself by demonstrating that they were not without friends and supporters in Canada and other imperial centres (whose elites otherwise tended, for commercial and investment reasons, to back white power).

That said, we also ruffled the feathers of the right people, corporate and governmental, here in Canada with our campaigns that targeted government complicity with racial rule and corporate investment in oppression. We hosted the liberation movements in Canada, we wrote and publicised the situation, through various media, a lot, we held endless meetings (including our popular "Cinema of Solidarity" series), and we mounted what we felt to be imaginative assaults upon such things as government support for Portugal through NATO, Canadian banks and their unconscionable loans to apartheid, Gulf Oil Canada's exploitative involvement in Angola, the Hudson's Bay Company and its pursuit of karakul pelts in Namibia, and Canadian mining companies like Falconbridge in a variety of regional settings. We know, for example, that, in retaliation, Gulf Oil infiltrated a corporate spy into our TCLPAC ranks during our public campaigns against the company in the 1970s, and though we caught and expelled him pretty quickly who knows how many others may have sought to follow in his wake; we were extremely open and transparent (and penetrable) in our activities after all. Who knows? Just last year, for example, when I finally managed to extract the CSIS file on TCLPAC/TCLSAC from the National Archives it was, quite legally but entirely immorally, stripped by the government of well over 50% of its contents – for security reasons, it was said, albeit 30 or 40 years after the fact! What remains does speak, furtively, to moments of governmental infiltration by individuals (names not revealed!) into our ranks, but who knows what else was on those whited-out pages!

It was the successes of the movements in the region itself that made the main running, of course. Soon the Mulroney government – though, fixated on "terrorists" and "reds," it remained extremely reluctant to give any aid and comfort to the liberation movements themselves, including the ANC – was faced with the reality of the latter's success, the parallel success of wide-spread popular resistance in the townships and beyond, as well as some continuing embarrassment at home (we liked to think). At that point, "official Canada" began to distance itself from apartheid (well before Reagan, before Thatcher, who were both more racist than Mulroney could ever be), becoming a prominent cheerleader for liberation as recolonisation. Our government now readied itself, in short, to egg on Canadian corporations to join in on the suffocating embrace of the "New South Africa" by the global empire of capital: business and exploitation as usual, hold the racism please.

So, by the end of the thirty years war for southern African liberation it was clear that we, in the region and beyond, had won a significant victory. And yet it was also a pyrrhic one: difficult, in short, to know whether to cheer or to cry, especially as the modesty of the ANC's intentions once in power became apparent. In Toronto we did keep our own magazine, *Southern Africa Report/ SAR*, going until 2000 hoping to be an active part in any on-going struggle in southern Africa that might be forthcoming. But, to most Canadians, the initial appearances of liberation were more graphic than was the sober reality apparently. Though many militants from the anti-apartheid days did move on to other fronts of the global justice struggle, the movement in Canada for equity and equality in southern Africa had, like apartheid itself, simply melted away.

What does this say about the Canadian political psyche? Although blatant racism mobilises anger and resistance, more complex debates over the nature of capitalism seem increasingly difficult to sustain in a popularised way. What can we do in Canada today to generate better and more widespread understandings of ongoing inequities in South-(ern) Africa?

National political psyches, I'm not sure I know how to think about those. But the problem you allude to is a real one, nonetheless – and I'm afraid it's not just germane to understanding our responses to southern Africa. For starters the situation in most of the Global South is the real issue here. And yet the truth is that for many – most? – Canadians, the gross inequalities that define the gap between the world's rich and the world's poor seems to be fielded as being, at best, the unavoidable common-sense of the marketplace and, at worst, a matter of mere indifference. The fact is that we're very far from being self-conscious members of a real global community, one built on empathy and mutual caring and respect, and the results of this you can quite clearly – if you care to look.

Mind you, the same is true even closer to home. Canada itself is a pretty unequal society and becoming all the more so all the time as our local chapter of The Architects and Beneficiaries of the System of Global Greed distinguishes itself ever more sharply in terms of income and lifestyle from the "creatures" set below it in the social hierarchy. My son is the executive director of a community food centre in West Toronto, and he lives such contradictions every day. His organisation is doing good work and helping make some difference, but he would love to make the accessibility of good healthy food for all a matter of right, not market-defined privilege – and not a matter of mere charity either. He finds it difficult enough work to make such points here; how much more difficult it is at the global level.

Of course, this global picture is the subject of much hand wringing amongst the "caring classes" – and even lefties can sometimes get discouraged. Thus a friend with a shared commitment to Africa writes to me recently that, if I may quote:

> I don't see how the South can ever liberate itself in the absence of a new socialist project becoming powerful in the North and

> I don't see that happening until people are hurting and see no prospect of meeting their personal needs under globalised neoliberalism, and until a new left movement with a serious attitude to organisation and democracy (to both, that is) emerges to displace the social democratic collaborators with capital.

His conclusion: "All of which means that very much against my will and my nature I feel very pessimistic."

As noted above, I'm not quite so inclined towards pessimism – although I can understand this kind of response. And my correspondent may also understate the will and the scope for local action, at once radical and transformative, in the Global South itself. But at least this letter has the virtue of bringing the problem right back here to our own doorstep. We must, of course, continue to support southern Africans in their efforts to help themselves by all means; many of us spent a lot of time over the years doing just that and we need make no apologies for having done so. But we must also continue to work to challenge and to change the global system from the centre, beginning right here in Canada too: work, in short, for equity and for the continuing viability of the global environment!

Unfortunately, our own national government refuses to hear the terrible tidings about injustice and ecological vulnerability and about the very real inability of the market to magically deliver fair and mutually beneficial social outcomes. What we actually need, I continue to think, is the more self-conscious challenge to the workings of the market – a real not rhetorical project of socialism – mounted by popular majorities committed to social and economic justice. I sense that many Canadians, old and young, are beginning to wake up to the pressing environmental challenges that face us… And, perhaps, they are also becoming more aware of the many other weaknesses and dangers of our market and dominant class driven system. So much depends on many more people doing so, both here in Canada and elsewhere.

I note the phrase "I continue to think," when you talk about the need to resist the logic of the market. Your commitment to this goal has been noteworthy in an era of trendy shifts in academia. What has changed for you intellectually since the 1960s and what remains the same?

I sense a whole other interview coming on, since this is, in itself, a very big question. But fortunately, it's also something I've written about elsewhere (most recently in "Is Socialism a Real Alternative?" in *Studies in Political Economy*, 2010) so I'll try to be brief. To begin with, my understanding of the logic of global capitalism that I first began to articulate with Giovanni Arrighi and others in my Tanzania days has remained, to the present, pretty much the same in broad outline. I simply see no reason to think of global capitalism as being developmental in any expansive and egalitarian sense of the word, but rather as having been and remaining primarily parasitical and hurtful in Africa. In short, "delinking" the central dynamic of the economy of Third World countries from the global marketplace is crucial, as Samir Amin emphasises.

Note, please, that this is not some simple-minded plea for autarky. There are, of course, useful and societally profitable external links an economy in the global South can and must avail itself of. But such links will not automatically make developmental sense in any sound and democratically meaningful sense unless these links are subordinated to a new internal logic for the economy concerned. And this must mean the primacy of conscious collective intervention that overrides any apparent market logic (a false, if seductive, quasi-logic that actually favours the strong in the world economy over the weak). This in turn would allow for crafting an internally-focused, not externally-focused, economy for the country concerned, one that links the city's productive activities and consumer needs to the productive activities and consumer needs of the countryside in an ever expanding set of exchanges – thus providing the basis for a "socialism of expanded reproduction," as Clive Thomas has effectively characterised it. Am I just being stubborn by sticking to my last on this and other economic and social fronts? Well, the fact is that capitalism just hasn't worked for the vast majority of the world's citizens and shows no signs of doing so. The socialist goal and vision therefore remain for me, in this and other particulars, the preferred option.

Of course, the socialist vision has itself taken a ferocious pounding, especially by the end of the twentieth century. And this has been not only the work of imperialism. For there have certainly been severe weaknesses in the so-called socialist camp itself. Here I do feel that, in my own negative take on the Soviet Union and its progeny, I was pretty consistent. But I was much too soft on vanguardism – as exercised, for example, in Mozambique (a country I thought I knew well). For there is no evidence that vanguards can be trusted for long anywhere, however benign their original intentions may have been. Leaders (for they have a role) simply have to be controlled democratically – from below, by the very populations in whose names they claim to speak. In short, socialism has to be profoundly democratic (although, at the same time, it must also be genuinely socialist, something that social democrats have forgotten time and time again – to our cost).

In short, I'm no less a socialist but ever more of an unqualified democrat than once I was. But I've adjusted my thinking on other fronts too. For example, I'm more open to expanding the definition of potential revolutionary agents along the lines I've suggested in quoting Post and Wright to you above: to include peasants, yes, but, especially, to embrace, in Africa, the full range of urban dwellers, well beyond the organised working-class. And I'm even less inclined to reduce resistances based on gender, race, religion, ethnic and anti-authoritarian political demands to their presumed class belongings but to see them as making rightful claims to expression and to redress in their own terms. They can, of course, give rise to political expressions of both right and left provenance. So just how they can be encouraged to intersect with class/socialist projects is a matter of creative political work – and negotiation and democratic interchange as well.

It also underscores the need to move away from mere revolutionary rhetoric and incantation as well – though not away from the cause of genuinely radical and structural change. Here I've found the thinking of Gorz and Kagarlitsky on structural reform especially suggestive and I've tried to expand on it elsewhere. Two points here, however. Firstly, any reform, to be structural in the sense I'm seeking to evoke, must be understood by those who press for and achieve it not as a single, self-contained event but, as a step taken, self-consciously, as part of a longer-term struggle for genuinely radical transformation. Secondly, the organisation and empowerment of the popular elements that prove necessary to realise any such short-term campaigns of would-be structural reform can also be seen as contributing to the broader and more general self-organisation that will prove necessary to the undertaking of even broader struggles for transformation in the future.

Moreover, such an emphasis on popular engagement and genuine empowerment once again implies a democratic process of revolution-making – a process that, as I have argued, can only have long term positive effects. At the same time, one mustn't be naïve: the side of resistance to revolutionary change – the dominant class, its military and its external backers (as in many of the struggles against white power during the initial years of liberation struggle in southern Africa) – will often play pretty violent hard-ball indeed. Then the escalation of confrontation may sometimes, of necessity, pass beyond the boundaries of anything like structural reform – with, unfortunately, long-term costs to socialist and democratic outcomes that, even if the "good guys" win, can be very severe.

Of course, the cost, human and political, of any such necessary escalation is one of the main reasons we in Canada and elsewhere in the West fight so hard (as we did during the stormiest days of the war for southern African liberation) against the state and corporate structures and class interests prevalent here that have so often put our governments on the wrong side of struggles for freedom in the global South – and continue to do just that. But this all evokes issues that demand continuing reflection on my part, and, no doubt, lots more to say in due course.

And finally, what is next for John Saul? Your works in progress suggest no quiet retirement!

I wouldn't hope for the latter certainly; in fact, once you have tasted the bittersweet fruit of knowledge as to the way the world actually functions there is no retirement you can easily permit yourself from the class struggle. Now, of course, my prevailing mode of struggle is through my computer (used as a glorified typewriter) – for as long, at any rate, as my physical and mental faculties remain sufficiently intact to permit me to form comprehensible sentences and coherent arguments. Such is my lot – and I ain't complaining.

Along such lines I last year produced a memoir, *Revolutionary Traveller* (from Arbeiter Ring in Winnipeg) – a memoir that was actually in large part a story of the southern African struggle and of our efforts here in Canada to support it. And I've just finished *Liberation Lite: The Roots of Recolonisation in Southern Africa* for India's Three Essays Collective and Africa World Press, a book that reflects on the aftermath of the southern Africans' victory over colonialism and on the region's future prospects. Meanwhile, wearing my present cap as historian, I have, at various stages of gestation, three more books I'd like to complete by the time I'm 80: a history of South Africa for James Currey; a recounting of what I call the thirty years war for southern African liberation, 1960-1990, for Cambridge University Press; and an evaluation of the world-wide, southern Africa-focused liberation support/anti-apartheid movement, once again for Arbeiter Ring. After that, he said jokingly (gallows humour!), we'll see.

For my wife and kids also take priority, and as befits my age, so do my four grandchildren, all of them here in Toronto at various ages and each a source of endless delight. I like to read, too, dozens of thrillers, but I also revel in George Eliot, Conrad, James, and Robertson Davies, Richard Ford, Colm Tóibín, David

Eggers and Jane Gardam, among many others. And I'm forging on with my Proust, determined to finally conquer it during my eighth decade.

In addition, I listen to a lot of jazz, go to the opera, Stratford and Soulpepper theatres, and watch an endless number of old movies at Cinematheque and on TV – from Stanwyck to Mitchum and Gabin, Randolph Scott to Eleanor Powell and Olivia de Havilland, and including such favourite directors as Michael Powell, Lang, Anthony Mann, Michael Haneke, Hawks, Oshima and Budd Boetticher – and various classic TV dramas on video: *Six Feet Under*, *Lost*, *Homicide*, *The Wire*. I didn't stop playing basketball until I was 70 either (it was at about the same time that I taught my last class at York), and, while I haven't found an equivalently satisfying form of exercise, I do still watch the game with immense enjoyment (including my grandson's team, coached by my son!). In short, there is life after retirement: it is called life in retirement – and it's also, for me, life in a struggle that continues!

2. Hakim Adi (2017), Pan-Africanism and Communism

Hakim Adi has spent years researching the African diaspora, Pan-Africanism and communism in the 20th century. He taught on these topics as a professor at the University of Chichester in the United Kingdom until 2023, when he was made redundant and his unique Master of Research programme on the History of Africa and the African Diaspora shut down.[2] On the anniversary of the 1917 revolution, he spoke to *ROAPE* about the significance of this historical event. For Adi, its significance lies not so much in how it helps us understand the past, but rather how it shows that the alternative can be created in the present and future. Adi also discusses his research, activism and politics more generally.

***

Can you tell us about your earlier involvement with activism and history? Can you speak a little about these experiences? What have your experiences been as a researcher and activist in UK Higher Education?

I suppose it could be said that it's impossible to be concerned with the history of Africa and Africans without also having to struggle against the prevailing Eurocentrism not just in Higher Education but throughout the education system and beyond, especially in this country. I have certainly found that struggle to be necessary and as Fredrick Douglass said without struggle there is no progress.

When I finally embarked on my own research on the history

---

2   Adi was the first person of African descent to become a Professor of History in the UK, and his programme was the only one of its kind in UK higher education at the time of his firing. For more information on these events, visit www.historymatters.online/save-mres-campaign.

of African anti-colonial activism in Britain it soon became obvious that there was very limited academic interest in such history. It was certainly not considered British history but then again it was not considered proper African history either. It remains almost totally marginalised and of course barely taught at the university level anywhere in Britain. What is also evident is that someone has decided that there should be a divide between the history of Africa and that of the African diaspora. That is the way that matters are presented in my experience, so African history is considered rather unimportant but the history of the African diaspora, especially in Britain, is not considered at all. As the history of Africans is marginalised in higher education it is, or was, almost totally neglected at the school level too. In other words, young people in Britain are being mis-educated about the history of the world in which they live and the lessons to be learned from that history. This has a profound impact on all young people but perhaps most of all on those of African and Caribbean heritage, who see themselves, or people who look like them, totally removed from history. The statistics show the consequences, as today only agriculture and veterinary science are less popular than history as a subject choice for black undergraduates.

So our activism, starting in the 1980s, was to attempt to change this situation, to change the national curriculum, to encourage more research, to work with museums, archives, libraries, teachers, as well as in universities, so that the history of Africans (as well as those of Caribbean and Asian origin in Britain) assumed its rightful prominence. It has its own history, but this is not the place to elaborate on it in detail. Suffice to say that there have been some advances and I think we have seen some significant changes in the last thirty years, the recent BBC TV series [*Black and British: A Forgotten History*] for example, but there is still a very long way to go. There are, for instance, still very few historians of African or Caribbean heritage in Britain and, at the moment, only one professor.

There has been a well-documented political retreat of the left in the UK and US academy, how would you see this? Has it affected the field of historical research you have worked in?

I'm not sure about such a retreat of the left. I think there is a general global retreat of revolution, if that is what is meant, and therefore the powers-that-be have been on the offensive in the recent period, especially in the Anglo-American world. This period has now been in existence for some time, it is certainly not the same now as it was in the 1960s and 1970s. It has certainly made a difference to academia in general, to job insecurity for example, but I'm not sure how much difference it has made to the field, in the sense that there are still so few people working in the field in Britain. It would be easy to say that perhaps historians approach the field from different perspectives today than they did 30 years ago, but I'm not sure that much has changed, perhaps it is about to change as more young scholars enter the field, but time will tell.

You started writing years ago about the history of the African diaspora particularly in the twentieth century. Can you talk a little about what you have written and how it has deepened our understanding of militant, left history outside (and inside) the continent?

My research has been mainly concerned with how those in Africa and the diaspora organised anti-colonial and anti-imperialist action in the twentieth century. I see history as the study of change and of people as the agents of that change and I'm interested in what approaches have been adopted by Africans to solve problems connected with liberation and empowerment in the past. My earliest work looked at how mainly West African students organised themselves politically in Britain during the colonial period in the early twentieth century. I found that some of the most significant anti-colonial activists Kwame Nkrumah and [Isaac] Wallace-Johnson, for example, were as politically active in Britain as they were in the Gold Coast and Sierra Leone. It was therefore impossible to fully understand the anti-colonial movement in West Africa without some understanding of its connection with the British anti-colonial movement. At the same time Nkrumah and Wallace-Johnson were Pan-Africanists, part of networks and in touch with other activists based in other parts of Africa, the United States, the Caribbean, Europe, as well as other parts of the world. They would have considered themselves internationalists too, concerned with the global human struggle for progress and of course both were strongly connected with the international communist movement. Wallace-Johnson like Kenyatta and others during the 1930s was partly educated in Moscow. So my research interests broadened to include the history of Pan-Africanism and the relationship between the communist movement and the anti-colonial struggle in Africa, as well as elsewhere.

There are several points that can be made about all of this. One is the important and often leading role played by Africans in the history of radicalism and the working class movement in Britain. This was the case long before the 20th century. The earliest African political organisations, such as the Sons of Africa formed in the 18th century, played a key role in the abolitionist movement, one of the first and largest working class movements in Britain's history. The other is the importance of what used to be referred to as scientific socialism as a weapon in the liberation struggle in Africa even before 1917 but certainly after, and the impact this has had on anti-colonialism, Pan-Africanism, national liberation and the struggles for empowerment and for an alternative today.

Recently you have written on communism and Pan–Africanism's influence on anti-colonial activism in Pan-Africanism and Communism: The Communist International, Africa and the Diaspora, 1919-1939. *Can you speak about the major thrust of this history and what new light it sheds on the period? One of the arguments you make is that Pan-Africanism and communism were not such completely separate currents in the inter-war period but became briefly, to some extent, connected in the struggle for black and colonial liberation. Is this correct?*

As I indicated above, if we look at the struggle for African liberation and advancement in the twentieth century at every stage the role of the communists, of the communist movement, of Marxism, assumes some importance. To some extent the same can be said about Pan-Africanism. With many, although not all, of the key Pan-Africanists, Padmore, Nkrumah, Kenyatta, Wallace-Johnson, Césaire, for example, one finds a connection with the communist movement, even if seemingly by accident as in the case of Kenyatta. Then there are other major personalities, Fanon, Cabral, Mandela, Sisulu who were influenced to a greater or lesser extent by Marxism. It can now be said that the latter two were communists but almost nobody presents them in this way. It could also be said that their adherence to Marxism did not prevent them adopting a Pan-African orientation at times if this served to advance things. Sisulu is an interesting example, since he planned to hold a major Pan-African congress in Africa in the 1950s around the same time that he visited the Soviet Union and China.

In 1956 the Pan-Africanist and former communist George Padmore wrote a book entitled *Pan-Africanism or Communism? The Coming Struggle for Africa* in which he argued that Pan-Africanism was a kind of third way, and in complete opposition to communism. He was and still is an influential figure, so his views still enjoy some credibility, even if the facts seem to suggest something rather different. The other thesis that Padmore advances is that communist activity in Africa was simply in the service of Soviet foreign policy, even though he had been one of the leading communist activists. Of course, Padmore's book was written at the height of the Cold War and he had his own agenda for writing it, in *Pan-Africanism and Communism: The Communist International, Africa and the Diaspora, 1919-1939*, I aimed to establish the facts, as best I could, in addition to reviewing Padmore's own communist career.

The main point that the book makes is that for a period

the Communist International itself adopted a Pan-Africanist approach towards the question of how those in Africa and the African diaspora would liberate themselves. This was the so-called Negro Question and from its earliest days the Comintern developed an approach to the Negro Question which recognised that Africans and those of African descent faced common problems and a common enemy and that in some ways their struggles were interrelated. It established special bodies to investigate and analyse this question and established an International Trade Union Committee of Negro Workers, at one time led by Padmore, with its own publication, designed to work with the various communist parties to address this question. The Comintern's orientation was particularly important in South Africa, where the only communist party in Africa was situated at the time, but it also made important interventions in West Africa, especially in the British colonies, amongst the African diaspora in Britain and France, as well as amongst African Americans and in the Caribbean etc.

In South Africa, as is well known the Comintern demanded that the Communist Party must be a mainly African party including its leadership and that the mobilisation of the masses of the people for liberation and majority rule was more important [than] the struggle of white workers for socialism. The perspective of the communists, that the masses of the people had to be organised and play a leading role in the anti-colonial or anti-imperialist struggle gradually became the accepted view not just in South Africa but throughout the continent. Similarly, many anti-colonial activists and Pan-Africanists recognised the need for the alternative to a capital-centred economy and a Eurocentric political system, issues also raised by the communists, although as we have seen since, recognition is one thing and implementation another.

What does your book tell us about the early days of the communist movement and its relationship to Africa/anti-colonial struggle? How might this help us today?

One of the important questions analysed by the early communist movement, and in particular by Lenin, was the relationship between the liberation struggle in the colonies and that waged by the working class in the most developed imperialist countries. Lenin's analysis of imperialism led him to stress the important role that the struggle of oppressed nations played in the anti-imperialist struggle, not just those oppressed nations in Europe such as the Irish but also the millions oppressed by colonialism in Africa, as well as elsewhere. Lenin called for an alliance between the revolutionary movement of the working class in the advanced capitalist countries and the anti-colonial movements and oppressed people in the colonies, including Africa, to undermine and destroy the imperialist system of states, pointing out that this system could be breached at its weakest link. In other words, there were not first and second class revolutionary struggles, it was not up to those in Europe or the US to liberate Africa and Africans but one humanity and one struggle, we are all our own liberators. I think that even today there is perhaps not enough discussion about this issue and the relationship between the struggles for empowerment in Africa and in Britain for example.

The analysis of the Comintern was very important, one could say that it elevated the importance of the anti-colonial struggle for every communist party. One of the 21 conditions for admission to the Comintern stressed that a communist party in a country possessing colonies, such as Britain, must demand an end to colonial rule, support every anti-colonial movement in words and deeds and cultivate a truly fraternal relationship between the workers and those in the colonies. To what extent this was implemented is perhaps another matter, but the Comintern was the only international organisation to act in this way and adopt such a position. In the inter-war period, it had a very significant impact on those Africans who came into contact with the communist movement and pointed to a way forward, exposing the widely promoted view that colonialism was a civilising mission that at most merely needed reform.

Of course, the communism of 1917 or the 1930s is not the communism of today. That communism was addressing the particular problems of the time and attempting to find solutions to them. The situation in the world is rather different today but not completely so, since in most African countries the anti-colonial struggle was not carried through to the end, it is the capital-centred economic system which predominates and Eurocentric political institutions. What was also emphasised at the time of the old communism was the great need for theory, which is for the summation of experience and I'm not sure how much of that goes on today. In some ways, it could be said that there is a need for a summation of the entire 20th century, or certainly the period since 1945. Of particular importance are the national liberation struggles where new people-centred states have been established, sometimes in partially liberated areas, in Guinea for example, or more recently in Ethiopia and Eritrea. Very little of this work seems to have been done. In Ethiopia, to mention one example, the experience of the TPLF [Tigrayan People's Liberation Front] is only just being thoroughly analysed and presented. But if this is not done, where is the guide for the future not only in individual countries but as a contribution to modern African political theory?

This year is the 100th anniversary of the Russian revolution. What is the significance of this anniversary for our understanding of 20th century African history?

As everyone knows the Russian Revolution was the most significant event of the 20th century. It divided the world into two, a division between the old and the new. Most importantly perhaps it showed that those who produced the wealth, who added value, could empower themselves, create their own political institutions and a people-centred economy which was the most advanced the world had ever seen. These revolutionary changes were of particular interest to Africans since they showed that even in relatively economically undeveloped parts of the world great strides forward could be made. There were also indicators of a new approach to what was referred to as the national question, how to guarantee the rights of nations and minorities in a multinational state. In this regard, even those who were critics of the Soviet Union at the time, such as Padmore and Clement Atlee recognised that significant advances had been made which further exposed the oppressive nature of the British Empire. Yet in Africa few of these changes have been possible with the exception of the right of nations to self-determination which is enshrined in the constitution of Ethiopia.

As mentioned above the success of the Russian Revolution ushered in the prospect of a new world that had a great attraction for many in Africa. It also served to further highlight the oppressive nature of colonial rule and exposed the secret treaties made by the colonial powers for the further division of Africa. The Soviet Union, which emerged from that revolution, especially in the first half of the 20th century, was the most steadfast opponent of colonial rule in Africa and was also a champion of anti-colonialism in the early years of the UN. The revolution also gave rise to the Comintern and its approach, as mentioned above, which had its own impact on Africa's history. So, one can look at the role of all those forces connected with the Comintern in regard to the anti-colonial struggle, or the fascist invasion of Ethiopia, for example, and evaluate the positive role they played. Then there is also the period of the defeat of fascism during the Second World War and the prospects that opened up for Africa and Africans. All of these things are very important.

Having said that, Africa's history has to be understood in its own terms, of course. In the twentieth century that history is mainly concerned with the struggle against colonial rule and its legacy, with the ways in which Africans have acted to empower themselves to bring about political change and create new societies which are people-centred. So, we can then ask ourselves how the revolutionary transformations in the world have impinged on those struggles for empowerment and change. Such a question would compel us to consider not just the first 50 year of the century but also the bi-polar division of the world, the role of Cuba and Cuito Cuanavale, as well as the current role of China: also consequences, to some extent and in various ways, of the 1917 revolution.

To my mind 1917 reminds us all that another world is possible, and that world includes Africa. I think of some of my own family in Africa and what life holds for them – the prospect of selling second-hand clothes in order to survive, pay medical fees and try to put a son through university. Or returning from a job that has been without pay since the start of the year to a darkened dwelling that has not seen a regular power and water supply for an even longer period. There is no doubt that the existing capital-centred system offers next to nothing in compensation and is accompanied with the almost total disempowerment that is referred to as representative democracy. This is the fate of those in one of Africa's richest economies and largest democracies. So, I think that the significance of 1917 is not so much how it helps us understand the past, or as a way of understanding Africa's history, but rather that it shows that the alternative can be created in the present and future. Revolutionary change is not just a hope or a theoretical possibility but, it could be argued, an inevitability in certain circumstances, as has been demonstrated many times since 1917. Those circumstances and conditions, 1917 continues to show us, can be created by the actions of the wretched of the earth themselves, if they can organise themselves appropriately, and find ways to deprive those who currently deprive them of power of the means to do so.

What is the challenge of a journal like ROAPE *today and how can it contribute to the debates and research in radical African studies?*

I would say that the challenge is how to make a difference, or to put it another way the question might be posed as to how to do more than just interpret the world but rather to seek ways to contribute more effectively to changing it. I suppose many of us struggle with this question and what it means to those of us in academia. It is particularly important at the present time, I think, when there is so much disinformation about everything. So even the struggle against disinformation, making a contribution to the dissemination and discussion of enlightened views about Africa, upholding academic rigour, etc, etc, all this can be considered very important and therefore a challenge. It may not be the stated aim of *ROAPE* to change anything but it's certainly an inferred concern. Perhaps it's a question that should be raised and discussed more often.

3. Victoria Brittain (2023), Lives Invisible to Power

Leo Zeilig speaks with the radical journalist, campaigner, and writer Victoria Brittain. Brittain has spent a lifetime exposing the lies and destructions of Western imperialism and celebrating the resistance and hope of those who fight back. For decades, Brittain worked and lived in Africa, and struggled to get the voices of the oppressed heard, and their lives seen.

***

Speaking personally, your journalism and writing on Africa was a revelation to me in the late 1980s and 1990s, as I became aware of the world, providing extraordinary and radical coverage of the plunder and resistance on the continent amid the narrative of coups, war, and famine in Africa presented by most media outlets. Can you tell us a little about yourself, and how you started writing, and your own politicisation? How did you become the radical writer and campaigner you are today?

Thank you, Leo, for your interesting questions and for pushing me to take time to think about the past and to explain things I didn't expect to. Actually, it is all about luck, and the kindness of strangers. I was helped too by being an outsider, as a woman reporter then was, plus the timing of working in a period of journalism on a small canvas, unimaginable in today's transformed media world with the huge commercial pressures, plus the mass output in social media, blogs, podcasts etc.

My first job was in a weekly magazine, *The Investor's Chronicle* – not a very likely place for someone no good at maths and with no interest in The City, but it happened because it was the only paper that replied to my many random letters to editors asking for a job. I think the editor gave me the job out of pity when he saw me for an interview – I was on crutches after a bad riding accident. In Tehran my horse slipped and fell with my foot still in the stirrup and I could barely walk for a couple of years. It was by chance and in desperation to find an independent life that I tried journalism – I had never read newspapers and had no knowledge of politics or the wider world.

Can you take us through your political background, and explain some of the formative moments in your work, writing and activism? I am thinking of the time you spent in Vietnam, reporting – along with others – on American imperialism and resistance to it.

In fact, I had no political background. I was the under-educated product of a poor boarding school and a silent home life. It was my good luck to arrive in Washington DC in 1968 and to find myself in an unimaginable new world of high drama as anti-Vietnam war demonstrations and violent police reactions played out on the streets of the capital and in cities and campuses across America. I shyly joined the crowds in Washington.

Gradually I learned new names of academics, poets, priests, and others who I heard speak out against the war: Professors Noam Chomsky and Richard Falk, Dr Spock (already my guru as a new mother with a baby), the Berrigan brothers Daniel and Philip, Jesuit priests and poets. I found the *New York Review of Books* with its elegant, scathing articles on the war, and I.F. Stone's wonderful weekly newsletter with its extraordinary exposures of wickedness in US domestic politics. I was surprised by the emotion which hit me at the assassination of Martin Luther King, just a year after his blistering speech in Riverside Church condemning the immorality of the Vietnam war. Exposure to the issues of the Vietnam war and the US civil rights movements had opened doors of curiosity that my rural conservative background had kept sealed.

By chance the well-known *New Statesman* correspondent, Andrew Kopkind, who I didn't actually know, asked me to cover his weekly column for a few weeks or months for reasons even now unclear to me. Had I perhaps met one of his friends in a demonstration? In early 1969 for the *New Statesman*, I found myself sitting on a bench in the street outside the White House with Ron Ridenhour, the young helicopter door gunner who had tried unsuccessfully to get US authorities and major media to report and investigate the US soldiers' massacre of an entire Vietnamese village of women, children and old men at My Lai, or Pinkville as the US soldiers called it. He finally got Seymour Hersh, then of *Pacific News Service* to publish the first incendiary story, which Hersh followed with much more research in articles and books for many years.

Listening to Ridenhour it seemed that hours went by, and I was overwhelmed by the unimaginable horror of the scenes he described. I was out of my depth and staggered at the scale of the official coverup as he explained it all to me and I put it in my notebook for the *Statesman*. I was frankly clueless (I certainly didn't know the word imperialism). But I really wanted to go to Vietnam and see this extraordinary world of America in Asia. I read and reread Graham Greene's *The Quiet American*, and I still didn't understand it, but I was hooked.

A little later, back in London, the ITN News editor decided on the then radical idea of hiring a woman reporter, in fact two, and, oddly, he came to my house and asked me to do it. I didn't like the camera and I was too shy to be any good, but I needed a job. One day he sent me on a three-week stint in Vietnam – my old dream. I went, entirely guided on the ground into soft short stories by my experienced and kind cameraman – he was Canadian and markedly different in his attitude from the patronising and hostile reactions I got from some of the British contingent. I wanted to stay in Saigon.

Another outsider, Louis Heron, foreign editor of *The Times* whom I knew slightly from my Washington days, gave me a chance when I approached him hearing his staff man was leaving. Louis took me to lunch, offered me a small monthly retainer and told me, "Remember, no story is worth dying for."

I left London, with my small son and one-way tickets to Saigon. Two things made my Vietnam a different experience from other Western journalists, who were nearly all men. Living with my son meant I was with Vietnamese and French mothers and children at school and at the swimming pool – another world away from the male journalists' social life.

Then, in the greatest stroke of luck, Mark Frankland, the distinguished, long-time *Observer* correspondent, passed on to me his exceptional translator and fixer, Mr Loc, to show me a Vietnam far from Western military and diplomatic briefings. Mark told me later that Mr Loc was hard to please, he would not work for a French or American journalist, he spoke French but no English, and he really only wanted to work with quiet, discreet, knowledgeable Mark Frankland. Mark promised Mr Loc I had the first two qualities and he, Loc, could work on the last.

Behind Mr Loc, riding pillion on his motorcycle, Vietnam's people, not just the war, opened up for me. I sat and listened to Vietnamese villagers and farmers, schoolteachers, monks, ousted politicians, displaced widows with their families, lost and wounded children and their carers. I had found what I wanted to hear and write about – oppressed people, the majority, whose lives were invisible to those in power. Later, the struggle to get those voices themselves heard unmediated was central to my work.

Everywhere I saw great natural beauty and America's unthinking destruction of place and people. I heard despair and what I would later learn to think of, in Southern Africa, as Dennis Brutus's *Stubborn Hope*.[3]

You were a direct witness, and fellow traveller, to some of Africa's liberation movements, not least the struggles in Angola against Portuguese

---

3   *Stubborn Hope: Selected Poems of South Africa and a Wider World* (1978) by Dennis Brutus and Heinemann. Dennis Brutus was one of Africa's greatest poets, political organiser, veteran of Robben Island and 30 years of exile in US academia. When he died in South Africa in 2019 Noam Chomsky called him "a great artist and intrepid warrior in the unending struggle for justice and freedom … a permanent model for others to try to follow."

colonialism (but also, of course, South Africa). Can you tell us about this period, and your experiences? What did reporting and writing over these years teach you about the role of British and American imperialism on the continent, and the experience of national liberation – not least the ways this liberation was terribly constrained?

I came to Africa in the late 1970s and spent two years in Algiers in the time of President Houari Boumédiène when Algeria was a central player in the Non-Aligned Movement and the Organisation of African Unity. After what I had seen of American horror in Vietnam, I was ready to embrace the steep learning curve of Cold War politics in Africa, where America and its allies – notably neighbouring Morocco, busy with a military takeover of Western Sahara from Spain – were always in the wrong. The Polisario delegation in Algiers liked to perch in the Reuters' office where I often was too, to watch the news ticker tape for news of the World Court ruling on Morocco's claim to their territory. We became friends, and when their declaration of independence of the Sahraoui [Sahrawi] Arab Democratic Republic (RASD in its French acronym) was announced in Addis Ababa at an OAU (Organisation of African Unity) summit, it was my birthday and their delegation insisted on a touching joint celebration. Visiting the desert refugee camp in Tindouf in southern Algeria, ignored beyond the Global South, later was an experience that combined the Sahraoui inspiration at miraculous creativity in making a dignified life for those in the camp, with shock at the overwhelming injustice they faced. The thought came to be familiar to me among the Southern Africa liberation movements: MPLA [Popular Movement for the Liberation of Angola], FRELIMO [Mozambique Liberation Front], ANC, and SWAPO [South West Africa People's Organisation].

When we left Algiers one Algerian minister, hearing we were moving to Nairobi said, with a sly smile, "perhaps you will enjoy life more in the perfect neo-colonial setting." He was right – five years in Kenya was privileged living, and between the beauty of the place and exceptional new friends cemented my love of the continent. The work, in the nearby countries of Uganda, Somalia, Ethiopia, Sudan, and even the Seychelles, covered coups, wars, famine and dramatic U-turns in geo-political alliances of the Cold War which were huge changing stories with so much to try to understand.

I was lucky again after Nairobi with a part time dream job in London at the *Guardian* in the 1980s editing an experimental page called *Third World Review* (*TWR*) where almost all the writers were from the Global South. I have written elsewhere about that unique experience which educated me on other continents beyond Africa and Asia, by people who lived, or were exiled from, them. As in Saigon, my, by then two, children gave me a different pattern of work from most journalists. I was at home in the evenings and many of these people came to talk to me there, long talks, not formal interviews. Some, like Mohamed Babu the Zanzibari Marxist, insisted on doing the cooking, others, like Abdul Minty, then leading the World Campaign against Military and Nuclear Cooperation with South Africa from exile in Norway, brought me a cooking pot.

It was a historical moment when revolutionary movements flared in countries of the Global South such as Nicaragua, Grenada, Ghana, and Burkina Faso and found resonance beyond the South in TWR. Ambitious US covert interventions, notably in Ghana in the Rawlings era, were revealed, and, obviously, denied. The experienced Cuban ambassador in Ghana, Niel Guerra, once warned me that there is a price for disturbing imperialism, but it is worth paying. He arranged an invitation to Cuba, among other things to see the various schools in the Island of Youth for children from the liberation movements, and newly progressive countries such as Ghana and Ethiopia.

At the same time, I was educated about a Britain beyond the small bubble of my past experience when the ANC in London and the Anti-Apartheid Movement sent me, reluctantly, to speak about Angola's grim realities to small audiences in British cities I wouldn't have known where to place on a map. There I met and listened to trade unionists and activists; often, and still sometimes today, people told me they were keen readers of the *TWR*. And on cold nights of demonstrations outside the South African embassy in London I listened to a cross section of people I had never seen before and discovered how solidarity was built.

For the first time, because of who and what came to me through the *TWR*'s open door, and what I knew from Angola visits, I felt at home in London as a city of radical exiles and their politics.

It was a decade when in the Global South neoliberal dominance, austerity and repression fired revolt against dictatorship, oppression, and economic crisis. Political prisoners, academics, opposition politicians, journalists, guerrilla fighters and writers like Ngugi wa Thiong'o and Babu from countries I knew became my friends. The modest Committee for Kenyan Political Prisoners produced small pamphlets and leaflets in late night work sessions in the Finsbury Park home of Caribbean activist, poet and publisher John La Rose's New Beacon Books.

A host of South African household names, some resident exiles, others passing through, were my world to listen to: Adelaide Tambo worked in a care home in Hampstead; Frene Ginwala (later First Speaker of Parliament) was assistant to Oliver Tambo; the unknown heroine of early underground action Eleanor Kasrils confided her terror as Conservative politicians publicly demanded the expulsion of her and her sons because of her husband, Ronnie Kasrils' leading role in the ANC's armed struggle against the apartheid regime. I met him in Angola and decades later we became, as we still are, close colleagues and collaborators on many projects, including Palestine.

Palestinians, Lebanese, Iraqis, and other Arabs came to *TWR* as the first Intifada and then the first Gulf War upended their world. Unsurprisingly, and following the Cuban ambassador's warning in Accra, *TWR* came under constant attack from the Israeli, South African, Kenyan, American and other diplomats in

London and their many friends in the media, including inside the *Guardian*. The editor Peter Preston finally decided the page was dated and had to go.

Luckily, I had by then a link with *AfriqueAsie*, the radical magazine in Paris, close to liberation movements. They published all my articles, initially under the more suitable name Alexia Ahmed, and gave me an intellectual and political home from home and the dear friends and colleagues who have been central to my life ever since.

Given that some of your work was in Lusophone Africa, can you talk about the colonial legacies in that part of the continent, and how these legacies were a handicap for post-independence politics, and continue to be? Many of us, including in ROAPE, had high hopes for liberation in Portuguese ex-colonies – the continent's great second wave of "radical independence" – and have been bitterly disappointed with the experience. Can you also speak of these disappointments, and how we can explain them?

Portuguese-speaking Africa, and Angola in particular, was the most intense part of my work in the 1980s. But for me it was not the appalling dehumanising colonial legacies of Portuguese settler economies, racism and fascism that were central, but rather the ruthless US-led war to control independent Angola's future, and with it apartheid South Africa's future. The US military project of the Reagan years in Africa, supported by Margaret Thatcher, was to use its client state Zaire, mercenaries from Western countries and South Africa's army to install Jonas Savimbi as a client leader in oil rich Luanda in 1975 as the Portuguese left. The goal was to safeguard Western economic interests in South Africa in particular, keeping apartheid alive, and Namibia maintained under South African occupation. A blind eye was turned to South Africa's military campaign of targeted assassinations, economic destruction, and destabilisation of the FLS (Frontline States) and the death of the high hopes of independent states across the continent. Without Cuba's historic intervention and its people's enormous sacrifices and courage beside the Popular Movement for the Liberation of Angola, Washington would have succeeded.

Western journalists were not often welcomed in Luanda, but in an act of kindness and trust, the radical historian of Africa Basil Davidson, who did not then know me personally, but knew some of my work, wrote letters to three Angolan leaders introducing me as someone who should write about the US/South Africa devastation being unleashed to cripple Angola's independence.

Those letters gave me extraordinary access to remote places and, in time, to friendships with remarkable people. I was able over the years to visit towns and cities besieged by UNITA, the rival movement supported by South Africa and the CIA. They were scenes of battered hospitals full of legless peasant victims of landmines, with infrastructure bridges, dams, roads, schools, blocks of homes built by the Cubans all reduced to rubble, and hundreds of thousands of hungry despairing people on the move. Think of more recent images of Fallujah, Raqqa, Aleppo, Grozny and giant refugee camps in Pakistan, Jordan, Lebanon.

In remote Angola I saw handfuls of Cuban and sometimes Vietnamese school teachers, doctors, nurses alongside the MPLA keeping humanity alive as the West tried to crush it. I met Angolan doctors and scientists later assassinated as UNITA targeted the local intellectual leadership. In Luanda I listened to MPLA leaders and Cuban generals talk of the shape of the social, economic, military and diplomatic challenges aimed at the progressive advances of the post-independence years were targeted.

After months of fighting around Cuito Cuanavale in southeast Angola from October 1987 a 40,000 Cuban and Angolan and SWAPO force, with Soviet supplies, confronted and defeated the South Africans in March 1988. Cuban engineers and Angola's new generation of army officers laid down two airstrips towards the border with Namibia, giving Cuban pilots air superiority. The epic battle around Cuito Cuanavale and in the neighbouring province of Cunene was won against the most powerful army on the continent. It changed African history.

This is the context that was followed by the political disappointment you talk about – decades of struggle for life against years of utter destruction, death and loss imposed by apartheid South Africa and the West. Angola and Mozambique opened their countries to the resistance of the ANC, SWAPO, and ZANU and ZIPRA (Zimbabwe People's Revolutionary Army) from what was then Rhodesia; Mozambique implemented Commonwealth sanctions on Rhodesia to the total detriment of the economy. Heroism and principle came with an incalculably high price.

Your work, books, and journalism highlight the role of imperialism. Can you talk about imperialism today, and how it manifests itself in Africa and elsewhere in the Global South? Are we correct to identify other imperialist players, including China, alongside the United States?

I don't think of my work as "highlighting" the role of imperialism. That sounds too purposeful and theoretical. I would say rather that I was for a long time living and reporting from inside countries being systematically wrecked by US imperialism's drive to maintain world control.

In Vietnam and Angola, the military aspect was then the most obvious. But control of financial systems, of science and technology, of communications, of information wars, of the systems of influence and funding which operate through NGOs, think tanks, diplomacy both inside the countries of the Global South and well beyond, all shaped, and continue to shape, the history, which has so disappointed you, and so many others, in the context of Southern Africa's political outcomes. (It could of course have been very different, as the examples of Cuba and Vietnam's social welfare systems of education, health and care of the elderly illustrate today.)

I believe these Western systems aim to keep most of the Global South in labour intensive production – and poverty. Let's remember that resistance across the Global South continues despite defeats – see Latin America and India, for instance. China, with its extraordinary successes in poverty reduction, can rightly be criticised for many things, but for me, it is not "an imperialist player" as you suggest.

Working on the continent, and meeting some of the giants of political struggles and liberation, can you tell us of these experiences and personalities? Who stands out, and what characteristics did you note specifically, in some of these political activists and politicians?

It was my great privilege to know Julius Nyerere, Lucio Lara, Thomas Sankara, and Ngugi wa Thiong'o as a political activist in London, and to meet others, like Oliver Tambo and Namibia's Toivo ya Toivo, with the same characteristics. What stood out was their integrity, their modesty, their habit of listening to the powerless, and their ceaseless hard work.

I remember watching President Nyerere once in his garden standing for a long time intently listening to the gardener who was sweeping the path. (And on his visits to London in the mid-1980s there was always an invitation to breakfast, and he would ask me for every detail of my visits to Luanda, so crucial for the Frontline States to understand through the language barrier.)

Similarly with Lucio, at his house in Luanda there were always humble people sitting waiting to talk to him. He always had time for everyone. Once, in two days spent travelling with him in Malange in 1984, driving round cooperative farms with local MPLA officials and seeing how South Africa and UNITA were encroaching on this rich agricultural province, I noted:

> through hours of sitting in farm courtyards Lara barely spoke, but listened as the complaints came thick and fast with no fear of the man in authority. The peasants were angry and asking for more military action against UNITA, against the South Africans… [I]t was a vision of what the party meant to people. Here the MPLA was the centre of people's lives, their security, their entry into a new world of organised farming, and their

faith in the leadership was touching and unmistakable.

I knew the private Lucio and his wife Ruth too. Pictures in my mind are of Lucio feeding his pet monkeys in Luanda or walking on the beach with his dog, Lucio on rare visits to London reading *Le Monde* for hours, walking for miles on Hampstead Heath and wanting to go to the ballet.

And sitting in his house in Ouagadougou with Sankara, at a different stage of life, I witnessed the energy and optimism, his thirst for knowledge, the piles of books he was reading, his torrent of questions, his urgent requests to have his speeches translated into English and given to Nyerere, to the ANC in Robben Island, Lusaka and London.

I knew Sankara because he had met Maurice Bishop of Grenada at the Non-Aligned summit in Delhi in 1983 and despite having no common language the two men had bonded, recognising the parallels in their bold projects of transformation for their tiny countries. Maurice's assassination in October of that year horrified Sankara, and mutual friends who knew that I had been in Grenada as the coup unrolled, and that I spoke French, invited me to Ouagadougou to explain to Sankara the treachery of a long-time close colleague – which would then be his own fate. In the four febrile years of social revolution until the same scenario ended his life, Thomas invited me several times – always with his agenda of work, translations, and discussions, plus presents of hand printed Indigo dresses.

Recently, in the last twenty years, your work has focused on Palestinian liberation and justice. Please tell us something about your current work, activism, and writing.

Nowhere better illustrates the power of imperialism than Palestine's shameful betrayal over more than a century. It was inevitable that after leaving Africa and coming back to live in London I would be drawn to Palestine's escalating drama. Palestinian writers and photographers were prominent in *TWR*, and Palestinian artists and filmmakers were central in my London world of exiles. I first went to Gaza at the invitation of its first and leading psychiatrist Dr Eyad Saraj who wanted me to write a pamphlet on his organisation, the Gaza Community Mental Health Programme (GCMHP), for fundraising in the Gulf. I had interviewed him in London when he had talked in particular about his work with adolescent boys traumatised by witnessing their fathers' humiliation and impotence in the face of violent arrests, house demolitions, disappearance into Israeli prisons.

It was 23 July 2002 and Hamas military leader Salah Shehadeh had been assassinated the day before by a 1-ton bomb dropped on his home in a crowded neighbourhood of Gaza City. Fifteen people were killed, including eight children and infants, more than 100 wounded, the area devastated. I spent the following days shadowing Eyad's staff in homes of the traumatised near the massive crater. Several were social workers who were veterans of Israeli prisons, quiet men bringing practical aid with food, water, clothes and above all emotional empathy in the horror they knew so well. Palestinian experience of injustice could never then be an abstraction for me.

After that terrible night 27 Israeli pilots signed a letter refusing to take part in such illegal and immoral targeted killings in civilian areas in the West Bank and Gaza. International condemnation went as far as a case brought under international jurisdiction in 2005 in Spain for Israeli war crimes by the New York based Centre for Constitutional Rights. In the end, as with the US soldiers in My Lai village, or the CIA and South Africans who devastated the lives of Angolans and Mozambicans (along with their own majority) over decades, there was largely impunity, forgotten history, indifference.

But Palestinians' resistance has only grown stronger, more visible, internationally supported over these decades. One of my activities on this front was 11 years of running the Palestine Book Awards from their inception. It was a period when more and more books came to us every year, new small publishers emerged, and the winners became overwhelmingly Palestinians – academics, poets, novelists, cooks, artists, photographers and writers of children's books. Nothing gives me more pleasure and optimism than the strength and creativity of young Palestinians. I am still close to GCMHP and other Palestinian projects and individuals. And I still study Arabic.

Palestine overlapped with my work during the years of the "war on terror". Post-9/11 in the UK [during] the jailing or putting under house arrest of Muslim men, deportations of some to US prisons, collaboration with US torture and detention in secret prisons across the world, and Guantanamo, I was writing and speaking in protest meetings constantly. It was my privilege to become close to many of the families involved in this tragedy, several of whom were Palestinians. I co-wrote Moazzam Begg's Guantanamo memoir *Enemy Combatant*, plays, other books, notably *Shadow Lives* on wives and daughters of men imprisoned in the US and UK in which the Palestine connection emerged clearly for me. Those women and their now grown children are still in my life, as are political prisoners in many places, including those still in Guantanamo.

But I have never lost sight of Africa, which has a special place in my heart, and I am happy today to be part of the editorial collective of *Afrique XXI* where we publish exceptional articles, interviews, video, and audio testimonies in French. One day we hope to publish in English too, like our older sister, *Orient XXI* which appears in French, Arabic, English and Persian.

Obviously, a life of activism, campaigning and investigative journalism never ends, but can you tell ROAPE readers some of the lessons you have learnt from a lifetime of radical engagement? What are some of the immutable(s) you have found, and that a new generation need be aware of, for example?

Given how very much better educated and generally informed today's generation such as *ROAPE*'s readers are, this is hard to answer. Let me give you words of others who inspired me decades ago, and whose historic actions still have unending resonance. And of course, actions of resistance, organising, tangible solidarity behind every popular struggle for justice, education, health, and food are obligations that can never end.

Ron Ridenhour, the Vietnam vet who exposed My Lai, wrote this in March 1993 in the Los Angeles Times looking back 25 years:

> There were several important lessons in this for me, personally. Among the most important and disappointing of them was that some people – most, it seems – will, under some circumstances, do anything someone in authority tells them to. Another is that government institutions, like most humans, have a reflexive reaction to the exposure of internal corruption and wrongdoing: No matter how transparent the effort, their first response is to lie, conceal and cover up. Also, like human beings, once an institution has embraced a particular lie in support of a particular coverup, it will forever proclaim its innocence.

Other words reverberate from Martin Luther King speaking in New York's Riverside church in 1967 (just replace Vietnam with Palestine):

> We still have a choice today: nonviolent coexistence or violent co-annihilation. We must move past indecision to action. We must find new ways to speak for peace in Vietnam and justice throughout the developing world, a world that borders on our doors. If we do not act, we shall surely be dragged down the long, dark, and shameful corridors of time reserved for those who possess power without compassion, might without morality, and strength without sight.

Let me end with a last quote, from a conversation with Lucio Lara in Angola in the mid 1990s. He said:

I don't have illusions about many things anymore. In the Angolan struggle perhaps, we didn't have philosophers or sociologists, but we had these words of Neto's, "the most important thing is to solve the people's problems". Once in the Council of Ministers I heard someone say that we should stop using this phrase. I thought that maybe he was right, because no one spoke out against him. In my opinion this was when the Party began to collapse. That was the time when the leaders felt they all had the right to be rich. That was the beginning of the destruction of our life.

Lucio sent my book, *Death of Dignity*, from which I quoted him, to Thabo Mbeki when he became South Africa's president. It was a warning of how political visions can be lost. Lucio died in 2016.

The historical work on the anticolonial archives of the MPLA in exile and in the bush until independence in 1975, is meticulously carried out, in Lucio's old house, first by his wife Ruth then by the family and close friends (creating the Tchiweka Documentation Centre). After Ruth's death the work was led by Lucio's son Paulo, who died last year, and whose life course was set by those days. Paulo at 19 was in the military front line in repulsing the South African invasion in 1975 and he became a general in the long years of post-independence war until the death of Jonas Savimbi. Lucio's daughter Wanda now runs it. There is also a treasure trove of filmed interviews by Paulo in the remotest of provinces with the people who lived those years. This website is a jewel, the richest record of a people's successful years of struggle against all that imperialism could devise to have them fail.[4]

---

[4] The website hosting the Tchiweka Documentation Centre can be found at https://www.tchiweka.org/.

4. Jesse Benjamin (2020), A Life of Praxis with Walter Rodney

Jesse Benjamin is a scholar-activist and professor at Kennesaw State University in the US. He is also a member of the Walter Rodney Foundation board and founder of the Walter Rodney Public Speakers Series. In the week that marked the fortieth anniversary of the murder of the revolutionary Walter Rodney, Benjamin spoke to Zeilig about Rodney's astonishing work, life and activism and how he speaks to the dehumanisation of Black lives everywhere. Rodney's work, Benjamin argues, remains vital for those now seeking to overturn the systems of oppression worldwide.

***

Firstly, can you tell us something about your own political and intellectual journey, how and where did it start?

I was born a citizen of the world, already with two citizenships due to my itinerant 1960s parents who had travelled and then started living in the Middle East. I had a third citizenship a year later when we got to rural Nova Scotia, where my brother was born, and my parents split up. Until I was 10, I then lived all over Toronto, from Etobicoke to Cabbagetown, from the "good school" neighbourhood of Forest Hills to years running between the recording studios and international vendors on the streets of Kensington Market.

I arrived to live in the US for the first time, just as the New York Islanders hockey team went on to win four Stanley Cups in a row – a literal miracle for a 3rd grade Canadian kid with every pro hockey player's cards in his collection, but it went almost completely unnoticed in upstate New York where we now lived, and wasn't even on TV. Almost four years in a rural small town situation was a new experience with some good friends and a new love for computers, physics and sci-fi, but before I was 13 we moved suddenly again, to Eastern Parkway in Brooklyn, surrounded by religious communities and the most shockingly new kind of overt and vulgar racism I had ever experienced within the confines of my then brief, ostensibly colourblind, ideologically liberal humanist upbringing. It was South African apartheid style racism in the schools and streets I was now on, and that was also formative.

I've traced my willingness to question and even stand against what is going on around me pretty far back. I recall failing only one class in Canada, my civics grade at a particular school, because I refused to stand or sing the anthem and the Queen-related song that followed it. I did do the subsequent state-mandated exercises to the piped-in music of Stevie Wonder every morning, but I did not want to align with the symbols of a single nationalism, even though I really liked Canada as a kid, it seemed ordered and largely fair compared to the adults in my world. I also remember anti-Pakistani racism from students and their parents within days of arriving to school in a more working-class immigrant community outside of Mississauga.

But the simmering race hatred we encountered in those early Reagan-era Brooklyn years was shocking and awoke me to my first attempts at more direct activism. Eastern Parkway was very white and Jewish on one side, and mostly Black and particularly Caribbean on the other side, and in hindsight as a young teenager I was one of the very few people with friends on both sides of this apartheid line around which violence could easily erupt on any given day and sometimes did.

By 1987 I'd dropped out of high school, relocated to the Middle East, gone through some pretty dramatic struggles, and improbably managed to join a radical Quaker international college in Jerusalem. I was introduced to Marxist theory, Paulo Freire and Edward Said, while doing fieldwork with marginalised

Bedouin communities in the Naqab/Negev and Sinai Deserts. The next year I made my way to my school's European Centre as a Marxist 17-year-old.

While studying in London I was lucky to have a series of mentors who I officially made my teachers and took courses with, starting with my primary advisor, professor and musician Vic Gammon, who taught me political economic theory and ethnomusicology. Then my development theory mentors introduced me to Ewan MacColl – a folk musician, leader in street and radical community theatre praxis, ethnomusicologist, lifelong Marxist theorist and activist who was the same age as my grandfather. He was then starting a Marxist theory class for his disaffected "capitalist" children, in his home in South London, together with his partner, folk singer Peggy Seeger. I joined the first session, as we read paragraphs aloud from the *Communist Manifesto* for several weekly meetings, then Lenin's *Imperialism*, some Engels, always illuminated in unparalleled detail by Ewan but also by the general conversation at this close-in level. Ewan's kids never showed, but he ran the group anyway, and he later insisted I take voice lessons from him to improve my diaphragmatic breathing, oratory, and "the way I carried myself." I tried to warn him that it might not be for everyone, but I did give it a serious shot and learned a lot from him in the process. He used a lot of Paul Robeson in our exercises, and I got to spend hours with their incredible record collection.

In my fourth year of college, I studied in Kenya for two years. I immersed myself in a coastal community north of Mombasa that was a mix of Mijikenda and Swahili cultures, including many descendants of formerly enslaved people from the brief plantation period that had emerged right in this area from the 1830s-1890s. Land and the struggle for it was central. The deeper my investigations went I discovered evictions of thousands of people into undocumented, largely hidden rural slums, the commodification of land as a resource in itself, and increasingly shady land dealings. This continued on as my dissertation research and is still an active area of my work. Underdevelopment was explicit in this setting, so Walter Rodney became a primary theoretical framework for me as an undergrad, because it provided even better answers than world-systems theory seemed to and provided direct explanations for the contradictions my studies were revealing.

So, underdevelopment became central to my thinking and has seeped into my work in many ways. To my knowledge, though it started with my unpublished 550-page undergraduate thesis, I am still one of the only people using underdevelopment as a primary explanation for the profound economic, political and cultural marginalisation of the numerically predominant non-Swahili, largely Mijikenda people of coastal Kenya. After the tripod-mounted machine-gunning British were largely defeated by Mekatilili and her Giriama rebels in 1913/1914 (because they levelled the playing field with spears dipped in one of the deadliest of all neurotoxins, produced locally of black mamba and deadly sea mollusc poisons), the British punished them for this humiliation by charting all subsequent colonial development to circumvent their territories. Thus, the Mijikenda hinterlands were deprived of roads or railways, schools and administrative centres, economic or any other forms of development, providing an unintended positive cocoon of cultural independence from the steady erosion of colonial cultures, but also producing undeniable long-term effects such as an almost complete lack of social science doctorates some seven decades later.[5]

Honestly, by the time I got to grad school in a more traditional state university setting back in upstate New York, in 1993, I not only had four years of serious fieldwork under my belt, I was also up to speed on most of the critical and radical theories of the day, and was already evaluating them on the basis of their applicability in real work contexts. So, I was probably a more intellectually aggressive and politically intense student than usual. I was also now a pretty experienced activist and, at least intellectually and morally, a self-avowed revolutionary. I quickly joined the growing

---

5   Jesse Benjamin, "Representation in Kenya, its Diaspora and Academia: Colonial Legacies in Constructions of Knowledge about Kenya's Coast," Journal of Global Initiatives 2(2), 2007.

social movements, was soon a campus leader, and we engaged in major social movements there for years, resisting arming of campus police, fighting to keep our co-op bus service, fighting state tuition raises and other regressive social policies, and mainly contesting racism and demanding a more diverse curriculum on campus in a cycle of incidents, actions, repressions, getting pepper-sprayed, building takeovers, marches and more occupations.

It became an education in and of itself, the struggles at SUNY Binghamton were almost a shadow PhD I accidentally enrolled in, as my closest comrades and I insisted on taking our classes into the world and our struggles into the classroom. For my first tenure track job, in Minnesota, I was hired to teach a required first year anti-racism course in a heavily white community with active racism and white supremacist organising, with the expectation of incorporating community activism into all my work. I didn't need the invitation, but I took it – we worked on dozens of issues like police profiling and brutality, and racist Native sports mascots, we fought to remove swastikas from the stone masonry of the regional Catholic cathedral and resisted anti-Somali and anti-Hmong violence. In Atlanta, my praxis came with me, as my colleagues soon discovered, and here one of my main groundings has been with the Rodney family and the Walter Rodney Foundation.

I am always on the lookout for activism and activist comrades, but I never expected the degree of involvement and movement we were a part of in Binghamton. But it was theory that truly reared its head unexpectedly when I needed it. In those same years I discovered coloniality and got to study with Anibal Quijano, and although we were in very different disciplines, Carole Boyce Davies was a significant influence as I deepened my knowledge of Pan-Africanism and Black radical thought, especially Black radical feminist thought. Rodney and Sylvia Wynter would be central in all of this.

How did you become involved and interested in the work of Walter Rodney? When did you first read his work and what were your first impressions?

Friends World College was a blessing on so many levels. I had survived a meandering transnational childhood, a religious cult, homelessness and drugs and now I wanted to understand the world in every way I could. Political economy, anthropology, philosophy became my primary tools, and for a few years I basically studied revolutionary thought and history. Every generative book that blew my mind in those early years led to a study of all the works in its bibliography, and so I studied the genealogy of revolutionary thought, from Marx and Engels to Che, Freire, Cabral. That is when Rodney's name first started coming up. At the idyllic job I landed in London, working the late shift at Regent's College Library, I talked to patrons of the Overseas Development Institute and basically anyone checking out any radical books, and in that context a dissident Eritrean PhD student insisted I read Rodney's *How Europe Underdeveloped Africa* that weekend in order to continue our already intense discussion about development theory. So, I did, with great appreciation. I remember being that radical librarian, who after reading this text, and Nkrumah's *Neo-Colonialism: the Last Stage of Imperialism*, politely but earnestly told everyone I could about the blood-soaked sugar slavery origins (Tate and Lyle Sugar Co.) of the stately Tate Reading room we were standing in as they checked out books with me. It was one of many times the world all around me was directly illuminated by Rodney.

His book was one of the reasons I decided to travel next to Africa, and my school had a Centre in Kenya. I read an immense amount of Kenya-specific scholarship, and then two years later as I worked to complete the ethnography that would be my senior thesis I returned to Rodney, along with Marx, Lenin, Robert Brenner, Fred Cooper, Wallerstein, Roger van Zwanenberg and anyone else who seemed to helpfully explain the neocolonial squatter evictions and land privatisation I was seeing.

Rodney was just so explanatory, his work provided the deepest of answers, and unmasked the dynamics usually left opaque or unexamined altogether. It used a nuanced and flexible Marxism and flexible thinking in general, to describe more than 500 years of history in Africa, and with a high degree of specificity for each region's details. While reading Rodney again in Kenya I remember figuring out that East Africa Industries, which produced a preponderance of staple products in all the stores (like Blueband margarine and Omo laundry powder), was in fact not local as its name slyly implied, but just a regional hub of the Unilever corporation, the largest and most colonial of Dutch/Anglo multinationals since the deeply colonial roots of the Lever brothers. Lloyds of London and Barclays Bank were also indelibly located within their violent imperial origins. It was the only book that evoked major reactions, mostly loving, when I took it on the crowded matatu rides to town. Everywhere I went with that book people who were touched by a lecture or a work of Rodney's announced themselves, started sharing their stories. That was a special experience in relation to a book unlike any I'd ever experienced.

Years later, in Binghamton New York, entrusted with my first ever solo-taught course as a now PhD student, I was teaching "Africa in the World System", and in the third week or so, we had occupied buildings in protest, and I was teaching my class in the occupied building, sitting in our discussion circle, each reading and then discussing paragraphs from our main text *How Europe Underdeveloped Africa*. There in the introduction was the statement about Rodney teaching in Michigan, Cornell and Binghamton to pay his bills, having been blocked from working in Guyana by the dictator [Forbes Burnham]. So, my class discussed how crazy that was, how we'd received no loving history of his presence on our campus, how the activists would be so empowered to know about him. We asked why no building was named for him, no study lounge, nothing. Few of my activists friends knew much about him either, and my own knowledge was still limited to three books and several articles, so I started a Walter Rodney study group with some other students, focused on Rodney and his writings, as well as his scholar/activist model, which we were already trying to embody a version of.

Walter Rodney Speaks was key to this time for me, for the blueprint and legitimation it provided for the radical academic life I was slowly realising I might actually continue working in long after my degree was completed. Rodney was a rare example of a truly committed intellectual, an important role model. We started monthly meetings around his scholarship, ran a petition and fundraiser to launch a scholarship, demanded the Student Union be named for him, and most consequently, after three years of work we held a major international conference on him and his work, run entirely by radical students, which became itself an historic event. That is where I met Patricia Rodney, Walter's wife, and Asha Rodney, his youngest daughter, who I was very excited to be on a young scholars panel with. Patricia Rodney riveted us with an intimate session about all she had lived through with Walter and the assassination, a night none in attendance will ever forget.

Eight years later, when I got a job offer to work in suburban Atlanta, they were the only people I knew in the region, and the prospect of their friendship and collaboration was a significant factor in our move. My informal mentorship with Carole Boyce Davies – more of me being a dutiful follower and student really – was foundational too, including her unparalleled scholarship, internationalism and willingness to engage with student movements, her rigorous example on both sides of the scholar/activist divide. Wynter was also a key part of this period for me. She was one of two keynotes at our Rodney conference, together with George Lamming. She also came to some of our early coloniality studies sessions and one of our first conferences, and honestly blew us all away with her brilliance, her intensity and unique style, her appreciation and recitation of Nas, that she chilled and danced with us until after midnight at the party we set up in her honour, or came to our house for dinner on another visit.

For readers of ROAPE *who may not be overly familiar with Rodney's work could you give us a brief overview?*

Rodney is both loved and appreciated all across Africa and the Diaspora, but too often pigeonholed into categories and limitations that suit the needs of contemporary scholars. He is an ancestor via martyrdom in the cause of his people's liberation, so interpreting his thought and ideas is, or should be especially sensitive. After achieving his PhD at 24, his body of work over the next 14 years made him one of the great Marxists and Pan-African scholars of the twentieth century, whose work is still insufficiently cited and engaged across a vast range of fields.

How Europe Underdeveloped Africa is by far his best-known book, still relevant and in print almost 50 years later because it dared to explain the fundamental relations of the world order like few other books ever have. He wrote erudite books like this for a broad general audience, and he also wrote refined historiographic works of anticolonial recuperation and reorientation that remarkably remain definitive in the historiography of both Guyana and the Upper Guinea Coast of West Africa. He was a peerless scholar/activist everywhere he went, an unusually solid example for us today, his concept and praxis of grounding providing a major pedagogic model. At a minimum, Rodney's work is central to discussion of underdevelopment, Marxism, Black history, race/class, world systems, Pan-Africanism, Guyana's politics and history, Jamaica's too, Caribbean studies, Tanzania's Ujama politics and the Dar School of radical historiography, Education theory, and I would also argue that he should be more central to modern genealogies of how we understand the politics of knowledge, coloniality and decolonial theory.[6]

You have recently coedited a book by Walter Rodney on the Russian

---

6   I've written a few short biographies of Rodney: "Walter Rodney," in Black Power Encyclopedia: From "Black is Beautiful" to Urban Uprisings, Akinyele Umoja, Karin L. Stanford and Jasmin A. Young eds., ABC-CLIO, June 2018; and with Robin D. G. Kelley, there is a biographical section in our long Introduction to Rodney's The Russian Revolution: A View from The Third World, Verso, 2018.

revolution, The Russian Revolution: A View from the Third World. *The book is based on the extensive and detailed lectures that Rodney prepared for an advanced course on the historiography of the revolution at the University of Dar es Salaam in the early 1970s. Can you tell us about how you came to put this extraordinary book together, the work that was involved and what you regard as its principal contribution?*

Different versions of the history and status of the work were out there. I heard little traces. Horace Campbell was the only person I knew who'd really written much about it, in a little-known essay, and Rupert Lewis in his biography. Rodney was at the height of his powers when he was killed, and he had many projects almost finished and ready to work on in his travels and various moments for research and presentations. Somehow, he was able to continue his major research projects while organising furiously and engaging in a steadily increasing battle with a dictatorship. Toward the end they were moving regularly between safe houses. Some of his unfinished works were confiscated from the Rodney home by the regime on the day of the assassination, others were saved and collected into what the family held together and preserved until it officially became the Walter Rodney Papers at the Archives Center of the Atlanta University Center Robert W. Woodruff Library.

Much later, while he was in town for a conference on race and integration in the post-WWII military industrial context of northern Atlanta/Marietta, I met with David Roediger who shared what he knew about the manuscript that Robin Kelley had worked on as a student of Ed Alpers in UCLA. And so, I got Robin together with Pat and Asha to form a plan and we worked to get the book out after that, over a few years, in conjunction with Verso. Rodney had written the book first as a series of lecture notes on the Russian Revolution, with the intention of developing them later as a book, and he used the same deep preparation for the class as the writing process, where he read the primary literature deeply and directly himself, taking meticulous notes on cards, starting from the ground up with his own independent evaluation of the history. Robin got to do a lot of work on the original handwritten drafts while they were in UCLA in the mid-80s in the care of Edward Alpers, before the Atlanta archive was set up. We now had the task of turning what was unfinished into a book, so we tried to leave it as close to the way it was in his papers, the reader gets to see the unfinished chapters in a few places, and wonder what other chapters he'd have added, what he would have revised before publishing. It's a fresh take on the Russian Revolution, with the clear point of what could be learned for then-contemporary revolutions, anticolonial struggles and non-aligned movement blocs. It's a snapshot of very critical 1970s thought, almost like a time capsule. For almost everyone it was an unexpected 10th book, a text which flows with a voice that feels closer in style I think to *How Europe Underdeveloped Africa* than almost any other of his works. Rodney frames the work as part of Black Studies, with the obvious but radical notion that any area of the world could be the legitimate subject of this newly ensconced academic framework. I also argue that his critique of bourgeois scholarship and its obvious biases compared to the largely more accurate technocratic records of the Soviets, encapsulated his original *Two World Views of the Russian Revolution* title concept for the book, which revealed the epistemic and cultural level of his work, parallel with critiques of knowledge/power in Michel Foucault and Edward Said.

Why do you think the Russian revolution held such interest for a radical activist and researcher working in Africa, and focused on the struggles of the Third World?

When I think of the 1970s and the transnational Non-Aligned Movement in which Rodney was a major presence, it was a similar moment to the one we are facing now, a period of unwritten possibilities based on unprecedented ruptures in the capitalist world system, where better visions emerge to confront colonialism, imperialism and outright fascism. When you think of the fight against Portuguese colonialism or the forward advance of apartheid South Africa and the resistance that frontline states had to put up, with the help of Cuba, these were transnational struggles against imperial fascism. Fascist dictators were ascendant in the Americas and elsewhere then too, creating stark choices, and from our vantage point we see that, with a few exceptions, the better side did not win.

The post-Vietnam era was characterised by "low intensity conflicts" and proxy wars, sometimes genocidal, often fuelled by clandestine drug and arms running operations, from Guatemala and El Salvador to Indonesia and East Timor. A lot of that imperial history has been coming home to roost for decades, as the US metropole reimports the only remaining industries it has, bringing the technologies of its imperial Third World domain back to the US. Things like debt manipulation, repackaged versions of structural adjustment and privatisation, infinite wealth disparities, militarisation of all varieties. Just as we must now assess our situation and draw from the best and also the most illustrative examples that history has to offer, Rodney wanted to understand every aspect of the Russian Revolution in all of its complexity. And on close examination there are innumerable parallels that help raise questions and ideas in relation to many African and Third World nations, and really people everywhere, regarding land and peasant production, industrialisation, ethnic and religious diversity, power and the state, power and the international arena.

You get a sense reading the book and looking through Rodney's archive in Atlanta of the phenomenal extent of his reading, his deep grasp of Marxism (and its various tendencies) and his knowledge of a wide-ranging literature on the revolution. What do you think the volume tells us about who Rodney was, how he worked and his political commitment?

How real and urgent his search for truth and answers was, but also how undoctrinaire and creative he was in his thinking. The groundings approach he already typified and then greatly refined during and ever after his Jamaican sojourn in 1968 was a very rigorous mode, one of self-reflection as to one's role and capacity in a given space, one of studying thoroughly the deep historical roots of each place, and then the process of decolonising our thinking sufficiently to the task of liberation. He mentions his interest in physics, he read about the natural world and the environment, he went wherever the questions and issues took him, and he was always independent in his thought, reading the original texts and forming his own analyses in the process, never skipping steps as a scholar, meticulous in his language and his argument. In his 20s he was openly contesting with the doyens of the field of African history and African studies in their peer-reviewed journals and remarkably holding his own. Really, he was boldly writing decolonial historiography and they were feeling threatened and therefore contending with him, not entirely successfully either. Because he was a prolific scholar and wrote in various media across his career, we can see many examples of his attempt to forge critical praxis wherever he was, grounded in Marxism and Pan-Africanism, always building his analysis from deep local roots and then navigating toward the primary contradictions, usually finding himself way ahead of almost everyone else, labelled a threat, surveyed. Already in grad school he and Pat were followed between restaurants and archives in Portugal where he was researching colonial history in his third or fourth language.

There is a balance of pragmatism and rigour on the one hand, and a creativity and realness on the other. When we read him, we find someone with the same questions as us: why is the world this way, and how can we understand it deeply enough to transform it? I am pained that we don't get to see his intellect contending with the powerful theories that have emerged since the late 70s. His praxis, the way he grounded, the way he went to the deeper truth and called it out, the way he was willing to reach unusual or challenging conclusions based on the evidence even if it was groundbreaking or unexpected, these are all licence for us in the present, models of how we can tend to the world and its contradictions today. And as you allude, even with the tragic loss of some of his work in the events around 1980, there is considerable work still either unpublished, obscure or little known, some of which will continue to flow out hopefully from the Verso loft. And scholars can seek his work, it is on all the servers and in journals which are increasingly accessible.

Rodney's research and writing, at all points, was marked by his commitment to putting ideas, teaching, books and articles to work in the vital and necessary struggle of continued liberation and revolution. How would you chart Rodney's intellectual and activist trajectory from the 1960s to his murder in 1980?

Relentless, multifaceted, unfinished, focused on numerous projects at once, focused on Guyana and its very specific geometry in the final years, and might have helped lead the country to freedom and unification beyond what has since seemed remotely possible. He was unusual in connecting organically and genuinely with people in all lines of work and at all levels of poverty and dispossession, he seemed to have no boundaries in that regard. In Guyana he crossed over racial lines and united people with knowledge of shared colonial histories. In Binghamton I met more working-class people who remembered him than academics, people who attended an open lecture of his or took one of his classes or knew him from some interaction in town. His praxis was so powerful in 1968 Jamaica, at such a significant time, that he was expelled from the country in under nine full months, leading to the Rodney Riots or Rebellion, an event of national, Caribbean and arguably world historical significance. In Tanzania he was a leading voice on campus and in the Dar School of Radical Historiography, and participated and was a leader in student social movements of national consequence, but he also left campus and taught and grounded with high school students, rural labour unions and collective farmers, and all sorts of groups that invited him.

Less seriously, but no less complexly, Rodney's thinking and work put him at odds with the government again, though he was close with President Nyerere. His transnationalism was off putting to nationalist party leaders, as were his withering but essential critiques of comprador petty-bourgeois elites and neo-colonialism, and he knew that his groundings would be deeper in Guyana than anywhere because it was his home society. His work there deserves more attention from PhD researchers and scholar visits to the archives, it was an incredibly rich grounding, probably his deepest of all. He produced his definitive *A History of the Guyanese Working People*, and the subsequent two volumes intended to follow it were done or nearly completed when they were stolen from his house. He produced the beginnings of an ambitious children's book series which was to cover the true historical stories of all the major groups in the country, to undermine the divide and conquer legacies that separated Guyanese communities. And his speeches to the Guyanese people, including "Peoples Power, No Dictator," are another set of documents altogether, some of his least known and most important, though his comrades have maintained a steady literature and engagement with this and all the literature in *Dayclean*, and more than a few other venues. He was planning to get out for a while, the complexities were staggering, political, legal, personal, familial; newly independent Zimbabwe had invited him and there was a plan to go when the bomb was planted in his walkie-talkie.

Where does this book, The Russian Revolution: A View from the Third World, *fit within Rodney's overall published work?*

As with *How Europe Underdeveloped Africa*, there's the methodological/theoretical modelling done here, which stands the test of time remarkably well, as the conditions it confronted remain largely continuous and expanded in new ways that need to be updated and can often be found in the pages of *ROAPE* and just a really select number of venues. At the level of specificities and historiographic details we see some inevitable ageing of facts and shifts of knowledge that reflects the passage of time. But even here many of the basics hold up in ways that reflect the depth of the basis on which his arguments were made, their original facticity and empirical, personally validated, experiential, grounded praxis. It's his most explicit work of Marxist theory, a window into his Tanzania years and his teaching practices. It's also an important contribution to his thinking on epistemology, Black Studies and decolonial scholarship.

Can you tell us something about the work you do as a board member of the Walter Rodney Foundation? What activities and events, publications etc does the Foundation carry out? Could you also mention the involvement of the family in the foundation?

It's a family foundation, first and foremost, and grassroots, which is to say, we operate on a very small local budget and have yet to land any large grants to support our work. We have an incredible group of community partners, with most of our work based in collaboration with the AUC Woodruff Library and comrades in the greater Atlanta area and well beyond, extending internationally wherever people find us really. Almost all our work and activities are therefore volunteer based. There is a lot of freedom in this model, but also a degree of grind on some of the main actors, including Pat and Asha Rodney, who do the lion's share of the actual work and leadership. I am one of a very dynamic Board, that already has its own history, and Atlanta is the perfect city to do the work we do, we fill a particular niche in the community and have room for many more to join us.

After the Rodney Papers were deposited at the AUC Woodruff Library, the family started an annual Walter Rodney Symposium, now in its 17th year (though our keynote speech and fundraiser with Angela Davis this past March had to be cancelled just as Covid-19 shutdowns arrived). This annual Atlanta tradition has attracted hundreds of guests each year, students and scholar research panels, artists and musicians, heads of state, and incredible recent keynotes such as John Carlos on the 50th anniversary of his Olympic protest with Tommy Smith, Mireille Fanon-Mendes-France, daughter of Frantz Fanon and a leading decolonial thinker and activist in France, and Ngugi wa Thiong'o, legendary radical Kenyan writer and theorist.

I started the Walter Rodney Public Speakers Series in 2013, which continues to grow. We have partnerships with The Charles H. Wright Museum of African American History in Detroit, the Walter Rodney People's Revolutionary Library in South Africa, the Young African Leaders Forum to name a few friends in our growing global network. We sponsor writing contests in the Caribbean, with a new writing project now in development in Jamaica. We are involved in the upkeep of the Rodney memorial in Guyana and a number of NGO and educational projects around the world. We have been working hard on the publication of his books. We have also built publications, first a *Groundings Newsletter*, and now a recently launched expanded version, with peer reviewed academic content, called *Groundings: Development, Pan-Africanism and Critical Theory*, at Pluto Journals.

For some years now, you have been organising a public lecture series on Walter Rodney's work and life. Can you give us some idea of how successful this has been, in extending and disseminating Rodney's work and ideas and raising some of the questions that were important to him?

The Walter Rodney Public Speakers Series is now eight years old, and our most recent guest speaker was Aaron Kamugisha, just before the shutdown hit. I was very happy to have Marc Lamont Hill and Walter Mignolo lined up, among other guests, and we plan to resume with them and many other friends in Spring 2021. We've had probably 80 events now, featuring student and community activism panels, discussions on the threats to Black Studies, and guests like Roediger, Kelley, Zwanenberg, Beverly Guy-Sheftall, Jesus "Chucho" Garcia, Cynthia Enloe, Kali Akuno,

Ajamu Nangwaya, Charisse Burden-Stelly and many more.

My own university sometimes tried to block me from bringing my suburban state university classes to the Black side of town for these lectures, and for college credit, so I've had to scramble to keep making this possible. Throughout, the public has been welcome to all lectures, high school students have participated, especially through our partner Project South, and undergrad and graduate university students have taken it for college credit at Clark Atlanta, Morehouse, Spelman, Emory and Georgia State, as well as being anchored at my school. The work has won awards, including the very meaningful Hosea Williams Community Activism award at Georgia State University, named for one of Martin Luther King's closest allies. This work has attracted small intimate groups of 20-50, and larger groups of 80-200 people over the years, and become a part of the Atlanta conscious landscape.

I have been pushing the idea that together with King and Du Bois, Atlanta should also be renowned for its Rodney relationship, the third of this powerhouse triumvirate, and whose work and legacies continue to overlap in Atlanta. One of those connection points was the Institute of the Black World, at which Rodney taught and worked over summers in the 1970s. It was launched by King's close ally and comrade Vincent Harding, in Du Bois's old house, just a few feet from where the Rodney Papers are now located. The earliest ideas for my series were inspired by Harding's visiting pedagogic model in 2012 at Morehouse, so I am happy that this work also serves to honour his legacy. These are important linkages we work to sustain and amplify.

Given Rodney's work on Black Power, and his deep involvement with the workers movements in Guyana, can you reflect on the contemporary relevance of his life and writing, for activism in the United States, and in a world increasingly controlled by the 1%?

This part of Rodney's work is powerful and really resonant with youth and activists today. It's central to all his work. I find *Ground-*

ings with My Brothers, for example, to be a great pedagogical tool in intro and more advanced classes, as is *How Europe Underdeveloped Africa*. Some Marxists falsely portray his work on race as "an embryonic precursor to his more mature Marxism of later years", but in fact he did not follow linear stages in his thought and development any more than human societies do. Instead, Marxism and racial analysis were things to be figured out in their specificities in different locations around the world, always in complex relation with one another.

Rodney is therefore one of our most brilliant thinkers on race/class questions and a major precursor to, and somewhat different tendency within coloniality and decolonial theory, which also seeks to elaborate what real world race/class continua are like in their actual complexities. Given the ongoing and abject dehumanisation of Black lives everywhere, and especially in the US police state, his work remains inspirational and important for those now seeking to overturn these systems of representation and oppression and provides critical historical groundings for us today. Rodney gives us a Marxism in which Black Power is central.

Less than a year after Rodney was murdered the great Caribbean activist C. L. R. James lamented that Rodney had "not studied the taking of power" – it seems to me more of a lament that Rodney was murdered, than a serious critique. Looking at Guyana and the Caribbean do you think there is any merit to James' observations?

It's a moment of personal frustration with James, honestly. I remember discovering it in the Alpers book in the stacks at Binghamton one night, no doubt one of those nights I came home after dawn to the chagrin of my partner. It was a blow, as I had come to love and appreciate James more than almost any other.

Either you take it as honesty in a moment of pain, as some no doubt do. Or you read it, as I think I tend to, as a moment of limitation, frustration at the loss of his student who had become an equal, a comrade with a parallel but different path, generationally removed but also different in more subtle ways. To me it signifies a shift between a more rigid and formulaic way of thinking in James (which incidentally reminds me of Ewan and my own grandfather, both born in 1917, and sharing an austere vertical formality in thinking regardless of which radical end of the spectrum they occupied), and a more creative and open way of thinking about epistemologies and categories of thought. But also, a matter of praxis, of grounding, and where Rodney lived his life in action as opposed to James who remained more in the metropole, often at a distance from the taking of power he so brilliantly theorised about.

We organised a major Rodney conference in 1998, the first of international scope after somewhat of a lull since the 1981 event at UCLA. And this question reverberated there as well, amongst the participants and the students. It's too big an unfinished and one-sided beef between some of our most revered leaders to leave hanging out there as a community.

One of the intended purposes of these assassination events is to send a public message of fear, a chilling effect. It's a potent weapon in fact, and it's a force we in the world have no choice but to acknowledge. Whether the silencing and chilling effects are successful remains an open question reflective of broader patterns of negotiations of power in various nations and regions. We are in our own ways all potential unauthorised and unexpected authors of alternate outcomes, limited only by our own grounded creativity, i.e., in many ways unlimited. Rodney's legacy, so ensconced within the lives of the people of this world, and resonant with profound and clear answers about our world, has unsurprisingly continued to grow. The conditions he illuminated and diagnosed continue to prevail and continue to need deconstruction and decolonisation.

What have the years of activism you have put into the study, legacy and politics of Walter Rodney taught you? How have you been marked by living so close to his work?

Deep questions. Honestly, it's a huge honour to be able to work so closely with the family and the Foundation, and although I never really expected something like this per se, I always did think about meeting or studying with the great scholars I read, each time I put down one of their masterpieces. Some I never met before they died, like Freire. In this case, not only did I meet the Rodney family, but they and those with whom they worked were truly great people steeped in the values and practices of Walter and his communities, so joining in was really an easy, organic choice. We have a beautiful family of activist friends and comrades for which we are grateful, but we are limited mostly to those who are willing to do the kind of work that requires institution building and low-budget activism without compensation, usually with few resources. One of the great privileges of supporting the WRF work, and then of building my own work around and into it, has been being able to be present for so many incredible speakers and guests, artists, musicians, scholars, activists, elders, youth and leaders who have come through to pay homage, to ground with us, to teach and to learn with us. My work there has also fused with my research, teaching and activism, and we've begun to articulate some of that and the emergence of a School of Rodney Pedagogy and Groundings Praxis here in Atlanta, particularly in a recent journal issue we did on Black radical pedagogy.[7] The work Rodney did remains fraught terrain, so much so that my own work encounters challenges and institutional resistance, all sorts of complexities. It's my activist background that makes this more navigable, but the grind is real, and it comes at certain costs which we have to weigh and try to balance.

What areas need to be developed on Rodney's work and how it continues to be used and read today?

I would argue that, with some irony and some predictability,

---

7 "Special Issue: Black Radical Pedagogy at the Limits of Praxis," Journal of Intersectionality, Vol. 2, No. 1, Summer 2018, p. 1-108.

Rodney's work itself has been underdeveloped, discursively and epistemically, and in terms of how the Academic Industrial Complex works and relates to it. What does it mean to decolonise Rodney, as we use him to decolonise history? What does it mean to work at this triple level, because Rodney already worked at a double level (writing history but also decolonising it), and now we have to work on him, and the production of work on him, while taking up his ongoing mission and methodology of decolonising history and thought generally. History in particular, as a discipline, still tends to avoid theory, but points to Novak when it goes in that direction, and has its own ways of talking about the politics of producing historical knowledge, but it largely fails to acknowledge or cite Rodney in these moments, or others before him, and it refuses to engage all the work he did to advance these very same questions. So that's an important disciplinary point of departure to consider.

This parallels in some ways *The Scholar Denied*, which revealed sociology's conspiracies to erase Du Bois and his original contributions. Apartheid structures of knowledge still haunt the academy, and Western and therefore hegemonic modern global thought in general. Rodney was a consummate scholar-activist, but the bourgeois pretence to illusory objectivity, and the resultant depoliticisation of scholarship, means that he is generally seen more as an activist and partisan than as a scholar in the academy, a glaring slight that should be challenged. One unintended benefit of this underdevelopment is that his work has also not been co-opted and mediated by the academy in the reductive ways that Fanon, James and Cesaire have been in the past three decades, so our freedom to interpret and engage his work is also greater.

What does it mean for the academy and the wider society if the greatest thinkers of the 20th century are not Foucault and Derrida but James, Rodney, Lorde, Wynter? What if our politics of citation take us not back to the slave owning and invested "founding fathers", but to the founding rebels who fought for every freedom we enjoy today?

Do you think there are any ways that Rodney's work and activism speaks to those protesting across the country and world today?

The issue of historical underdevelopment is foundational, it's a framework for understanding everything we are seeing. Tamika Mallory gave a powerful speech a few days ago about how America has been looting Black people, and this is the basic truth. Rodney pointed out the relational nature of our lives. When we see Black poverty, we know that it is there because it is making someone else rich. Underdevelopment means extraction of labour and resources so others can be overdeveloped. This happens on a local and domestic axis, and also transnationally.

Western societies tend to focus on the actions of individuals, as though individual Black and White choices and behaviours could account for the grossest disparities of wealth we have ever seen. Rodney helps us achieve an historical structural analysis that accounts for the mechanisms that create and perpetuate systems of inequality. In the absence of such a robust structural explanation for the chasm of unequal life quality, experience and wealth between racial communities in the US, what possible explanation can people reach other than the tired racist tropes that blame the victims of oppression for having dysfunctional cultures, families or behaviours that supposedly bring suffering down upon themselves? Are people, beyond the Murdoch/Breitbart world of openly racist discourse, willing to defend the idea that the different outcomes are actually because of the behaviours of different races? Increasingly I have confronted my students and colleagues with this stark choice, because there really is no middle ground, we are either racist (and it's a wide spectrum), or we develop capacity to see and articulate how systems produce different racial experiences and outcomes, and join the fight to change those systems (in everything we do, how we fully live our lives, not just once in a while).

Covid-19 is an expected but unpredictably timed world-historical crisis of its own, which continues to unfold even as the US is in open rebellion. With a racist president working overtime to disenfranchise and assault communities of colour, now an illness that attacks the pre-existing conditions of oppression and dispossession is predictably having a disproportionate effect on all oppressed communities, Native, Black, migrant labourers, industrial meat and factory workers, the undocumented, the homeless, the newly unemployed, workers choosing between lethal risk at work or rent and food. The profound mishandling of the pandemic in the US and the UK, and in so many countries around the world, adds another profoundly destabilising impact at all levels of our world systems.

We are looking at dereliction of national duty so severe and at such horrifying rates of death that it bears comparison to the eugenicist planning of the 1930s in terms of outcomes and the range of callous elitism, with widespread discussions and even supposedly rational heartfelt speeches about sacrificing our elders en masse, and people with health issues and disabilities for the good of the economy. Covid and its rising death toll, as something we all face, but very disproportionately, is having a politicising effect akin to the Vietnam War, helping clarify the divides in our society into clearer warring camps, those grounded in reality and collective good will, and those who refuse to distance, preferring to traffic in conspiracy theories without concern for the dead as a category.

The uprising against racist dehumanising policing in the US confronts the core fact that police treat people of colour as non-humans, as Sylvia Wynter told us in her Open Letter in the aftermath of the Rodney King beating and the L.A. Rebellion. The police had been openly responding to calls in Black and Brown neighbourhoods with the code NHI, or "No Humans Involved," literally codifying their at-war mentality with an enemy they no longer considered human. Police and civilians have both driven into and over protestors in New York City and many other places this past week, and threats of driving over protestors remains a popular theme on TikTok and are being heard on police channels. Between the pandemic and its orchestrated and amplified unequal impacts, and the war on Black and Brown people, the US is at a critical juncture in terms of its capacity to function.

The consent of the governed is badly shaken and/or withdrawn, and the state apparatus of violence is insufficient to protect private property like it normally does. Meanwhile we all see the response to legitimate protest of the most grotesque police brutality is met with historic levels of more police brutality, including the latest advanced new technologies of violence. It's gone global because it's so recognisable and familiar everywhere. And as the hegemonic empire for 80 years now, what happens in the US is watched closely globally, in the event that one of its crises is also a crisis in the whole world system, signifying a shift to a new world order.

These are the historic moments that produce such shifts, and the US is completely unprotected at the moment from these implications, its executive actively fuelling the decline in status and power almost daily, while also exploring the possibilities of more fascist alternatives. Wynter would hasten to point out that the crisis could also this time be not just limited to the cycles of world capitalist hegemons, but might also be a crisis of the capitalist system itself, and a crisis of the legitimating liberal humanist epistemology that has governed with it for 500 years, through inquisitions, indigenous genocides, mass enslavement of African peoples, violent colonisation, and now a network of neocolonial puppet dictators. The kind of decolonising of the mind Rodney and Ngugi wrote about.

Rodney also warned us that fascism is the product of capitalism in crisis, which could not be more relevant today. Trump just declared Antifa – the correct idea of being anti-fascist, rather than a formal organisation – to be illegal and terrorist, while failing to name white supremacy, which is now ascendant at historic levels, burning and accelerating whatever violence and chaos it can. Young people especially are discovering the disenchantment of the two-party corporate oligarchic system, amidst a global death cult that may never respond to the spectre of total environmental apocalypse, so that too is an accelerant to consciousness, again akin to Vietnam and the cascading sociogenic ruptures of the late 1960s.

The electoral hope of defeating ascendant fascism and racism in the US is now in the hands of the woefully lacklustre Biden/Democratic National Convention, and mail-in ballots are being blocked in the first germ-warfare inflected election season since 1918. Critically, the centrist liberals are unequipped to fight this war and inevitably abet the right agenda in almost all their actions. The US therefore faces the very real prospect of open fascism if Trump wins re-election. It will be a long hot summer of protest. The forces of the Right are actively seizing this conjuncture to foment their agenda, and the Left is largely fractured in its response, due to internal differences, engineered divisions, ideological mistakes, and mainly decades of repression aimed at removing leaders and organisational structures. Because the US sees fascism only in its enemies, it is incapable of seeing its own proximity to fascism, its own descent. So now is the time for increased vigilance, the looming election is actually critical for not just the US future, but for the world. Even more important is the direction this new movement takes, and what gains it can rip from this moment. This is going to be an especially intense year, reminiscent of 1968 globally.

When I think of Rodney in moments like this, I think of a truly brilliant and passionate thinker in search not of professional gains but of the actual truth, of the actual understandings that could help us navigate to social justice in the present. And in that spirit, I look at this uprising and I know I am feeling like I want something new. I'm grounded in but also slightly distrustful or tired of the usual way we do these things, largely within the parameters prescribed by our race/class enemies. It's time for this generation to define new horizons for us all. The rupture is world systemic in nature, the economy is crushing people as its baseline starting point, the grind of capitalism is felt everywhere in the world. History is unwritten right now, at a very perilous time, on the precipice of resurgent fascism on its widest and most industrial scale since World War II. We also have the possibility of shaking loose from systems of control so rooted they appear to be inscribed in nature. We are in that rare moment where, as Marx and Engels said, "all that is solid melts into air." The illusions holding our societies together are ruptured, because the humanity of the majority is being so visibly and systemically denied that for once most of us experience some measure of it and/or know it to be that way, and so the myth of civilization and democracy and gallant lofty bourgeois notions generally [are] shattered – for those who still harboured any such ephemeral hopes. The all-important but usually invisible consent of the governed is being everywhere withdrawn, an unwanted shift in the calculus has been forced by what the bourgeois and property-identified misname looting.

The four imperial circuits of hegemonic world historical capitalism (Spanish/Portuguese, Dutch, British/French, US) have created contiguous un-remediated patterns of inequity that are easily visible in the lives we live, the relational wealth and poverty, the (over)developed and underdeveloped. Power ensures that the "over" in overdeveloped is silent, invisible. Instead, it's always just stated as "developed", the posited natural baseline or optimal state. Immaculate, somehow, in its arrival, as if by its sheer force of will or character or special Cartesian rationality – though some argued it was virility and manhood, some cranium size, there were many bizarre scientific versions – but always a unique human quality that only select white bourgeois Europeans somehow managed to have. Which of course also required the total erasure of all of African history and all of American, Asian, Pacific and Indian Ocean histories. These issues of relational power and immiseration are instituted in obvious and clearly visible ways, industrialised in our modern world, built into our radically disparate infrastructures and currency valuations.

More than half of us go in abject want of food and housing

and water and education, while we have long had and continue to have far in excess of enough for everyone in the world to have all their basic needs completely satisfied and the basis of life thus completely altered. Yet this is hardly conceptualised and pursued as a goal, so beset with antihuman capitalism as an epistemology and total way of life that alternatives have become almost unthinkable. But within and between nations these deep patterns of colonialism, neocolonialism, and oppression can all be traced, and we can demand and institute reversals of the flows and expenditures, to rebalance but also to undo. Why stop at reparations, why not a universal bill of human rights that includes freedom to travel anywhere on earth, honouring of indigenous and collective land holding nations first, provision by any of numerous means of food, housing, work, education and opportunity for all, as basic human rights? Demilitarisation and inter- and intra-regional cooperation to solve our real needs would shift productivity in unknown ways, so many resources and so much potential could be freed up. It's utopian, but in these conjunctures, we need to think big about what is possible. Our enemies can only think small, to fascist manoeuvres and regressive horrors; it is up to us to create something new, which is always utopian until we make it real.

5. Anne Braithwaite (2021), Walter Rodney and the Working People's Alliance

When Guyanese Revolutionary Walter Rodney returned to his home country in the mid-1970s, he joined a socialist organisation called the Working People's Alliance (WPA) to fight against Forbes Burnham's dictatorship. By 1979, the WPA's advocacy for bread, justice, and unity between Afro-Guyanese and Indo-Guyanese drew thousands of Guyanese working people into its ranks. The WPA also attracted support from members of the Guyanese and wider Caribbean community in England. One of them, Anne Braithwaite – who today is the co-chair and treasurer of the Walter Rodney Programme in London – spoke to *ROAPE*'s Chinedu Chukwudinma about her experience as a founding member of the WPA Support Group UK ahead of the 41st anniversary of Rodney's assassination. Braithwaite charts the history of the support group from its emergence in the 1970s to its slow petering out following Rodney's murder. Braithwaite explains that though Rodney was betrayed, then assassinated, his body destroyed and concerted efforts made to tarnish his record, people around the world continue to develop and build on his immense legacy.

***

Tell me about your early years in Guyana and the UK, how did you become politically involved, where did it start?

In Guyana, I was not politically active at all. Guyana gained independence when I was in the middle of high school in 1966. Looking back, I'm amazed that I didn't do more and that I wasn't more engaged with independence. I think having fun really was my main thing at school and between school and coming to England. Not a lot of political engagement at all. My parents were sort of typical, you know, I guess working class with middle class ambitions. My mother was a nurse and was meant to be very good at school. She was one of those really bright girls. She was that kind of hard-working person, but not herself directly political. My father came from what would be considered [the] aspiring middle class, but he himself never exerted himself too much about getting into the middle class. He was somebody who was into enjoying life and, you know, just doing what he liked. He was a security guard and was happy with that.

Going on to school, I spent [my] formative years in primary school in a village in Guyana called Victoria. I realised later on that one of the teachers must have told my parents that they should put me in for the scholarship as it was called at the time. And so, they decided to send me to school in Georgetown where my aunt was a teacher, which was quite far from where we lived at the time. My parents lived in Lodge while my aunt lived in Kitty. So, it was quite a long distance to get to school. But I went to school there and managed to get a scholarship to go to Bishop's High, which was the elite girl's school. In the early days, it would only have been white folks and light folks who went there and the children of diplomats and the planter class who would have gone. I started at Bishop's High in 1963. It was a delayed start because in 1962 we had a big explosion of racial violence that was very disruptive.[8] Like Covid-19 is now, it was very disruptive for schooling, and there was a general strike. They were major disruptions, and the start of the new school year was just one of them. But I started school in 1963, Guyana got independence in 1966, and I left school in 1969.

After leaving school I worked for a couple of years in Guyana[at] Wales Sugar Estate, which has been closed down now. But at the time, it was a functioning sugar estate. I worked there for

---

8   Anne is referring to one the racial conflicts that occurred during the People's Progressive Party's (PPP) term in office from 1961-1964. In February 1962, strikes and riots erupted against the PPP government's Budget bill. As the protest spread, they often took the form of violent clashes between members of the Afro-Guyanese and Indo-Guyanese communities.

a while, which meant leaving home very early in the mornings because I had to get two to three forms of transport and then a ferry to get there at seven o'clock. I subsequently got a job in Georgetown, which was much more attractive because it was much easier to get to. The job was with another state institution, which was the Guyana rice board. It was called the Rice Marketing Board at the time. It was an admin job, bookkeeping and mainly accounting.

I realised afterwards that I got both jobs because of my privilege. Even though I didn't know it at the time, I had two forms of privilege going for me, one, I was a Bishop's high school girl. The second one, I was black African. By that time, the government that was in power was the People's National Congress (PNC) of Forbes Burnham, which was backed mainly by African Guyanese. And the PNC had changed the senior staff in most of these state-organised workplaces because Indian Guyanese or supporters of the rival People's Progressive Party (PPP) had usually staffed these workplaces.[9] So there was an active attempt to get African people in. It was not until much later that I realised why I got hired. I got hired really easily as I didn't have to ask anyone. Usually in Guyana, the way things work is that you have to know somebody and ask somebody to help you. I simply wrote applications or turned up. I don't think I even told anybody about it, I just applied for jobs and got them. Because they were my first jobs, I didn't realise how lucky I was and how privilege was playing to my advantage.

Shortly before I left Guyana, privilege also played to my advantage when I got hired at the CARIFESTA in Guyana, which was

---

9   The People's Progressive Party was the party that led the anti-colonial movement in the 1950s. It was founded and led by the Marxist Indo-Guyanese dentist, Cheddi Jagan, and the African Guyanese Lawyer, Forbes Burnham. However, the two leaders split in 1957. Forbes Burnham created the People's National Congress (PNC), which relied on support from the African community, while Jagan's PPP relied on support from the Indian community. Burnham's PNC defeated the PPP in the General Elections of 1964, rising to power before Guyanese independence from Britain in 1966.

the first Caribbean Festival of Creative Arts. I was then working at the Rice Board and I was told that I received a secondment to work for the festival for six months – I was working with the CARIFESTA secretariat. The crazy thing was that I actually got my salary from the rice board but also got paid as if I was doing a separate job at the festival secretariat. I got tickets to everything going, so was really popular with my mates. By that time, I bought a car and life was wonderful.

When did you end up going to the UK, then?

I wanted to leave Guyana partly because of the racial violence that had happened in 1962. And, in general, it was considered [that] anybody in Guyana who was going to be someone had to go away to do something, usually study. I got a letter from a cousin of mine who lived in London inviting me to come in 1972, and that was the choice that I made.

Life for me in Guyana was, apart from working, just having fun. That was the mindset that I arrived in London with. Within a couple of days of me being in London, another cousin of mine said she was going to take me to a party. I'd literally been here just for a matter of days. And I think it was at the International Students House around the Bloomsbury area, where I met quite a few other Guyanese. The party was in somebody's room in the hall of residence. That same cousin took me to another party at a student centre where there was a bigger space and a much larger crowd. And I met a whole lot of other people, one of whom was a sibling of Walter Rodney. And he eventually introduced me to Walter. He also introduced me to Jessica and Eric Huntley and that's how I kind of started being aware of things and being politicised. Jessica Huntley and I became really good friends and I would help out at the Bogle-L'Ouverture bookshop in Ealing on free evenings and weekends.

When exactly did you meet Walter Rodney, what did you like about him and his work?

The first time I met Walter Rodney was in a house in the early 1970s. He didn't live in London anymore – he lived in Tanzania. But he [was] always travelling back and forth. His relatives would tell me when he's coming to London, and we would go and see him. We turned up to the house at which the Rodney's were staying, that's how I met Walter, his wife Patricia and their young kids.

He just seemed like a regular nice guy actually, both him and his wife, they just seemed like regular nice people, and they were Guyanese. I knew that he had written a couple of books. But I had no real idea of the importance until I started getting reactions from other Guyanese, when I mentioned that I met Walter Rodney, they would say, "you mean, you met Walter Rodney!?" I realised then that he did history. He was a historian. I'd heard people say Walter was bright. But in my colonised mind, if you were bright, you'd become a doctor or a lawyer. Only somebody who wasn't bright enough would do something like history. And I really did not have a concept of how you made a career of being a historian apart from being a teacher, and you became a teacher if you couldn't do better. So him being special and bright was not at the forefront of my mind. He just seemed to be a regular nice guy.

I think one of Rodney's greatest strengths was that he could understand and talk to people at every level with clarity, but without condescension or without using complicated language. By every level, I mean from people who had no formal education – people who literally could not read and write – to people who were very sophisticated academics and professors and who considered themselves the intellectual elite. He could relate to everyone in a clear and respectful way without patronising them. That is why even as a student in Jamaica, he had attracted the attention of the security services. But because of his clarity and [his] ideological and political stance at the time, elements within the university did their damnedest to make sure that he didn't stay there.[10] I guess they would have seen him as a loose cannon as he wanted to go listen and talk to the Rastafari community.

I'm guessing that from your interest in Guyanese politics you came to support Rodney's political organisation the WPA from the UK. When did the WPA Support Group start?

Mid-1970s was when things were becoming politically and economically difficult for working people in Guyana. Reports of repression there were rife. But there were also other things happening. Companies were being nationalised and the government was inviting Guyanese who were leaving in droves to come back home, and calling itself radical, socialist and supporting liberation struggles and so on. I was beginning to become curious about what was really happening at home. That was really the origin of my interest. I realised that one or two people I'd gone to school with were saying things that seemed very strange to me, including identifying Indians in Guyana as the enemy. I found that really upsetting in a way because it reminded me of what had happened in 1962. I felt this is the time that I've got to decide: am I going to support this or am I not? That was when I started thinking actively about politics. I wasn't interested in Britain – I was primarily interested in understanding Guyana and what was happening there.

The WPA Support Group started in 1979, the same year the WPA became a political party. But before the formation of the WPA Support Group in London, I worked with an organisation called CARIG, Committee Against Repression in Guyana, which both Leland De Cambra – another WPA SG UK founding member – and I were part of. That group of mostly African Caribbean activists, with a Guyanese core, started agitating against political developments in Guyana.

---

10   Anne here is referring to when Walter Rodney went to teach in Jamaica in 1968. The Jamaican Government banned Rodney from the island because of his Black Power agitation among students, Rastafarians and unemployed youths.

I was really hungry to learn and to understand what was going on in Guyana. Unlike others there who were politically active before, I had no ideological background. All I knew about ideologies was what the propaganda had got into my head in my early days in Guyana, which was [that] the PPP was communist and they were bad and had to be gotten rid of. And the PNC was the party for me. That was probably the extent of my ideological awareness. Until I began to read things, write and talk to people and meet other activists involved in liberation struggles and other struggles, it was then that I decided with others to form a WPA support group. In short, I think CARIG had ideological issues with the WPA becoming a political party in Guyana. WPA supporters were therefore pushed out of CARIG, although CARIG continued agitating against Guyana's escalating political repression.

The WPA message that resonated the most with me was the genuine wielding of power in the interest of working people, and in particular about ethnic division not being the way to go. And so I was able to support them and over time come to learn a little bit more about what was happening and to understand why they were opposing the PNC government. When there was talk about WPA needing support groups I said, "Yes, I want to be part of it!"

How many people were involved in the WPA Support Group and who?

Initially, I would say maybe a dozen members, rising to scores at its height. We organised the first meeting at my then home at 80 Sistova Road, Balham. By that time, I had become so convinced by what the WPA was saying that I thought it would make sense to most of my friends, and most of the people I knew. I remember rushing home early from work that first evening; myself, Leland De Cambra, Makini Campbell, Horace Campbell, and a few other people waiting around to start. But then the phone started to ring with apologies and excuses like "sorry I have to work late" or "I can't come". That was my first really tough lesson: I thought we were not going to have enough room for people to sit, but that certainly was not a problem at that first meeting. I was disappointed, but it was the start of a steep organising learning curve.

Can you give me a few examples of the various activities that the WPA Support Group did in the UK?

Apart from having planning meetings, we would have public meetings exposing the PNC dictatorship and its neocolonial nature, organise fundraisers, cultural events, dances, film screenings, and connect with radical groups from around the world. We also maintained close contact with the WPA in Guyana, hosting and organising public platforms for visiting members and supporters like Josh Ramsammy, Clive Thomas, Moses Bhagwan, Eusi Kwayana., Rupert Roopnarine and Andaiye who resided in the UK for two years in the early 80s as an WPA international secretary. We also distributed WPA literature and its newsletter, *Dayclean*. Meetings in those days was hiring a school, community or church halls, Ritzy Cinema and Abeng Centre Brixton, getting invited by students, trade unions or other radical groups and disseminating information about what was happening in Guyana and showing solidarity with other campaigns. Those were the priorities at the time. Burnham's PNC government was showing itself up as dictatorial. They had been shamelessly rigging elections, and were duplicitous with Guyana's working people, doing really progressive and popular things like supporting African liberation struggles while at the same time being a despot at home.

Did the WPA Support Group organise these meetings with African or Indian community organisations? Or even left-wing and student groupings?

I think it was very much a case of whatever and wherever the support group could do, and with whomever. We collaborated with Caribbean, African, and many other student activists all over London, the Midlands, Sussex; with Labour and Liberal party activists, NGOs like CAFOD, Friends of The Earth, Amnesty International [which were] interested in the erosion of Guyana's political, civil and human rights. These contacts assisted with disseminating reliable information on Guyana and the WPA, organising legal election observers and briefing journalists, MPs and other activists.

What we were doing all the time was trying to say to people what's going on in Guyana and why. That certainly was my focus. We would say, "we formed this group and are happy to come and talk to you about it." So some students somewhere would invite us to come and speak at something that was already going on, or we would just organise meetings and do flyers and put them out. I remember events at the old Africa Centre in Covent Garden on King Street. That was like the second most important central venue for African and African-Caribbean activists after the Earl's Court Student Centre. Those were the two venues if you wanted to meet black activists, progressive kinds of people. The Earl's Court centre was predominantly Caribbean people while the Africa Centre was predominantly Africans.

That leads me to another question because Burnham in Guyana in the late 70s supported this so-called "cooperative socialism" and made a reputation for himself abroad as a progressive leader, especially in various black radical circles across the world. Did that fact make it difficult for the WPA support group to gain respect in the UK among elements of the black community?

It was not so difficult to get respect, because at that time people were very receptive. However, when non-Guyanese realised we were criticising the Burnham government, they became confused. Guyanese people understood it, because then they knew either directly or from family and friends in Guyana what was going on. But for other Caribbean and African and progressive people, anywhere, really, one had to do a lot of explaining, to explain how somebody who is seen as progressive in the Non-

Aligned Movement was anti-democratic and rotten at the core. In the 1980s, I remember going to the Houses of Parliament here in London with a WPA leader, Clive Thomas, to meet MP Bernie Grant. Clive Thomas was attempting to garner support for the WPA and Bernie Grant at first was supportive, but then said, "… the thing is, man, I can't criticise Burnham as a black leader." That was the biggest struggle that one would have with black activists in the UK, trying to explain to them "Yes, Burnham is a black leader, but…" Rodney's explanations helped me understand those contradictions and the WPA in Guyana had a well thought out position to counter the PNC's carefully cultivated progressive, radical pan-African image.

The primary focus of the PNC, in all their rebrands (now APNU), has always been about usurping state power to develop a base to enrich themselves and dispense patronage, mainly to an African-Guyanese elite. Classic manifestations were the nationalisation of Guyana's sugar and bauxite industries; their notorious, well documented election rigging during the 1960s to 1990s to keep out the PPP with CIA collusion [for which documentation has now been released], and their astonishingly foolhardy attempt – in full public glare – to steal the March 2020 election which they lost, citing historical economic deprivation of African Guyanese. Their reckless desperation to retain control of Guyana's nascent oil and gas industry precipitated today's sad pictures of PNC old men [mostly ex-military in sharp suits] embarrassing themselves.

Did a lot of members in the WPA Support Group write and publish any pamphlets or maybe news briefs on the situation in Guyana?

We did a lot of that but virtually all of them came from Guyana, because we were gathering information, and accurate and reliable information was always an issue. We would get, by various means, information from Guyana – it could be sent to us by post, or it could be people travelling and bringing stuff and we would reproduce them here and there. There were quite a lot of documents that we would reproduce; *Dayclean*, which was the WPA's regular publication, and other particular speeches and publications like *Sign of the Times, People's Power, No Dictator*, and other pamphlets and booklets.[11] It was the sort of material that they would have circulated in Guyana because reading material was always at a premium and newsprint was banned. Part of the repressive nature of the Burnham regime meant that you were starved of newsprint. So, reading material was always in premium demand.

One of the things, if you were Guyanese and you were travelling, is that you tried to tell as few people as possible that you were going back, because otherwise everyone would ask you to take a letter and the letter would turn out to be a big carrier bag full of something. That has to do with the fact that there was always a lot of shortages in Guyana, of basic foodstuffs, also other basic things so that somebody was always desperate, almost anything that you take for granted now would have been either scarce or unavailable in Guyana.

In one sense it was easier to get WPA pamphlets reproduced in the UK. We just had to go to a printer's and get it paid for, or some of us would use facilities where we worked. I worked at one time at a place where I was allowed to use a Gestetner machine (an old duplicating machine), where I could print a flyer and type it up on a stencil and then run it off on the Gestetner machine. I think that was the only way we duplicated pamphlets because photocopying was far too expensive. And the WPA Support Group never paid for the Gestetner because we received collections from meetings and fundraised for everything we did. Or we'd ask people to do it at work or try to get reduced prices somewhere. It was our hustle.

The Working People's Alliance in Guyana became a political party at the height of strikes and mass protest against Burnham and the People's National Congress in the summer and autumn of 1979, known as the civil rebellion. How did you and others feel about the civil rebellion and

---

11 Anne is naming some of the speeches Walter Rodney made in Guyana in 1979-1980.

its impact on the working people, whether African or Indian?

I think there was unity. Absolutely! I think that unity was what alarmed both PNC and the PPP because, in an incredibly short period of time, Rodney and the WPA had actually succeeded in uniting working people in Guyana. That is when Burnham and the PNC decided Rodney had to be permanently removed because cross-community unity undermined their whole foundation of political power.

When a doctor family friend who lived in London learned that I worked with the WPA Support Group, he summoned me, sat me down in his surgery and asked: "Does your mother know what you're doing here?" I tried not to laugh and said, "Yes, I believe so." He could no longer contain himself. He became totally exasperated with me, wagged his finger actually touching my forehead and said, "I'm warning you about those Indians, child!" But that's the kind of experience not uncommon to Guyanese working for grassroots power across the ethnic divide.

My other question is, you know, between the members of the WPA Support Group, did you have any political debates? If so, what were those debates about?

Absolutely! For example, one of the major early debates was on whether non-Guyanese people should be allowed as group members. I had to overcome my own nationalist limitations, then work to persuade others. Makini Campbell, an American and Horace Campbell, a Jamaican, among others, were founding members. But most members were of Guyanese heritage, an exciting microcosm of Guyana's multi-ethnic possibilities. Other debates were around how we advocate for WPA in Guyana, which UK community, activist and political groups to collaborate with, and how, given their various ideological nuances.

I was working full time and also had a part-time job, yet I had a very full social life, with lots of politicking. Yet a good rave remained an agenda feature. One of the things the support group often did was to host combined events [cultural, rally, rave] at particular venues that were suitable, like the Covent Garden Africa Centre, Clapham Common Methodist church hall which was also the Queen Mother Moore Saturday school and the Abeng in Brixton. Turning political meetings into parties became a really good way of recruiting.

Walter Rodney was somebody who loved partying, and I was probably with him more at parties than any other place. In parties those days, you'd have floor-to-ceiling speakers so any conversation on the dance floor was impossible. We called parties where you hold your glass in one hand, nibbles in the other, and chat, English parties. We did not do English parties.

I was told that Rodney and WPA did not address people by proclaiming their socialist ideology or using complex jargon and concepts in Guyana. It seems like they always spoke to people in a language the people could understand.

An issue for me within the WPA Support Group was when others who would have studied various political theories and ideologies ask, have you read this or that? And I would say no. They might then reply with a smirk and say "You mean, you've not read *The Wretched of the Earth*, you've not read this, you've not read that. You want to be an activist and you haven't read these things!" And that used to irritate me so much that it made me less inclined to read that kind of stuff.

Rodney often said things that made me want to think, but I recall him using few "isms" in public meetings or private discussions that I was part of, nor in my conversations with him. So, I did not feel put down by the way Rodney spoke or related in ideological terms. People in Guyana who listened to him at public meetings were able to understand and tell you what Rodney had said. When I visited my village, people there like my grandmother, who had no discernible prior political interest, would say things that would make me think again, oh, she's listening to Rodney. So yes, Rodney had a huge communication gift.

There were some ideological tensions in the Support Group, but I would mostly tune out of those. When it came to what to do next, I would re-engage. And when we had to write stuff, put out event leaflets etc, that was quite challenging for me to be clear and not use wrong terminology. I would always have others do it or check what I wrote.

So, if we come to the tragic moments when Walter Rodney was assassinated in June 1980. How did you feel when he passed? What did you and the Support Group do in the aftermath?

Of course, Rodney's assassination is imprinted on my mind. The Support Group had only been going for a short while. I had accounting exams all that week, and finished on Friday 13 June 1980, with a wonderful celebration dinner with friends from Barbados who were honeymooning houseguests, it was an indulgent evening. The telephone woke me at about 3am with the horrible news: Rodney was assassinated and his brother Donald seriously injured. The WPA Support Group convened an emergency meeting early that morning to plan action.

Rodney's murder was a massive shock worldwide, and particularly frightening for those on the ground in Guyana. But anger and rage soon took over and intensified the Support Group's work here. Many Guyanese, Caribbean people, radical activists would have said, "no, no, Burnham would not kill Rodney." WPA supporters and others were attacked and killed before: Father Darke, Ohene Koama and Edward Dublin, but they won't dare kill Rodney. There was all kinds of harassment and terrible things happening, but they were people who believed that Burnham would kill other people, but not Rodney. People who were supporters of Burnham and his PNC party saying "No, he won't kill Rodney." There was one particular person who couldn't speak to me after the murder, because he was one of the people who swore loudly that they wouldn't kill Rodney. I think very few PNC supporters believed that it was anything other than an assassination by the state, which was masterminded by Burnham. Although people found ways of making excuses or justifying it, there was never much doubt about who killed Rodney.

The WPA Support Group's activities in England intensified. In 1982 when Princess Diana and Charles got married, Prime Minister Burnham came to the UK to attend the wedding and meet with the Guyanese community. The Support Group picketed the Grosvenor House Hotel meeting as attendees arrived, then circumvented security to enter and break up the meeting. That was an important and effective symbolic confrontation. On another occasion, Burnham was in London for Commonwealth heads of government meeting, I think. PNC supporters organised a huge meeting at Battersea Town Hall. That meeting too was picketed and we broke it up.

Wow! Really, you broke up the meeting?

Oh, we broke up many meetings! Anytime the PNC attempted public meetings that we heard about, especially when senior politicians or big names came from Guyana we planned for them. So, eventually they were restricted to small, semi-secret events. We also regularly picketed Guyana's High Commission around repressive events in Guyana. Some Guyana high commissioners had a particularly difficult job at the time. Whenever they attempted any public appearances, we would challenge them and picket. I mean it was a normal part of what we did.

The WPA Support Group seems to have operated long after Rodney's death and well into the 1980s...

One of the things that really helped to sustain our work here was that Senior WPA members from Guyana would often come to London for fundraising, academic or personal reasons. People like

Joshua Ramsammy, Clive Thomas and Moses Bhagwan. Usually senior WPA men, Andaiye being the exception. After Rodney's assassination, Andaiye spent a couple years in London as WPA International Secretary. So we had a reasonable flow of senior people back and forth. And of course, one would have meetings with them. Everyone in Guyana had [and still have] close family residing outside Guyana. Many who lived at subsistence levels in Guyana would travel, if only to buy goods abroad and resell them in Guyana. So, a lot of travel overseas was part of the ordinary Guyanese life. London was also quite an important hub for travelling to other places like Europe and North America.

On a tangential matter, Guyana's emigration epidemic since the 1960s – believed to be the worst of the Caribbean – remains unaddressed.

When and why did the WPA Support Group's activities come to an end?

It was a slow petering out rather than a sudden stop. Andaiye was here, as I said, as international secretary for a couple of years. And we continued working, campaigning, fundraising. There were various campaigns that some of us worked with like the Justice for Walter Rodney campaign which Helena Kennedy and then Richard Hart chaired, also the Campaign Against Waste Dumping in Guyana (CAWDIG). Lots was going on.

The difficulty the Support Group had was that communication and information from the WPA had all but dried up after Andaiye's return to Guyana. There was no email or internet in those days and telephone calls were very expensive. No materials, no *Daycleans*. With hindsight I recognised that Rodney's death had dealt the party itself a fatal blow, and by the late 1980s it had ceased to be a mass party, or even a pressure group.

In the early 1990s when Clive Thomas was visiting London, some of us arranged a public meeting. Thomas wowed a packed Commonwealth Institute audience, talking about Burnham's PNC government's disgraceful plan to import toxic waste from the United States. An elite Guyanese friend of Guyana's government had negotiated a lucrative deal with private US companies which was being sold to the Guyanese as "we can burn it to generate electricity and end blackouts forever". Some people in Guyana were saying "Yeah, if it means no more blackouts, we want it." Quite reminiscent of current oil and gas and other natural resource exploitation and environmental protection concerns. It was only by raising the alarm with information unearthed by Friends of the Earth, that Burnham's government quietly dropped the plan.

At that time, I thought that that was like old Support Group times – a full house and a great meeting.

It seems that the WPA had lost its soul with Rodney's murder. They were never able to rekindle Guyanese working people's interest, nor engage with workers' struggles on the ground. There were no WPA public meetings, no workers' campaigns, no discussions, no party manifesto. A flurry of activity in 2005 to commemorate the 25th Anniversary of Rodney's assassination took some overseas-based WPA associates to Guyana and produced some material.

In 2010 the WPA rump (mostly a tiny, old male elite) decided that the way to remain relevant was to join the PNC. Most of the earlier senior WPA women had left the party and were either doing social activist work in Guyana or had emigrated. That so-called coalition with the PNC[12] was hard to believe. And the PNC has done what it has always done with previous coalition partners, namely isolate then destroy them.

In the UK, I think there are WPA-related documents, such as pamphlets, pages of Dayclean *and press releases that came from the WPA Support Group, which have been stored at the London Metropolitan Archives and the George Padmore Institute. I wanted your opinion on what you think has been done so far to honour Walter Rodney's legacy?*

---

12   A Partnership for National Unity – was a coalition formed in 2011 and comprised the PNC and the WPA.

You find that people continue referencing Rodney and his work internationally, in every continent in the world. I think to myself, this guy died at age 38 and continues to inspire. Yet he never held senior office anywhere, never held any lofty positions outside his family. That in itself is a huge legacy that he's left, and that people can continue to recognise his work and his contribution all this time and that his work remains relevant in 2021. When I travelled to places like Malaysia, or Thailand or Japan, let alone Zimbabwe, essentially everywhere I go, you can meet people who knew Rodney or knew his work. I just found that really amazing.

In Guyana, the PNC, in assassinating him, removed his body. What they also attempted to do was to destroy his legacy, and they continue to try to do that. I think their position now is to say things like, "Oh, yes. You know, Rodney was very bright, but maybe a bit impetuous." It depends on who they're speaking to. If they think they're speaking to intellectuals, they say, "his work was brilliant. But he didn't understand working people and practical organising on the ground. The people weren't ready." To African nationalists they say, "but you know, he was trying to destroy a black man, a black leader."

But I think Rodney's legacy in Guyana is massive. It's huge, because at least senior politicians are now acknowledging that there are ethnic issues in Guyana. In Guyana in 1972 Burnham's PNC was saying "there's no race problem here in Guyana. Look, we have Indian friends in our party, too." The PPP would do the same. But the leadership of these parties are still just thinking about how they can use their position at the top of the race-based parties to leverage state and resource power to enrich and glorify themselves and dole out patronage. It's all about how the elites are going to get their hands on the "corn". Rodney's legacy exposed that deception.

In Rodney's name we must continue to ask these questions: is multi-ethnic organising, independent of the two ethnic-based parties that have comprehensively failed Guyanese for the last six decades, possible? Or is Guyana doomed to decades more division and destruction?

What was your favourite moment in the WPA Support Group?

Moments that stick out in my mind are times when we challenged the PNC here in London. We broke up their meetings and faced them down to the extent where I think the PNC wouldn't attempt to do too many big public things here, even when they were in office. President Granger [PNC President of Guyana from May 2015 to August 2020] only had one public meeting here while he was president for the last five years. I don't think they would have the nerve to do it, simply because there was too much opposition.

Everyone in Guyana feared Burnham. People in London would say to you, "I can't picket because I'm on a scholarship. And my scholarship will get taken away." Scholarships got taken away anyways, whether these people came to the pickets or not. But being able to go into meetings and challenge them to their face was to puncture that god-like image that the PNC ministers had. That meeting we disrupted in Battersea Town Hall in the 1980s was one of those meetings that people still remember.

Importantly "big man" politics was effectively challenged and there remains the hope that youth will carry on the struggle.

Rodney was betrayed, his body destroyed, and concerted efforts made to tarnish his legacy. But I am most proud of the WPA-Support Group UK's role in nurturing young community and scholar-activists to develop and build on Rodney's immense legacy.

6. Georges Nzongola-Ntalaja (2021), A People's Historian

ROAPE's Ben Radley speaks with the Congolese historian and scholar-activist Georges Nzongola-Ntalaja. A professor at the University of North Carolina in the US, Nzongola-Ntalaja is the author of many seminal books on Congolese history, including *The Congo from Leopold to Kabila: A People's History* and *Patrice Lumumba*. Here, he explains that the overriding motivation of his work is solidarity with the oppressed and an uncompromising quest for the truth to elucidate the political history of the Congo and Africa generally from the colonial period to the present.

***

Can you please describe to us your memories and experiences growing up as a child in the Congo under Belgian colonial rule, coming of age during the national liberation struggle, and how these experiences shaped your early politics and student activism?

Growing up on the American Presbyterian Congo Mission station of Kasha, some 10km from the state post of Luputa and a major railway station on the BCK network between Lower Congo and Katanga, the first experience I remember from my childhood was the consciousness of skin colour. As Frantz Fanon has described all colonial settlements, this mission station was built as a Manichean city, with whites on the one side with modern houses and electricity, and black people on the other side in thatched roof houses lit with kerosene lamps on unlit streets. A large *cordon sanitaire* or a huge open space comprising the church, the medical centre, school buildings and the football field and other sports facilities separated the city of light from the city of darkness, which rejoiced only under moonlight.

Since our parents worked for the mission in various capacities as teachers, nurses, maintenance workers and domestic servants for the American missionaries from Dixie, we as their children could play with the few white kids present. By the time we all attained puberty, these children's games ceased, and it was not unusual to hear the white kids calling us by the N-word. Racial consciousness evolved on both sides, and this was reinforced for the Congolese each time we went to Luputa to catch a train or to shop at the stores owned by the Greek, Italian and Portuguese merchants. While in Luputa, we also witnessed whipping of prisoners by the police under the stern watch of the Belgian administrator at 6:00am or 12:00 noon near the flagpole with the red, yellow, and black Belgian standard. At the train station, black people stood in a long queue under the sun to buy tickets, but a white person could simply walk straight to the ticket box and walk away with his or her ticket in a minute.

You briefly held a number of academic positions in the Congo in the early 1970s, shortly after Mobutu came to power, and before beginning your long period of exile from the country. What impact has having spent such a long time away from the Congo had on you?

I had spent eight years and a half in the United States completing one year of secondary school, four years of undergraduate studies and three years of postgraduate studies, from July 1962 to February 1971. During this period, I had the opportunity of spending two months and a half in the Congo during the summer vacation of 1965, which allowed me to visit my very large family, and to even visit newly independent Zambia for a week. It was therefore very difficult to spend 17 years and a half, between December 1973 and August 1991, without seeing members of my family. Both parents and one sibling had passed away during that period. But those years of exile strengthened my commitment to the struggle for political change and genuine democracy in the Congo. I participated in numerous meetings and spoke on the Congo in the United States and Canada, Europe and several African countries.

This self-imposed exile from Mobutu's Zaïre was due to the harassment and threats I had experienced from the regime during my two years of work at the Lubumbashi campus of the National University of Zaïre, including a four-hour interrogation by the security police in November 1973. The harassment was renewed in Washington DC in the 1980s when I became actively involved in supporting the mass democratic movement led by the Union for Democracy and Social Progress (UDPS). In 1989 my passport was confiscated by the Congolese ambassador to the US, Mushobekwa Kalimba wa Katana, following my request for a renewal. After several months of inaction, I received a letter dated 26 December 1989 from the ambassador stating that he took away my passport on the grounds of my opposition to the regime. Although I did get the passport back after the liberalisation of the system on 24 April 1990, I still introduced a complaint against Mr. Mushobekwa for violations of my rights as a citizen through the Foreign Affairs Subcommission of the Political Affairs Commission at the Sovereign National Conference on 29 June 1992. He appeared before the subcommission and admitted that he had indeed violated my civil rights but added that he had acted on orders from the secret police in Kinshasa. It was, for him, a question of a choice between renewing my passport or losing his job. The subcommission cleared him.

You were heavily involved in the Sovereign National Conference in 1992, which represented the culminating moment of around a decade of resistance to Mobutu's dictatorship in the struggle for multiparty democracy. Can you describe the atmosphere in the Congo at that time, and the meaning and significance of that historical moment, both for yourself but also politically for the country and for the Congolese?

It is almost 29 years now since I joined the Conférence Nationale Souveraine (CNS) in April 1992 as one of seven "scholars of international renown" co-opted by the Conference to make their contribution to this nationwide palaver. Following my general policy statement on 14 May 1992, my name became a household word in the Congo. My declaration was one of the most popular speeches at the CNS, judging by the number of applauses. Cassette recordings were made and sold in the Congolese diaspora in Belgium, and in a country where the post office was no longer functioning very well, over 500 letters were sent to me by young people from all over the country. On a trip to Goma from New York in April 2007, an immigration official looked at my passport and said to me: "Aren't you the Professor Nzongola of CNS fame?" When I said yes, he started chastising me for having abandoned the struggle by returning abroad. Even today, people over 50 in Kinshasa would recognise me because of the CNS.

I have given a comprehensive assessment of the CNS in my book, *The Congo from Leopold to Kabila: A People's History*. Most of [the CNS'] 23 commissions and over 100 sub-commissions produced excellent reports on what had gone wrong in the past and proposals on charting a new path for freedom, peace, and well-being in the country. As a member of the Political Affairs Commission, I had expressed interest in chairing the sub-commission on external affairs. But the people who had advanced the foreign agenda in the Congo like Justin Bomboko and Victor Nendaka did their best to exclude me from that sub-commission. As a consolation, they allowed me to chair two sub-commissions, on current affairs and political files, the latter being basically the rewriting of Congolese history by revisiting all the major political events in the country since Independence on what happened, why it happened, and what we should do to prevent such events in the future. When the late Professor Ernest Wamba-dia-Wamba joined us, I managed to pull him from the Scientific Research Commission to make him the rapporteur for Political Files. He wrote an outstanding report on our deliberations.

The CNS succeeded as an educational forum and a political mobiliser, for all plenary meetings were carried on national radio and television. In most places of work, people did what they could do between 7:00am and 12:00pm and went to sit by their radio or television to follow the deliberations at the Chinese built People's Palace, home of our Parliament. However, the CNS failed to achieve its immediate objective, which was to remove the dictator Mobutu from power and put the country on the path of multiparty democracy, economic recovery, and the improvement of the living conditions of ordinary people. The main reasons for that failure were the reluctance of Mobutu and his clique to leave power and its attendant privileges, the weakness and immaturity of the opposition, and the lack of support from the major Western powers for radical change in the resource-rich centre of the African continent.

I illustrate the latter factor with the way the international community refused to accept the democratic decision of 4 August 1992 by 2,842 delegates at the CNS, representing all strata of the Congolese population to abandon "Zaïre" and to go back to the majestic name of "Congo." This was a confirmation of a decision by another popular assembly, the Constitutional Convention of 1964 at Luluabourg (now Kananga), to make the official name of the country "The Democratic Republic of the Congo". In May 1997, the same international community had no problem accepting the actions of Laurent-Désiré Kabila who, by the stroke of a pen, changed the country's name to DRC and proclaimed himself the new president of the country. The major powers, beginning with the United States, accepted this unilateral decision, like Mobutu's earlier decision imposing the name "Zaïre" in October 1971.

Today, the CNS remains a major historical reference for political and social change in the DRC. None of the numerous conferences, dialogues and consultations that have been held since then have brought anything new in terms of democratising the political system, cleansing the state of its deadwood and corrupt oligarchs, and empowering the people to ensure that they are not only the primary sovereign, but also the beneficiaries of state action. In accordance with Etienne Tshisekedi's credo, the business of government is *"le peuple d'abord"*, or the people first. This is the popular and progressive legacy of the CNS, and the alpha and omega of democratic and developmental governance in the DRC.

We have recently marked the 60th anniversary of Patrice Lumumba's murder, and to commemorate the occasion ROAPE published an extract of a keynote speech you gave in 2018, in which you discuss Lumumba's rise and influence as both a nationalist and pan-Africanist leader. Before discussing Lumumba, I'd like to briefly touch on the late Etienne Tshisekedi, the main opposition leader to Mobutu in the 1980s and 1990s, and father of the current President Felix Tshisekedi. You served at one point as a diplomatic advisor to Etienne Tshisekedi, who himself was an advisor to Lumumba's Mouvement National Congolais (MNC) in the late 1950s. How do you position Etienne Tshisekedi in relation to Lumumba and the broader emancipatory struggle of which they were both a part?

Yes. As a law student at Lovanium University, Etienne Tshisekedi wa Mulumba served as an advisor to the newly created MNC for one year, 1958-59. Thus I do assume that they did get to know each other, given the fact that only seven years separated them in age, as Lumumba was born on 2 July 1925 and Tshisekedi on 14 December 1932. In September 1959, the MNC split into two separate wings, the radical and unitarist Lumumba wing, known as MNC/L, and a more moderate wing led by federalists under Albert Kalonji, known as MNC/K. Following his service on Mobutu's College of general commissioners from 14 September 1960 to 9 February 1961 as deputy commissioner for justice, Tshisekedi went to work for Albert Kalonji in secessionist South Kasai, where he served as minister of justice.

Tshisekedi's stoicism in the face of unending persecution and humiliations by Mobutu, Laurent and Joseph Kabila, [and] his steadfast fight for democracy, the rule of law and the instauration of a government that works for the people, was exemplary. His courage and persistence recalled those of Lumumba. This made him very popular among the people, who reverently called him "Moses," in the Biblical sense or, more affectionately, as "Ya Tshitshi" or "Big Brother Tshitshi." By his courage, stoicism, and intransigence on key principles of democracy, justice, equality and service to the people, he was the Congolese political leader closest to the character of Lumumba. As for the son, he is nicknamed "Tshitshi Béton," or someone as hard as concrete and capable of facing any challenge, including getting rid of the Kabila dictatorship.

Moving onto Lumumba, then, how strong an influence do you think his political legacy continues to hold in the popular Congolese imagination today, and across Africa more broadly?

Given the lack of regular polling on the knowledge and attachment that people do have about Patrice Lumumba and his martyrdom, it is difficult to assess the strength of his political legacy in the Congolese political imagination today. People do frequently hear his name on national radio and television, which remind them of his eminent status as our national hero and the 17 January, the day of his assassination along with Sports and Youth Minister Maurice Mpolo and Senate Vice President Joseph Okito, is a national holiday.

In Africa, boulevards, major avenues, squares, and streets are named after him. In most of the countries I have visited, the place I like the best is the African Heroes Square in downtown Bamako, Mali's capital, which has a very impressive statue of Lumumba. When he was killed, many parents across the continent gave his name to newly born sons. Two of them were serving as members of the Nigerian Parliament when I lived in Abuja in 2000-2002. Kenya has a distinguished professor of law who goes by the name of Patrick Lumumba. Finally, many literary and nonfiction books were written in honour of Lumumba following his death.

Lumumba's Independence Day speech remains a major treasure for African freedom fighters, even among the lost sheep. In the 1980s, during my days as a professor at Howard University in Washington, I had a visit to my office one day from Roberto Holden, then exiled leader of the National Front for the Liberation of Angola. I asked him if it was true that he had always been a paid collaborator of the CIA. To refute this accusation, which was nonetheless well-established, he and his assistant stood up and recited Lumumba's famous speech in its entirety, in French. I was so moved by this gesture that I momentarily forgot about his crimes in Angola.

60 years after Lumumba's demise, the people who really know about his leadership and his trials and tribulations, in the Congo or elsewhere in Africa, are generally past the age of 75. The two generations who came after 1961 may have heard tales about him, read books and articles on him or seen films and videos about him, but they have very little knowledge of Lumumba because they live in countries that – in most cases – are ruled by political leaders who have no interest in progressive and visionary leaders determined to put people's needs above their own selfish class interests. Patrice Lumumba was such a leader, and most of his peers in this category, including Kwame Nkrumah of Ghana, Mehdi Ben Barka of Morocco, Eduardo Mondlane and Samora Machel of Mozambique, Amílcar Cabral of Cape Verde and Guinea-Bissau, Thomas Sankara of Burkina Faso, and Ruth First and Chris Hani of South Africa, were destroyed by imperialism and their cronies in Africa through military coups d'état and/or assassination.

Lumumba's name was also associated, positively or negatively, with the popular insurrections of 1963-68 for a "second independence." This was a movement based on the grievances of peasants, workers, secondary school students and lower civil servants, including teachers and nurses, whose organic intellectuals had clearly shown that the flag independence of 1960 was a sham. Politicians had promised everything under the sun during the electoral campaign of May 1960 but delivered nothing in terms of expanding freedom and improving the living conditions of the population. Since they were no different from their Belgian predecessors, the Congolese rulers constituting the new privileged oligarchy were in the eyes of the people the new whites because they were just as brutal in their repression as the former colonialists, on whom they continued to rely for military support, and liars because they excelled at making false promises.

The popular movement for a second independence was led by the former lieutenants of Patrice Lumumba. It had two distinct wings and fields of armed struggle, the Kwilu revolution, led by Pierre Mulele, Lumumba's former minister of education and a Marxist-Leninist, and the Eastern or Simba Rebellions, led by Christophe Gbenye, Lumumba's former minister of internal affairs and successor as head of the MNC/L. This is the wing that also included Laurent-Désiré Kabila, Thomas Kanza and Gaston Soumialot. Of the two wings, Mulele's was the most politically successful by its revolutionary engagement and commitment to ordinary people's interests, while the Gbenye wing was more militarily successful but betrayed Lumumbism by its brutal and unprincipled goal of regaining the power Lumumba's lieutenants had lost in Kinshasa at any price.

Once they conquered a city, the first thing they did was occupy the residence of the provincial governor or district commissioner to find the loot, which included gold, money, and fine alcohol; they paid no consideration to people's needs and interests, while pretending to be fighting for ordinary people. Rhetoric aside, they were no different from the new oligarchy led by army general Mobutu, intelligence chief Victor Nendaka and perennial foreign minister Justin Bomboko. Later, Gbenye would remain head of one of a dozen MNC/L factions and joined Mobutu's and Joseph Kabila's political coalitions; Thomas Kanza would become Mobutu's candidate for prime minister at the CNS in 1992 and a minister in Laurent Kabila's government; Gaston Soumialot became a very successful farmer with Mobutu's support; and Laurent Kabila overthrew Mobutu with military support from Rwanda and

Uganda in 1997. The multiple errors of the second independence movement and the co-optation of most of its leaders by the MPR, Mobutu's ruling party, weakened Lumumbism as a political force, but the hold of Lumumba's legacy in the Congolese imagination has remained strong thanks to Congolese popular music and popular urban art.

In June 2021, the return from Belgium of what is left of Lumumba's remains, namely a tooth that one of the Belgian police officers who cut up the bodies of the three martyrs of 17 January 1961 took as a souvenir before dissolving them in sulfuric acid, will be observed with national honours in Kinshasa. In a continent in which funerals occupy a very important place in our culture, President Félix Tshisekedi is doing everything possible to lay Lumumba to rest in a manner befitting a great chief and warrior. This is another event that should have great impact in strengthening the hold of Lumumba's legacy in popular Congolese imagination today.

For those readers interested in my views on Lumumba's leadership, his legacy for Africa, and the role of the CIA in his assassination along with the Belgians, the British M16 and corrupt Congolese leaders, a good place to start is my blogpost published by *ROAPE* on 15 January 2021.[13]

I'd like to move on to discuss your scholarly work. What has been the motivation for your historical enquiry over the years, and what do you regard as your most important work and contribution?

I am not a historian by training since none of my university degrees are in history. I have a BA in philosophy (Davidson College, 1967), an MA in diplomacy and international commerce (University of Kentucky, 1968) and a PhD in political science (University of Wisconsin-Madison, 1975). Despite my training as a political scientist, only six years of my academic teaching since 1971 have been in a department of political science: one year at the Congo

---

13 This post can be found here: https://roape.net/2021/01/15/patrice-lumumba-and-the-unfinished-business-of-liberation/.

Free University in Kisangani, DRC, two years at the National University of Zaire, Lubumbashi Campus, two years at Atlanta University (now Clark-Atlanta University) in Atlanta, USA, and one year at the University of Maiduguri in Nigeria. My longest two jobs as a teacher have been at Howard University and at the University of North Carolina at Chapel Hill, since 2007.

I taught in the Department of African Studies at Howard, a unit of the Faculty of Social Sciences, offering MA and PhD degrees in African studies with a focus on public policy and development. At Carolina I am teaching in the Department of African, African American and Diaspora Studies, which offers undergraduate degrees. Moreover, I have held the presidency of both an interdisciplinary professional organisation, the African Studies Association of the United States, the largest scholarly organisation of Africa-area scholars in the world, in 1987-88, and a disciplinary one, the African Association of Political Science, 1995-97. With 33 years spent teaching in interdisciplinary departments, I see myself as an interdisciplinary scholar, and I am above all a scholar-activist.

As a youngster whose political awakening coincided with the struggle for independence in the Belgian Congo, and whose dream of becoming a medical doctor was derailed by my own choice to participate in civil rights demonstrations against racial injustice and discrimination in Charlotte, North Carolina in 1963-65, political activism has been an integral part of who I am since I was expelled from the United Secondary School (Presbyterian-Methodist) of Katubue in April 1960 for participation in protests in favour of Congolese independence. Consequently, my scholarly work has been focused on the political history of the Congo and Africa, with the aim of understanding colonialism, African resistance to foreign rule, the independence struggle and the betrayal of the people's expectations of independence by the new African oligarchy, which is more concerned with enriching itself and clinging to power to protect itself from political and economic crimes. My first major scholarly article dealt with the role of different African social classes in the struggle for independence, and it was published as the lead article in the December 1970 issue of *The Journal of Modern African Studies*, while the French translation appeared three months earlier in the *Cahiers Économiques et Sociaux*, the social science journal of Lovanium University in Kinshasa.

This article, along with my very first article published in the December 1969 issue of *Mawazo*, a Makerere University journal, on the massacre of university students in Kinshasa on 4 June 1969, set the tone for all my subsequent publications. The most important work in these publications is *The Congo from Leopold to Kabila: A People's History*. This book, which I finished writing while working for the United Nations Development Programme in Nigeria, won the Best Book Award from the African Politics Conference Group, an affiliate organisation of the African Studies Association and other professional groups. It is an organisation made up mostly of American political scientists studying Africa. To make it available to Congolese and other Francophone readers, I published an updated French version of it as *Faillite de la gouvernance et crise de la construction nationale au Congo-Kinshasa: Une analyse des luttes pour la démocratie et la souveraineté nationale* (ICREDES 2015), which is translated in English as "Governance failure and the crisis of nation building in Congo-Kinshasa: An analysis of struggles for democracy and national sovereignty."

This is the main thread running through my work and comes out clearly in my major books and articles, such as my presidential addresses at the African Studies Association in 1988 and the African Association of Political Science in 1997 entitled "The African Crisis: The Way Out," and "The Role of Intellectuals in the Struggle for Democracy, Peace and Reconstruction in Africa," respectively. The first address seeks to answer a question that many African scholars have raised but which is best articulated by Claude Ake in the London magazine *West Africa* of 17 June 1985 with a simple interrogation: "Why Africa is not developing."

The American sociologist Barrington Moore has provided

the correct way of approaching such a question. Generally, he argues, intellectuals analyse society either from the standpoint of the dominant groups, which have a vested interest in mystifying the way society works, or from the perspective of ordinary people, who have nothing to lose from truthful analyses of their predicament. For him, it is this latter class perspective that comes closer to objective scientific analysis. He writes: "For all students of human society, sympathy with the victims of historical processes and scepticism about the victors' claims provide essential safeguards against being taken in by the dominant mythology. A scholar who tries to be objective needs these feelings as part of his ordinary working equipment".

At the same time, sympathy with the popular classes does not mean creating other mythologies that have nothing to do with reality. Here I take advice from the French phenomenologist Maurice Merleau-Ponty on the social responsibility of intellectuals, which includes thinkers like Socrates, Karl Marx, and Cheik Anta Diop. According to this tradition, intellectuals are to be philosophers and, as such, critics of the status quo. For, to philosophise, Merleau-Ponty maintains in his book Éloge de la philosophie (*In Praise of Philosophy*) – his brilliant inaugural lecture at the Collège de France in 1953, implies that there are things to see and to say. And what a philosopher sees and says may not agree with society's conventional wisdom and dominant interests. This is a position that is in perfect agreement with the Socratic view of philosophical practice as an uncompromising quest for the truth. A quest, it must be added, that involves a critical appraisal of all ideas, values, and conventions. According to this view, the philosopher is one who investigates and announces the results of this investigation regardless of the price to be paid for her/his commitment to the truth, the ultimate price being, as in the case of Socrates himself, giving up one's life.

These are the two basic principles of my scholarly practice and contribution to knowledge: sympathy with the oppressed and uncompromising quest for the truth. I have attempted to rely on them to elucidate the political history of the Congo and Africa generally from the colonial period to the present.

Which political figure from Congolese history do you think has been the most misunderstood or overlooked, and is deserving of greater attention today?

In terms of political history and social analysis, the one intellectual who fits this category the best is Mabika Kalanda. A philosopher and a political activist formerly known as Auguste Mabika Kalanda, he received an excellent education in the classical Greek and Latin curriculum of Belgian schools at the famous Catholic secondary school of Kamponde in the Kasai province of the Belgian Congo. In 1954, he was one of the first Congolese to enrol in a full-fledged university at Lovanium in Léopoldville (now Kinshasa). He graduated in 1958 with two undergraduate degrees in psychology and education and political science. After one year of professional training as an assistant in the Ministry of Interior and the provincial government of Brabant in Belgium, he returned to the Congo as the sole Congolese member of the European-only corps of territorial administration officials.

Four years later, he would become the second person to hold the post of Minister of Foreign Affairs from 14 April 1963 to 8 July 1964. When Pierre Mulele returned to Kinshasa on 3 July 1963 disguised as a West African following his training in guerrilla warfare in China, he apparently received support from Minister Mabika Kalanda, who gave him a new Congolese passport and helped facilitate his return to the Kwilu bush on 27 July. The popular insurrection for a second independence was about to start. A Lumumbist and a strong advocate of Lumumba's vision for the Congo, Mabika Kalanda was head of one of the MNC/L factions at the CNS in 1991-92.

Mabika Kalanda wrote several books on different topics, ranging from the intra-ethnic conflict between the Lulua and Luba-Kasai to mythology, but his most important book with respect to postcolonial Africa is *La remise en question: Base d'une décolonisation mentale* [*Questioning: The Basis of Mental Decolonisation*] (1967), in which the author calls for mental decolonisation in Africa by the calling into question of ideas, values and behaviour inherited from colonialism. The manuscript was sent to the publisher in 1965, but the book did not appear until two years later. By the time Kalanda began writing it in 1964, he had already dropped using his Christian or "European" name of Auguste, nearly eight years before Mobutu launched his "recourse to authenticity" drive in February 1972, which ordered his compatriots to use African names only and to promote African culture. Before that, in 1963, Mabika Kalanda had written a book in Tshiluba, one of the four national languages in the DRC, entitled *Tabalayi*, or open your eyes, for the Lulua and Luba-Kasai who are not fluent in French, but who share the same mother tongue, to resist the manipulations of ambitious politicians who were stoking the fires of division and war for their own interests.

Today, when you go into academic forums in the United States and in Anglophone Africa, you hear scholars heap praise on the distinguished Kenyan writer and academic Ngugi wa Thiong'o, formerly James Ngugi, as the person who first came up with the concept of mental decolonisation in his book *Decolonising the Mind* (1986), although Ngugi himself gives a lot of credit to Frantz Fanon for this idea. Unfortunately, both Anglophone and Francophone scholars in Africa know little or nothing about Mabika Kalanda and his work. One can understand why Anglophone scholars could not have heard of him in the absence of translations. In the case of Francophone scholars, on the other hand, the main issue is the fact that we seem to notice great African intellectuals only after they have been discovered by Europeans or Americans.

When reading your work, and especially your most seminal contributions, the spirits of Frantz Fanon and Amílcar Cabral are ever present. Could you talk a little about their influence on your intellectual develop-

ment and writing?

I discovered Frantz Fanon in 1964 at Davidson College and Amílcar Cabral in 1968 at the University of Wisconsin-Madison. One day, while walking past his office in the main building of the college, Dr Richard Gift, then a professor of economics at Davidson, called me in to show me the 1963 Grove Press edition of *The Wretched of the Earth*, Fanon's masterpiece. He asked me whether I knew this revolutionary thinker of African descent. He was surprised by my ignorance and told me that every Third World student must study Fanon. I took his advice seriously and went to the college library, where I found the original of Fanon's book in French (*Les damnés de la terre*, 1961), other books by him, and several of his articles as well as critiques of his work in French scholarly journals.

Since then, Fanon's writings have influenced my intellectual outlook and my analysis of African politics. I was greatly inspired by his central message to African intellectuals, that they should follow the path of revolution by going to the school of the people rather than be captured by the bookish knowledge of the ivory tower, to transform the inherited structures of the economy and the state to serve the interests of the wretched of the earth instead of those of the imperialist bourgeoisie and its lackeys in Africa. This message rang so true in my mind not only because it reinforced similar messages from other great intellectuals such as Karl Marx, Antonio Gramsci, and Barrington Moore, but also and more importantly because it reminded me of the martyrdom of Patrice Lumumba in the Congo.

With reference to Amílcar Cabral, I came across his brilliant address on "Presuppositions and Objectives of National Liberation in Relation to Social Structure," which is best known as "The Weapon of Theory," in 1968. This is the speech he had delivered on behalf of the peoples and nationalist organisations of the Portuguese colonies to the First Solidarity Conference of the Peoples of Africa, Asia and Latin America held in Havana on 3-12 January 1966. This and subsequent readings of Cabral's other speeches and writings confirmed his affinity with Fanon's central message. As a trained agronomist, his writings were fact-based and he combined a high level of empirical analysis with a very clear theoretical compass for understanding social realities, in addition to being a great strategist in the armed struggle against Portuguese fascism and colonialism. His writings on imperialism and national liberation were so superb that they were cited as an inspiration by the young Portuguese military officers who carried out the democratic coup d'état of April 1974, which is better known in Portugal as the Carnation Revolution.

The Amílcar Cabral Foundation learned of my appreciation of Cabral's scholarly work at the 25th anniversary meeting of the African Studies Association, which was held in November 1982 in Washington under my leadership as the Program Director and chief organiser, that they invited me to the First Amílcar Cabral International Symposium held on 17-20 January 1983 in Praia, Cape Verde. These dates were chosen to coincide with the assassinations of Lumumba and Cabral himself, the first in 1961 and the second in 1973. I have had the privilege of participating in the second symposium in September 2004 and the third in January 2013, all of which were held in Praia.

Lastly, it seems we are living through a period of some hope in the Congo – where, in the first instance, the courage, activism and sacrifices of Congolese people taking to the streets and in some cases laying down their lives made it politically unfeasible for Kabila to fulfil his desire to change the constitution and continue for a third term (and beyond) and, more recently, the current President Felix Tshisekedi (Etienne's son) has pulled off a succession of significant strategic moves to weaken Kabila's political coalition and grip over the country, replacing it with what he is calling a Union sacrée de la nation (Sacred Union of the Nation). This is all very much ongoing as we speak, but what is your initial reading of the current political moment, and do you share the view that this is indeed a period of hope?

Africans tend to be eternal optimists, and I am one of them. In

April 2019, on his first official visit to the United States, President Tshisekedi told a Congolese audience that he sees his job as that of ousting or taking down (*déboulonner* in French) the dictatorial and corrupt system that he found in power. Lots of people laughed at this statement, but he was dead serious about it. He started the process by unleashing the judiciary to let them do their job without being dictated to by Kabila and his cronies, and the prosecutors went after the President's own chief of staff. Next came changes in the military high command and the Constitutional Court. The Kabilists overreacted with insults and acts of insubordination, particularly by the Justice Minister and the Prime Minister, and fell into their own trap. The President stopped collaborating with them and cancelled the weekly cabinet meetings. Meanwhile, he appealed to patriotism and organised consultations with all strata of the population for a full month to gauge the spirit of the nation. The result was overwhelming support for breaking the coalition with Kabila's political group and the desertion of hundreds of MPs from Kabila's camp to the Union Sacrée de la Nation, the new parliamentary majority.

There is no doubt that some of the MPs who have changed political camps have done so in the hope of getting ministerial and parastatal posts. While fragile, the new majority made up of the pre-2019 opposition and the deserters from the Kabila camp will help the President in the short term in reorienting the country towards the rule of law and fiscal discipline likely to improve revenue collection to allow the state to pay civil servants and to provide to the population basic services such as water, electricity, health care and free education in primary and secondary schools. This will create a new departure for DRC citizens, who are tired of living in a banana republic but one with an enormous wealth in the natural resources necessary to ensure decent livelihood. Popular support is one of the main reasons for the success of Tshisekedi's political gamble, and the majority of the population stands behind the son of Etienne Tshisekedi. It is also the main reason for hope. Our politicians are aware of this reality. Being human, they do not want to see the people's anger directed at them.

7. Reinhart Kössler (2016), Namibia, Genocide and Germany

Heike Becker speaks to the celebrated German scholar-activist of Namibia Reinhart Kössler. Kössler has extensively examined and written about German-Namibian relations, with a particular focus on the violent colonial relationship and its consequences for a racist ideology, which prepared the ground for the genocide of the Ovaherero and Nama in 1904-1908. Here, Kössler reflects upon his intellectual and political engagement in national liberation on the continent.

***

Firstly, can you tell us about your intellectual and political involvement with African nationalisms and national liberation movements? How did it start? What were your inspirations and motivations at the time? What are your current interests?

When I entered Heidelberg university to study sociology and social anthropology in 1967, my choice of subject was strongly influenced by a concern for general Third World issues. In 1965/66, I had spent a year as a high school exchange student in Youngstown, Ohio. Apart from forthcoming hospitality, I became appalled by the many identity and race-based divisions I was more or less directly asked to follow. In a way, this experience was complemented by discussions I enjoyed with other exchange students, particularly from Brazil, who related some of the situation in their home countries. I also experienced first stirrings of resistance against the Vietnam War in what you may call a US backwater. When I returned to West Germany, it was clear for me that I should shelve my earlier plans to study archaeology. Something had to be done, and I wanted to contribute. This was of course a somewhat naïve idea of scholarship. One further push was the fatal shooting by police of the student Benno Ohnesorg, during a demonstration against the presence of the then Shah of Iran in Berlin on June 2, 1967. This became a clarion call for many of my generation, which also sent me to the streets for one of my first vigils.

In Heidelberg, I got involved almost instantaneously in the emerging student movement. Confrontations ranged over a wide array of issues and so did our study of the theory of imperialism or reading Rosa Luxemburg on the mass strike. Remember: Paris in May '68 was literally next door – these were exciting times! In spring 1969, I took part in an awareness raising campaign about the liberation struggles in what then still figured as the Portuguese colonies in Africa. On that occasion, I also made connections, sort of, with some Portuguese and Mozambican comrades. A little more than a year later, this apparent sideline of the Heidelberg student movement erupted into a major turning point. The World Bank, whose president was then Robert McNamara, held a conference in a classy hotel in the very centre of Heidelberg – just imagine that today! One prominent participant was Erhard Eppler, then Minister of Economic Cooperation, and arguably the most progressive person ever to have held that post. However, we held McNamara – who of course as a former Secretary of Defence, was seen as one of the masterminds of the Vietnam War – along with Eppler, above all responsible for planning at this venue the Cabora Bassa Dam, now known as Cahora Bassa. We perceived that as a huge project of counterinsurgency, involving large scale removals of the local population, and the settlement of huge numbers of settlers from metropolitan Portugal. Our demonstration under the slogan "Eppler is planning with his dam, here a new Vietnam!" was banned by the police, but it took place, nonetheless, to the front of the Heidelberger Hof. It became the most militant demonstration to date in Heidelberg, and the state government of Baden-Württemberg responded by banning the local SDS (Sozialistische Deutsche Studentenbund), the last surviving chapter of the formerly national radical student organisation.

All of this was very influential for me politically and intellectually, but did not generate an immediate, sustained interest in Africa. This happened only in 1979 when I landed my first formal job as Executive Secretary of the Information Centre on Southern Africa (ISSA) in Bonn. ISSA had been created as a Centre for counter-information, serving the broad anti-apartheid movement. Among other tasks, I edited a monthly magazine and ran a small publishing venture where I was responsible for both editing and salesmanship. I delved into the relevant issues, did a lot of journalistic writing, and was helped in all that by the fair amount of material that was streaming into ISSA's little office, or could be found in its archives. It was tremendous to observe the amount of work and energy that came out of these shabby little offices, which were run by grossly underpaid staff, in Bonn, in London. In Amsterdam, the situation was a little better.

Then, at the end of 1979, I got a university appointment, but remained with ISSA as a board member and frequent contributor. I still am. At the Institute of Sociology in Münster, where I was employed, I continued to pursue African issues, but these really started only to take centre stage from 1991 onwards and resulted in a number of projects, mainly in Namibia.

For now, I have realised that after the publication of my book *Namibia and Germany: Negotiating the Past* in 2015, I cannot steer free any time soon from the issues. In particular there has to be a proper German apology for the 1904-08 genocide, committed in what was then the German colony of South West Africa, and consequent reparations to the affected communities. This is an obvious case for activist scholarship.

Were West German scholars and solidarity activists like yourself connected with activists elsewhere in Western Europe?

As long as I can remember, there were lots of links with like-minded individuals and projects across Western Europe as well as the US and partly also Japan. Apart from relations with Third World countries, [relations were] largely represented in Europe by students from these regions. I myself have not belonged to a political organisation since 1972, so links tended to be rather on an individual level, and unfortunately, I was not always able to sustain them over a long period of time, so there were a lot of breaks and shifts.

An important contact was established late in 1976 with *ROAPE* – at the time, the acronym was still *RAPE*. It involved a bit of adventure. A colleague, Werner Biermann, and myself had come up with the idea of a radical Third World quarterly in German, and so we decided to find out about role models and attend the editorial conference of *ROAPE*. To share costs, we took along an Eritrean colleague, who however had not cleared transit through Netherlands, Belgium and France, or entry into Britain. After an arduous journey, we made our way to Dover, only to be detained there. Eventually us Germans were, reluctantly, allowed to proceed, but our friend was taken back across the Channel. The meeting was very interesting and fruitful, with people like Doris Burgess, Ruth First, Peter Lawrence, Colin Stoneman and last [but] not least Lionel Cliffe in attendance. Lionel was very thin at the time, since he had just got out of prison in Zambia. The main topic was the situation in Zimbabwe, which remained important for my contacts with the group, including a seminar held in Leeds in summer 1980 to assess the recently won independence.

Apart from your own involvement you have also carried out research on the solidarity movement in West Germany, as it were. Can you describe who came together and how they campaigned for solidarity with Southern Africa?

An important strand of the solidarity movement came out of the student movement, where Third World solidarity was once important, though by no means the only component. But there were others. They included, with considerable overlap, church people, partly from missionary societies once these had turned, quite fundamentally, towards a critique of colonialism by the late 1960s. There were also development aid workers who had returned from stints abroad, groups in the unions, particularly the youth organisations, also civil society groups like Amnesty International. During the 1970s, the various student parties of communist pretensions, the Maoist K-groups, and also the re-established German Communist Party, the DKP, which was close to the East German government, played prominent roles, both by engaging in spectacular actions like "arming a ZANLA (Zimbabwe African National Liberation Army) detachment up to their teeth", and by their pervasive sectarianism. This had been a serious problem for my predecessor at ISSA, where we tried to work with the entire range of solidarity groups. There was repeatedly a need to moderate between the broad Anti-Apartheid Movement, the AAB, and a group called the Organisationskomitee, OK, which was close to some of the K-groups. When I took over in January 1979, the K-groups were already dissolving. Many of their activists who had engaged in Third World issues continued work in the Green Party or in structures of the Protestant Church.

Apart from OK, which relied on sections of the Maoist left, AAB was the most important and largest group. It was formed on the initiative of people who came from the various strands I just mentioned. One important core was Mainzer Arbeitskreis Südliches Afrika, MAKSA, which had been formed by a group of Protestant pastors and their wives who had spent some years in South Africa and Namibia. Most of them at some point had been expelled by the Apartheid regime. Besides opposing Apartheid more generally, these people also opposed the collaboration of the German Protestant church with the Apartheid regime, and in this sense, they still stick to their guns even today, now that they are octogenarians. Soon after AAB had been formed, it entered into a close working relationship with ISSA, although the relationship had its own problems. AAB insisted throughout the 1980s to closely reflect the positions of ANC and SWAPO, whereas ISSA took a broader view and during the later 1970s tried to reflect a greater range of groups in Southern Africa, while trying to take a more critical stance in their solidarity, even while unquestionably supporting the mass struggles of the 1980s.

One particularly painful instance concerned the so-called SWAPO spy drama, which cost many activists their lives. What had been happening was fully realised only once survivors made their appearance in Windhoek in mid-1989, during the run-up to the independence elections. Even then, responses by supporters remained divided and there was considerable controversy at the time. So the more considered, critical efforts actually failed.

Did the specific situation of Germany being divided between the major blocs of the cold war era impact on the solidarity activism?

One must keep in mind that in contrast to the Scandinavian countries, but also to some others in Western Europe, the solidarity movement in Germany was always clearly opposed to the state. This came out especially around the issue of nuclear cooperation with South Africa. The enormously dedicated research of a small group of activists, many of them based in West Germany, unearthed proof of these deals, and the stiff denial of the Schmidt government was shamed once the official facts emerged in 1994. I would venture to say, however, that apart from adherents of the DKP, the existence of East Germany was of minor importance to the activists. Only very few ventured to East Berlin to visit missions of national liberal movements, or such. On the other hand, the structures close to the DKP were clearly nurtured by the GDR.

How did Germany's past colonial rule over Namibia feature in the West German solidarity movement? Did it feature at all?

Seen from the vantage point of today's postcolonial concerns and initiatives, one is struck by the very small role Germany's colonial past played at the time. The facts were certainly known, but they were not addressed in any consistent way. Of course, the Federal Government was criticised for maintaining a consulate in Windhoek or for sending commissions to administer end-of-school exams at the German high school. Yet this was related to the illegality of South African occupation of Namibia, rather than to the legacy of German colonialism.

Namibia's independence coincided with the end of the cold war. Did this, among solidarity activists, change expectations for post-independence developments, as compared to earlier when Zimbabwe or Mozambique gained independence?

I feel this is difficult to assess. Some of us had already analysed the performance of liberation movements in power for some years and had realised the chasm that existed between the dreams of some Western intellectuals and the reality on the ground. Of course, this did not mean that one presaged the pervasive triumph of neoliberalism right on November 9, 1989, the fall of the Berlin Wall. For the great majority of those in the solidarity movement, in particular members of AAB, things look different. Membership of AAB rose steeply during the late 1980s, only to plummet [almost] as swiftly after 1990. Obviously, many of these people felt that there was a job well done, and they could shift their commitment to other issues or maybe have some rest. This was precisely what we at ISSA tried to counter, arguing for the need to continue our critical solidarity by closely monitoring liberation movements in power. Obviously, this had little effect as far as the erosion of the broader movement was concerned, except that ISSA and its journal still exist today, while AAB found its demise some 20 years ago.

Many of us who used to support the liberation struggles in Southern Africa have been disturbed by the forms of social and political rule reproduced by national liberation movements in power. What do you think have been the reasons for that?

Well, Third World liberation struggles – not just those in Southern Africa – tended to become something of a foil on which people on the left, who did not see a realistic chance for their aspirations to come true at home, projected their frustrated dreams and hopes. This attitude may have been understandable, but it was obviously deeply flawed. One might even say, this was a specific, well-meaning kind of Orientalism. Once people awoke to reality, despondency and cynicism were likely responses. It seems that attempts to reach an understanding of liberation movements in power, in my case, since about 1980, were not effective in changing this.

In more mundane terms, there has been a tendency, at least in the West German solidarity movement, to shift attention to other countries and regions rather quickly. Thus, after 1975, few people would concern themselves any more with Indochina, thereby of course ignoring what was happening there. Concerning Southern Africa, probably more people were aware of the crises and needs in SWAPO's camps in Angola, than seriously cared about the fates of socialism there, of the modalities of political rule, or even human rights.

As you have pointed out, national liberation movements were regarded as the most radical form of fight against colonialism and imbued with high hopes for overcoming colonial legacies. With decades of liberation movements in power this hope has certainly lost its shine. You suggest that, beyond evaluating the hegemonic governing practices of national liberation movements in power in the dominant party states, Angola, Mozambique, Zimbabwe, South Africa, Namibia, which has been done by Roger Southall and, for Namibia specifically, Henning Melber, and others, we need to rethink, more profoundly, nationalism as legitimising postcolonial modes of rule. Can you elaborate on this?

In important ways, the 20th century has been marked by ideas and projects of emancipation and liberation veering towards nationalism – not exclusively but in decisive ways in the processes of anti-colonial movements and decolonisation. Amílcar Cabral noted that such nationalist movements were marked by suspending or even by denying social cleavages within the nation. Cabral stated explicitly that such cleavages would break up once again after independence had been attained, and dubbed this as the return of the erstwhile colonised into history. The practices of post-colonial governments of various shades tend however, up to the present, to continue laying claim to national unity and cohesion and [to] deny social conflict. In this way, social conflict is to a large extent de-legitimised and its articulation has been framed as a criminal act in a number of cases. Still, the claims of the nation have their substantive basis. Let's just think of the quest for security, which relates to what people may hope for, such as protection for a state's citizens in foreign countries. Also, some state-sponsored solidarity which was present in the – now often defunct – welfare state; think of rudimentary forms of social security such as old age pensions in Southern Africa. Then there is the provision of infrastructure, education, and the like. All this may appear quite fictitious from today's African vantage point, but it forms the substantive basis of what people expect from the nation state. Just think of the linkage between democracy and development that became apparent in many democracy movements in Africa during the 1990s. We can say, where the state proves unable to deliver on such promises and expectations, it will be delegitimised in the short or medium run.

Over the past twenty-five years you have spent a lot of time in Namibia. Can you tell us a bit about the situation there in the early 1990s, the immediate post-independence years?

There is little doubt that, upon the attainment of independence and during the years immediately following it, hopes were running high. At the same time, the brokered transition stood for continuity, above all in everything relating to the socio-economic structure. Compared to today, there was less cynicism, less concern with ethnicity, and more civic commitment. How the opportunities of this situation were lost is an important question. There were factors working towards demobilisation of civil society, but there was also the concern of SWAPO in government to let bygones be bygones and get on with their own goals. Apparently this has not resulted in overcoming the structural constraints that must be considered the legacy of apartheid, above all extreme social inequality, which is still patterned predominantly along racial lines.

In Namibia, SWAPO has claimed to embody anticolonial and post-colonial nationalist politics – even the United Nations declared it the sole legitimate and authentic representative of the Namibian people. As your research on memories and anticolonial struggles of southern and central Namibian communities has shown, this hegemonic declaration of legitimate nationalism still has problematic consequences. Can you say a bit more on the underlying contradictions?

The basic issue may be phrased in how to operationalise the standard slogan of "unity in diversity". To date, SWAPO does not seem prepared to acknowledge the very diverse trajectories and experiences of different Namibian regions under colonialism. Only the central and southern regions were subjected to settler colonialism while the northern regions did not experience land dispossession, even though the migrant labour system impacted enormously on social structure and basic features, such as gender-related division of labour, or the standard male biography. Again, "native reserves" in the centre and south meant very close surveillance and constant meddling into even petty affairs of residents, while indirect rule in the northern regions was invasive at points, but this could not compare to the situation in the zone of settler colonialism. The genocide committed by the German colonial power in 1904-1908 lies at the root of these experiences, mainly of the Ovaherero and Nama, but certainly felt as well by Damara and San. Recognition of such difference has been slow and uneven and is not evident, in particular, in the current negotiations with Germany about the consequences of the genocide. The Namibian government's stance of claiming to be the sole representative of the nation is grounded in the formal legal position but ignores the specific situation of Namibia as a whole and of the victim communities – Ovaherero and Nama in the first place. The Namibian government's stance here reflects a rather rough and unsophisticated idea of national unity.

8. António Tomás (2023), Amílcar Cabral's Life, Legacy and Reluctant Nationalism

To mark the 50th anniversary of Amílcar Cabral's murder in 1973, Chukwudinma spoke with Cabral biographer António Tomás. Tomás, who teaches at the Graduate School of Architecture at the University of Johannesburg, speaks about Cabral's political development as well as his abilities as a teacher, revolutionary diplomat and leader. But he also discusses his insecurities, shortcomings and the myths surrounding national liberation in Guinea-Bissau.

***

What motivated you to write a biography of Amílcar Cabral in the 21st century?

When I wrote the first version of the biography on Cabral I was in Portugal, and I wrote the book in Portuguese. The introduction is different from the one in English. I don't see *Amílcar Cabral: The Life of a Reluctant Nationalist* (2020) as a translation. I prefer to say that it is the English version of the book that was written in Portuguese. When I started working on this book project in the early 2000s nobody, at least from my generation, was talking about Cabral in Portugal.

But Cabral, his generation and all the people fighting for the independence and liberation of Africa were students in Lisbon. Most of them lived in Lisbon. Cabral was married to a Portuguese [sic]. So he was pretty much part of the debate about blackness in Europe, and blackness in Portugal as a student. When I started writing about Cabral in Portuguese (*O Fazedor de Utopias – Uma Biografia de Amílcar Cabral*, 2007) I was just trying to understand, as a black man, how to think through and engage with Cabral and his struggle in the context of race, not so much that of independence, which is the kind of stuff I became interested in after I went to the United States and did my PhD at Columbia University. I was trying to understand the place of race and blackness in Lisbon in the context of black Portuguese or African immigrants.

Many years after, I changed a few things in the English version of the book. The initial debate on race and racism is less there. But what is interesting now is that the Portuguese version is sold out in Portugal. It has been sold out for many years. I'm now preparing a new edition where I bring back the debate on race because we have a lot of developments: a right-wing party in Portugal and an emerging and very strong black movement, formed mostly by people who want to bring debates on racism and the legacies of colonialism to the national agenda. It is a good moment to get back to these original questions that drove me to the quest of Cabral's legacy.

In what ways do you think Amílcar Cabral's life and work have relevance to the young people developing their racial and political consciousness in the aftermath of the Black Lives Matter protest?

He's a very important figure, either you like him or you don't like him. If you compare him with Walter Rodney, they both moved back to Africa and they were involved with questions of societal transformation, and racism. It was not just about critiquing imperialism and critiquing colonialism. Particularly for Cabral, it was about how to create new societies and how to go about creating societies that go beyond the ways in which these countries came into being through colonialism. It is important to appropriate these figures and to bring them into discussions about what is going on now with issues such as Black Lives Matter, structural violence and racism.

But it is important to put these thinkers in their very particular context and to do the sort of exercise that David Scott did with *Conscripts of Modernity: The Tragedy of Colonial Enlightenment* when he says we have to find not the answer, but the question

Cabral's Life, Legacy and Reluctant Nationalism   131

that they asked in relation to their context. But it's very important to engage with these figures and to learn, but also to understand that they were fighting in different times using different resources like Cabral using armed struggle and so on.

One thing I like about your book is your refusal to tell Cabral's story in retrospect as if everything he did since a child was destined to turn him into a revolutionary leader. Can you tell me a bit about who Cabral was? How did he become politicised and politically active?

I'm from Angola and I grew up in Angola during communism. People of my generation (I was born before 1975, the year of independence) grew up with all these traditions of big men, like Agostinho Neto, Brezhnev, Tito, and Che Guevara. Even today the toponymy of the city [Luanda] reflects that, with streets named after Kwame Nkrumah and Amílcar Cabral. The biographies of these figures have been recorded in a very problematic way. They are talked about as if their lives were linear. They don't have challenges, they don't have doubts, and they know from the outset what they are going to do. They have a destiny, and they fulfil it. But what you see in my book on Cabral, is that life is not like this. Leaders like Cabral had to make really hard choices. Most of the time they were thrown into situations that were not of their choosing. It's the conflation of circumstances that brings them to these moments when they have to make hard choices.

Cabral was born in 1924 in Guinea-Bissau to Cape Verdean parents and moved back with his family to Cape Verde in 1932 and then to Lisbon, in 1945. Cabral was not the most politicised of his generation of African-born students in Lisbon. Agostinho Neto, who later became the first President of Angola, was by far more politicised than Cabral. He was already [imprisoned] by the Portuguese secret police even before Cabral knew anything about what he would do as a nationalist. Cabral was just trying to do the best he could in the circumstances that he found himself. He had his radical friends; he was trying to help his friends. By the time his friends were being harassed and arrested by the police, he was the only one that had a formal job working as an agronomist for the colonial state. So he could travel in the Portuguese empire, go to Angola and Guinea-Bissau, link people, and distribute money and letters. But it reached a situation where he could no longer do that. So he had to take a stand. And that was in 1959 or 1960 in London when he wrote these very famous documents, "Facts [About] Colonialism", which is how he introduces himself as a nationalist.

What is interesting is that because he was not as politicised and devoted to politics as many others in his generation, like Mário Pinto de Andrade or even Agostinho Neto; he had time to draw from other resources, such as his training as a scientist and his writings. All of these allowed him to do the kind of stuff that nobody had done in any other place fighting Portuguese colonialism, such as creating the liberated zones during the anticolonial war in Guinea-Bissau and promoting an approach to gender equality throughout the struggle. Because he pushed back the moment to become a full-fledged nationalist, he had time to bring much more to the fight.

My descriptions of what Cabral was doing in 1959 convey the sense of hope that Africa's time had arrived. It was the time for Africans to show the world what they could do. It was the time for Africans to build societies that could deal with and go beyond all the structures that colonialism and imperialism imposed upon them. And then there was the 1960s – a wonderful decade in Africa. Of course, things got worse in the 1970s and particularly the 1980s with the IMF and structural adjustment. but it is a very important time in Africa, and I think we should revisit that formative moment and perhaps try to recapture a little bit of the optimism of the 1960s.

Your book points out the discrepancies between the myths and the actual reality of the national liberation struggle. I remember when I was learning about Guinea-Bissau's struggle at university, I enjoyed reading

Lars Rudebeck who paints a very idealistic picture of the struggle, and Basil Davidson as well. What are the discrepancies that we should know about?

This is a very important question. Reading authors such as Lars Rudebeck and Basil Davidson and getting to know how the struggles in Africa were understood in the context of global struggles for freedom. But this comes with a problem. These liberals and progressive writers were so involved with the struggle, particularly Davidson, that they lost objectivity. For them, these struggles for liberation in Africa were seen as part of ideological struggles going on in Europe. For them, it was sort of mandatory to make the case that everything was going well and that the national liberation movement would prevail. About the critical decisions that had to be made, you won't find much in their writings. But the struggle is a very tough business. Whenever violence needs to be used to liberate a country, there will be people dying. In the case of struggle in Guinea, which you don't see in the writings by these authors, that war was conducted in the context of historical rivalries between Cape-Verdeans and Guineans within the national movement, the PAIGC (Partido Africano para a Independência da Guiné e Cabo Verde). So, the questions were then: who was fighting and who was leading?

Cabral's decision to start the war was a very heavy one to take. First Cabral did not have any military training. If he could, he certainly would have pursued the liberation of Guinea-Bissau and Cape Verde in a non-violent way. He resisted pressure to start it in 1961 when the anticolonial war was starting in Angola. It was only when his men were caught smuggling military equipment by the authorities in Guinea-Conakry and his companion was imprisoned by Sekou Touré in 1962 that he had no other choice than to show the uses of the smuggled guns. If he had not shown Sekou Touré that the weapons and military equipment were to fight the Portuguese, Touré would certainly have thought that it was a way to arm one of the groups against him.

To come back to your question, I think the ways in which liberal and progressive writers were engaging with the struggle have also contributed to obscuring our knowledge of the killing of Cabral. A lot of people who were writing about Cabral were people that were invested in Cabral's theory and practice, Cabral's ideology. So they were not paying much attention, or they were not interested in understanding the killing of Cabral in relation to the contradictions that the national liberation movement had brought to the fore. The idea that António de Spínola, the Portuguese governor in Guinea-Bissau, had ordered the killing, or that the PIDE (Polícia Internacional e de Defesa do Estado) had plotted it, was a good explanation. However, I also think that this explanation prevented a lot of these scholars from really engaging with the contradictions of colonialism and the contradictions of post-colonialism. And this is part of what I tried to do in my understanding of Cabral.

There is a contradiction between those petty-bourgeois Cape Verdeans, some of whom lead the PAIGC, and the Guinean masses who are much poorer comparatively. How does this contradiction play out throughout the liberation struggle and at independence?

Cabral tried to think through this issue with what he proposed as the class suicide of the petty bourgeoisie. He knew that there was a contradiction, and he knew it was very difficult for people to overcome these contradictions. Cabral proposed that the petty bourgeoisie had to transcend who they were. They had to put aside all the privileges and embrace the masses. But how do you do this in practice, when you have very deep structures that put people against others, in terms of language, in terms of culture, in terms of the mechanisms that the Portuguese created to differentiate people, such as the native laws? These laws fostered the overwhelming distinction between natives and civilised. The central idea behind this legislation is that a group of people were given privileges because they were able to assimilate a way of life that the Portuguese deemed civilised: they could eat with utensils, they could speak Portuguese and dress like Europeans. Those who could not demonstrate these abilities were placed under the statute of native.

It was for Cabral a difficult task to bring these groups together. Guineans would resent Cape Verdeans because they considered them agents of colonialism. Many Cape Verdeans would not be comfortable around Guineans because of their different languages, customs and traditions. For Cabral, it was how to dilute these cultural differences. And then there was the Portuguese colonial power finding ways to exacerbate these differences to create even more problems in the national liberation movement. If the suicide of the petty bourgeoisie was something difficult to consider during the struggle, it was even harder after independence when the postcolonial states became machines for accumulation. So you start to have a sort of differentiation between the haves and the have-nots.

I called the Portuguese version of this book *O Fazedor de Utopias*, "The Maker of Utopias", because of the odds of making the national liberation movement a functional and operational machine. It was hard to bring different people together. Reality is too complex for that. People are too complex for that. Humans are for the most part comfortable with what they have. This is one thing. But the other thing is that we must give credit to those who think that transcending difference is possible. It is difficult, of course, but it is worth dreaming about and aiming for. We still need to believe that a world without racism and discrimination is possible.

Can you talk about Cabral's political identity? You called him in the English version of your book a reluctant nationalist. What does that actually mean?

Cabral was reluctant on many issues, and he hesitated on a lot of issues. The Cubans wanted Cabral to finish the anticolonial war by invading Bissau. He had numbers. But to do that, you would have to bring more people, more violence, more killing and more blood. So he was hesitant. In terms of the "reluctance" of his nationalism, there are two reasons to consider. When he started to get involved with political activism, the notion of nationalism, for black Portuguese, was not there. Cabral was married to a Portuguese, Maria Helena, [and] in their correspondence that was recently published there is something to allow us to understand Cabral as the product of a different identity. He is a black Portuguese. He was Cape Verdean, which was a culture, not a nationality. The whole idea of no longer being a subject of the Portuguese Empire could give you a nationality that was not Portuguese but was conceivable as a second-class citizen Portuguese because, in 1951-52, Portugal changed the Constitution to get rid of the notion of the colony and replace it by an older one, overseas provinces. So there was the idea that Angola, Mozambique, Guinea-Bissau and Cape Verde were provinces of Portugal. Those born in these territories were Portuguese, but they were not like white Portuguese, they were second-class Portuguese. If you read Cabral in Portuguese, what he wrote at that time, he considers himself black Portuguese and there is an important tradition of black Portuguese since the 1920s. So this is the first idea behind Cabral being a reluctant nationalist.

The second idea is that when Cabral had the chance to put forward a notion of nationalism, he did not have any. He was not talking about a nation. He didn't believe in nations. He believed that he could create a bi-nationality bringing Cape Verdeans and Guineans together because he thought that Cape Verdeans originated from Guinea – their ancestors had been brought to the island of Cape Verde during the Slave Trade. Unless you can convince me otherwise, the kind of nationalism that Cabral was proposing is not in any form a traditional nationalism that Benedict Anderson would write about in *Imagined Communities*, around the culture and language.

What place does Pan-Africanism have in Cabral's mind?

He was highly influenced by this movement. And if you are black Portuguese, you knew what went on in New York during the Harlem Renaissance. All these wonderful poets, such as Langston Hughes, were part of the conversations that African students were having alongside jazz music. Because Cabral could speak French, he could read what was coming from Paris with the Négritude. In the thinking and writing of black students in Lisbon from Africa, there are all these influences. You see the influence of Aimé Césaire, you see the influence of Du Bois, of Garvey's going back to Africa.

But what is interesting about Cabral and many of these authors, Du Bois, Nkrumah and Senghor, is that they are on both sides. Because they were the ones writing about "imagine what an independent Africa would be like!" Then they were on the other side as leaders trying to come to terms with the formation of these new countries and new nationalities. It was a very difficult position to be in. Guinea-Bissau only became independent in 1973. Cabral was certainly thinking about how to avoid dictatorship and one-party rule because he was watching what was going on in Africa, with the spread of coup-d'états and political violence at the time.

What was the influence of Marxism on Cabral?

The Portuguese Communist Party (PCP) was very strong in Portugal and it was a great part of the resistance to Estado Novo, the fascist regime in Portugal. The most organised illegal opposition to Estado Novo was the Portuguese Communist Party. So, it was just natural that everyone that was against the Estado Novo would gravitate around the PCP. Cabral and many other students were seduced by communism and Marxism. In almost everything Cabral has written you see the mark of this intellectual tradition, with a lot of contradictions as well. The Communist Party were against Estado Novo but they didn't side with the independence of African countries. It took a long time for communists in Portugal to have a clear position about independence in Africa.

To what extent were Cabral and his guerrilla army influenced by the Soviet Union, China and Cuba?

The Soviet Union with Lenin had the struggle against imperialism as central in their policies. Lenin and Mao have written about imperialism, Fidel Castro was interested in the liberation of Latin America from the yoke of imperialism. It was clear, they would support any national liberation movement fighting against any form of colonialism and imperialism in Africa. What Cabral did, in coming to terms with his insurgent strategies, was to use all these experiences. The influences are clear for instance in the kind of support he received throughout the war. In the early stage of the war, because of the geographical conditions of Guinea, based for the most part on rice production, the nature of mobilisation was based on China's Maoism. But towards the end of the insurgency, in the late 1960s, the whole organisation leans more towards the Soviet-Cuban model, in which you have the separations between the structures of the whole organisation and the cadres. So the cadres, those doing political work, were above the military elements in the PAIGC. This structure was also handy for Cabral. He was not a soldier. Throughout the war and until his death in 1973, he was always trying to find ways to subsume the power of the military under the power of civilians.

Reading your book and thinking of Cabral's actions and internationalism, he gives the impression of being more of a revolutionary diplomat than a soldier. Someone who is able to manage complex relationships with leaders of other nations. How accurate is that depiction?

The most interesting trait of Cabral's personality was his penchant for diplomacy. Because it was a very crazy world. With the

Cold War, it was very easy for many leaders just to take sides. But Cabral didn't take sides. He tried to use his diplomatic skills to bring everyone together or to bring everyone behind his movement. He had very good relations with the left Portuguese people fighting against Estado Novo. He had very good relations even with the Vatican. During the 60s and so on, he had very good relations with northern Europe – countries like Sweden and Norway. He received humanitarian support from the religious denominations around the world. He got a lot of support from associations and groups in France as well. Towards the end of his life, he was trying to get the hardest group to convince to support his struggle against colonialism: the Americans. He made a few trips to the United States. He spoke at the Congress. It is always fascinating to see how Cabral dealt with diplomacy in the Cold War. One day he was giving a speech at the anniversary of Lenin at a congress in the Soviet Union and a few days later he was talking at the Congress in the US. There are not many revolutionary leaders that have done that. Diplomacy was very important as a tool to get things done. It was the strongest side of Cabral. And even bringing together Cape Verdeans and Guineans was also part of his diplomatic effort to work through differences.

What I liked about Cabral from reading your work was his quality as a teacher. Especially in how he trains the PAIGC recruits and spends a lot of time helping them understand the society they are trying to change. What can you say about that ability of Cabral?

Through the years, there is a lot of effort and a lot of people trying to see Cabral as the theoretician of the revolution. But Cabral was not like that. He was an organiser, but he was particularly – as you say – a teacher. He was very, very good at explaining very complex ideas, scientific ideas, to people that didn't have any sort of education. A great part of what Cabral [has] written, that we now read as theoretical contributions, are in fact teachings. Almost everything is Cabral talking to his soldiers, his companions.

He's someone who had been to Portugal and had the opportunity to learn. And trying to explain all these very complex ideas to people that hadn't been exposed to anything. Besides his diplomatic abilities, the teaching and the sharing of knowledge was the strongest part of Cabral.

I wonder what you think can be generalised from Cabral's writings and speeches for today.

That is a good question, it is such a different time. That is the difficulty. It is easier to read Fanon and to engage with Fanon because there's all the psychoanalytical side and he was a brilliant writer. He was part of a very profound philosophical school and, if you read Fanon, you'll find all the resonances to everything that was going on in French literature and French philosophy with Jean-Paul Sartre and Existentialism. You find none of this in Cabral. Unlike Fanon, Cabral was not a speculative writer. He was really trying to write about the day-to-day in Guinea at that time. In that regard, it's very hard to find things in Cabral that you can easily use and easily apply to the struggles that we have today. Even in terms of the post-independent state, how to think of it, and how to understand it, you will not find a lot of instances in which Cabral would talk about how he imagined independence. He talked about unity, he wanted to create a country bringing together Cape Verdean and Guinea. But the whole stuff about how that would function is not to be found in Cabral's writings.

A huge part of his personality was his ability to learn from the mistakes of others. He started the war in Guinea and didn't want to replicate the same kind of mistakes of other movements and national liberation struggles. That gave him a lot of space to do stuff to push forward something very original. But this raises questions: what kind of post-colonial leader would Cabral have been? What would Guinea-Bissau and Cape Verde be with Cabral as a leader? We will never have answers to these questions.

9. Pascal Bianchini (2018), Senegal's Street Fighting Years

ROAPE's Remi Adekoya speaks with the researcher and activist Pascal Bianchini, who lives in Dakar, Senegal. For years, Bianchini has been researching and writing on protest, activism and the left in Senegal and Burkina Faso. He is widely recognised as an expert on student movements on the continent. Here he discusses the major events in Senegal in 1968, and the impact on the left in the years that followed. He sees the explosion of student and worker resistance that year as triggering the growth of radical left politics and organisations in the country and region.

***

So how did your story with Senegal start?

For me the story has been quite long, going back to the 1980s when I came here for my PhD fieldwork to investigate the social struggles within the school system as well as education policies connected with these struggles. Right now, I teach at a secondary school in Senegal and am still trying to gather information about the events of 1968 and their aftermath during the 1970s, which was a very interesting period of what we could describe as revolutionary politics. Of course there are challenges to gathering this kind of information, as these events happened fifty years ago and many of those who actually witnessed them might not always remember so clearly what exactly happened in which month, week etc. Also, many of the political pamphlets being distributed during these events have disappeared as people were afraid to keep them after the government crackdown started soon after the events in 1968.

Could you briefly recall for us the sequence of events that led to the mass strikes?

A very important event before the 1968 strikes was the overthrow of Kwame Nkrumah in February 1966. This was a major incident in Dakar as well and students went to demonstrate in front of the American and British embassies who they blamed for the coup. Another major event that year in Senegal was the country's hosting of the World Festival of Black Arts. These two combined events represented the moment when the student movement started to rebuild after being suppressed by President Léopold Senghor in the early 1960s. For instance, the Union générale des étudiants ouest-africains (General Union of West African Students) was banned in 1964, but in 1966, the government was forced to accept the existence of the Union des étudiants de Dakar (Dakar Students Union) and the Union démocratique des étudiants du Sénégal (Democratic Students Union of Senegal). They helped create an anti-imperialist atmosphere along, of course, with some other things going on outside Senegal such as the Vietnam War, the Portuguese colonial wars in Guinea-Bissau and Angola and Mozambique etc.

The spark for the actual events of 1968 was the government's decision to cut scholarships for university students, some by half, some by one third. This got students angry and they started a strike on 18 May. They were quickly joined by secondary school pupils who attended the campus strike meetings. On 27 May, the students started an all-out strike yet two days later Senegalese police raided the campus – it was very violent with many injured and one person killed. Hundreds of students were arrested and sent to a military camp in Ouakam, a small place near Dakar. This was a shock for the country and workers quickly joined the movement in solidarity. The government responded by arresting trade unionists who were sent to Dodji, a military camp in the north of the country.

However, due to mass riots mainly in the capital city of Dakar, the government had to release the activists and start negotiations with them in June. Wages were increased and some other concessions made to reduce tensions. The same thing had to be done in September with the students – so the events of May 1968, in reality, spread across the rest of the year. In 1969, the following year, there was a virtual remake of the crisis, but the government was better prepared to deal with it and prevented the general strike from spreading.

Yet the main consequence of the 1968 events was that people saw that the regime of Léopold Senghor was not as strong as they had thought it was. Prior to that, Senghor had been able to suppress all opposition to his government and silence his rivals including through the arrest and imprisonment of Prime Minister Mamadou Dia in 1962. But in 1968, the whole country saw that his regime had been weakened and destabilised. This gave young revolutionaries in their 20s the hope and inspiration to commence what I would call the street-fighting years which lasted from 1968 up to the mid-1970s. During this period, there was a lot of unrest and active opposition to a government considered by many to be neo-colonial. The radical left also believed Senghor's government could be overthrown.

However, Senghor was a shrewd politician and his regime eventually adapted to the situation. He was conscious about his image abroad and did not want to appear as a dictator. By 1974-75, he started to realise he needed a legal opposition. At first, he tried to limit the number of parties that could participate in the political system and in effect choose his opponents. For instance Abdoulaye Wade, who [was] elected President in 2000, was allowed to launch his Parti démocratique Sénégalais in 1974.

So, in the years 1974-75, the multiparty system was essentially limited to four parties, including one Marxist-Leninist party, the Parti africain de l'indépendance (PAI) whose historical leader Majhemout Diop was allowed to return from exile and to launch a "legal PAI" whereas most of the PAI members continued to operate in secrecy. The system started to open up and many groups challenged the limited nature of the multi-party framework.

By the time Abdou Diouf succeeded Senghor in 1981, the country had abandoned this limited multi-partyism and accepted a full multi-party system which at the time was not that common in Africa. We can see how an internal process, started in 1968 and driven by the left, led to major political changes in subsequent years.

What is the condition of the left today in Senegal?

It is in a state of confusion today unfortunately. One of the consequences of the multiparty system was that after one or two decades, various leftist movements and groups entered into alliances with neoliberal parties with all the ideological consequences of that alliance. Many of them also suffered internal splits, not necessarily because of ideological disputes but over personal struggles for leadership. In this complex web of alliances and counter-alliances, it is difficult to grasp what actually remains of the left today. So, to be honest, I am not so optimistic about the left today in Senegal.

However, there is still a political culture of struggle that we could describe as a legacy of the 1968 years. The ideological atmosphere today is different, but that culture of social struggle is still very much alive and the problems essentially remain the same. Just a few weeks ago, a student was killed by the police during a demonstration triggered by delays to payments of scholarships for students, so the exact same issue which led to the 1968 events. In fact, because of the tensions on university campuses, the organising committee – maybe thanks to some of its members who are close to the government – decided to postpone commemorative events for the 1968 strike till July, by which time they hope things will be calmer. So we basically have an echo of the 1968 events though, of course, in an entirely different ideological atmosphere.

The reasons for the resistance remain but, as I said, the situation is different. For instance, today various Islamic religious movements are active on Senegalese university campuses whereas student unions no longer exist in the same form. Also, as I mentioned earlier, since the 1990s many of the activists of the 1970s and 1980s have been or are now in government or close to government circles. Yet the fundamental issues that provoke opposition remain strikingly similar. For instance, there is the issue of a trade agreement between the EU and Senegal (and other African states) that will essentially see EU goods coming into Senegal without tariffs. There is strong opposition to that in Senegal and in other African countries where such moves are being considered. Also, there is the issue of the CFA currency, which is seen as a colonial currency. So there are many anti-imperialist sentiments on the ground.

Driving around the streets of Senegal, you can see painted slogans saying "France get out" ("France dégage!") in reference to the many French companies and other French influences many people feel exist in their country. Recently, we have also witnessed the emergence of a movement called Faidherbe Must Fall,[14] similar to Rhodes Must Fall… Still, I would not describe today's atmosphere as revolutionary – no.

So, what is the future for the left in Senegal?

For years there have been attempts to build a united left, but the reality is that in practice you either accept the neo-colonial reality with heavy French influence or you stay away from government circles. There are still a few leftist groups with a clear political position, but they are in the minority. For now, the situation doesn't look very promising but sadly this is by no means peculiar to Senegal. However, the spirit of struggle and resistance lives on in the country.

---

14   Louis Léon César Faidherbe was a French colonial general and administrator, responsible for much brutality in Senegal.

10. Explo Nani-Kofi (2016), Rawlings and Radical Change in Ghana

Explo Nani-Kofi was born in Ghana where he started his activism as a socialist organiser for popular democracy. He coordinated the Campaign Against Proxy War in Africa and the IMF-World Bank Wanted for Fraud Campaign. Here he describes his involvement in a period of radicalisation in Ghana in the 1970s and 1980s, under the charismatic leadership of flight lieutenant Jerry Rawlings. His recollections offer a sense of some of the experiences for activists on the ground, along with insider analysis of the aspirations and the shortcomings of the period.

***

Can you first of all tell us briefly who you are and your political background in Ghana?

I am Explo Nani-Kofi and at present the Director of Kilombo Centre for Civil Society and African Self-Determination which is a research, education and advocacy institution, which I have been developing as a social justice practitioner and grassroots organiser. Through that I coordinate the International Conference on Africa, Africans and Social Justice every September in Peki, Ghana. I come from Peki and was born in Anfoega, both in the Volta Region of Ghana. When I was a child, relatives, family friends and neighbours were officials in Kwame Nkrumah's Convention People's Party (CPP), so I grew up in an atmosphere of CPP influence.

In secondary school, I got involved in the Current Affairs Society and came across *The Dawn*, published by CPP overseas, and *Amanee* published by the Central Union of Ghana Students in Europe, which were Nkrumahist-oriented publications which were being sent discreetly into the country. All this was given as orientation when I was starting secondary school in 1975, when my teacher was the Marxist-oriented Mahama Bawa. I then founded and became President of the Students Movement for African Unity (SMAU) in my school, Mawuli Secondary School in Ho.

Having been in SMAU, when I entered university I looked out for the SMAU branch. Initially there was a SMAU note on the notice board and when I followed it, I was introduced to the Pan African Youth Movement then led by Chris Buakri Atim.[15] Atim was the Acting President of the National Union of Ghana Students (NUGS) and I ran errands for him to the other universities often circulating press statements. By the time of the 31 December 1981 coup d'état, I was the first National Vice President of NUGS.

Can you describe the atmosphere in Ghana at the time, in the 1970s and 1980s?

On 24 February 1966, the first post-independence government of Ghana was overthrown through a coup d'état by police and army officers of Ghana with what has been shown now to have been influenced by western intelligence services. Ghana was then ruled by a military junta of the National Liberation Council (NLC). The NLC organised elections in 1969 which were won by Dr K. A. Busia and the Progress Party (PP) which was the successor party to the United Party (UP) which was the right-wing opposition to Kwame Nkrumah's government. The Nkrumah regime was the First Republic, so this became the Second Republic.

The 1970s started with the devaluation of the currency by 48% on 27 December 1971 after the Pan-African atmosphere created by Nkrumah's government was disrupted by the introduction of the Aliens Compliance Order policy which expelled Africans from Nigeria, Mali, Niger and other countries who had been living in

---

15 Chris Bukari Atim later became co-plotter with J. J. Rawlings in the 31 December 1981 coup in Ghana and also a leading member of the ruling Provisional National Defence Council (PNDC).

Ghana. Radical student movements brought up the question of the declaration of assets by the politicians of the Second Republic. In response to this situation the right-wing government of Dr Busia was overthrown by the Ghana Armed Forces. The military government was initially popular with its Operation Feed Yourself programme, and a declaration was made that we will not pay imperialist imposed debts and we will support African liberation movements. Gradually, the military regime grew corrupt and institutionalised the bureaucratic structure in 1975 by dissolving the original council and replacing it with a council of military generals. The military regime tried to institutionalise its rule and stop any transfer to civilian constitutional rule with the campaign for the so-called Union Government. As the regime became corrupt, the student movement grew more radical.

Before 1976, the external wing of the Ghana students' movement was led mostly by those who won scholarships to study outside during Nkrumah's regime. In 1976, the external students' movement (Central Union of Ghanaian Students in Europe) integrated with the students' movement back home under the umbrella of the NUGS and adopted scientific socialism, which created a crisis as the students' movement was a mass organisation of all students in a neo-colonial state and such a programme and commitment seemed inappropriate.

The students' movement together with professional bodies mobilised against the military regime. The students of Ghana had a national demonstration against the military regime and its Union Government campaign on 13 May 1977 resulting in the closure of the universities. Since that day, the week including 13 May each year came to be celebrated as Aluta Week with demonstrations and other activities. The military regime had a referendum on its Union Government in 1978 and rigged the referendum results declaring that the population had endorsed it. Further opposition created a crisis in the military regime leading to a palace coup that year. In 1979, during the Aluta Week, a hitherto unknown Air Force flight lieutenant by the name Jerry John Rawlings took advantage of Aluta Week and attempted a military uprising on 15 May 1979 which failed. He was arrested and together with others brought to trial.

How do you assess the legacy of Kwame Nkrumah?

Kwame Nkrumah rose to become the main leader of the struggle against classical colonialism since his return to the Gold Coast, as Ghana had been named by the colonial power, in 1947 upon invitation by the United Gold Coast Convention. In 1949, he led a breakaway which constituted itself as the Convention People's Party and became more rooted in the masses of the population and was also more radical in its demands for self-government. Another great plus of his legacy is that the party was national in character and not dominated by a particular ethnic group, as has been a weakness of certain political parties and "nationalist" movements in other parts of Africa. As the immediate post-independence government, the Nkrumah administration embarked on the construction of infrastructure, provided social services to the population, developed an industrialisation programme and provided employment in a way that cannot be compared with any government since. Nkrumah's commitment to African unity, liberation and self-determination raised his stature throughout the African continent and the African diaspora triggering a movement for revolutionary Pan-Africanism. He wrote books together that made an enduring contribution to revolutionary Pan-Africanist theory. All together this posed a threat to the efforts by the west to continue the neo-colonial control they had in Africa. As a result of this the CIA influenced his overthrow on 24 February 1966.

After his overthrow, the political class – including some who had worked with him – came to a consensus that lacked his vision, an agreement I have referred to as the "24 February 1966 Consensus." A number of the leadership and activists of his party integrated with others who had fallen out with Nkrumah to constitute new political parties. Any form of resistance was patchy.

Four people were tried for a plot to bring him back to power. There was a counter-coup attempt on 17 April 1967, but it is still unclear whether it was linked to Nkrumah. The only political party which departed from this consensus and maintained a genuinely pan-African vision was the People's Popular Party led by Dr Willie Kofi Lutterodt and Johnny FS Hansen. This party brought together CPP elements who refused to accept the 24 February coup as a fait accompli and a group of activists with links to internationalist socialist movements.[16] However, Nkrumah's influence developed among a younger generation of activists within the youth and students. By 1981 there were so many organisations inspired, in one way or another, by Nkrumah's legacy and politics.[17]

The conflict between Rawlings and these organisations during his rule from 1982 to 1992 led to a collapse of many of these organisations. In lieu of a movement, the dominant application of Nkrumah's politics in Ghana today is to use reference to pro-Nkrumah politics to attack one of the main opposition parties as a group responsible for his overthrow. That has not helped in practice but has rather been a distraction that creates confusion about the emergence of the two main political parties in 1992, despite their struggle for (and against) Nkrumah's legacy. What determined the political divide in 1992 was the attempt to shore up the neoliberal tyranny of Rawlings' regime against the struggle to open the democratic space to enable genuinely civilian rule. Rawlings' regime succeeded in infiltrating the pro-Nkrumah movement by taking advantage of contacts they had with the left's tragic flirting with Rawlings' fake radicalism in the 1980s. In the

---

16   This party was banned and prevented from contesting the General Elections in 1969.

17   These groups included the African Youth Brigade, African Youth Command, June 4 Movement, Kwame Nkrumah Revolutionary Guards, Kwame Nkrumah Youth League (formerly part of the People's National Party Youth League), Movement on National Affairs, New Democratic Movement, Pan African Youth Movement, People's Revolutionary League of Ghana, Socialist Revolutionary League of Ghana, and Students Movement for African Unity; each had an orientation close to Kwame Nkrumah's vision.

process there are a number of people who were in pro-Nkrumah movements but became members or supporters of the neoliberal New Patriotic Party (NPP) that was founded in 1992; they saw the NPP as the only effective way to stop the military regime's structure reorganising itself into a party under the umbrella of the National Democratic Congress also set up in 1992.

You were involved in the left movement in Ghana. How were you engaged?

I was involved in the Kwame Nkrumah Revolutionary Guards (KNRG) which emerged as a result of the People's National Party, it was perceived as the successor party to Kwame Nkrumah's Convention People's Party. The KNRG was formed by Nkrumahists (adherents to Kwame Nkrumah's Pan-Africanist and socialist-oriented vision of politics) who were disappointed in the PNP so decided to organise as Nkrumahists with the guidance of his revolutionary Pan-Africanism vision of socialist transformation. I also organised students and youth under the banner of the Students Movement for Africa Unity which I was a member of since my secondary school days. The KNRG organised events to mark Kwame Nkrumah's birthday and memorials for his death and on those occasions reflected on and analysed the national and international situation and looked to advance the cause of socialism and Pan-Africanism. One important forum which brought together all left-wing forces was the Progressive Forum of 3 October 1981.

From June 1979 to September 1979, the Armed Forces Revolutionary Council (AFRC) under the chairmanship of Rawlings, which was a populist regime and reduced prices, executed military officers for supposed corruption and was very popular with the radical forces. This presented a very difficult situation for the successor civilian regime as the shops had been emptied. The experience under the AFRC raised the expectations of the Ghanaian population which could not be met under civilian constitutional rule, conditions which were totally different from the populist military. The situation worked to the advantage of the Rawlings regime as people developed a sort of euphoria for the AFRC days and therefore Rawlings became increasingly popular.

There were a number of groups sympathetic to Rawlings – like the June 4 Movement, New Democratic Movement, Movement on National Affairs, Pan African Youth Movement, People's Revolutionary League of Ghana – the majority of these groups became sympathetic to Rawlings with only the Movement on National Affairs (MONAS) coming out openly against him. MONAS supported a call for a probe of the AFRC and also stressed the anti-communist statements of the AFRC as well as his attacks on Kwame Nkrumah and support for the overthrow of the Nkrumah regime. I was close with groups on both sides with some of my closest friends in MONAS.[18]

You were involved in an initiative of setting up workers committees in the Volta region under the June 4 movement before the 31 December 1981 coup d'état. Can you give us some personal background to these initiatives and explain what happened and what went wrong?

In August 1981, through a meeting involving the June 4 Movement, Pan African Youth Movement and Kwame Nkrumah Revolutionary Guards with the support of Prof Mawuse Dake, a programme of Workers' Committees was launched under my coordination.[19] These were decision-making and mobilisation

---

18 My closest friend and comrade was Kwasi Agbley, the International Affairs Spokesman of MONAS who was arrested when the PNDC came into office and was imprisoned in the military detention cells and later the Nsawam Medium Security Prisons, the most notorious prison in Ghana for almost two years. We were both students of Mahama Bawa, who was the Secretary for the State Commission for Economic Cooperation under the PNDC. When the Left came into conflict with Rawlings, our teacher, Bawa, was in the Castle military detention cell and I was in military detention.

19 Mawuse Dake was a progressive politician who was a Vice Presidential candidate of a political party in general elections in Ghana in 1979 called the Social Democratic Front and became a minister in the PNDC

committees of workers to raise consciousness and also to work as a group on political issues. These committees were political discussion groups, they organised communities and workplaces, were involved in clean-up activities and also holiday classes for students as well as revision classes for those who had failed school certificate examinations and were resitting.

After the 31 December 1981 coup d'état, the People's and Workers' Defence Committees were established as organs of popular power. Chris Atim, under whom I worked in the students' movement, became a member of the ruling Provisional National Defence Council (PNDC) and national coordinator of defence committees. He appointed me the Regional Coordinator of the defence committees in the Volta Region. A former editor of the NUGS, Zaya Yeebo, was appointed PNDC Secretary for Youth and Sports. I was also appointed the Regional Political Coordinator of the National Youth Organising Commission. Being responsible for the defence committees and the youth movement made me the main contact with mass organisations in the region.

With the help of the committees, we organised the Defence Committees as units of community and workplace decision making. They helped with the distribution of goods and services. They arranged to get implements for work on farms and equipment for fisheries. They were also a forum for political discussion where national and international issues could be raised by ordinary people.

As this involved the political activity of a left-wing nature it was mainly based in bigger urban centres like Accra. Yet I made efforts to get experienced organisers from the capital city to assist us in the Volta Region. I requested the release or secondment of cadres from the capital. It was in this respect that I worked with Kofi Gafatsi Normanyo and Kwame Adjimah from the National Secretariat of the Defence Committee in Accra, and the secondment of Austin Asamoa Tutu from his workplace, the Architectural and Engineering Services Company, to work with

---

regime but like most left-wing activists fell out with Rawlings.

our regional secretariat of the Defence Committees.

However, the way we did things was different from how the bureaucracy wanted things to be done – our involvement directly radicalised the government. For example, when there was water shortage in the city, we didn't see why we should have water where we stayed in student accommodation whilst ordinary people didn't have water in town. So we opened our university accommodation for the ordinary people to come and draw water from the university. We tried to break down the barriers between ordinary people and political leaders.

Contradictions in the regime and with its support base became intolerable. It turned out that the PNDC Chairman, Rawlings, wanted to have a typical military junta and did not want to see genuine popular organs of power but to have them just as supporters to shore up the military junta. This and other issues led to a total breakdown and misunderstanding within the ruling council on 28 October 1982 and Rawlings felt that he and the two members of the council most active in the defence committees, Chris Atim and Alolga Akata Pore, had to go their separate ways, but the exact details were not known to the public – including to organisers like me. After that conflict, Atim addressed a public rally in Ho where I was based.

When there was a coup attempt to overthrow the PNDC on 23 November 1982, which failed, Rawlings took advantage of the situation to frame those he considered to be his enemies. In our naivety, many of us didn't know that we had been declared enemies. So, on 24 November, Rawlings descended on the official residence of the PNDC Secretary for Youth and Sports with a helicopter and a fully armed platoon of soldiers. I was there at the time. He insisted that all of us he found there kneel down in public with guns cocked at our heads. After that, he declared two of our colleagues – Nicholas Atampugre and Taata Ofosu – were under arrest and directed the soldiers to take them away to be detained. Later, on 7 December, I was invited to a meeting at the barracks and when I got there I was arrested and told that the

Army Commander had directed that Kwame Adjimah and I were to be arrested and detained by the military. With the division in the ruling council, things started taking regional and ethnic lines. My closeness with Atim, who is from the North, was interpreted to mean that I was an obstacle to Rawlings being in control of his home region. It was felt that I had to be removed so that it would be easier for Rawlings to control his own region. This was a tragic ethnic turn by the regime.

At the time many saw Jerry Rawlings together with Thomas Sankara in Burkina Faso, in the north, as figures committed to radical transformation in Ghana. This was never your position. Can you explain why you took such a stance on Rawlings? How did you characterise him (as opposed to Sankara) at that time and now?

There are substantial differences between Rawlings and Sankara. Sankara was a visionary because he took theoretical study very seriously as a sympathiser of communist groups in Burkina Faso. This is why we can quote Sankara today on issues like third world debt, African self-determination etc. Sankara was also very clear about the anti-imperialist struggle. Rawlings didn't have the discipline or the theoretical mind of Sankara. When Rawlings was recruited into the Free Africa Movement, he saw such study and discussions as a waste of time and rushed recklessly into an attempted uprising on 15 May 1979 which failed woefully and put the lives of all he was associated with in danger. He was a populist who incited the population without any clear vision of a way out. For those outside Ghana, who didn't see his weaknesses, recent revelations that he received financial gifts from the corrupt Nigerian military tyrant, Sanni Abacha, expose Rawlings' opportunist character. Facts which are available today show that Rawlings is an opportunist who had other frustrations with the military authorities. These included his financial problems as a result of spending too much money on drinks and his army book shows his difficulties in passing promotion examinations and even the inability to handle his household responsibilities that senior officers had to intervene in all these matters.

After a very difficult period you travelled to Czechoslovakia in 1984 and then to London in 1989. Can you explain your experiences there? What did it teach you about the communist bloc? What were your impressions, experience of racism etc?

Having fallen out with the Rawlings government in 1982 I was in military detention until a military uprising and jailbreak on 19 June 1983, in which political detainees from three major prisons in Ghana and various military guard rooms managed to escape. I joined the military uprising and jailbreak. The military instructed that anybody who saw those of us escaping should shoot us on sight. Some of my comrades were caught and killed but I was able to escape to Togo by the end of June that year.

In 1982 I was awarded a scholarship by the International Union of Students (IUS) to study in Czechoslovakia, but I didn't take up the award. But once in exile, I appealed to the IUS to revive the award and they did. As I never wanted to leave Africa, I didn't even have travelling documents. I had to arrange an emergency Safe Conduct document to join the aeroplane to Czechoslovakia. As the Eastern European countries were sympathetic to the Rawlings regime, they were unprepared to grant political asylum to its opponents. I lived in Czechoslovakia for one year without a residence permit. Through the award, I went to Czechoslovakia in 1984 to study and completed my studies in 1989. I was admitted to a PhD programme but as I wasn't sure of the post-1989 regime's support for the IUS, I sought asylum in the UK where a number of my comrades were in exile.

Despite the official declarations and documents, the majority of people in Eastern Europe didn't feel attached to the socialist governments – certainly not by the 1980s. The ruling class was very unpopular and treated with scorn as well as being totally alienated from the population at large. It had a negative effect on many of the foreign students as well. I was, therefore, not surprised when the experiment collapsed in 1989.

Briefly can you talk about your life in the UK, your political involvement and activism?

In the UK, I have been active in the left movement. Initially we tried to organise the left opposition to Rawlings from London, but the pressures of exile made London the centre for divisions in the Ghanaian Left. In 1991, a group editing the *Revolutionary Banner* published in the paper that Atim and I were agents of the Rawlings regime in exile as a way of trying to destroy us through a smear campaign. With the collapse of the Ghana left, I participated actively in the general left movement in [the] UK. I was a member of the Stop the War Coalition Steering Committees for five years. I contested the Greater London Assembly Elections in 2008 on the left platform Left List.

How have you maintained your involvement in African politics and movements?

In London, I was the Secretary of the Afrika United Action Front which was a coalition of Pan-Africanist organisations. I was also the coordinator of the Kwame Nkrumah Memorial Lectures, the International Campaign to Un-ban Kwame Nkrumah's Convention People's Party, IMF & World Bank Wanted for Fraud Campaign, Campaign Against Proxy War in Africa and the African Liberation Support Campaign Network. I also managed and edited a pan-Africanist journal known as the *Kilombo Pan-African Community Journal*. Through these roles I networked with others involved in African politics and movements.[20]

---

20 Most literature on the history of the left ignores the 1930s when the trade union movement started and the Communist International sponsored Negro Worker publications. During the period, the West African Youth League led by I. T. A. Wallace Johnson emerged, linked with the Communist International. Some UK based Ghanaians also joined the Socialist Party of Great Britain and the Communist Party of Great Britain

What are some of the principal challenges to a radical agenda and politics on the continent? What sort of projects are needed?

Until recently, a lot of the post-colonial world was looking to Latin America as a model to address the issue of neo-colonialism. Recent developments there give us further lessons, the importance of winning over and being rooted in the population at large and knowing that the capitalist class will always be on the offensive to stall efforts at social justice.

In Africa, liberation movements have either not been able to adjust to administering and managing or have been overwhelmed by the reality of the post-colonial state. The left or radical forces seem to have been cast to the margins and even those who were once major forces have become a shadow of their former selves.

I'll often return to a definition between left and right by Emmanuel Hansen in his analysis of Ghana at the time of the 31 December 1981 coup d'état where he wrote:

> Among progressive groups and individuals there had for some time existed the idea that Ghana's post-colonial problems were such that only a revolution could change them. What exactly this revolution was to imply has never been precisely articulated. There is, however, a consensus that it involves termination of the control of the local economy by foreign multinational companies, changes in the structure of production and production relations, changes in the class structure of control of the state, creation of political forms which would make the interests of the broad masses of people predominant and realisable and a programme which would initiate a process of improving the material conditions of the mass of the people. Those who broadly shared this position I would identify as belonging to the left. Those who entertained the

---

(CPGB). It is difficult to say whether those involved became integrated with the CPP but there is evidence that some of the activists in the trade unions fell out with the CPP between 1952 and 1954.

opposite position that there was nothing basically wrong with the nature of the country's structure of production or production relations or the nature of economic relations with Western capitalist countries or the structure of power, class relations or the nature of state power, and that only certain aspects of its functioning needed to be reformed. I would identify as the right.

I think Hansen is correct and I have long seen myself as being part of the "left" in this definition.

Can you explain, through the long period of exile and hardships you faced in Ghana, Czechoslovakia and the UK – witnessing as you did the murder of comrades – how you managed to survive? What forces in your life keep you going?

My father was imprisoned by the PNDC and my mother had travelled to the Republic of Togo with my younger siblings when the PNDC took over. In these difficulties I put the commitment to the cause above personal pain, and I have never lost that internal driving force. When I fled into exile my mother was with me, and when she was returning to Ghana she told me that if she was arrested as a tactic of the regime to lure me back to Ghana – that I should never return and that she was prepared to die. My family's support has strengthened me. My comrades who have been murdered haven't done anything that I have not done, I was supposed to die with them. I think the only tribute I can pay to them is to continue on the path we were on before they were murdered. The other thing that keeps me going materially and psychologically is the unlimited generosity I have had from a number of compatriots. In addition to this, is the recognition I receive from comrades for my contribution to the development of the broad left in Ghana. All these strengthen my commitment.

11. Mosa Phadi (2018), *Understanding Steve Biko*

On the anniversary of Steve Biko's murder, *ROAPE*'s Remi Adekoya spoke to South African scholar and activist Mosa Phadi. Phadi has worked for years on questions of race and class. Here, Phadi reflects on the legacy of Biko's radical thought, but also discusses how he did not consider cohesive alternatives that could now serve as a counter to neoliberal ideas. In a wide-ranging conversation, Phadi also looks at the political and economic crisis in South Africa, the Economic Freedom Fighters, the failures of the ANC, and the possibilities of a solution in the militancy and consciousness of working-class struggle.

***

Today is the anniversary of Stephen Biko's murder by apartheid state security operatives. He has since become a hugely symbolic rallying figure for many black people, especially in Africa, but not only there. What is your take on Biko's legacy today and how he is being historically positioned?

I have a problem with how Stephen Biko is positioned by the likes of Donald Woods, his friend and biographer, who ascribes the whole philosophy of black consciousness to Biko as if he emerged in a vacuum. His argument is basically that at the time Biko emerged, the Pan-Africanist Congress (PAC) and the African National Congress were both banned organisations, and so Biko's arrival filled a void in the struggle for black freedom.

However, if you think about the historical context of that time, this was not the case. Biko along with other students started the South African Students' Organisation (SASO) movement in 1968. If you think about 1968, this was a year of global protests; you had the anti-Vietnam war protests, huge civil rights demonstrations, student protests. Also going back, there was the background of Ghana becoming the first African country to gain independence from colonial rule in 1957 – an event which bolstered other pro-independence movements across the African continent. There was Julius Nyerere in Tanzania talking about an African socialism.

Prior to the 1960s even, there was the 1954 Women's Charter in South Africa demanding equality between men and women, there was the Women's March of 1956, the Sharpeville massacre in 1960, civil disobedience during that period and many other instances of struggle against oppression. So portraying the South African struggle as essentially being fought by the PAC and the ANC, and thus once these organisations were banned, there was some sort of a lull in the fight against oppression and apartheid, is a false analysis.

Another underreported issue about Biko and the era he came of age in is how caught up it was in the unravelling contradictions of Stalinism and the Soviet Union in general. Clearly this was no longer an alternative as many had imagined after WWII and most black activists, including the Black Panthers, were thinking about stretching Marxism, using its insights when it came to party organisation but viewing the lumpenproletariat in primarily racial terms as Fanon did.

There are similarities between Biko and Stokely Carmichael in terms of organising students initially using non-violent tactics but later becoming militant and asserting blackness or "reclaiming blackness" as Stokely would call it. At the same time Malcolm X was also in the picture, claiming blackness as the oppressed but also as the revolutionary agent. Workers were also organising.

Acting as if nothing existed before, during or after Biko is a failure in analysis. It is important to emphasise that he emerged in a period when a splintering of ideas and ideological eruptions were occurring elsewhere and these in turn informed his ideas.

Biko's idea of black consciousness, even though original in the context for South Africa, was very similar to Carmichael's ideas. My point is that I am critical of those who try to sanitise that history by decontextualising the progression of his political ideas.

Having said all that, Biko was a very important thinker whose ideas have been adopted by many movements. His ideas of Black Consciousness were important in focussing on what apartheid did to the psyche of black people. He talked about reclaiming blackness, but also put thought into how we as black people in South Africa should relate to coloureds[21] and Indians as the oppressed. He emphasised that while there was a hierarchy of racial oppression, we all needed to approach the system as an oppressed collective.

Black Consciousness is an idea that works best in a racist white-supremacy capitalist setting. However, its interpretation today is very neoliberal. You hear talk of "black excellence" for instance, there's nothing wrong with that per se, but it is a concept tied to a neoliberal framing that focuses on the individual. Such an approach will not help break with the system, but rather perpetuates inequalities, as capital by nature produces these inequalities. If you view yourself as an individual focused on achieving black excellence forgetting about structures which produce inequalities, then you are not helping solve the problem. If such views prevail, then a few successful individual blacks will be put on a pedestal by black people as symbols of black excellence and black power while a system perpetuating inequalities continues to produce mass poverty.

Biko's solutions to black problems were twofold: Black Consciousness and black economic empowerment. The second part is much emphasised recently, we see this even in the now popular "township economy" in South Africa which is fundamentally neoliberal in its philosophy. The provincial government in the economic hub of South Africa seeks to encourage entrepreneurial culture in various townships. Hence, it wants to support black businesses. This idea of growing black businesses was part of Biko's emancipatory approach. Biko wanted to create black markets and expand black business ownership. Once a radical

---

21   South African ethnic/racial classification referring to people of mixed African, Asian, and European ancestry.

idea it is currently used to justify elite formation especially among politically connected individuals.

Biko's ideas, while radical at that time don't get me wrong, nevertheless played into this bourgeois democracy we find ourselves in, his ideas were radical and important at that time, but he did not think much about cohesive alternatives that could now serve as counters to neoliberal ideas.

Which of Biko's ideas are popular today among South African intellectuals?

His death in 1977 sparked militancy amongst people, for example when you think of the 1980s insurgence, I think part of the courage emerged from black consciousness ideas of reclaiming Blackness. His thoughts about what black freedom should look like, what type of mentality we need to achieve it and via which methods, still permeate today through various social movements. For instance, the Fees Must Fall student movement sparked in 2016 about statues which still perpetuate symbols of black inferiority quoted Biko extensively and his views were manifest in their demands. They demanded that first and foremost statues of people like Cecil Rhodes must go, the curriculum must change and there should be a higher representation of intellectuals who look like us teaching us, for example.

People still gravitate towards Biko today because when you read his work you can relate to it as a black person. Even though he wasn't a traditionalist who believed in fixed cultures, he was very aware of the role cultural norms and values play for everyday Africans in their everyday lives. For instance, he knew religion was important to people and his spiritual outlook moved beyond Christianity and incorporated ideas of ancestors. He talked about how music can enlighten the wounded soul, he tapped into daily experiences realising the potential of everyday culture to radicalise and galvanise people into action. When you read him, he sparks the radical spirit in you to say: "yes, we can fight the system, yes we have the right to fight the system." But then apart from this, you need to think what kind of world you want to replace the current system with. This is where his limitations were. But as a light to spark action, he was very important.

What are some of the most popular ideas among South African intellectuals today regarding the way forward for the country?

In academia, especially after the Fees Must Fall movement, the most popular issue is that of decolonisation. Seminar after seminar, conference after conference and article after article have been written on this. The main inspiration comes from Latin American scholarship emphasising the need to decolonise, for example, the knowledge system amongst other broader structural issues in South Africa which are inherently Western-oriented and steeped in racism. This is the most popular school of thought today.

Marxist ideas have been rejected, as indeed Biko rejected them in his day. The link between class and race has not been integral in our analysis; Marxism failed to incorporate race into the equation. Meanwhile, issues centred around our history and oppression are very important to people. People use terms like "triggers" to refer to pain that has been inflicted upon us in the past and emphasise that we need to remedy that. However, Marxism in South Africa is unable to offer an analysis of how a history of racial oppression and being black frames how people relate to various struggles beyond the workerist approach.

Julius Malema's Economic Freedom Fighters (EFF) are quite popular today both among the working classes and some black intellectuals. This is due to the failure of ANC to radically change people's lives in the townships where there is huge unemployment. I come from a town called Kagiso. When I go home, on a weekday, it seems like a weekend there, young men and women on the streets with no jobs. There are protests virtually non-stop, people demanding services. In the 1990s, people waited patiently for change, but by the 2000s, they started realising it was not happening. This has sparked some xenophobic attacks like recent ones on Pakistani shop-owners which were looted by people complaining they were selling stale food. Taxes have increased, VAT was increased this April leading to steep hikes in food prices. There is tension everywhere.

This is the crisis we've been in since Ramaphosa became the president, squeezing not just the poor but the middle-class as well. This has created space for EFF, especially with Malema forcing the conversation about race into the public forum. Up till then, the left had been fixated with class while the conversation about race had been muted. The left focussed on economic structures, neglecting the everyday manifestation of being black. They missed the feelings young people had about being not just poor, but poor and black as well. Malema exploited this very well. He too uses Black Panther methodology, utilising a Marxist-Leninist model of party structures combined with Fanonian elements incorporating race and treating the racially oppressed individual as a revolutionary subject. Again, this goes back to 1960s ideas before and during Biko's activist period. Although embroiled in some corruption scandals themselves, EFF has attracted young unemployed people, mainly men, but also some middle-class people who have experienced racism in the corporations they work in, which are still largely owned by white people. Some black intellectuals have also been drawn to EFF.

However, many of the protests on the streets demanding basic services like water and electricity are not organised by any political party or movement, they have no specific policies, they simply want services. The new student movements, meanwhile, are not only using Biko as a symbol, but also challenging gender dynamics, ideas of feminism have become key debates in struggles with power and patriarchy. Women are protesting against domestic violence and patriarchy, again taking us back to the ideas of the 1960s which are coming back in different ways. In general, revolutionary ideas about race and gender dating back to the 1950s and 60s are returning – the only difference is that they are emerging today in modern form and style, especially with the proliferation of social media which can be used to spread a message very rapidly.

Is there any party who, in your opinion, if they came to power, would best deploy that power towards the betterment of the people? You've mentioned EFF in a rather positive light but said yourself they have been implicated in corruption scandals too. On what basis do you associate them with any hopes of true positive change for downtrodden South Africans? As you know, history is replete with examples, plenty in Africa unfortunately, of people riding to power on the back of all sorts of equalitarian slogans only to gorge themselves on the state's resources once they get there.

Well, what are the options? There is the Democratic Alliance, which is a very liberal party, so you are assured of a set of liberal economic policies if they get into power. Additionally, they seem to place no emphasis on our history and don't recognise the psychological scars apartheid has left on black people. Ideologically, this is thus not a viable option for me. Then you have the ANC and the EFF. EFF wants state capitalism. They should be understood as a party that is left of the ANC, not that leftist you understand, but simply left of the ANC. I will vote for them. Not because I believe they, or any other party, can emancipate the working class. No, the working class have to find the agency in themselves to fight for themselves.

No politician or political party will save the working class or the poor, let's not be delusional. For me, the hope is that the working class will organise and fight for themselves. EFF wants state capitalism, and this can go two ways as history shows. It can become very authoritarian or focus on building new forms of elites. EFF is important for debates linking race to class, but I don't naively believe they will be our saviours. As always, the working class will continue trying new parties, hoping for something better. But only their militancy can force change. EFF is a child of the ANC, and they cannot break away from the corrupt links of the ANC.

What then would be the value added of the EFF for regular South Africans were they to one day win power?

If they come to power, of course there will be reforms – they wouldn't be able to just rule in a business-as-usual fashion. They would have to make concessions to the poor. The land question would be addressed, land would become state-owned. With regards to key financial sectors like mining, they are currently trying to propagate a three-way ownership system in which the state would own say, 50% of a mine, the community 10% and the rest would be privatised. They want to show capital they are ready to negotiate with it while at the same time trying to sustain their radical image.

But they have opened a space in the debate, emboldened people to believe they have a right to push. I know the militancy they came with can't be sustained if they win power. If they win, there will be some big reforms, but there would be contradictions too, no doubt. And yes, there is the danger of dictatorial tendencies in them. That is the risk involved with them. Yet, I still think the working class should vote for EFF demanding some specific reforms.

So, basically, you accept they are a risk but think they are a risk worth taking?

Yes, I do. Also, one major issue they deserve credit for pushing onto the agenda as well is that of land reform, the idea of the expropriation of land without compensation. Even though there were various landless people's movements in the 2000s, EFF emboldened that demand and now parliament has passed a resolution to amend the constitution allowing for land expropriation without compensation. However, right now, public consultations are being held, expected to end with a report by [the] end of September.

If President Ramaphosa eventually signs that amendment into law, is there any plan in place for how exactly this process would look?

No, right now there has not been any debate on who would get what and on what grounds. The politicians are simply caught up in the militancy of the people who are demanding reforms. This whole land issue also reflects ideas popularised by Biko years ago. Apart from the physical desire people have to get their lands back, it is also part of a psychological recognition that this is your land. The planning of our cities today is still the same as it was under apartheid with developers able to keep certain areas exclusively rich and white. Or even in the rural areas, you have a situation where all the best farmland is owned by whites, so they are the farmers while the blacks are simple village residents with a few black people who managed to carve their space in the agricultural sector. People are now imagining a different kind of space, a different kind of South Africa and politicians are rushing to respond because they want votes. But the discussion about who will get what and whether this process will really empower the poorest South Africans has yet to be started.

12. Tamás Szentes (2018), To Be Bravely Critical of Reality

Tamás Szentes, Professor Emeritus of the Corvinus University of Budapest (the former Karl Marx University), was one of the early contributing editors of *ROAPE*. Between 1967 and 1971, he worked together with *ROAPE* activists and researchers at the University of Dar es Salaam. Here he talks with Tamás Gerőcs about the years he spent in Tanzania, the hope and political possibilities of the period, and his extensive contributions to development economics.

***

What was your intellectual or political background before you went to Tanzania? And why to Tanzania? Where did you work before 1967, and did you publish anything related to Africa earlier?

After having graduated at the Karl Marx University of Economic Science in 1955, where I wasn't employed for political reasons, I got a job thanks to my professor of the history of economic theories, Antal Mátyás, in the Publishing House of Economics and Law as an editor. My first publication (in 1959) was about the views of David Ricardo. But I wrote quite a lot for myself and a few friends, not publishable, [which was] moreover very risky in the early 1950s (such as a study of the real nature of the Soviet system in 1951). As a matter of fact, my interest has always focussed on social science theories and social systems – not only from an economic point of view. From my professor Mátyás, who also ran a seminar on the three volumes of Karl Marx's *Capital*, I have learnt to approach both historically and critically all theories, even the best ones, as none of them can fully capture reality which is infinitely complex and ever changing. After the Year of Africa, in 1960, when a number of colonies gained independence, my interest turned to such countries – particularly those somehow attempting a pattern of development different from both the capitalist West and the communist East.

Owing not only to this interest but also to the fortunate fact – namely editing the book of a dean of my university, who helped to secure me a senior lectureship in the Department of International Economic and Political Relations – [that] my new job involved research and teaching on Africa and the Third World. Besides several book-chapters and articles, I authored a monograph on East Africa (in Hungarian), published in 1963. As a result, I was heavily involved in the operation of an Afro-Asian Research Group at the university and what followed in that of the Afro-Asian Research Institute of the Hungarian Academy of Sciences that was established in 1963 and renamed as the Institute of World Economics in 1973.

When Professor Knud Eric Svendsen, an appointed head of department for the newly established but not yet operating University College of Dar es Salaam, was mandated by Julius Nyerere to recruit professors in Poland and Hungary, known to be rebels against the Moscow-line, and relatively independent of it, I was one of those recommended to him and was interviewed. Soon I received an offer and contract for four years to become the Head and Professor of the Economics Department.

As your book in English, The Political Economy of Underdevelopment, *obviously grew out of your experiences and work in Tanzania, how and to what extent were you intellectually inspired there to write it?*

I must say that the conditions for research as well as the atmosphere both politically and intellectually were excellent at the time at the University of Dar es Salaam. My department, as well as the Economic Research Bureau led by Gerry Helleiner, had considerable funds to order books, documents, etc, to make field research and to contact people involved in political leadership in the country. We also had regular staff seminars to discuss research results and to exchange views. The very fact that in those years, after the Arusha Declaration, Tanzania attracted a number of highly qualified and progressive minded scholars obviously contributed enormously to the exceptionally good intellectual atmosphere in Dar. While the academic staff itself involved such eminent members, among them not only those already mentioned but also Arnold Kettle, Robert and Ann Seidman, John Loxley, Leonard Berry, Walter Rodney, Reginald H. Green, Ian Livingstone, G. Routh, M. A. Bienefeld, etc, several other internationally well-known scholars came also to participate in conferences, to deliver public lectures. Such as Paul Streeten, Dudley Seers, Samir Amin, Immanuel Wallerstein, René Dumont, Brian van Arkedie, Dharam Ghai, etc. President Julius Nyerere and his aim to develop democratically a genuine type of socialist system of society different from those in the East had obviously gained not only wide-spread interest internationally but also – among progressive thinkers – a great sympathy.

You mean among left-wing people, don't you?

Mostly but not exclusively. Anyway, nowadays "left-wing" is not an unambiguous term.

But did you belong to the obviously leftist theoretical stream which blames Western capitalism for the underdevelopment of the "South", and explains it by dependence?

Yes, but also no – or not precisely. Prof. Paul Streeten in his articles on the two, opposite theoretical streams of development economics,[22] honoured me in mentioning my name among those eleven scholars[23] who share the views expressed by André Gun-

---

22 See "L'évolution des théories relatives au développement", *Problemes Économiques*, No. 1546, 9/1977, and "Development Economics: The Intellectual Divisions", *Eastern Economic Journal*, Vol. XI, No. 3 /1985.

23 Namely Samir Amin, E. A. Brett, F. E. Cardoso, Frantz Fanon, Celso

der Frank and also Raul Prebisch, Hans Singer, Gunnar Myrdal, Albert Hirschman and Francois Perroux, rejecting the theory of linear development to stress the responsibility of the rich developed countries for underdevelopment of the poor. What I have obviously shared with them, besides the rejection of the concept of linear development and the historical responsibility of the colonial powers, is a very critical evaluation of the prevailing world order as well as the existing social systems both in the West and the East.

However, the views among these scholars were quite different in their details – particularly regarding solutions; if a new world order was required for example, and mine also differed from theirs (even from those of my friends, such as Samir Amin, Gunder Frank, Immanuel Wallerstein or others). Thus, I complemented my critique of the conventional theories of development economics, which appeared in my first book in English, by a critical survey in other books[24] and each of the different main theoretical streams they seemed to belong to (such as the school of *Dependencia*, neo-Marxism and New Left stream).

Does it mean that you denied the dependence of underdeveloped countries and disagreed with the world-system approach?

Not at all, but I found it insufficient and one-sided to point to dependence and explain underdevelopment by external factors only – because the latter are interrelated with internal ones and dependencies have different forms, varieties which provide chances for manoeuvring, or even reducing its overall intensity. While [the] world-system approach is necessary, it should not be exclusive and must not mean that national economies are merely

---

Furtado, Johann Galtung, Keith Griffin, Colin Leys, Ann Seidman and Osvaldo Sunkel.

24   See *Theories of World Capitalist Economy. A Critical Survey of Conventional, Reformist and Radical Views* in 1985, and *World Economics 1: Comparative Theories and Methods of International and Development Economics* in 2002.

virtual units or the level of analysis and actions should be limited to the global system.

Taking up this last point, and looking back from today, how much can Tanzania's modernisation and economic transformation under Nyerere be regarded as successful? Did the Nyerere Government have the power to carry them out, or were there any external or internal obstacles that kept the country on a dependent path? Where can we place the "Nyerere Years" or the "Arusha Declaration" in history?

There were considerable achievements in modernisation and economic transformation, albeit not without shortcomings (some of which were discussed in our staff seminars). Nyerere's aim to create a kind of socialist system based upon traditional collectivism (like *ujamaa*) has obviously failed, for both internal and external reasons.[25] I considered the objective manifested in the Arusha Declaration as one, and perhaps the most sincere and honest, of those similar attempts in the 1960s and 1970s in the Third World which all failed partly because of the international conditions, forces and effects and partly due to mistaken policy of the domestic ruling stratum.

At the Dar es Salaam conference organised by *ROAPE* this year, an interesting debate emerged about whether the regime built by Nyerere was a state-socialist one which sought to break away from the dominance of capitalist powers, or was it a state-capitalist regime which promoted modernisation and the development and integration of a capitalist national economy? We also have similar debates on the left in Eastern Europe: whether 1949-1989 was a state-capitalist or a state-socialist experiment.

I think we have to be careful in making use of the terms "state-socialist" or "state-capitalist" in distinguishing a socio-political or economic system from another one, partly because

---

25   Ujamaa was the name of the concept that formed the basis of Julius Nyerere's developmental policies in Tanzania after independence. The term means "familyhood", referring to the type of socialist development that differed from Soviet-type socialism.

capitalism as such has many different variants and is permanently changing, while socialism in reality has never and nowhere come into existence yet – and partly because the above terms substantially refer to the role of the state, particularly in development and modernisation. Both terms primarily indicate a transition only, the direction of which may be declared and expressed in ideology, but the outcome of the transition process is necessarily questionable and undetermined.

Oversimplifications go hand-in-hand with over-generalisations, which characterise ideologies and are to be refrained from in science – such as the purist perception of capitalism versus socialism as independent entities contrasting each other in all respects, the transformation of which cannot succeed by gradual reforms. Systems with exclusively and perfectly compatible components exist in pure models of ideologies only, not in social reality. The existing socio-economic systems of all countries of the world (as well as the world itself) incorporate heterogeneous segments, combine mechanisms governed by different rules and reconcile opposite needs or principles.

What is called state-capitalism is a particularly mixed and changeable phenomenon with contradictory elements and tendencies. It may pave the way for the unfolding of capitalism proper (by substituting state accumulation and investments for private ones) or may turn to the so-called state-socialism (by setting limits for private capital and decreasing social inequalities). These two variants have also common features and can easily change over from one to the other.

Socialism-orientation, or state-socialism, in underdeveloped countries necessarily faces a double task [representing] more or less contradictory requirements – namely, to catch up with the developed countries (often called "modernisation") and to reduce social inequalities by helping the poor and disadvantaged. Such systems, if isolated and confronting a hostile capitalist environment, may, almost inevitably, become militarised, dictatorial and bureaucratised (like the Soviet one under Stalin), or if they remain open to the outside world, cooperating with dominant forces of foreign capital, can easily be undermined by the latter and their domestic clients resulting in violent coups d'états or replacement of the leadership. The most typical and frequent oversimplification undoubtedly follows from the divorce of the external and internal factors in the explanation of the rise, defeat or transformation of social systems. It obviously neglects the historical changes in the international conditions of national development, the widening and deepening of global interdependencies.

How and in what sense did your personal experiences in Tanzania and other African countries influence your views, theoretical orientation and academic career? For what can you be grateful to Africa?

I can thank Africa for a lot. My experiences there have certainly reinforced my deep interest in social science as a whole, beyond economics, and my very views [and] increasing conviction about the requirement of a historical, critical and dialectically holistic approach to reality. I also made invaluable acquaintances, numerous friends there who also helped my career later on. Thanks to them and also to the success of my book in the following decades, until almost the end of the century when I stopped travelling abroad, I was regularly invited as an expert in various advisory, expert and steering committees to many different international bodies (such as [the] International Labour Organisation, UNESCO, IDEP, etc) and as an invited speaker in many conferences of various international scientific associations and funds (such as the Association of Third World Economists, Lelio Basso International Foundation, International Foundation for Development Alternatives, the South Centre, etc).

How did your African experiences affect your teaching and academic activity at home, in Hungary?

Having returned to my university in Budapest, I initiated and led an alternative multidisciplinary bloc of courses called development studies which became so popular among students that we had to limit their number. With a colleague of mine and one of my best students, namely Ferenc Miszlivetz (today Professor and Director of the Institute of Advanced Studies in Kőszeg, Hungary) who actually initiated it, we produced a semi-samizdat series of readings under the same title which presented the students selected writings of foreign scholars (e.g. Immanuel Wallerstein, Paul Streeten, Arghiri Emmanuel, etc) otherwise unavailable for them at that time. We included the writings of Samir Amin and Gunder Frank whose works were not publishable because of their anti-Soviet stand. After the "system-change" when an English program was established at the university, for several years I had regular courses on development economics too. Later on at the Academy, when I was the head of the social science section for two terms, I initiated a permanent committee on international and development economics, which is now the interdisciplinary "International and Development Studies." (I am its Honorary President.)

Let us return to the case of the University of Dar es Salaam, where ROAPE held a workshop on radical political and economic transformation, the intellectual birthplace of the review! What innovations, if any, did you suggest or realise there at that time – for example in the teaching program, as compared to that of the other two East-African university colleges? Did you replace the standard Western teaching material by readings of Marxist-Leninist political economy, for example?

As to the teaching of Marxist-Leninist political economy only, while it was expected – particularly by some militant leftist colleagues – I taught the fundamentals of economics in a historical framework embracing all the main theoretical streams (from mercantilism through classical, Marxian, and Keynesian theories to neo-classical economics, including also institutionalism), evaluating each of them critically but also pointing to useful lessons from each. As a matter of fact I have always rejected any exclusiveness, and while I have always appreciated and been heavily influenced by the works of Marx I had been – from the very beginning – critical of such Marxism as represented by Marxism-Leninism, particularly in its Stalinist sense.

What readings did you use and recommend? And were the students able to attain the required knowledge in such a course?

I had to make cyclostyled readings for which I partly wrote, partly translated some text from the book of Antal Mátyás. Our students, by being exempted from learning some irrelevant details, concepts or models, performed very well in general, so that the same external examiner also examining the university colleges of Uganda and Kenya at the same time noted as a surprise in his report that our students understood the fundamental concepts and methods of economics better than those in the other regional colleges. Anyway, it was my strong conviction that our primary role was in teaching students to think instead of presenting them ready-made universal formulas and mathematical models. In the 1969 international conference on the teaching of economics in African universities, I stressed that "one of the greatest mistakes would be to teach only one particular theory... Instead, all important schools in economic theory should be taught... [I]t is necessary to put the theories into a general historical framework and to explain their origin and interrelations..."

Were you against mathematics as a language of economics?

By no means. Quite the opposite. As another innovation, quite contrary to conventional practice elsewhere, I made it compulsory for all those students choosing an economics major to also take mathematics and statistics. In the same conference in 1969 I also stressed that "any attempt to diminish the significance and weight of the economic mathematics and statistics in teaching would inevitably lead to a decrease in the quality of the new graduates." While I also noted that "mathematical formulas, no doubt, have the advantage that it is easier to memorise them, and they give a direct basis for practical calculations." Yet I called attention to "a tremendous danger in teaching economic principles and concepts by and through mathematical formulas" because such formulas and models necessarily simplify the economic interrelations, conceal the original presumptions, and give the impression of scientific exactitude.

What was your relationship with the students like? What was the most interesting experience you had as the head of the department of economics?

In the first weeks of teaching I experienced what I had been told beforehand to expect, namely the lack of discipline manifested in wandering in and out during lectures. To overcome it I introduced the practice that, after having arrived a few minutes before the lecture was due to start, I would stand with my back to the students until the last second, and then turn around to face them, and always interrupted my speech whenever a student came or left the lecture theatre. Surprisingly not only for others but even for myself, very soon the students' discipline was better than at my home university. Students also helped a lot in my work, particularly their elected representatives who forwarded majority opinion on the teaching program and lecturers when participating in department meetings. This was, by the way, another innovation that time, almost causing a scandal, as student representation was not yet an accepted institutional practice in any university.

After a half century, what would you send as a message to the students or the lecturers at the University of Dar es Salaam, many of whom will certainly read this interview?

I send, of course, my best wishes to them and their country. If I

To Be Bravely Critical of Reality 179

can suggest anything in general, it follows from my life experiences: let them be bravely critical of reality, both of society and politics, and let them do their best to improve both.

13. Frej Stambouli (2021), When I Was a Student of Fanon

The Tunisian sociologist, Frej Stambouli, remembers his teacher Frantz Fanon. Stambouli is a scholar of urbanisation, migration and the urban poor, and worked for years as a Professor of Sociology at Tunis University. Here, Stambouli describes Fanon's lectures at the university in Tunis in 1959, and his unique conception of psychiatry and promotion of open psychiatry as a "pathology of freedom". Stambouli considers Fanon's legacy and his anger, reason and kindness, recalling, "I will never forget the generosity of Fanon".

***

You were in Tunisia in the late 1950s. Can you explain how you came to be there and what you were doing?

I am Tunisian, born in December 1935 in a prestigious small city called Monastir, which lies on the Mediterranean coast. I am married to a Finnish woman, Anja Toivola-Stambouli, whose career was in the International Red Cross and Red Crescent Movement. We are now both retired and have lived in Helsinki since 2008, with frequent visits to Monastir, Tunisia.

At an early age, in 1942, I was hiding with my parents in a small tunnel dug by my maternal grandfather in his field. This was during the Second World War when the Germans were attacking the French in Tunisia. I had just started my primary school, run by a French headmaster. For me, it was rather hazy what was going on. My parents were illiterate. They just told me that it was a battle between Europeans.

While I went to school and learned French, my sister, who was younger than me, remained illiterate. That was the mood of the time: girls do not go to school. Also, my two older brothers did not finish primary school. My father owned one hundred olive trees and was a merchant of olives. In addition, he rented three houses to officers of the French army in Monastir.

In Tunisia, where a nationalist movement was on the rise, the struggle against French domination intensified until the nation gained its independence in 1956. Just after, in 1957, I finished secondary school in the city of Sousse and left for Tunis for my first year of university. In the late 1950s, the university offered only two years of education, for this reason I went to Paris in 1960 and obtained a master's degree in sociology. I then finished my doctorate in [the] College de France under the well-known orientalist Jacques Berque in 1964.

While in Paris, I discovered the influence of Fanon there – having been his student in Tunis in 1959. Unhappy about the timidity of the French political left concerning the Algerian revolution, Fanon met with Jean-Paul Sartre and Simone de Beauvoir and convinced them to act. I could now personally witness Fanon's influence; I saw Sartre in the Latin Quarter of Paris distributing leaflets in favour of Algerian independence and spoke with him. I also invited him to talk to the Tunisian students about the Algerian revolution. Later I asked Simone de Beauvoir to talk about the condition of women in Algeria. With Gisèle Halimi, the talented lawyer of Tunisian origin, she was defending the Algerian woman fighter Djamila Bouhired.

From 1964 to 2000, I taught sociology at Tunis University where Michel Foucault was in 1967 my colleague and friend. During that time, I did field research in Tunisia on regional development, urbanisation, and slums in the periphery of Tunis. I wrote several articles that were published in journals and edited books on these topics.

As you know, Frantz Fanon and his wife Josie and son were in exile in Tunis. Fanon worked as a psychiatrist in the capital but he also taught. You were one of his students. Please tell us a little of your experiences with Fanon, how you first met him, your personal impressions and your direct contact with him?

Fanon arrived in Algeria for the first time in 1953. A year later, the Algerian revolution started while Fanon was working at Blida Hospital. The French colonial administration feared his influence on the events, leading Fanon to resign from his post two years later.[26] Pierre Bourdieu arrived in Algiers in 1955 and was teaching and doing research there until 1960. He was critical of Fanon, whom he never met.

It was in Tunisia during the years 1956-1961 that Fanon came to fully develop his political engagement for the liberation of the Algerian people. This was precisely when I became a student of Fanon, attending his lectures at Tunis university in 1959. I followed a course of social psychopathology. Fanon was critical of the somatic conception of psychiatry and promoted open psychiatry as a "pathology of freedom." He also spoke about his time at the Blida hospital in Algeria and his fights with his orthodox colleagues there.

I rarely came across a fascinating personality like Fanon. An intelligent and sharp man, passionate and fully mastering his discourse, Fanon spoke with elegance, conviction, and a superb art of persuasion. In particular, he made you realise the ferocity of the colonial system and the necessity to fight against barbarity, violence and injustice. As first-year students of sociology, it was for us an unsurpassable introduction to our future specialisation.

We were surprised that Fanon's lectures were attended by a non-student public, such as medical doctors, academics, Algerian militants, and politicians, creating an unusual atmosphere that fascinated us as students. After his lectures, Fanon would invite us to be present at some of his consultations in the psychiatric hospital. We were enormously impressed by his ability to listen to his patients and his art of making them talk without fear. It was often about trauma while fighting in the Algerian mountains

---

26 See Fanon's letter to the French colonial minister in Algeria, Robert Lacoste, in his posthumous collection.

during the revolution.

The patients were invited to verbalise their symptoms freely, explain their problems and learn to make contact with reality again. As for Fanon, "social therapy helps free the patient from his phantasms and confront reality." I will never forget the generosity of Fanon with his patients and his ability to free them from anxiety and guilt.

Can you talk us through the years you were in Tunisia, and your contact, experience of the Algerian exiles, and FLN (Front de libération nationale) members at the time?

In 1956 Tunisia had just won its political independence under the leadership of Habib Bourguiba, having fought for it since the birth of the Nationalist Party in 1934. Bourguiba was a great leader, very popular, realistic and pragmatic. He was born in Monastir and came from the educated petty bourgeoisie. This was the time when Tunisia became the safe haven for the Algerian political leadership and a great number of political activists. An intensive beehive!

In 1957 Fanon, using Dr Fares as his pseudonym, arrived in Tunis, which became the main harbour of the FLN in exile. Ferhat Abbas, a moderate Algerian nationalist leader, founded in 1958 in Tunis the Provisional Government of the Algerian Republic (GPRA) in exile. He also used to meet with President Bourguiba for deliberations. Later on, in 1961, he joined the most revolutionary wing of the FLN led by Ben Bella and Boumediene. Great figures of the Algerian political spectrum were based in Tunis, such as Reda Malek, Ahmed Boumendjel, M'hamed Yazid, Mohamed Harbi, Abane Ramdane, Pierre Chaulet, and others.

From time to time, I interacted with some of them. Reda Malek, who later on would have several ministerial positions, was a fine man. Bitter about the timidity of the French left and especially the betrayal of the communist party, he was rather happy to be in Tunisia – praising the active solidarity of the Tunisians with the Algerian people. Dr Pierre Chaulet, expelled from Algeria in 1957 along with his wife Claudine, used to visit us at the university, where I met them in 1959. (Pierre had introduced Fanon to the FLN.) Claudine sometimes joined lectures on sociology in the department where I was studying. Both were passionate about the Algerian revolution. Pierre Chaulet was also writing for *El Moudjahid*, a daily newspaper of the Algerian revolution since 1956, available in Tunisia but, of course, banned in Algeria. He even conducted secret operations under the strong leader Abane Ramdane.

Fanon became a fierce political speaker of the Algerian FLN. He was a brilliant polemist and active journalist for *El Moudjahid*. There were papers of Fanon published in *El Moudjahid*, which are available in a book called *Pour la Revolution Algerienne* (published in English as *Towards the African Revolution* in 1967), edited by Maspero in 1964. In some of them, one can feel the strong attacks of Fanon against the timidity of the French political left. Fanon's style is a unique synthesis of passion rooted in rigorous national analysis. Several journalists who approached Fanon described their impressions. The famous Giovanni Pirelli from Rome speaks of his "burning eyes which cut my defences."

One can conclude from his articles how much Fanon represented the left of the Algerian FLN, contrary to the first Algerian President Ben Bella. Fanon's dream was a future Algeria leading the way to a revolutionary Africa, secular and modern. Here, Fanon underestimated the Islamic dimension of Arab-Algerian society which he did not master. During the terrible decade of the Algerian civil war in the 1990s, I met some of the modernist Algerian intelligentsia who had fled Algeria. For example, Ali El Kenz joined my sociology department of Tunis university in 1993-94 and Faysal Yachir – a leftist. The three of us joined Samir Amin as members of CODESRIA (African Council of Social Sciences and Development) in Dakar.

The whole position of Fanon regarding religion is very peculiar. In particular, he was too quick and too optimistic when he wrote, "The old Algeria is dead, and a new society is born." One should remember here two decisive sinister heritages from the colonial time in Algeria and elsewhere in the Maghreb: the extension of illiteracy and the marginalisation of the Islamic patrimony, which started early in the process of colonisation.

Until 1954, [the] illiteracy rate in Algeria was about 86%. The country lost one hundred and fifty years compared to European societies. This is probably the most catastrophic heritage of colonialism, and the origin of what analysts will later on call under-development. Jacques Derrida, who was born in Algeria, denounced such scandalous trauma. Albert Memmi, born in Tunisia, characterised bilingualism in a colonial context as a "linguistic drama." In order to identify the nature of present-day Algerian society, one should consider not only the colonial legacy but also its specific Arab-Islamic matrix – Islam being simultaneously a society, a state, and culture: the well-known Din, Dawla, Dunja.

While in Tunisia, Fanon enjoyed meeting the famous radical scholar Jacques Berque and listening to his analysis of North Africa and the Arab world. Berque talked about Fanon, *"sa colère, sa raison et sa bonté"* ("his anger, his reason, and goodness").

Can you explain what happened to you after 1961, and in the subsequent decades? How do you measure (or weigh) this early period in terms of your life and its trajectory?

Because I belong to an in-between historical period and generation, I can clearly see the advantages and the inconveniences of such a position. My generation had better access to universal and global knowledge than the previous ones. I was trained in Paris, Sorbonne, in the sixties and later for one year in 1973 at LSE, London, under Ernest Gellner. I also had the chance to spend one year in 1987 as visiting professor at UCLA, Los Angeles, and a similar period at Ann Arbor, University of Michigan in 1991.

The shortcoming of such an itinerary is that my rootedness in my own culture and history remained insufficient. I realised it clearly when I started teaching at Tunis University in 1964. I was lecturing on the sociology of North African societies, which I had not sufficiently mastered. My knowledge of my own civilization – Islam and Arabism – was simply not sufficient.

I was not ready to understand, for example, the failure of the Arab armies in 1967 against Israel, nor the spectacular success of the Islamic turn of the Iranian revolution of 1979. The massive return of political Islam was an unforeseen surprise. I had to work hard to catch up and adjust to my own history. This is one lesson among others about the ravages of alienation and dispossession of our history from colonialism, which Fanon has scrutinised all his life. Despite all these shortcomings, I still feel privileged in contrast to the present-day challenges of our societies in nearly every domain, including education, health, employment, etc.

Albert Memmi, who wrote a book on Fanon, is intrigued by our societies' present-day stagnation. "Why such failure?", he kept asking in a book called *Decolonisation and the Decolonised* in 2006. "In formerly colonised peoples, fifty years later, nothing really seems to have changed, except for the worse." And he adds: "The gulf between the rich and the poor grows wider... [A] police state and tyranny maintain an oppressive system".

Since decolonisation more than 60 years ago, the global political configuration of most Arab and African societies remained similar to what Fanon analysed: a micro-bourgeoisie controlling its wealth and power inherited from the direct colonialism era with the help of the army and a party regime.

Here and there, there are small changes, new variations, but the overall scenery remains unchanged. For example, the Arab spring of 2011 had been an uprising by the excluded, such as the peasantry of the interior regions, but also and especially the proletariat and semi-proletariat around the main cities, in rebellion for a share of wealth and for respect of their dignity and for justice. But the weakness of their organisations and their internal division did not allow them to win.

As we know, in all of Africa south of the Sahara, the historical heritage is as complicated as it is across the Arab world: manipulation of the frontiers by colonialism and hence arbitrary separation of communities and people. It is impressive how Fanon had dealt with these structural characteristics of Arab and African societies in *The Wretched of the Earth* under the title "Pitfalls of the National Consciousness".

Fanon was fully aware of all the complexities of these societies. In his last book in 1961 he wrote: "One should get away from the ethnic and tribal dictatorships and promote a national policy in favour of the periphery and the masses."

Therefore, the road to liberation of the oppressed is still long and tortuous. But Fanon has offered precious tools and hope. His contribution to the liberation of the oppressed (Mustathafin in Arabic) is infinite. And his optimism for the future of humankind is energising. Fanon's humanism is refreshing. It purifies history from segregation, racism, humiliation (Hogra in Arabic) and injustice and opens the door of freedom for every human being, regardless of race, culture or religion. Recognition of the hominisation of human beings (Hegel) leads to a revitalised universality. Time has come for an alternative civilization – this is what Fanon teaches us.

The most recent protest movement in the US, Black Lives Matter, shows how much Fanon's struggle for the liberation of humankind is alive, and his ideal for justice and dignity will never be defeated!

14. Jean Copans (2019), Radical Scepticism

Jean Copans is an Africanist anthropologist who specialises on Senegal, the social sciences of development, and the history and methods of anthropology and sociology. He is a long-standing comrade and collaborator of *ROAPE*. Here, Zeilig asks him about a lifetime dedicated to research, activism and writing on Africa. Determined always to carry out serious investigation in his own research, Copans explains we must ensure that our radical understanding is not completely divorced from the real world.

***

Can you please give us a description of your early politicisation and work in the 1950s and 1960s?

My parents – an American father and a French mother – had been communist sympathisers since the 1930s, having met and married in France where my father was studying for a doctorate from Columbia University. They returned to the US on the outbreak of war but after 1945 they finally settled in Paris – my father having landed in Normandy in June 1944, serving with the US Army Office of War Information because of his French language skills. This explains why I was born in New York in 1942. My father went on to work initially for Voice of America, then for French national radio where for a quarter of a century he presented programmes on American music – mostly black music and jazz.[27] We always had plenty of newspapers at home and I followed from afar the wars in Korea and French Indo-China, and the early stages of the Algerian War. In May 1958 I also experienced first-hand, you

---

27 See *Un amour* (Les Films d'Ici, 90 mins, 2014) – the very personal film made by my producer/director brother Richard Copans about our parents, in which I do not entirely recognise myself. See also the Wikipedia article on Sim Copans.

might say, the coup that brought General de Gaulle to power.

With a view to returning to the US, I started my education at the American School in Paris before moving for my secondary years to the private École alsacienne. The people and atmosphere there were so bourgeois, with very few *gauchistes* [leftists], that I wanted to attend a regular *lycée* (and one I believed, wrongly at that time, would be more "popular"). So, in the autumn of 1959, I started at the Lycée Condorcet, near the Gare St Lazare. There I met Jeunesse communiste (JC) activists, including their leader, Alain Krivine, who was in my class and became well-known in national politics. Alain and one of his brothers had already joined the Trotskyist Fourth International and were pursuing its familiar tactic of entryism. When we started university at the Sorbonne in 1961, in the Faculté des lettres et sciences humaines, we all joined the UEC (Union des étudiants communistes).

During my three years of undergraduate studies (history, geography, ethnology and sociology of sub-Saharan Africa), I spent much of my time campaigning for an end to the war in Algeria (the ceasefire came in March 1962); against neocolonial interventions in newly independent francophone Africa and the former Belgian Congo (independent since 1960); and lastly, via the very reformist student union UNEF (Union nationale des étudiants de France), for improvements in student conditions.[28]

My activism evolved on several levels, layered one inside another like Russian dolls: the PCF (Parti communiste français), which I subsequently joined for a year in 1964-5; the *gauchiste* tendency within the UEC; the Fourth International; and from 1961 or 1962 the Pabloite tendency, a splinter group named after the pseudonymous "Pablo" – its Greek founder and leader, Michel Raptis.

The Pabloites adopted a very militant position towards the Third World and its national liberation movements, which I found increasingly attractive as an undergraduate studying these

---

28 The UNEF later helped to spearhead May '68, but I was not involved as I had been in Senegal since January 1967 conducting my anthropological fieldwork.

regions. Particularly influential was my Certificate in Human Geography course, which had a strong Third World focus and was taught in part by the geographer Yves Lacoste, author of a title on the Third World for the Que-sais-je? series and husband of the ethnologist and Algerian specialist Colette Lacoste-Dujardin.

Through Alain Krivine and other comrades, I had also become involved in providing clandestine support to the Algerian FLN. This was low-key practical assistance – mainly logistical and financial – and in truth my activities were somewhat limited as my father was still a US citizen. This Pabloite engagement with the FLN explains why my comrades came to play such an active role within post-independence Algeria, remodelling its administration after June 1962. Whatever their precise affiliation, all these militant revolutionaries were known as *pieds rouges* rather than *pieds noirs*, the name given to white European settlers in colonial Algeria.

Your first political years were spent in the French radical (and Trotskyist) left. You were also inspired by the struggle for national liberation by the Algerian people. Can you speak about your direct experience during this time?

I went to Algeria in July-August 1963 to try and understand what was happening on the ground, but I declined the chance to become a *pied rouge*. In the months between the ceasefire and the immediate post-independence period of summer 1962, rival FLN factions had engaged in violent military clashes, raising doubts in my mind that were only confirmed by my visit. Victory went to the Ben Bella clan, which had long enjoyed Pabloite support for its programme of socialist self-management (the programme that had prompted the Pabloite split with the Fourth International which remained very statist and Leninist). I turned down the offer of a teaching post at the University of Algiers – partly for the reasons given above, but also because I then had only two of the four certificates needed for my degree. Ten years later I made a similar decision in refusing to go and teach at the University of Maputo after the liberation of Mozambique – a state that was clearly part of the socialist bloc and ultra-Stalinist in its administration and ideology (an analysis amply confirmed by my subsequent visit in 1983).

Late 1963 thus saw the end of my period of intense political militancy and the start of my professional career in African studies, ethnology and sociology. I read the works of Georges Balandier, who encouraged me to study for a doctorate under his supervision and in January 1965 appointed me as secretary of his political anthropology research group. Perhaps I should add that on 24 December 1964 I had married a secondary-school teacher who did not work in Paris, which brought some changes to my lifestyle and routines. Through my contacts with fellow researchers – Marxist and non-Marxist! – my engagement subsequently became more intellectual and ideological.

From 1959 onwards I was reading most of the French communist and Marxist journals and frequenting the bookshops that stocked this literature. I was also a regular at the Salons du livre Marxiste – book fairs that were then pretty popular and well attended. The late 1950s and 1960s saw powerful movements of internal criticism growing within the PCF and its academic and trade union affiliates. My new life as a militant intellectual also became public at this time, as in December 1964 [I] published my first paper – an extended discussion of two monographs on social class in sub-Saharan Africa, by Jean Ziegler and Raymond Barbé respectively. The paper appeared in *Sous le drapeau du socialisme*, the new monthly journal of the AMR (Alliance marxiste révolutionnaire), the official title of the [Pabloite] splinter group described above. By then I had been working on AMR publications, in practical and editorial roles, for at least two years. I had discovered my passion for writing and the critique of ideas, and also for the real world of publishing and even printing (in the days of linotype).

How did you move from these interests into research on Senegal? What explains the emergence of these interests and how were they tied to your activism on the left?

In the 1960s, the research interests of French Africanists (in ethnology, anthropology and sociology) reflected Anglo-American trends in these disciplines and the majority of our reading was in English. Contemporary undergraduates and doctoral students had greater expertise in Nigeria, Ghana, Kenya or southern Africa than in Côte d'Ivoire or Senegal. In the 1950s French Africanists had really only just begun breaking ground, which is why in 1965 I had neither a field nor a domain for my doctoral research project. The Centre d'études africaines was based at the École pratique des hautes études VIe Section, which in 1974 became the EHESS (École des hautes études en sciences sociale). There the leading lights were Georges Balandier and Paul Mercier, whose main preoccupations centred on social and cultural change, the political anthropology of Africa (traditional, modern and post-colonial), under-development and current development initiatives.

In late 1965 I spent three months in Côte d'Ivoire, working on an applied social science project for a private research organisation. I was investigating agricultural modernisation initiatives in the peri-urban zone of Abidjan, a topic in line with the dominant theme of contemporary Africanist research – understanding rural societies and the modernisation of the peasant farmers who would be vital to the economic take-off of the new nations. There followed several twists and turns in my professional and personal life before I left for Senegal in January 1967. Among these was my son's birth in December 1966, which delayed my family posting. My mission came under the auspices of ORSTOM (Office de la recherche scientifique et technique outre-mer – now the Institut de recherche pour le développement – a national research organisation founded in colonial days (1943) and active throughout the former French territories worldwide. I had gone to study social stratification in the Mouride Brotherhood, a Sufi confraternity deemed to be hierarchical and perhaps totalitarian in structure – happily a hypothesis that turned out to be completely false!

My move into research was not accompanied by any militant engagement in support of the revolutionary struggles ongoing in Africa in the late 1960s. Several factors were in play here. The intense mobilisation provoked by the Algerian War had not prompted a similar degree of activism in support of newly independent Algeria. Elsewhere in francophone Africa, in countries by then independent for several years, the erstwhile nationalist reform movements that came to power had been co-opted immediately by the French authorities and lost all potential for radical action. The only exception was Guinea which, despite its geopolitical alignments, had become a dictatorship and was thus socialist in name only. Movements in non-francophone Africa were off-limits to French militants who lacked any contacts there. Finally, the focus of the ideological, political and theoretical debates that sprang up around Marxism's new directions were anti-Stalinism, Sino-Soviet confrontation and the romantic opening-up of Cuba. My activism thus became more academic and conceptual, yet at the same time more empirical and practical: how are we to discern the process of class struggle in societies of which we know almost nothing? What do we need to think and do? How are we to conduct the essential fieldwork? And the result was an attitude of radical scepticism towards dogmatic assertions of the theoretical benefits of Marxism, totally at odds with the so-called revolutionary realities of the new Third World nations.

You were researching social and economic change in Senegal in the late 1960s, specifically the Mouride Brotherhood. There are a few questions here. Can you describe life in Senegal (a relatively newly independent country) while you were there? Could you also speak of your impressions of the immense uprising in the country in 1968 and its consequences? What was your direct involvement?

Influenced by my reading, education and early fieldwork, as well as by experienced researchers like Jean Suret-Canale, Maurice Godelier, and especially Claude Meillassoux, I began to rethink the anthropology of pre-capitalist societies, the nature of post-colonial capitalism, and especially the structure of the new nations and neo-colonial states – social groups, modes of production etc. I believed it absolutely essential to clarify our understanding of these areas before devising any kind of political programme. The extreme numerical and sociological weakness of the working classes, the absence of private agricultural landowners – these were vital characteristics that demanded investigation before committing any serious militant support to parties or groups whose boasted radicalism seemed completely divorced from the real world.

Late 1960s Senegal was still a very colonial society, with a large French administrative and military presence at least 30,000 strong and an export-oriented economy dominated by a groundnut sector in the midst of technological modernisation while remaining within an ostensibly socialist system of cooperatives, rural development and so on! My study of the Mouride Brotherhood prompted me to question the existing Third-Worldist (René Dumont) or Marxist (Samir Amin) approaches, which failed to distinguish between different levels of national political control, market-driven economic exploitation, and religious and ideological submission to religious leaders or marabouts.

While May '68 in Senegal had some strictly local roots, others were in a sense pan-African through the University of Dakar's multinational recruitment policy. I was involved very indirectly in these events through contacts of my wife, who was enrolled in the Faculty of Arts and Languages at the university (where in 1968 the teaching staff was still all white) and was the only one of the white (French and Lebanese) students to go on strike. I believe there were 5,000 students in all at the time. Of course I met some of these militants, whose programme combined extreme corporatism (in favour of higher grants) with a highly abstract anti-imperialism. We were careful, nonetheless. At the request of President Senghor, France had repatriated two professors of sociology – Louis-Vincent Thomas, the Head of Faculty, and Jacques Lombard – whose only crime had been to defend their students against violent state repression. By contrast, because I had a reputation as a *gauchiste* militant, my ORSTOM colleagues came to ask me about the potential impact of May '68 in France – a May '68 whose roots I did not fully understand after eighteen months away.

Can you discuss what you did after you returned to France after your period in West Africa? How did your work develop during that period and what was the influence/involvement in France and Africa?

A year after I returned to France in 1970, I secured a post as a tenured research fellow and immediately expanded my politico-professional activities. I popularised the "Anthropology, Colonialism and Imperialism" debate started in the US by Kathleen Gough and fellow anthropologists, particularly in the pages of *Current Anthropology*. I edited dossiers for the journal *Les temps modernes*, followed by a substantial anthology for François Maspero, the radical *gauchiste* and Third-Worldist publisher. In 1973 I defended my doctoral thesis from a Marxist perspective, in line with current debates in French Marxist anthropology. Teaching at the EHESS, I also became a very militant trade unionist, leaving the ultra-Stalinist and PCF-controlled Syndicat nationale de l'enseignement supérieur and joining the Syndicat général de l'éducation nationale, which was aligned with the Confédération française démocratique du travail and espoused a reformist Christian left ideology that was shared by three-quarters of the unionised staff. As an aside: the highly corporatist communist-leaning labour unions were seeking revenge on the left of May '68, detesting the wholly exceptional solidarity displayed by the EHESS staff. In effect, doctoral students, administrative and technical staff, junior faculty, directors and professors had all combined to form a single labour union, thereby calling into question the legitimacy and authority of PCF-appointed union bureaucracies. This type of vertically integrated unionism lasted throughout the 1970s, and as a result I led delegations and negotiated with individuals like Fernand Braudel and François Furet, who disagreed profoundly with the staff yet respected us absolutely.

The 1970s were the years of the first great West African droughts, leading to significant urban migration and the onset of famine. In 1973 a group of colleagues signed a petition denouncing France's neocolonial policies, which were aggravating the situation, and established a Comité Information Sahel (of which I was treasurer). Over the next two years the Comité maintained a high public profile: in 1974 Claude Meillassoux and I edited anonymously *Qui se nourrit de la famine au Sahel?*, a highly critical work published by Éditions Maspero, while in June 1975 a day of protest in the Bois de Vincennes attracted at least 3,000 people. The book went into a second edition, selling 15,000 copies in two years! Reprisals followed, more or less overt, and unlike other colleagues I received no promotion for the next two years. Alongside the book for the Comité, however, I had also edited a two-volume work for *Dossiers africains*, a popularising series published by François Maspero and co-directed by Marc Augé and myself. This work, *Sécheresses et famines du Sahel*, was much more academic in tone and enabled me to expand my contacts among British and American Africanists mobilised by the same topic, especially with regard to northern Nigeria and the Horn of Africa.

This international collaboration was extremely productive, so much so that by accident I became the "Mr Famine" of the French Sahel. While I was working at Johns Hopkins University in 1975-6, I was visited in my office by medical scientists engaged in nutritional research, and I also conducted an active correspondence with British and Canadian anthropologists. I published half a dozen articles or notes in English at a time when, apart from the academics mobilised by the Comité, French institutions and research groups seemed indifferent to the crisis. This apathy confirmed my enduring belief in the need for anthropological and political activism, albeit an activism more analytical in character than ideological or organisational. I would add also that the book's most active promoters were Catholic associations and NGOs like the Comité catholique contre la faim et pour le développement.

The late 1970s saw two further engagements on my part: the first was the study of Africa's working classes, where for twenty-five years I became the French specialist – again as part of a group of international collaborators, Canadian, American, British, Dutch and African (particularly South African). It was Peter Gutkind who first involved me in this venture in 1975 following our debates in the pages of *Cahiers d'études africaines*, and I also was engaged with the Canadian journal *Labour, Capital and Society* with Robin Cohen, Peter Waterman and Edward Webster. For over a decade, ORSTOM hosted a very active research group, my EHESS seminar became the centre for internationalist studies, and a newsletter was launched which led to the publication of several titles between 1987 and 1997. I published an article in 2014 that explored the reasons underlying this success and its subsequent demise around the turn of the century. In the past year, however, I have noted a revival of interest among a new generation of French Africanists. I have played no part in this new ideological and militant mobilisation but its motivations clearly differ from those of its predecessor thirty years ago.

The second was African political studies, in anthropology as well as political science per se. This was the movement embodied in the journal *Politique africaine*, which I helped to found in 1980. I also served as a director in 1983-5, before leaving to spend four years in Kenya. I worked very closely with Jean-Francois Bayart, then known only for his "politics from below", the theory that transformed leftist and also Marxist analysis – initially of state machines and modes of political control, and subsequently of the underlying meanings of popular social movements. Despite all these academic and editorial engagements, my links with African militants – union officials or political activists – have been very few. I limited my contact because nearly all these individuals were assimilated within state or institutional hierarchies, prompting an enduring mistrust on my part. This was true in Senegal but also in Mozambique, where I had several introductions from students or from AMR contacts like Aquino de Bragança, the adviser of Samora Machel. I should emphasise, however, that as a doctoral supervisor, unofficially at the EHESS from 1977 and officially at the University of Picardy (Amiens) from 1990, I have had only one or two African students researching the working classes – tangible proof of the sharp decline in working-class activism since the 1980s.

ROAPE was born from the struggles of a second wave of independence in the 1970s, mostly in Portugal's ex-colonies, and the hopes of a generation in a more critical and Marxist-inspired independence, leading to a transition to socialism. Were you similarly influenced by these movements – specifically in Tanzania and Mozambique?

I took a very critical view of Portugal's ex-colonies despite my contacts with students from these countries and my interests in Africa as a whole, not just its francophone nations. I even published an article, later translated into English, proposing the hypothesis that the old socialist states and Africa's young Marxist-Leninist states shared a number of similarities in sociological terms. In the case of Tanzania, I knew enough of the researchers published in *ROAPE* to recognise the need to differentiate between the ideas of its leaders, the prevailing political ideologies, and the everyday workings of African bureaucracies. A first visit to these countries in 1983, before my longer stay in East Africa, confirmed me in my views. In fact, from the late 1970s, it was South Africa and the different anti-apartheid movements that mobilised me in particular. I had some collected papers by Mike Morris, Harold Wolpe and Martin Legassick translated into French and published by François Maspero, but to my regret this evoked no response among French Africanists nor more generally among Marxist economists specialising in the Third World. When Eddie Webster invited me to defy the boycott and travel to Cape Town for the congress of South African sociologists in 1985, it was 100% Marxist!

My engagement with South Africa took several forms: leading a Centre national de la recherche scientifique research group (in succession to Claude Meillassoux) in the 1990s; co-directing an EHESS seminar on southern Africa for twenty years; and in the mid-1990s, helping to establish the Institut français d'Afrique du Sud for research in the social sciences (modelled on identical bodies in Nairobi, which I ran, Ibadan and Addis Ababa, to mention sub-Saharan Africa alone). Yet these initiatives enjoyed only moderate success in mobilising French academics who continue to prioritise the countries of francophone Africa. We can debate how far such institutional and administrative engagement is truly activist and militant, but I have always felt that concrete action is required to extend the professional Africanist culture of my students and colleagues, all too often reluctant to stray beyond their own backyard. African students in particular are more tightly bound than most by a methodological nationalism with deep roots in the colonial past.

Part II: Weapon of Theory

15. Samir Amin (2017), Revolutionary Change in Africa

Samir Amin was a Marxist economist, writer and activist, who died on 12 August 2018 – just over a year after this conversation took place. He remains one of the continent's foremost radical thinkers, who spent decades examining Africa's underdevelopment and Western imperialism. With great originality and insight, he has applied Marxism to the tasks of socialist transformation in Africa. In this conversation with Zeilig, Amin reflects on a life spent at the cutting edge of radical theory and practice, African politics and the legacy of the Russian revolution.

***

So, can I first ask you to tell me a little bit about your political background? How you developed politically, how you became a communist and a Marxist, if you can go back to those early days?

I considered myself a communist already at secondary school. Probably we did not know exactly what it meant, but we knew it meant two or three things: it meant equality between human beings and between nations and it meant that this has been done by the Russian revolution, the Soviet Union. That was our definition, and at secondary school in Egypt at that time there were about 40%, say, of the youth who claimed to be communist in that sense. 40% claimed to be nationalists – that the only problem was getting rid of the British occupation and nothing more. And there were 20% who had no opinion.

Both the two politicised groups considered the 20% as inferior human beings [laughs]. But the two groups, we were fighting every day, and fighting from the age of 12 or 13 to the age of 16 or 17 in vocabulary but also [laughs] physically. Immediately after my secondary school, I got in contact with the communist party in Egypt and I joined it.

So, I have been a communist since then. When I was a student in France there was a rule at that time, that if you were a communist you had to be a member of the communist party in the country where you were. It was a very internationalist principle, even if you were a foreigner and belonged to another communist party, so I was a member of the French Communist Party during all my time as a student in France. Then when I came back to Egypt, of course, I remained a member of the communist party.

These were Nasser's years. It was a very, very difficult time. I went back to Egypt in 1957 after both the Bandung Conference and after the move, relatively speaking, to the left of Nasser. We had very strong arguments, which opposed the Egyptian communists to Nasser on the ground that the struggle was not just a national liberation struggle; it has to be associated with radical change on the road to socialism.

Now, we were not supported by the Soviet Union at that point. For diplomatic reasons, they wanted to support Nasser and did not want to have an independent communist party. So they pressured, they exercised their pressure, that we should accept the theory of the non-capitalist road and support Nasser. Now the communist party at that point in time was divided. Probably the majority, a small majority, accepted the Soviet view of the non-capitalist road, but I was one of those who did not; so, a strong minority, perhaps 40%, did not accept it and, of course, I moved to Mali as of this time. That is my history as a communist debutant.

And I continue to consider myself a communist.

If I can ask you a question about this period from the 1950s when you returned to Cairo in 1957, through the 1960s and even longer than that, you saw your role as an intellectual but was also someone, if I'm correct, who needed to support projects of radical transformation on the continent where possible?

Yes.

Where there was space? And you worked as a Research Officer in Cairo in 1957?

To 1960.

Working specifically on questions of how this sort of change came about?

I was working with a state organisation which was created for the purpose of managing the whole enormous public sector, but we had to look at the entire edifice of state enterprises and companies and to see if their policy was consistent, was radical enough etc, etc. For that reason, this institution was full of communists! The director was a communist, Ismail Sabri Abdullah, and I was second to him. But Ismail got arrested precisely for that. What I learned there was very important for me. I saw how a new class was emerging. I had to represent the state in the boards of companies, of public companies, and I saw how the public companies were being captured by a small, tiny class, a kind of bourgeois caste, a corrupt class, including financing indirectly through their private enterprises. That is what I learnt later, in Russian, was called the Matryoshka pattern – Matryoshka, as you know, is the Russian dolls, yes?

That is, you have the state – the big doll – but inside you have smaller private interests. That was exactly what was happening, so I learnt a lot about that process, and I became even more radicalised. This is why, when in 1966, there was the Cultural Revolution in China I supported it. The slogan of Mao was "fire on the party headquarters", which means the leadership of the communist party itself. Mao said at that time, you are – which meant we, the communist party – building a bourgeoisie, but remember, he said, the bourgeoisie doesn't want socialism – they want capitalism. Restitution.

Can I ask you now to look at ROAPE and some of the issues that were discussed in the first issues from 1974? You wrote in the first issue on accumulation and development, and you were part of that project along with Ruth First and others. Can you recall the spirit of that first issue, what you were trying to do as an intellectual and as a communist with the journal? What was the project of ROAPE?

You see, I had a problem at that time. I discussed it with some of the early members of the *Review*. First, why [the] use of this word "radical"? Why not "socialist"? Since the only meaning that we can give to radicalism is to be anti-capitalist and socialist. However, my starting point was that we cannot entertain this illusion of the big revolution at a global level or even a big revolution in the advanced capitalist centres as Trotsky had it.

Revolutionary change will necessarily start, I argued, in the peripheries, and it is not pure chance that it started in Russia – a periphery or semi-peripheral country, call it as you want, but certainly not the most advanced centre of capital at the time. It moved to a more or less peripheral country in China, and it succeeded in other peripheries as well – in Vietnam and Cuba. And this was not by pure chance because really existing capitalism is highly polarising and uneven and has been from the very start, and continues to be extremely polarising. Therefore, out of all the contradictions within capitalist societies, these contradictions are more acute, more violent in the peripheries of the system and therefore there is less legitimacy or impossible legitimacy for any capitalist system. Capitalism is therefore not only weak, subordinate, dependent, but also not really legitimate in the eyes of the majority in the Third World. However, I also argued in those early days that the majorities in these countries, in Africa are not the proletariat of advanced industries but a mass of peasants, poor peasants, working in very small units of production and so on…

So we asked the question how to construct a positive block for such transformation, and we looked to Russia and then China, and then Vietnam and Cuba which we believed were succeeding to do it. This was the intellectual and socialist environment we were operating in when *ROAPE* was formed.

Did you see ROAPE – and its first editorial board – as a militant publication that could help build the movements and politics that were necessary on the continent?

Some of them were, but not all, and even those who were militants, they considered themselves more academics than militants. A socialist review should call upon other people, not necessarily academics, who are directly involved in politics, in leadership of movements, social movements and parties and so on.

So let us accept that radical meant at the time being open to a critique of capitalism, and that was accepted at that point by everybody. But to what extent? A vision that capitalism is there forever, or is there for still a long, long time, and that therefore what has to be done is to criticise it in order to compel it to adjust to social demands. I was not interested in that; let the leaders of the Social Democratic Party do that, if they want [laughs]. We may support some of their demands, but we have no illusions in the capacity of the system to be reformed. Therefore, there was always this tension in *ROAPE* and with the changes that have taken place in the world – this academic vision has been reinforced within the journal.

What was exciting about that period was that the journal was conceived as a contribution to the projects of radical transformation that were taking place on the continent, so it was no coincidence that it was founded at about the time that Mozambique and Angola were reaching towards independence. And this second wave of radical independence that wasn't going to make the mistakes of the first wave, but that was going to infuse into national liberation, socialist transformation, gave that project a new energy and initiative and the journal was certainly part of that hopeful project. Did you see things in that way? Did you see the shift on the continent?

Yes, you see, my whole life I would say, in Egypt, after having finished my university studies, and then in Mali, and then at the head of Institut Africain de Développement Économique et de Planification, and then as director of the Third World Forum in Dakar, I have maintained a radical critique of society – otherwise none of those institutions would have been able to survive, succeed even, in doing many things. We have not changed the world but we have kept the flag flying, which is important also.

Like some others at the time, I saw a long historical transition from capitalism to socialism and that this is a process that starts in the peripheries – in Africa – and it will continue probably to be so. But in the peripheries, there are phases. The first phase was the struggle for reconquering political independence, a process that extended from the 1950s to the 1970s and which had to be successful everywhere. But there was unevenness between weak and strong independence. These movements for independence were variously associated with social change, progressive social change, more radical in the case of Nasser in Egypt, similarly in Algeria, in the case of Angola and Mozambique, Cape Verde, Portugal's ex-colonies; yet alongside these radical projects there were others far less radical in countries like Mali, Uganda, Tanzania, Congo-Brazzaville, and almost nothing elsewhere, including South Africa, which has seen no real social change.

But the challenge for all of us, at that time and now, is how do we find the practical policies and strategies for progressive social change? And what are the changes which are needed and possible at each stage? It was here that I came to the idea of a "long road"; if the transition to socialism is a long road we should not be surprised that it is full of "thermidors"[29] and even restorations. This is clear when you look at the apparent victory of monopoly capital with the breakdown of the Soviet Union, in China after the death of Mao, and Deng Xiaoping – because Deng Xiaoping

---

29   Since the French revolution the word "Thermidor" has come to mean retreat from the radical goals in a revolution.

was a transitional figure who moved China towards participating in capitalist globalisation etc – we have entered a new stage of contradictions, so we have been always dealing and discussing those problems.

What does social progressive change mean today? Does it mean the possibility of "moving up" within capitalism, or do we orientate in the opposite direction and intensify the contradictions between an anti-capitalist alternative and what capitalism can offer – in a word are we able to strengthen socialist consciousness?

Can I go back a little bit to something that you said yesterday when you were talking about Marx and Marxism, because it seemed to be that you were describing Marxism as a developing and growing theoretical approach and that it's something that you've contributed to in your writing and in your activism...?

Do you smoke?

No. Your own contributions to develop Marxism are very considerable across a whole range of different areas. Perhaps the greatest moment in human history was the Russian Revolution 100 years ago, as an extraordinary demonstration of the self-emancipation of ordinary people. I wonder whether you could talk a little bit about the significance of 1917 and the revolution, its victories and defeats in the decades afterwards for the continent?

The Cold War started in 1917 and never ended. After the hot wars of intervention to crush the revolution, then from the 1920s to WWII, we saw different processes. When, after Munich, Stalin wanted an alliance with the democratic countries of the West, Britain and France, against Hitlerism, it was the democratic countries which preferred concession to Hitler – even encouraging Hitler to start the war against the Soviet Union. We should never forget that.

The postwar world, with the formation of NATO and other

anti-Soviet institutions which came out of this period, was targeted at the Soviet Union and sought to maintain the colonial system, which was only defeated by internal anti-colonial forces in the countries of Asia and Africa. Despite the propaganda it was always a polycentric system because it had at least four participants: the Imperialist West, more or less united behind the US with NATO – that is the US, at that time Western and Central Europe, capitalist Europe – Japan, plus Australia and Canada, the external provinces of US, one close and the others far geographically, then you had the Soviet Union with its dependent countries of Eastern Europe just as Western Europe was dependant on the US. This was important and a direct legacy of the 1917 revolution.

Then there was the Chinese revolution in 1949. So you also had the non-aligned movement, which means all the countries of Asia and Africa achieved their independence under the leadership of the most advanced amongst them. All of this means that we had in that time, not a dual power, but a polycentric system, unequal but with a margin of manoeuvres.

It has been the strategy of imperialists from 1991 or so to make it impossible to rebuild such a multi-polar, polycentric system – not only by newly globalisation and so on but, more important, through the tool of military interventions. But US imperialism has proven to be unable to achieve its targets, because it has created even more chaos. And it has been unable to establish reliable allies...

So what I am saying is that the system, which had been in its short triumphant phase from 1990-1995 – say five years, labelled, you'll remember, as "the end of history", blah, blah, with commentators arguing that capitalism was a permanent, stable feature of the modern world and associated with democracy and peace. But what we have actually seen is the opposite: collapse, chaos, crisis generalising and extending across the world at an increasing rate.

What were the abiding lessons or experiences of that successful revolu-

tion for the continent?

There are many lessons. The major one is that we have moved into a long transition where it is possible to start moving towards socialism in many places in the world. That is one. That is fundamental. Second, it has to be a strategy of stages – one after the other. Instead of calling it revolution I call it revolutionary advances, which means that we achieve revolutionary changes but which only create the possibility of later, further revolutionary advances. Yet it means that the revolution can be stopped and decline in one place, and this is what has happened in the Soviet Union.

Another lesson is that revolutionary changes were successful in October 1917, precisely because the Soviet Union was able to construct an alternative united bloc which was the workers-peasants alliance.

My one worry is that the effect of the failure of the Russian Revolution was to set back in ways that perhaps we didn't expect in the early 1990s, the language of socialist transformation, of revolution, of social revolt.

Yes, and we should learn that the forms of struggle which were probably correct in their time – last century, almost 100 years ago now – are no longer blueprints for us. There are organisational forms that no longer respond to our questions today, so there is a question today – terribly difficult to answer – of how to organise, in what type of organisations. However, my friend, Abdulrahman Mohamed Babu, used to say that "You organise or agonise".

[Laughs.] You don't agonise about organising?

Yeah, but simultaneously I reject completely the naïve view that we can change the world without seizing political power; that is changing state power. On that point I remain intransigent, I would not say dogmatic but I would say this principle is the evidence of all history – so the problem is now how to conceive of the organisation of the movements which could crystallise into a political force, able to challenge and ultimately change political power.

There's the wonderful metaphor in Trotsky's History of the Russian Revolution *where he talks about the Piston Box. The Piston Box is the revolutionary organisation, but without the steam of mass participation the Piston Box is an inanimate lump of metal.*

Very good image.

It's a powerful image, so what are the forms of organisation for today?

This is what we are discussing continuously. I have no blueprint or easy answer. There are a good number of leaders and activists within the social movements who are drawing lessons from their relative failure.

Can I talk just briefly about two of your – what I consider – very significant contributions, ones that made a big impact on me. You referenced this yesterday where you talk about Marxism as a living theory, a living philosophy. You contributed to the understanding of Marxism and history very significantly in Eurocentrism, *a book that was written in the 1990s, which challenged a Stalinist notion of stages of historical development. What were you trying to do in that book and what were you trying to say? It seemed to me that one of the things you were saying is that the transition from what had been understood as feudalism to capitalism was actually a far more complex process, which you described as the tributary system that took various forms across the world. Could you just mention something about your argument and what you were doing?*

We see in the transition to capitalism, to European capitalism, and the transition from capitalism to socialism in the revolutions of the Soviet Union, China and others, a consciousness and a political strategy. This was the case very clearly in the French Revolution, much more than in the English revolution for example…

So, I said there had been three great revolutions of modern time: the French, the Russian, the Chinese, and these three big revolutions are big precisely because they have given to themselves targets which go far ahead of the objective problems and needs of their societies at the time of the revolution. That is the definition. So I was – in part – arguing that we are at a time of big revolutions, in that sense, even for smaller countries.

Your argument in the book was that it was a weakness of state formation, a sort of underdevelopment, in Western Europe that allowed the transition to capitalism to take place to a certain extent. So you were reversing an argument, a Eurocentric argument that's often made.

Yes, I dared even to write that the most advanced parts of the pre-capitalist world were not where change starts. It is rather at the peripheries. Now, the most advanced system before capitalism spread across the world was not in Europe – it was in China and that has been recognised again today, though it had been recognised in the 18th Century. China was the model for the Europeans. They were aware that not only had China, if we use the economistic language of today, higher levels of productivity of labour than Europe at that time, but it had better organisations across all layers of society.

Democracy was not on the agenda but China had invented, ten centuries before the Europeans, a civil service. You have to wait until late in the 19th Century to have a civil service in Europe – the idea of recruiting bureaucrats and civil servants of the state by examinations and so on, which was invented a thousand years ago in China, was unheard of.

I would argue that there are the same type of contradictions today. The power of the most advanced, the US today for example, also cripples the developments of a new society… The US is the most advanced capitalist country, but it is the country where socialist consciousness is at its weakest globally. The ideas of socialism are close to zero even as compared to European countries today, where it is not far from zero but it is not quite zero.

Can I ask you now about a second very important book that you wrote in the mid-1980s, I think in 1986, Delinking? *In the book you argued for the need to escape from the constraints of a global capitalist system and therefore countries in the periphery had to break those connections which had strangled any hope for economic development.*

Delinking is a principle of strategy. It is not a blueprint. So it means that instead of adjusting to the needs of capitalist, global expansion – which involves deepening underdevelopment, polarising the world more and more – that the pattern has to be broken instead of what I called [it] in my PhD dissertation in 1956: "permanent adjustments of the peripheries to the needs of capital accumulation in the centres". I used this phrase, these exact words – underdevelopment is a way of describing what is in fact permanent adjustment. What do all banks say today, structural adjustment or change – this is now a permanent state. With the World Bank I put it in a slightly polemical way: I said it is requested that the Congo adjust to the needs of the US, not for the US to adjust to the needs of Congo. So it's that adjustment which is simply one side adjusting. Now, delinking means you reject that logic and therefore you try to, and succeed, as far as you can, to have your own strategy, independent of the trends of the unequal global system.

You were, in the 1970s, perhaps unfairly criticised by some on the left as promoting a national bourgeoisie. Yet it seemed to me that you were saying that the project of delinking needs to be one powered by popular forces.

If it is led by bourgeois forces it will never go beyond a small class.

However, if it is a process powered by popular forces it will lead to other questions, namely industrialisation and reviving peasant agriculture, as a means of having, ensuring food...

Security?

More than security, sovereignty – and having policies, economic policies including control of foreign capital. This might not mean that you reject completely foreign capital, but you control it... Now this is the programme that I call today a sovereign popular national project for African countries...

So, in that case, can I ask you to speak directly as an activist, Samir – what is the agenda and project for radical or socialist transformation on the continent today?

The people, all the peoples of Africa are today facing a big challenge. So their societies are integrated in a pattern of so-called globalisation, that we have to qualify because this is not globalisation – it is capitalist, imperialist globalisation. This is control[led] by financial monopoly capital by a set of imperialist countries – principally the triad: the United States, Western Europe and Japan, which are strong enough to control the processes of economic life and production and therefore also political life at a global level, and we are invited by the World Bank and others simply to accept it and to adjust to it.

Now, we must move out of this pattern of globalisation. That is the meaning that I am giving to the word, "delinking". It means rejecting the logic of unilateral adjustment to the needs of further capitalist and imperialist expansion, and trying to reverse the relation and focus on projects of development ourselves. I think if we start we will succeed, that we will compel imperialists to accept it and that would create a logic, a possibility of further advances.

This is what I am calling a sovereign popular national project for Africa. National not in the sense of nationalist, but with the meaning that political power must be changed, and political power can only be changed in the frame of the countries and states as they exist today. It cannot be changed at global level or even at a regional level before being changed at national country level. It will be popular in the sense that this is not a bourgeois, capitalist project, yet these steps cannot be achieved while accepting the pattern of globalisation and capitalism.

Finally, can I ask you how you have been able to maintain your own phenomenal positivity and energy over the years, in the face of the failure of progressive movements?

Well, one reason is that I was condemned not to survive my first years and that compelled me to develop a terrific will of struggle in the 15 first years of life. I think it was turned to an advantage of having been weak, physically weak. But since then, I have had good health. I have been smoking now for 65 years and I had a recent examination. One doctor who did not know how long I had been smoking said you are a beautiful example of somebody who has never smoked. I said, "Thank you for the result of the examination but you are mistaken doctor, I am a long-time smoker."

Okay, but then there are some political reasons. My struggle in the Egyptian Communist Party between the Soviet line and the Maoist line also compelled me to try to be rigorous and continuously on the frontline, politically and ideologically.

I also continue to be active in different places: in the Third World Forum, and the World Forum of Alternatives, living in both Dakar and Cairo. I happen to also be the chairperson of the Egyptian – so-called Arab – Centre of Research which is radical in the sense of being a socialist centre, not only in Egypt but in the whole Arab region. I am active – action is key.

I also remember yesterday about how, as Marx says in one preface to Capital, *when he hears that later editions were being read by workers that nothing could make him happier. And you said yesterday* Capital *required considerable work and there's no greater evidence or need for that than the constant study necessary to understand and change the world.*

And this is not making something vulgar, or simple. Vulgarisation is a very dangerous thing. It is trying to translate a complex problem into a simple one, and that's dangerous because the people have to understand that a complex problem is a complex problem but they have to understand it – that's the whole difficulty, but one that can be achieved.

16. Issa Shivji (2021), Let a Hundred Socialist Flowers Bloom

Socialist activist and writer Issa Shivji taught for years at the University of Dar es Salaam and has written more than twenty books on pan-Africanism, political economy, socialism and radical change in Africa. He is a long standing member of *ROAPE*. Here, in conversation with Freedom Mazwi, Shivji discusses the peasantry, capitalist development and socialism. He argues that those who predicted the end of history have been proven woefully wrong. Capitalism and the planet are in deep crisis. For the first time in decades people in both the South and the North are openly using the ideas and slogans of socialism – even if they have divergent ideas.

***

Let me start by asking you to define the peasantry. We know that it is a debated concept. There are various views on the peasantry, its characteristics and why it is important.

Thank you, Freedom. I think you have raised a very important issue. I would like to briefly start with the traditional Marxist take on the peasantry. Karl Marx himself, based on the European experience, thought that with the development of capitalism, the peasant – basically meaning the smallholder who survives on land, produces on land – will disappear, and a large mass of people will become the industrial proletariat. It was in this regard that when it came to politics, we have Marx on record calling peasants a "sack of potatoes" because he did not see a lot of potential in the peasantry for revolutionary change. Although that was based on the European experience, Marx did talk about countries of the South – particularly those in Africa. He however talked about them in relation to primitive accumulation of capital. But that was, for him, the original condition in developing his model of capitalism. Since then, we have had some theoretical and political developments. In this regard we must mention Rosa Luxemburg who disagreed with Marx. She argued that capitalist accumulation is not simply self-contained. Her position was that for capitalism to continue reproducing itself, it always needs non-capitalist sectors on which to feed for accumulation. She saw many of our countries as feeding capitalism through primitive accumulation.

That was the initial argument during those debates. The second point that I think Rosa Luxemburg made, which is also very important for us, was that Marx's formulae saw primitive accumulation as the original condition and once capitalism has developed, we get what is called capitalist accumulation. It is based on labour and capital. The former is exploited to produce the surplus value and part of that surplus value is accumulated for the second cycle of expanded reproduction. Rosa Luxembourg's argument was that primitive accumulation does not actually come to an end with capitalist development, but rather continues because exploitation of the non-capitalist sector based on primitive accumulation is essential for capitalist reproduction.

Subsequently we had other developments starting with Lenin, going on to Mao and so on. And contrary to the predictions of the earlier Marxists, the socialist revolution happened not in the centre but in the semi-periphery, i.e., Russia.

Russia of the time still had pre-capitalist relations in the countryside and also a mass of peasantry. That is where Lenin politically located his thesis of worker–peasant alliance. Previously the peasantry had been seen as a conservative force but, for Lenin, the working class could rely on the peasantry and lead the peasantry for revolutionary transformations and changes. This thesis was developed much more in the periphery, particularly in China. The Chinese argument about the role of the peasantry makes a very important contribution to Marxist theory and politics. It has been pretty prominent in discussions of Marxism in many countries of the Global South. But Mao still worked within the Marxist paradigm, and we should not forget that – initially at least – he saw the revolution happening in stages. First the national democratic revolution and then the socialist revolution. Later on, Mao developed a thesis of some kind of continuous revolution thus more or less abandoning the stageist thesis. That is where I will end my introductory remarks.

Now let me come to the question you raised in the context of the debates in the South. More recently, I would say in the last two or three decades, we have developed a thesis in the South, particularly in Africa, that exploitation by and accumulation of capital, which is dominated by the capital from the centre, is primarily based on the extraction of surplus from the peasantry. The dominant producers of surplus are the peasantry. As a matter of fact, the history of capital destroying the peasantry by turning them into a proletariat has to be modified when applied to many countries in Africa. Here, capital preserves the peasant form – the form of petty commodity production – but integrates it in the web of world-wide capital circuits. The dominant form of accumulation is primitive accumulation in which the peasant producer cedes to capital a part of his/her necessary consumption. Within this context, exploitation cuts into the producer's necessary consumption. In effect, therefore, labour subsidises capital by taking on the burden of reproduction.

This thesis has increasingly been debated among African intellectuals and more recently within our own Agrarian South Network. Dramatically, this has proven to be so under neoliberalism. My argument has been that many of the efforts that were made by independent governments essentially tried to move away from the dominant tendency of primitive accumulation of the colonial period. This was for the purposes of attempting to install some kind of capitalist accumulation by, for instance, abolishing migrant labour, raising wages and initiating some social services like education, health etc. This contributed to the social wage and the adoption of some or other form of industrialisation, albeit in many cases, import-substitution industrialisation.

This was justified, rationalised and presented in a variety of nationalist and developmental ideologies. Regardless of what these countries called themselves, capitalist or socialist, the underlying driving force of their policies was to move away from primitive accumulation as the dominant tendency of accumulation. This was done to try and install some kind of expanded reproduction of capitalist accumulation. That project of capitalist development in the image of the historical European development, for various reasons which I am not going to get into, did not succeed. It failed. And neoliberalism, through which imperialism has now assumed an offensive, in my view, has brought back primitive accumulation as the dominant tendency.

Before I proceed, you asked me the question of how we define the peasantry. For me, when we say the peasantry, I am thinking of smallholder producers on land. This includes not only those who cultivate and produce crops but also pastoralists. I will include them because very often we forget that pastoralists are a section of small producers on land. Pastoralists and the peasantry, directly or indirectly, derive their subsistence and incomes from land. That is where the centre of the agrarian question lies. Now having defined it so, a number of our scholars and intellectuals have tried to understand small producers within the specific political economy of our concrete situations. I also wrote an article in the 1980s arguing that capital, in this case monopoly capital, does not only destroy the so-called pre-capitalist relations but also preserves them. The so-called pre-capitalist sector is in essence capitalist in the sense that it is integrated in the world-wide accumulation of capital. For this reason, the so-called pre-capitalist is only that in form.

Under neoliberalism, we are witnessing new forms of primitive accumulation that include the privatisation and commodification of the commons. This also includes privatisation and commodification of public goods such as education, water, health, energy, finance etc. In essence, this is an attack on the production of public goods whose production was not subjected wholly to the market. That does not mean that the classical type of primitive accumulation, such as enclosures, has not continued. More recently we have witnessed, for example, a new wave of land grabbing. An important point to keep in mind is that when the land grabs occur, the smallholders who are thrown off the land do not become the proletariat since the expansion of industrial production and manufacturing is not happening. What happens is that they become landless and unemployed slum dwellers in the ghettos, as well as street hawkers and vendors. Large numbers of our youth between the ages of 14 and 25 buy goods from merchants and hawk them in African cities and towns. They practically subsidise merchant capital and thus are subjected to a kind of primitive accumulation.

In the countryside, the peasant is exploited. Based on this, I developed the thesis that the peasant is subjected to primitive accumulation in that the peasant producer cedes part of the necessary consumption to capital. Consequently, capital is subsidised because the reproduction of a peasant household/family is on the shoulders of the peasant household itself, largely women and children. The peasant, therefore, does not only produce surplus for capital, but also reproduces the peasant household by cutting into its own consumption and exerting super-human labour to be able to live sub-human lives. These are the processes which have intensified under neoliberalism. You will notice that all the programmes of land or agricultural reform put forward are meant to further entangle and integrate peasant production in the capitalist circuits and therefore reproduce the exploitative relationship I have talked about.

If you were to ask my opinion, using the Marxist method, the way Marx derived the revolutionary potential of the working class, similarly my analysis of the current financial capitalism which manifests itself as neoliberalism, I think we can derive revolutionary potential of the peasant, small producers, small entrepreneurs, street hawkers and a whole group of people including those sometimes known as the lower-middle class. I have tried to amalgamate these groups in the concept of "the working people." Therefore, the agency of transformation is the working people.

This has a different political nuance than the traditional working class (proletariat) concept but is derived using the same method of Marxism. Of course, the concept of the working people is still in its putative form and sounds somewhat abstract. We have to do a concrete analysis of each of our social formations and see what social classes and groups in our societies have a revolutionary potential of transforming our societies away from capitalism. Such analysis and empirical study should help us theorise the concept of working people in a more rigorous fashion.

Many scholars like you, Samir Amin and Paris Yeros have taken the capitalist crisis into consideration and have indicated that we have reached a point where we can take this struggle from capitalism and progress towards a socialist future. In your view, what would it take to reach that socialist stage, and how many decades would it take? What should progressive activists do to ensure that we achieve that?

I think that is an interesting question. This is a kind of question you are frequently asked. When you give a response about socialism as a possible alternative, you are immediately confronted with a follow-up rhetorical question – where has socialism ever succeeded? All the countries which tried socialism failed. The problem is that our interrogators cannot even imagine what Samir Amin called the Long Road to Socialism. When we are talking about socialism, we are talking about an epochal change. We are not talking about years and decades because we are talking about overthrowing a system that has lasted for five centuries. So, to answer the second question about the failure of socialism, I would say this: the socialist revolutions that took place in countries like Russia, China, Cuba, Vietnam etc were what one might call revolutionary advances. No doubt, these countries did make revolutionary advances. That is undeniable. These, however, were only glimpses into the socialist future, not fully-fledged socialist societies. The fact that these advances failed in the countries that we described as socialist is nothing new in human history.

Take the analogy of the development of capitalism, and the transition from various pre-capitalist modes of production – like feudalism and other forms of tributary systems – to capitalism. Those places like Venice and Portugal etc in which capitalism first appeared are not the countries where capitalism ultimately succeeded. It succeeded in Britain. So long transitions with a zig-zag trajectory, from one epoch to another, are nothing new in human history. Compared to the development of capitalism, revolutionary socialist advances had a shorter period. The Soviet Union lasted for only seventy years. China, from which we can derive lessons, despite many internal changes and struggles that have taken place, cannot be fully described as capitalist. The jury is still out. We have seen a small country like Cuba surviving all these years, despite the ups and downs. We have also seen initiatives taken in Venezuela, as well as initiatives of major land reforms in countries like Zimbabwe, etc. We have also seen bitter struggles in South Africa on the question of land which remains unresolved, yet it was a central question of the liberation movements.

Based on these examples, I would say the era of revolutionary advances and struggles towards socialism is not over. It will, of course, take long, not just decades, yet we are witnessing major shifts and changes in the world. Those who predicted the end of history, and that capitalism was here to stay, have been proven woefully wrong. Capitalism is in deep crisis. Its very mode of existence is wars – from one war to another. Increasingly, and for the first time since the post-war period of the golden age of capitalism, people in both the South and the North are openly using the ideas and slogans of socialism, even though different people mean different things by socialism. Why not? Let a hundred socialist flowers bloom!

The second point I would like to make in this regard is that in the last ten to fifteen years we have witnessed major crises of capitalism. Neoliberalism, for example, which made its entry in the 1970s, and became politically significant in the 1980s, is already discredited. Its triumphalism has been whittled down. It is almost in its last leg of existence. For how long did neoliberalism last, thirty years? We then witnessed a major crisis in 2008, which of course, took different forms in different countries. The crisis is not only economic. It is also a political one of political legitimacy in both the North and the South. One of the backlashes to neoliberalism is right-wing in the form of fascist tendencies that have been witnessed in countries like Brazil, India and some countries in Africa. But that is one tendency. Broadly, there also is a progressive left tendency. Youth all over the world are exploring and revisiting socialist ideas and developing new forms of struggle like the Occupy movement or the upsurge of the Black Lives Matter movement or the farmers' movement in India. All in all, there are rays of hope all over.

In Africa, we have progressive tendencies emerging. Our problem is that our progressive forces, particularly the Left, remain largely unorganised. Organisation is the foremost task before us. For many years we have been talking about World Social Forums at the international level and civil society organisations (CSOs) at the local level. The impact of the latter has been marginal at best, and diversionary at worst. Theoretically infected by the liberal virus, and socially constructed by the middle classes, CSOs have failed to make a breakthrough. They have failed to resonate with the hearts, minds and real-life struggles of the working people.

How do you organise the working people and how do working people get organised themselves? What kind of alternatives do you pose, what demands do you make and what are the sites of mass politics, for politics [that] are where the masses are? In my view, those are the burning issues before the African Left.

More recently I have been arguing that one of the important demands of the working people that can be put forward, and around which the working masses could rally, is reclaiming the commons. Though not only the commons as traditionally understood to mean land and its resources, but commons in a new sense. By the new commons, I mean strategic sectors of the economy like education, health, finance, energy. These should also be considered the commons. They should be taken out of the realm of the law of value, that is, the market. These are the commons which we must struggle to reclaim. Why am I putting this forward? It is because it will sound feasible and doable by the working people. Thinking of land and its resources as the commons, not subject to private ownership, would not be new to many societies in Africa. The concept of ownership of land was introduced by colonialism.

Secondly, arguing for health, education, water, finance, and energy as commons not subject to private ownership, but essentially producing public goods, also cannot be considered new because privatisation of these sectors has caused devastation to the working people. It has polarised our societies into small classes of a few who are filthy rich, and large masses of the poor who cannot afford paid education, health, water, electricity, etc. This can be the basis of organising the working people and it could be a political demand to the existing states. That is where I think the struggle stands. As I said, this is only a suggestion which requires further discussion and theorising. It is only after theorising that we can develop ideologies based on those demands and also understand how we can then learn from the experiences of the people to mobilise and take the struggles forward.

Moving on to another question that is almost linked to the previous one on alternatives, I would like us to spotlight Tanzania's ujamaa – a collectivisation project that was implemented by Mwalimu Julius Nyerere. This project has been vilified by a number of people who have argued that the project does not work and therefore had discouraged developments that take that kind of path. As someone who went through this experience and followed it closely, what would you say was the major undoing of ujamaa? I still think at some point people can try to relook and redefine it to make it work, but that can only be after a process of analysing its pitfalls. Did it really fail and, if so, why?

That indeed is an important initiative that we should table and discuss further. You will remember, Freedom, that *Agrarian South: Journal of Political Economy* produced a special issue that looked at both a hundred years of the Russian revolution and fifty years of the Arusha Declaration. In the publication, we tried to revisit both issues. I would like to say, first and foremost, that *ujamaa* was undoubtedly a very progressive initiative in Africa. Secondly, both in its conception and implementation, it was a nationalist project, not a socialist one. The architect of the project himself often said that for him nation-building was primary, socialism secondary. If I were to put it in some kind of Marxist language, in *ujamaa* social emancipation and class emancipation were subordinated to national building which in turn meant giving primacy to national unity.

The social question was subordinated to the national question. The (national) unity of all classes trumped (social) class struggles and politically speaking, as we have argued in our biography of Mwalimu Nyerere, in book three, that partly explains the so-called undoing of *ujamaa*, because it was not seen as a social question. The national question was privileged. Within *ujamaa* and within the political class, we ended up accommodating all kinds of tendencies including rightist tendencies which had no interest whatsoever in *ujamaa*, and even went as far as to sabotage it. When the crunch came, this proto-bourgeoisie turned against *ujamaa*. That is the thesis of book three of the biography. Of course, we can say a lot about the shortcomings at the policy level, referring to failures of implementation etc, but that discourse does not take us far. Inevitably, it becomes tautological. For example, although the Arusha Declaration talks a lot about workers and peasants as the movers of the project, the truth is it was a top-down project. The agency to carry out this project was the state bourgeoisie which developed on the heels of *ujamaa*. Ironically, the Arusha

Declaration ended up creating a new class in its wings, so to speak, a kind of bureaucratic state bourgeoisie. It was this class that was supposed to drive *ujamaa*!

Secondly, although we kept declaring that agriculture was the backbone of our economy, we did not transform agriculture. It remained the same agriculture of peasants using the same age-old instruments and implements. It is also important to point out that the peasants continued to be exploited to the maximum and without any support going back to the farmers. This issue has been analysed in the context of the land question and the truth and reality is that we failed to transform agriculture and we failed to address the agrarian question. The peasant was sucked dry.

You are right when you say there was a time when *ujamaa* was very much demonised as a titanic failure (to use the late Mazrui's hyperbole). The truth is, like many other African countries, whether capitalist or socialist, Tanzania found itself in a deep crisis in the late 1970s to the 1980s. All these countries had to submit to the so-called Structural Adjustment Programs (SAPs) to survive. I will not get deeper into this because we all know what happened. What I can say is that the consequences of adopting SAPs and neoliberal policies are now being dramatically seen and felt, and people (not only the masses but the so-called educated classes too) are revisiting the Arusha Declaration with nostalgia. If you read the Arusha Declaration today, you will realise that it was a pretty revolutionary document during its time – in spite of what happened in its implementation. There is a lot to learn from it.

That is a very interesting point. In the interest of time, let us move to another important issue which you and many others have raised. When we started this conversation, we talked about how an imperialist system disadvantages the South. In your writings you have gone further and postulated that the solution is to delink. May you please provide clarity on this concept of delinking because some might interpret it to mean that we should not have any links with the outside world.

Firstly, delinking does not mean that there should not be any relations. Not only that it is impossible, but it is even undesirable. Delinking means subjecting your policies to the logic of national development not to the logic of imperialist and capitalist development. That is what you are delinking from. Simply put, you may say the kind of decisions you make and the policies you implement are meant to subject your development to the internal logic and not that of world capitalism. That is the meaning of delinking. How you do it is a different matter. Is it possible to do it? Yes, it is possible to do it and that is a political question. It does not happen mechanistically but depends on how well the popular classes are organised and mobilised to sustain the project of delinking.

We have the experiences of some emancipatory tendencies which were nipped in the bud. For example, Amílcar Cabral did not see national liberation as a stage but rather, a continuous process. If I may paraphrase him, he said "as long as imperialism exists, independence can only mean the national liberation movement in power". This is a very profound statement. What are its implications? Take the example of South Africa and the stageist theory of some of its proponents. On the other hand, we had someone like Chris Hani who had a different vision of South Africa. He was killed. Amílcar Cabral was killed. These were strategic killings. Let us not forget them because in such struggles, individuals do matter. While we know that individuals do not make history, they do matter and play a critical role in certain circumstances. The turn that history takes does depend on the role of individual leaders. If you examine, and that is what we need to do, our history of national liberation, you'll find that at very strategic moments, strategic people who had a different view of liberation were bumped off. Cabral and Chris Hani are examples. Would these countries have taken a different path had they lived, one cannot say.

There is a point of view which is arising now which totally rejects the national question. It views the national question as the colonial question. That is also problematic. I do not think that the national question has exhausted itself but, I will go along the line that in our present state of the struggle and politics of the left, the national question needs to be subordinated to the social question. If we do not do that, we are likely to be identified with right-wing nationalisms and that is problematic.

Today in South Africa, for example, you cannot simply continue harping on the national question. The question which is very much on the table is the social one. It never addressed the social question. Capital, white capital, stayed with its privileges. In that situation, it is now important to discuss the social question and not simply stick to the national question or pontificate on some woolly idea about all-inclusive democracy. So the national question exists, it has a role, yes, but where do we place it.

Before we end, Freedom, I would like to make a couple of remarks. First, I want to suggest, I am of course thinking aloud, that we need to shift away from some of the dominant vocabulary. There is also an NGO vocabulary which many of us, unconsciously or unintentionally, tend to adopt. That is problematic. Here I am opening up myself to criticism. Is the term "alternatives", for example, not very much part of the NGO discourse? I ask because in Marxist ideology, we talk of a "new world view". In this ideology we do not talk about alternatives, but we talk about building a better world with a new world view. I know it sounds abstract and utopian, but the world's history was made by utopias.

The second point I would like to make is this: maybe we cannot explore this a lot here, but it is relevant when we are discussing the land question. There is a lot of debate about private individual ownership versus communal ownership and many of us think that the latter is progressive. I would actually want to suggest that we should move away from the concept of ownership altogether. That is why I am trying to develop, and maybe we can debate it, the concept of the commons. The commons are not communally owned. They are only managed by the community through its democratic organs.

Finally, there is the question of the classes which I would want to address to my fellow comrades from the Marxist tradition. Many of us think that radical political economy and the analysis of classes is a Marxist method. It is not. Marxism was a critique of political economy, not its affirmation. The concept of class was developed by the classical political economists before Marx. What was specific to Marxism was the concept of historical materialism and the central problematic of historical materialism is class struggle. The question of class struggle has been discarded in our discussions. I would therefore like to suggest that we need to dig deeper in our work to understand better the question of historical materialism because, if we disregard it, we open ourselves to a very common criticism that Marxists are reductionists who only talk about economics and not politics. We also become susceptible to the criticism that Marxists talk about the "rule of capital" but not how capital rules.

17. Lena Anyuolo (2021), Politics, Poetry and Struggle

Lena Grace Anyuolo is a Kenyan writer, poet and social justice activist with Mathare Social Justice Centre and Ukombozi Library. Talking to Zeilig, Anyuolo discusses her background, politics and writing. She explains that when our environment is trauma, and we are forced to survive under impossible conditions, it is hard to love. Activists are exposed twice – first to our personal demons and then to the task of fighting for socialism while living the crisis of capitalism. Only the transformative power of revolutionary work can save us.

***

Can you tell ROAPE *readers about your background and work?*

I am a writer, a poet and feminist. I am a member of Ukombozi Library. I grew up in a small family. My mother was a teacher and my father a computer engineer. There was a culture of learning in our home. My sister and I were encouraged to explore our environment through reading books, watching films and plays. I am a proud alumnus of Donholm Catholic Primary School. My teachers were kind people. I loved my friends. Many of the aspects of my early learning environment encouraged analysis. I went to a national high school. It wasn't the best experience to be so far from home, at a boarding school.

Writing was nurtured in me from an early age. My early childhood mentors encouraged imagination. My sister, my friends and I would make up games to play, by myself I would make up fantastical stories in my head some of which I'd write down. In high school, I felt my creativity stifled. It was a blow to my confidence. We had a heavy workload of memorising irrelevant things so that we could pass our examinations and maintain our "ranking". There were few avenues to blow off steam apart from one hour of optional physical education once a week.

My self-esteem took a big blow when my mother died when I was still young. I was in class seven and my sister was in class five. I was really scared because I felt alone in the world. We lived with different relatives over the school holidays. My social life was suddenly heavily disrupted. I went from having a bevy of friends to struggling to find and keep hold of friends because of all the movement. I grew exceptionally close to my sister because of it. She felt like the only family I had. It wasn't a perfect relationship because we were doing our best to grow up, be there for each other, and fit the expectations of our relatives so that our material needs would be met. We did our best to make it work under such stressful conditions. She remains my dearest friend.

University was rough. My world was getting bigger, and up until then my entire being had been pegged on academic success and the approval of my relatives. In university, it didn't matter what my grades were or how overachieving I had been in high school. I ached for a mentor. I desperately wanted to write but lacked the creative confidence to do so. University felt so big. It also challenged my belief systems, and ambition. The initial excitement to be at university wore off very fast. I had imagined an intellectually stimulating culture, but in the end I felt drained and exhausted by the bureaucracy and tedium.

I took on a number of odd jobs and that helped me to diversify my interactions. I read a lot and it expanded my world view. I ended up at Ukombozi Library because of a love for books and libraries. The dreamer in me was excited to explore. The rebel in me was elated because it was a subversive space. I wouldn't say I was interested in local politics. I had already given up all hope of expecting change from the government. I was apolitical because I didn't know or couldn't see how we could possibly get ourselves out of the fucked-up order of things. Yet, at the library, the atmosphere was hopeful. The centres overflowed with optimism.

People didn't have the answers, but everyone was doing their best to analyse society and come up with a strategy for change.

I would debate a lot in high school and at university, and the period after that. I still do. Our discussions were quite philosophical. I have fond memories of fiery debates about the US elections, and our capacities for change in the current electoral climate. This was around 2013. My best friend at the time introduced me to feminism and she encouraged me to read Frantz Fanon's *The Wretched of the Earth*, and bell hooks. On long afternoons with another close friend, I would debate intensely about the application of these ideologies to our reality. I was enriched by these women in my life.

You are an activist and writer, and have been involved for some years with Mathare Social Justice Centre, can you tell us something about your activism and how you became politicised?

I began human rights work and political work at the same time. I was strongly inclined to political work because of the examples of audacity that I read about in the resistance of Muthoni Nyanjiru, Wangari Maathai, the Kenya Land and Freedom Army, the Kurdish Women's Movement, Che Guevara, Celia Sánchez, Dandara Palmares. I could write an endless list of these people. I was impressed by the legacy of Rosa Luxemburg and her analysis of the women's struggle.

The social justice centres were an ideal space for experimentation with these political theories. They were an organised, organic, grassroots movement of workers. We faced the task of ideologically grounding the centres to grow from human rights theory to scientific socialism. I was challenged by the practical ways in which my comrades dealt with extra-judicial executions, water scarcity, gender-based violence. I was inspired by the persistence and collective effort of the social justice centres to document these violations, conduct community dialogues and disrupt the status quo in civic spaces dominated by NGOs, human rights organisations that were based in upper-class neighbourhoods.

I became politicised through various study cells at Ukombozi Library, and Mathare Social Justice Centre.

Though you are also an environmental activist, you describe yourself as a socialist. What role does socialist politics – and anti-capitalism – play in your activism and political thinking?

They are tools of analysis. Capitalist education and religion have conditioned us to believe that the oppression of the many by a few propertied individuals is natural. It is a deeply depressing, fatalistic worldview. The ideology of workers is optimistic because we are practically, daily engaged in class struggle for a better world in which the means of production are controlled by our labour. Scientific socialism removes the evil veil of capitalism revealing to us that this is not a natural world order – it is the great, indeed historic adversary of capitalism.

You have spent long years struggling with depression and a diagnosis of ADHD, you have written powerfully about these episodes – can you tell us about your depression, and how you view depression in the context of our struggles under capitalism?

Depression is a monster. As I reflect on my life, I am able to see that much of my struggle with it was directly linked to my material conditions. The structure of capitalism and patriarchy does not support healthy relationships of any kind. Family is considered the bedrock of social justice and freedom, yet it is also the place where peace is first disrupted. Our environment is trauma. We survive under impossible conditions. Nairobi makes it hard to love. As activists, we are double exposed. First to our personal demons and then to the task of organising for socialism while living the crisis of capitalism in these concrete prisons. Depression leads to a very slow death. The medical industry in Kenya is ultra-capitalist, from the insurance company to the hospitals. It is a privilege to gain access to healthcare with any sort of dignity.

Through study, I now know that capitalism is quick to put a stamp of illness on behaviour that does not conform to the picture of the ideal robotic worker. Capitalism profits from the trauma that capitalism and patriarchy itself causes in us. It turns psychiatrists into drug dealers, eager to medicate for profit.

I knew my primary home environment was highly abusive and directly linked to my depression and suicidal ideation, but I lacked the material means to find a place of my own. So I used pills prescribed by the medical profession to cope, the medication would flatline me emotionally and deaden my feelings. To me that was better than having to be fully aware of the reality of my living conditions.

However, I am hopeful that we can heal but there is no easy panacea. There is also a good amount of effort that must be put into developing healthy mental practices.

My greatest appreciation goes to my comrades, organising together has helped to chip away at some of my despair. It is an exhilarating process because I was able to see practically that even an individual has a role to play in history. No resistance is too small, and we are not condemned to hopelessness. It is capitalist trauma to always perceive doom and gloom. We have all the power in our hands to destroy capitalism and build socialism from its ruins. We must do this in order to survive as a species. The poem by Langston Hughes, "I look at the world", sums up the transformative power of revolutionary work.

I appreciate now, for example, that better planning of my finances can alleviate some of the anxiety of survival. It can help to have a little extra to cultivate a small hobby. Constant, persistent self-cultivation in a study circle continues to sharpen one's worldview and that in-depth knowledge of our situation helps us remain optimistic about our revolutionary potential and future.

One way you interpret the world and express your rage against its horrors and how we live our lives is through poetry. Can you tell us about the importance of poetry and creative writing in your life, and how it speaks to our battered lives and revolutionary hope. How do you see the "uses" of poetry in our movements, and lives?

I mentioned earlier that at some point it felt like I had lost my creative confidence. One of my mentors is Mama Wangari. I am so grateful for her presence. Whether she knew it or not, she slayed a big part of my enforced creative shyness. Even the messages, letters, emails we wrote to each other, are pieces of incredibly valuable writing. That was an epiphany. I saw my notebooks in a different light. They were beautiful precious pieces of text. These were my points of release. I am a firm believer in the political flowing from the personal. You must be able to tell your story honestly whether you are telling it to yourself or to others. When we tell our story truthfully, we can inspire others.

Can you tell us a little about your most recent collection and what the poems mean to you?

This collection is based on reflections from 2020. That was a wild year for me in terms of organising. I felt like my life had been distilled into the intensity of the months between March and November that year. I had to talk about it because it was a lot to deal with. There was a lot happening in my personal life in addition to organising during the pandemic. I became a workaholic because I was trying to postpone dealing with myself.

Inevitably I came undone, so I had to face up to myself whether I liked it or not. My comrade, Maryanne Kasina, the convenor of Women in Social Justice Centres, urges activists to try and come to terms with themselves. To tell the truth to ourselves and accept who we are – as flawed and broken as we might be. There's no escaping this aspect of humanity otherwise we may end up causing quite a bit of harm. It's not as if we will reach an actualised version of ourselves. I don't believe in that. But we must retain the belief in our capacity to change and grow.

Fanon says that out of obscurity we discover our mission. Dialectical materialism teaches us that the world is in a constant state of flux – even in our individual biology this is occurring. So, there are no permanent or irredeemable mistakes. Toni Cade Bambara writes that there is no such thing as an instant guerrilla. We have to face up to uncomfortable realities. The good thing is that if we have cultivated safe communities, then we won't have to go through this process alone. We must remember not to be harsh to ourselves or each other when we falter, we can correct ourselves and move forward. This collection which is being published next year is a reflection of that time. There is grief and rage, cheekiness too. It is precious. A drop of my being.

In the aftermath of Covid and the continuing devastation of our planet, what is the future for activists and social movements in Kenya and the region?

Mona Eltahawy writes that we must emerge, not regress. We are definitely not unscathed, but we must continue drawing on the lessons from our practice. We need to be really aggressive about organising against patriarchy. It is urgent that we do so because sexism is causing deep harm to ourselves and our communities.

I am optimistic about the future because of the existence of Ukombozi Library, the organic intellectuals movement, the ecological justice movement, Vita Books, Women in Social Justice Centres, Matigari Book Club, RSL (Revolutionary Socialist League) study cells, Cheche Bookshop… The list is endless and that reflects that we are a young, politically aware group of people eager for lasting change.

18. Max Ajl (2021), A People's Green New Deal

Max Ajl is an associated researcher with the Tunisian Observatory for Food Sovereignty and the Environment. In conversation with Zeilig, Max Ajl discusses his new book *A People's Green New Deal* and explains that environmental justice and change is a revolutionary project. Ajl argues that the expansion of southern or Third World sovereignty is a critical element of Third World environmentally sustainable development.

***

Could you introduce yourself to ROAPE? How did you become involved in questions of climate change and ecological justice and what's been your scholarly and activist trajectory?

I have been interested in the environmental cause since I was very young, mostly through reading and some climate change journalism. Politically, I have been primarily engaged in anti-Zionist and anti-imperialist work but have always focused scholarly efforts on agriculture, ecology, agrarian questions, and popular development. I studied at Cornell for my doctoral work, under Philip McMichael, who specialises in historical sociology and agrarian questions. Cornell was and remains one of the best places in the United States to focus on the political aspects of agro-ecological development. For me, all these issues are intertwined: we need a good and clean environment for people to have good lives, taking care of the environment starts with taking care of agriculture and food provision, the major human interaction with the surface of the Earth and finally countries and peoples need first of all to be able to determine their own paths in the world in order to set out to build up their societies.

Your book A People's Green New Deal *details a radical project, a revolutionary one, for environmental justice and change. You argued for "local democratic economies built on appropriate technologies and sovereign industrialisation and local control of renewables." Can you talk us through some of the main arguments in your new book?*

My book starts by making what I think is the basic point that in order to have a just and revolutionary transformation of the world, we need a holistic understanding of how this world was created and made unjust, particularly as it relates to resource use and environmental issues. Furthermore, we should depart from plans for a just transition which have come from those most oppressed, excluded, and harmed by our current system. The book starts with a criticism of many right-wing and social-democratic plans for a great transition, and shows points of convergence between them. I then go on to consider and try to show empirically how to transform certain critical sectors which I know something about, especially agriculture and a bit about infrastructure, construction, and manufacturing. Above all, I want people to see how we can have non-hierarchical – or communist – extremely complex societies, with a high degree of social interdependence, an extremely high level of technology, complex social division of labour and specialisation, yet without them being enormously destructive to the environment. Such societies obviously need certain baselines, including local control of renewable technology (where possible), locally-sited industrialisation so that people can democratically decide and remediate the damage from industrialisation, and technologies which are appropriate to a permanently sustainable modern and non-hierarchical society. That includes in many ways a process of re-skilling to allow for more distributed and decentralised control over technologies. It also includes local control over agriculture, as a mechanism of landscape management, a way to draw-down atmospheric carbon dioxide, a way to protect biodiversity, a way for human communities to generally feed themselves mostly locally, at least within reason, and a way to smoothly integrate humans into nature.

You describe at the start of the book a dizzying array of Green New Deals (GND) and how the idea of the GND has proliferated. Can you describe how this idea has exploded, some of the proposals on offer and also what is deeply problematic at the core of many of these, seemingly radical, initiatives?

The GND entered the household discussion because of the legislation from Senator Edward Markey and Congressperson Alexandria Ocasio-Cortez who has been invented as a democratic socialist. This GND essentially tried to bring together issues like employment, housing and carbon dioxide emissions, and to build a new industrial century for the US, with some attention to social needs and covered with anti-racist rhetoric. It has exploded because of the wide unease with the environmental crisis, but also because capital is attempting to carry out a great transition from above and has increasingly publicised the climate crisis for its own purposes. The more social democratic proposals essentially call for a partial or full conversion to renewable energy by 2030 while remaining within the green Keynesian paradigm – the state as a large spender and economic coordinator, the endurance of private property relations. Uniformly, the more visible progressive proposals – like that of Robert Pollin and Noam Chomsky – ignore the Cochabamba demands for climate debt repayments, assert that the North has the permanent right to use more electricity than the South and disdain any struggle against capitalism. They also sidestep the broader environmental crisis, linked to biodiversity, soil erosion and damage, overuse of nitrogen fertilisers, etc. All of these measures are very much reminiscent of attempts from the 1980s to arrive at North-South development agreements without reckoning with ongoing northern exploitation of the South: that is, they are not even anti-capitalist let alone anti-imperialist.

Max, you write early on that capitalism has an inbuilt "inability as a historical system to respect the earth-system and the tenuous, delicate and easily shattered niche it has for many billions of humans". Though this may be obvious to many readers, including of ROAPE, can you explain why you see capitalism as "unreformable" in terms of any serious environmental transformation?

Capitalism is based on treating use-values as fungible: one thing is as good as another thing provided they exchange on the market. Once we see that this can create an equivalence between, say, sustainably-harvested lumber, or a house made of such lumber and capital secured from selling phosphate-based fertilisers, or from oil capable of completely changing the composition of the atmosphere, the problems of unlimited fungibility of use-values through market exchange should be clear: such a system is capable of causing almost limitless damage to non-human nature. Because capitalism is based on the massive expansion of value and profit and limitless accumulation, it is naturally unable to respect that earth systems have survivability thresholds. If they are pushed too far, exploited too much, doused with too much poison or if fisheries are extracted from too much, they will simply collapse. Now, I think what is important to keep in mind is not merely that capitalism has run roughshod over the natural world, causing enormous damage – especially on North-South lines of concentrated damage in the South. It's also worth pointing out that capitalism is now threatening to shift to a different kind of hierarchical regime, a point that Immanuel Wallerstein spent many decades of his life making. Such a system could well preserve nature because it would be based far less on indefinite expansion of exchange value, and would instead pay people a pittance to preserve nature as a use value and be based on stable oppression rather than expansive exploitation and endless accumulation.

Interestingly, you state that "we" in the north have a responsibility, "specifically in preventing our own governments from imposing by violence their political values on other countries" – this dimension of the fight for anti-capitalist climate change is important. Can you explain what you mean and the nature of this responsibility?

Very often anti-imperialism or the national question are phrased in terms of supporting X bad figure: for example, those who opposed the US war on Iraq became apologists for Saddam Hussein. I want to make the simple point that each nation has to essentially start from minding its own business, and that non-intervention in the affairs of other nations needs to be the starting point for world-wide environmental justice and environmental revolution. Quite simply, the US/EU do not have the right to decide who rules other countries – especially but not only in the Third World. This is a necessary element for an anti-capitalist just transition on a world-wide level, because we need to fight for other countries' rights to determine their own paths and assess how our own countries are obstructing the exercise of that. Such an assessment is simple, since the US, EU, and the UK intervene constantly world-wide. What follows are serious campaigns to put a stop to that intervention, in other words, by demanding respect for international law and the dismantling of northern militaries.

One of the exciting elements of the book is that you challenge seemingly radical figures and projects including the celebrated Alexandria Ocasio-Cortez, the US congresswoman, and the GND she advocates. What specifically are its problems in contrast with the Democratic Socialists of America, for example?

In particular, that document which she proposed envisions sending public money to private corporations through state-private collaborations, sometimes softened with "appropriate ownership stakes." Now, whatever that is, it is certainly not a socialist program. Another major issue: she calls for the US to be a green-tech leader, and for this to be the main mechanism for international action within the GND. In fact, this means replacing climate debt payments and putting in their place a new program for the US to be an industrial powerhouse based on renewables exports. She really does not mention class very much in the document: it refers to phantasms like "frontline communities" to receive special funding. There is no call for the takeover and dismantling of the oil companies. And finally, there is no mention of demilitarisation. So it's important to highlight that the plan basically ignores the most central sectors of capitalism and is not even remotely anti-capitalist.

You outline a Southern platform for an ecological revolution – can you describe the nature of such a programme and how it goes beyond the climate to protect Mother Earth?

Capitalism and imperialism deeply damage the environment, and that damage extends well beyond climate – it means cancer plagues, the pollution of aquifers, microplastics, a biodiversity crisis. In Tunisia, for example, two of the major disaster zones are Gabès and the area near Monastir, each soaked with chemical residues from textiles and phosphate processing. Cancer rates are astronomical. Tunisia is emblematic of a larger pattern of uneven accumulation which has systematically dumped the most polluting industries in places with the fewest safeguards, particularly in the Third World, in effect making the Third World pay the environmental costs of capitalist industrialisation. People need to be able to have choices about what kinds of production their societies are engaged in, what the costs of different choices are, and what are the feasible alternatives. In many ways, even the Third World societies are both over- and under-industrialised: insufficient access to electricity, insufficient existence let alone capacity to manufacture machine tools and mass transport systems yet burdened with export-industries primarily to the profit of northern capital. So we need to change that system, based on southern demands, in order to construct a just world system that takes care of ecology.

In what ways do you see existing GNDs as Eurocentric?

Existing GNDs, even progressive ones, tend to share the following traits: one, little to no mention of climate debt, the absolutely essential demand from 2010 from the Third World. Two, a techno-fetishism extending to lab meat and biofuels – two frontiers for renewed primitive accumulation of the South. Three, insufficient interest in agriculture which is at the core of southern questions of development but must also be far more central – eventually – in northern productive systems. Four, lack of interest in appropriate technology development. Five, total lack of engagement with highly developed theories of environmentally uneven exchange which show that the South has always paid the environmental price for northern development. Those lenses bring the nature of the actual world-system into focus, and if we do not deploy those lenses we will produce GNDs that are false remedies to a poorly investigated crisis.

You mention how a supposed internationalism actually silences the South, and undermines any real project built on climate justice. Why is the national question central to your approach and to ecological transformation? How is this approach a key part of achieving climate justice?

The national question, very simply, means that national liberation is the *sine qua non*, the antecedent, to further national-popular development efforts. This is very visible in the case of Palestine: how can Palestine expect to develop unless it as a nation has sovereign control over its national productive resources, including land, investment decisions, technology, and so forth? Now, the international system is structured to remove those decisions from southern nations and to remove control of resources from southern nations. So the national question reminds us that countries need not just political sovereignty or liberation, but also economic liberation, in order to have just and ecologically sustainable transformation. The national question reminds us that national sovereignty is the necessary political shell, or frame, within which to resolve those questions. And that frame imposes particular obligations to activists and militants in the North, in particular – to seriously come to terms with and contest how our governments violate southern sovereignty, and our monopolies drain southern wealth.

Can you speak about your theoretical framework – you use dependency theory which positions the focus of global political economy into centre or core nations and the periphery. You write, "the West has systematically shifted its dirtiest industrial plants to the semi-periphery ... even in the core the dirtiest waste processing is often sited close to Black neighbourhoods". You also use the term "Environmentally Unequal Exchange" – can you explain these terms and the ways it helps to enrich our understanding of the processes underway and what needs to be done?

Simply, core, semi-periphery and periphery are best understood as relative positions in the world division of labour and accumulation on a world scale. World accumulation is by its nature polarised and continually polarising. Wealth concentrates in some places: the core. And it is produced, yet flows outwards from, the periphery. Semi-peripheries, such as China, may import value from places like Vietnam yet on the whole they are exporters of wealth and value to the First World. These terms remind us that overall, most wealth and value comes from the working classes – popular classes – of the periphery, and most of the material components that are inputs into value come from the periphery; and finally, the periphery unequally suffers from environmental pollution including unequal use of or access to world space for CO_2. In that way we can see that the nation, and of course classes within nations, are part of the structuring units of our world system, and even working classes in the core and the periphery may, at least without intercession, have different interests because of different levels of access to world wealth. Those obstacles are superable, but superseding them must start by recognising them and the problems they impose on planning for world-wide transformation. In particular, the core left has to do a better job on defending demands from the periphery – including ones which seem tough at the moment: climate debt payments, for example. Otherwise, the world-system will remain permanently uneven.

On the other hand, environmentally uneven exchange and dependency theory remind us that those suffering the hardest impact of climate change, environmental degradation, and capitalism are in the periphery, not the core. This includes those outside the formal labour market, or indeed who are involved in subsistence based social reproduction as Lyn Ossome has argued. Such people in fact are central to creating what Archana Prasad calls "socially useful nature," on the one hand and, on the other, are central to producing human beings who become a labour reservoir. Thus, these sectors of people are absolutely central to the world-wide accumulation of capital. Insofar as such sectors successfully defend the land and territories from unwanted environmental degradation and produce sufficient use-values for their own purposes, and then take part in sovereign popular-ecological development strategies, they will be the fulcrum for a transformation in the world system. So, these populations are absolutely central to a just transition on a global basis.

You see national sovereignty as central to the protests of progressive movements across the world. From this, you argue that the rights of subjugated nations must be central also to climate justice. Can you talk us through this argument?

This is a question of defending the positive achievements of struggles against war, racism and colonisation. The UN Charter and the anti-colonial national liberation struggles and covenants from the 1960s, 1970s and 1980s were all crystal-clear that subjugated peoples under occupation and colonisation had the right to achieve full political sovereignty, the right to form nation-states fully as equal as other nation-states within the international system. A modern corollary is that nations should have the right to be free of unilateral coercive measures, including sanctions; and perhaps these sanctions or other coercive measures may soon include forms of unilateral environmental protectionism or invasion under the aegis of rights to protect the environment, as has recently been advocated in for Venezuela. We cannot accept discourses of the environment being used as a justification to violate national sovereignty, any more than we can accept discourses of humanitarianism or development or civilization, and because the default ideology in the core states is to accept the ruling class propaganda of the right to intervene, it is necessary to insist on this point rather than accept the refrain "we are all against intervention." It is absolutely not the case, including within the metropolitan left.

At the centre of the book is an anti-capitalist eco-socialism which is revolutionary but also pro-Third World sovereignty. This last element is missing from most accounts. Why do you see this as key?

The classical arguments for Third World sovereignty went well beyond political or state sovereignty, to questions of natural resource sovereignty. They also saw economic national liberation as flowing organically and extending the achievements of political or legal independence. The Iraqi re-nationalisation of its natural resources, for example, flowed organically from its re-acquisition of national sovereignty in 1958. It was a continuous process which lasted some decades and led the US to set in motion the destruction of Iraq in 1980. Colonialism is in large measure about the denial of Third World states to have the full right to dispense of their natural resources, which certainly includes the capacity to set prices for them through commodity cartels (something that people like Robert Vitalis apparently fail to understand). Furthermore, if you look at investment treaties they often constrict southern self-determination and sovereignty when it conflicts with the newly written rights of the large monopolies – overwhelmingly based in the North.

So the question is achievement of, defence of, and expansion of southern or Third World sovereignty as a critical element of Third World, environmentally sustainable development. Indeed, the entire range of arguments for Third World development from the 1970s and 1980s rested on individual and collective self-reliance and planning for this reached a fairly advanced stage, at least in the Arab region. Clearly, such sovereignty goes well beyond legal ascension to statehood but implies the full exercise of sovereign rights – including the right to make alliances and erect alternative economic, and environmental, architecture.

Unfortunately, there is a common conception that to lift up sovereignty is to downplay internal class struggles. But it is the opposite: internal environmental class struggles need sovereign states within which they can advance. Furthermore, many social scientists and planners – from the 1970s – saw that certain northern conceptions of environmentalism were being parlayed into a denial of the South to develop. As the Founex Report, for example, stated: "concern for [the] environment must not and need not detract from the commitment of the world community – developing and more industrialised nations alike – to the overriding task of development of the developing regions of the world," since development in the periphery would better allow for countries to overcome environmental problems.

What role does the struggle of the oppressed and working classes play in the North in advancing and championing eco-socialism?

To begin, although the oppressed peoples and working classes of the North are unlikely to lead the struggle for eco-socialism – a struggle whose programmatic elements were laid out in 2010 in the Cochabamba People's Agreements – this does not mean northern working classes can be excluded from strategic plans and horizons. It simply means that we cannot lapse into an economism which looks at those demands in the absence of internationalist horizons, normalises the blindness to the Third World which is the default ruling class ideology in the West, forgets demands for Land Back from Indigenous movements and accepts that blindness as simply the "normal" ideological basis for building up better lives in the core.

However, organised labour can be central to a just transition insofar as the move – for example – to change the nature of first world industrialisation goes hand-in-pen with the demands from the periphery: climate debt, prior consultation and informed consent for resource extraction. Take, for example, the heavy presence of electric cars in the Bernie Sanders proposal for a GND. That emerged from trying to get the large amount of organised labour in the auto industry on board. However there is no reason the target for that industry could not be nationalisation, and conversion into producing the vehicles for nation-wide public transport, with a far lower environmental impact. Those are political decisions.

On the other hand, agriculture is a sector which – if done sustainably – in principle involves no extraction from the Third World. There are some small collaborations between ranchers and Indigenous people in the US West around sustainable landscape management, for example. And the move to entirely convert US farming to carbon-dioxide-absorbing agro-ecological production could create a community of interest between the migrant labour force, especially if massive minimum wages and agrarian reform are part of the agenda, family farms and indeed consumers, who prefer healthy meat and produce from entirely ecological farms. There are opportunities to suture the interests of separated sectors, which are themselves the product of capitalist alienation of production and consumption. However, those sutures need to be carried out through political organising which keeps the long view in mind.

Finally, what role do you see industrialisation playing in the eco-socialist future?

Unfortunately, far too much of the debate around industrialisation is trapped in false binaries: between an anti-industrial anti-extractivist or post-extractivist position, for example, and a high-modernist super-industrial position. We should not treat that false debate as innocent. Indeed, one can find precisely the same set of journals and institutions – *Historical Materialism*, Verso, etc, and behind them German foundations like Rosa Luxemburg which fund and platform the set of intellectuals who crystallised the theory of "extractivism" – simultaneously blasting the Bolivian government for investing rent in infrastructure or just using gas proceeds for popular needs, criticising that same government for not having immediately implemented an agro-ecological revolution – while also platforming Aaron Bastani to talk about space mining and the Green Revolution, and bizarrely totalling ignoring agro-ecology or the agrarian question as Third World development strategies except when useful to berate Bolivia. Such a debate is fundamentally unserious and antagonistic to serious political thought and practice.

It's actually necessary to clear away this deliberately created confusion in order to have a real discussion. First, what is industrialisation? Following Colin Duncan, we can say most essentially, industrialisation is the transformation of abiotic, or dead material like lead, copper, oil, gas, iron, into various things humans want and need. It differs in principle from manufacturing or agriculture in that the latter do not produce wastes and can be smoothly integrated into the environment while industry produces poisons – illusions of industrial ecology [and] circular economies to the side. So ideally we want an eco-socialism that is extremely modern in the sense of socially interdependent with complex divisions of labour and with an extremely sophisticated and highly technically advanced, yet controlled industrialisation. We want and should treasure industrialisation, but industrialisation within the limits of what we can remediate, clean up and control using existing technologies, not prospective technologies which justify current environmental degradation. That probably means overall on an absolute basis, a less industrialised but far more evenly industrialised world, assuming we demand roughly equivalent per capita access to public transport, computers, energy and advanced medical care – some of the sectors which need industry. On the other hand, many things which are made using industrial methods – like textiles, for example, or furniture – can be made using far less industrial methods, using natural materials at a minimum. Think oak cabinets instead of metal ones, or linen and cotton clothing instead of polyester. How much of a change that implies remains to be seen – we will make the path by walking it.

19. Ndongo Sylla (2022), Economics and Politics for Liberation

Ndongo Samba Sylla is writer, researcher and activist based in Dakar, and a long-time collaborator and comrade of *ROAPE*. Here, Sylla speaks with Zeilig about his work, French imperialism in Africa, and the struggle for economic and political liberation in Senegal and the continent. Ndongo continues Samir Amin's search for anti-capitalist political alternatives grounded in a radical analysis of trends and developments across Africa, and the Global South.

***

Comrade, can you introduce yourself to ROAPE readers? Please tell us a little about your background, activism and work.

I was born in Senegal and educated there, primarily at the Prytanée Militaire de Saint-Louis. After I obtained my baccalauréat I was offered a grant-aided place at a prestigious French military academy, with the assurance of becoming an officer in the Senegalese army after five to six year, but I decided instead to study social sciences in France, an option that also fitted better with my burgeoning "career" as a French-language Scrabble champion (four world titles between 2000 and 2016).

I've always been fascinated by the issue of work from philosophical, sociological and economic perspectives. On the strength of my master's thesis, a critique of the concept of employability, I was recruited by one of my tutors to assist on a project evaluating the European Employment Strategy while my subsequent doctoral thesis in economics examined gender inequalities in the Senegalese labour market.

After returning to Senegal, I worked first as a technical advisor to the Presidency of the Republic (2006-9) then as a consultant for Fairtrade International and now at the Rosa Luxemburg Foundation, where I am currently the Senior Programme and Research Manager.

You have worked on a broad array of areas in radical political economy and African politics and economics. How would you describe your research and writing and its motivation, what are its overriding elements and purpose?

My writing has focused in part on topics relevant to my professional career. It was natural to write about fair trade as I was briefly active in this field, while my interest in social movements has grown since I joined the Luxemburg Foundation. My writing also tackles issues I've considered over the years. For example, as work is so central to modern societies, can we apply the Western model of decent wage employment to developing countries characterised by stark under-utilisation of labour and sustained population growth? What does the word democracy mean? What is the relationship between democracy and development? How does the CFA franc work and what problems does it pose in a development context?

In each case my aim is first to understand the issues, then to form my own opinions and test the dominant narratives. So I need to challenge Eurocentric approaches, mobilise more critical perspectives and engage in dialogue with them. No matter how complex the subject, I always try to write clearly and intelligibly. Heterodox economics and alternative approaches that question prevailing intellectual orthodoxies are already marginalised, and hermetic language only reinforces this. Thus, I would argue that my approach is generally consistent with an economics for liberation perspective.

You are also engaged in various radical initiatives in Senegal, where you live and work – not least Economic Saturdays. Am I correct in describing these Saturdays as radical (and frequently Marxist) study classes in political economy? How were they formed and what do they signify?

In March 2013, with financial support from the Rosa Luxemburg Foundation, the Senegalese economist Demba Moussa Dembélé and I launched Economics Saturdays, a monthly forum for economic discussion and debate. We first met on 15 October 2012 at the Senegalese Social Forum, at an event marking the 25th anniversary of Thomas Sankara's assassination. We remarked how neoliberal economic thought dominated teaching, research and public policy in Senegal, and how Dakar lacked any kind of platform for heterodox views on political economy.

Alongside Marxist and pan-Africanist intellectuals and activists, we welcome students, civil society activists, politicians, journalists, comrades from the North etc. We've been honoured to invite personalities like Samir Amin, Cornel West, and Mamadou Koulibaly (former Minister of Finance and President of the National Assembly of Côte d'Ivoire). The papers presented at Economics Saturdays appear in collected volumes under the title *Deconstructing the Neoliberal Discourse*. We've published five volumes to date covering a wide variety of subjects including local problems, global issues, topical questions and tributes to prominent individuals.

For a number of years, you were a close comrade and collaborator with Samir Amin. Can you describe your collaboration, and how Amin's writings have influenced your work? What are the main questions and issues that Amin helps us with today – how does his understanding of political economy, and Marxism in Africa and the Global South, help us to elucidate the nature of the current epoch?

Samir Amin had his "headquarters" in Dakar, where he'd been Director of the Institute for Economic Development and Planning and Executive Secretary of CODESRIA. The Third World Forum, which he ran until his death, is also based in the city. His prolific output, the positions he held, and his involvement with the great struggles of his day undoubtedly make him the most influential economist among progressive African intellectuals. He paved the way for the majority of us. One of his greatest strengths is that he produced a fertile body of thought rooted in the history and concerns of the Global South: he asked the right questions and suggested fruitful directions for intellectual debate and political action.

We first met in Dakar in early 2013 and often afterwards at conferences in the city. He gave the inaugural address at our Economics Saturdays and spoke there many times. He reviewed my work on fair trade and democracy, which I regard as a huge honour. Our last intellectual correspondence concerned Moishe Postone's monograph, *Time, Labour and Social Domination*, a significant contribution that, based on the *Grundrisse*, offers a new interpretation of Marx's thought.

What can Amin teach us today? His central idea views capitalism as a historical system (which is thus doomed to disappear) based on polarisation between nations and between social classes within a nation. For this and other reasons arising from the specific development paths taken by the western nations and Japan, the nations of the periphery are unable collectively to "catch up". This does not imply that the periphery cannot make economic progress, simply that economic development here must be differently conceived. This view has since acquired empirical support in the literature on unequal ecological exchange.

Amin believed that the nations of the periphery must strive to escape the role assigned to them by the international division of labour. Rather than prioritise exports of primary and low-wage products, they must focus instead on expanding domestic demand. Industrialisation must be based on agricultural development, especially of peasant agriculture, but also on local technical innovation and on a coherent relationship between the industries producing capital goods and those producing mass consumption goods. To achieve this, peripheral countries need greater control over centralising and subsequently allocating their economic surplus. In other words, they must reject the dictates of free trade and financial liberalisation. In terms of domestic politics, work is required to tilt the class structure towards an anti-comprador alliance. Regionally, we must encourage new forms of regionalisation in line with national development plans. And globally the countries of North and South must ally to challenge the power of the financialised monopolies that, in Amin's view, should be nationalised. He outlined a vast political project that to me remains relevant in the context of what he describes as the "long march towards socialism".

You have written powerfully about the continued imperial control of countries in West Africa, subjected to the straitjacket of the French imposed and directed CFA franc. Please explain the issues and tell us why this remains a vital question for the sub-region's development, and possibilities of radical and socialist change linked to a removal of the CFA franc.

The CFA franc is a colonial currency still circulating in 14 African countries, mostly former French colonies. For many years a taboo issue, since 2015 certain intellectuals and pan-Africanist movements, on the continent and in the diaspora, have brought it into the public domain, as French journalist Fanny Pigeaud and I discuss in *Africa's Last Colonial Currency: The CFA Franc Story*. My thanks go to *ROAPE* for publishing my first English-language article on this subject, which has since been quoted often as an introductory text.

It is fair to say that in recent years the advocates of monetary liberation have won the intellectual debate around the CFA franc. Most of those interested in the subject acknowledge its anachronistic and colonial nature, the severe restrictions imposed on its users, and their fairly disastrous long-term economic performance. The most important task now is one of political strategy: how best to escape this monetary straitjacket?

Some favour abolishing the CFA franc but doubt the ability of African leaders, given their perceived or actual shortcomings, to manage an independent currency. Others suggest avoiding an exit to national currencies, relying instead on the projected ECOWAS – Economic Community of West African States, a grouping of 15 countries including the eight using the West African CFA franc – common currency, the ECO, whose planned launch in 2020 has been postponed to 2027. As the ECO was conceived within neoliberal parameters as a tropical euro, I would prefer a system of solidarity-based national currencies. Each CFA country should, if it wishes, have a national central bank that would issue the national currency. Rather than a monetary union, we would have economic and monetary cooperation: a regional or even continental payment and settlement system, a pooling of part of the foreign exchange reserves, and common policies for food and energy sovereignty.

I believe that reform of the CFA franc must occur in the broader context of delinking: regaining national control over currency, finance and economic resources, and transforming the economic structure through industrialisation and the expansion of domestic demand, in particular via an ecologically sustainable agricultural development policy and a full employment strategy. On these points in particular, I believe it is essential to combine the ideas generated by Modern Monetary Theory with those on the need for delinking.

Can we now talk about Senegal? Senegal's radical politics have forced the pace of change many times before, most remarkably in compelling Leopold Senghor – the first president – to call for the French to intervene after a mass uprising across the country in 1968. Behind the transition in 2000, which saw the ruling socialist party defeated after forty years in power (and the election of president Abdoulaye Wade), was a social movement ready to take to the streets for the change that they wanted. And once more, in 2012, when president Wade faced the anger of the streets in the "Y' en a marre" [we have had enough] movement.

Ndongo, can you tell us about the social movements in Senegal, and their relationship and independence from political parties?

In the volume I edited on *Liberalism and its Discontents: Social Movements in West Africa*, I identified five major logics of protest: liberal (campaigns to defend minority rights), corporatist (some of the campaigns led by trade unions, students), proletarian (working-class campaigns against the high cost of living or land grabs), republican (campaigns for public accountability, respect for the Constitution) and cross-cutting (combining different elements of the above).

In Senegal, as so often in West Africa, republican campaigns mobilise the greatest numbers and attract the widest geographical and political support. In general, during these campaigns, social movements and ordinary people, as guardians of political legitimacy and the public good, offer autonomous support to opposition parties. Neither necessarily shares the political agenda nor the ideology of the opposition parties, but they accept a conjunctural alliance in the name of the common good. This has often been the case in Senegal. The *"Y'en a Marre"* movement, which embodied the face of protest against Abdoulaye Wade in 2011-12, contributed indirectly to his replacement at the ballot box by Macky Sall in 2012. Today, however, this movement and its leaders are experiencing a rocky relationship with the Sall regime.

I would argue that the Senegalese have always been actively and appropriately involved in the major moments of national life. They've acted as a democratic brake on despotic excesses from Senghor to Macky Sall and have facilitated two peaceful transfers of political power (in 2000 and 2012). However, we should not be too idealistic. In my own, highly critical, view, the social movements are not radical enough in their demands. Being a radical, we should note, is to tackle issues at the root. Being an extremist, by contrast, is to surpass all reasonable limits. The extremist is the enemy of the radical.

The cyclical recurrence of the issues that provoke popular

mobilisations, e.g. the presidential third term, demonstrate this lack of radicalism. In other words, no institutional or sustainable solution has been found to a problem that provoked previous campaigns. The social movements also often operate in reformist mode, improving a dysfunctional system rather than laying the groundwork for an alternative democratic politics. Even while acknowledging the limitations of the political parties, they seldom question the electoral system that underpins the power of those parties. By failing to challenge the right to govern of the dominant political parties, they cede the political initiative. Once in power, former opposition parties are not obliged to implement the reforms advocated by the social movements.

In summary, while the social movements play an important role as political regulators, in practice they've done more to resolve conflicts within the political oligarchy than open up new horizons for a genuine democratic politics. However, given the inequalities and suffering linked to the Senegalese model of growth without development, we can expect that they will become more radical in their demands. This is especially true of their economic demands, such as access to decent employment, which the politicians continue to ignore.

Can you explain why Macky Sall is so despised across Senegal? No one, except for the state media, has a good word to say for him or for his coalition, Benno Bokk Yaakaar. Taxi drivers, shopworkers, informal traders, students and trade unionists are united in their disgust at what they see as a government that has taken from them, massively enriched itself and delivered nothing except price rises and crippling poverty.

Domestically, Senegal's current president, Macky Sall, is opposed by progressive movements, political parties and intellectuals alike. Yet he remains the great darling of the West, a status that gives him an important advantage in suppressing dissent. It is common knowledge that Western diplomacy and media are usually very tolerant of the repressive measures deployed by "friendly" regimes against their people and their political opponents.

Although relatively unpopular in Senegal, since 2007 (when he was prime minister) Sall has topped the poll each time he has stood for election. The explanation for this apparent paradox lies partly in the Senegalese electoral system, which – as in most countries around the world – is not designed to reflect popular preferences. Young people and urban dwellers, who in general vote for opposition parties, are under-represented in the electoral register. In Senegal, the 18-20 age group represents 11% of the voting age population (over one million), but just 1% of that population (under 70,000) are listed in the electoral register.

The opposition normally wins in the capital, Dakar. However, its majorities are kept low by the modest increase in the size of the electorate. The population of the Dakar region grows by almost 60,000 adults a year. Between Macky Sall's election in 2012 and re-election in 2019, the potential electorate thus could have increased by almost 400,000. Yet official figures suggest otherwise, with an increase of less than 130,000 voters in the Dakar region over this period, and indeed a fall of 18,000 in the department of Dakar, which accounts for over a third of the regional population. By contrast, in rural areas and departments that favour the current government, the electorate has often grown significantly since 2012. Thus the choice made by urban dwellers, young people and intellectuals voting to reject the current regime is easily counterbalanced by the less populous departments that vote in its favour.

Control of the electoral register, so acquiring an advantage even before the election takes place, is a venerable secret jealously guarded by any regime that aspires to longevity and sometimes leads to a significant gap between majority opinion and the final poll.

Currently Senegal is being rocked by protests and major political upheavals. For a time, demonstrations were called by the opposition coalition Yewwi Askan Wi and the leader of the opposition, Ousmane Sonko, to protest the violation of the constitution and the electoral law by the president Macky Sall. Ahead of legislative elections at the end of July this year, the ruling party interfered with the list of candidates, refusing to allow many to stand. Can you describe what is going on?

In late July 2022, Senegal saw the most contested legislative elections in its history. Through an error of its own making, the main opposition coalition (Yewwi Askan Wi) had its list of incumbents rejected by the Constitutional Council. On 17 June 2022, in protest against this decision, the coalition organised a demonstration that was banned and suppressed by the government which argued that the country should not be held to ransom by a handful of individuals. Three deaths were recorded that day.

Looking at the state of the radical left, social movements, and the opposition, do you think that the movements from below need to find their own voice, independently of opposition leaders, like Sonko, even when these leaders seem to speak of popular transformation? How seriously do we take Sonko's national development project?

In recent years Ousmane Sonko has become the phenomenon of Senegalese politics. The former tax and property inspector became known to the general public as a whistleblower over issues of financial transparency. He became a member of parliament in 2017 and came third in the 2019 presidential elections with 15% of the vote. Subsequently, he has gathered political momentum and established himself as the leader of Senegal's political opposition. After initially presenting himself as a pragmatist who transcends the usual ideological divides, he has gradually developed his pan-Africanist credentials and given a more left-wing focus to his political discourse.

A rape allegation still pending before the Senegalese courts was the pretext grabbed by the current regime to drive him permanently from politics. This attempt to eliminate a political rival failed when Sonko called on the Senegalese to resist tyranny. Against a backdrop of the various frustrations caused by measures taken to combat the Covid-19 pandemic, young people responded in a massive nationwide mobilisation over five days in March 2021. The situation spiralled out of control, demanding a political solution beyond the capacity of an overwhelmed police force. Macky Sall broke his silence and released Sonko in an attempt to bring calm. Since then, Sonko's popularity has continued to grow – especially among young people and members of the diaspora. They believe in his project to set Senegal on the road to transparency, good government and a form of development based on reclaiming the instruments of sovereignty, including the currency.

Sonko is thus the champion of everyone who aspires to a Senegal with greater autonomy from France, including some left-wing parties and movements. For his supporters, he represents the hope of building a new Senegal that might extend its example to the rest of the continent. For his fiercest opponents, notably the proponents of the neocolonial order, he is the greatest threat they have faced. Tensions seem likely to remain high between now and the February 2024 presidential election. Macky Sall still refuses to say if he intends to stand, although he is now in his second, and in principle final, term of office.

Looking across the continent, how do you assess the role of French imperialism in recent developments?

In the post-independence period, French imperialism in Africa has been organised around the CFA franc, a system of trade preferences, diplomacy (with French advisers in presidential cabinets) and regular military interventions. Today, French imperialism is in crisis. The relative decline of France within the world economy is visible in its own "backyard", where it has lost market share to new economic competitors (notably China). Given the failure of repeated French military interventions, countries such as Mali and the Central African Republic have turned instead to Russia as a diplomatic and military partner.

While Africans have nothing against ordinary French people, they are increasingly expressing their opposition to French policy in Africa. They want to break from a French neocolonialism made all too apparent by French officials making derogatory and often racist remarks about African leaders, African women and so on. On the streets and social networks of francophone Africa, more and more young people are chanting *"France Dégage!"* ("France Out!"). In Niger and Burkina Faso, young people have blocked the passage of French military convoys. In Senegal, where France still dominates foreign direct investment, the premises of major French companies (like Orange and gas stations of TotalEnergies) were ransacked and looted during the March 2021 demonstrations.

In the context of the current revolt against Françafrique, the French government and sections of the French media are seeking to caricature popular African desires for emancipation as anti-French sentiment, co-opting in support a number of public intellectuals of African origin. These intellectuals offer a postcolonial discourse that distances itself from anti-imperialism and remains critical within the limits allowed by the former metropolis. They are there to serve as a screen for the ex-metropolis regarding the growing desire of African peoples for self-determination. Often their tactic is to marginalise the outstanding and canonical intellectual figures of continental Africa, or to misrepresent or dilute their thinking. Some are active in developing the Afroliberal project – Africanising neoliberalism by invoking pan-Africanist jargon.

France can sense that Africa is slipping from its grasp. Desperate and thus potentially destabilising or even brutal manoeuvres on its part cannot be discounted.

Much has been made of the French intervention – which has recently ended – in Mali. The crisis in Sahel is a combination of factors that link climate change, jihadist terrorism and capitalism. What are the most useful ways of understanding these developments?

Mali summarises many of the ills suffered by post-independence African countries. These include underdevelopment within a neocolonial framework, pursuit of neoliberal policies, a mixed record on regional economic integration, failed state-building, and communal conflicts over land and climate change. A review of its balance of payments speaks volumes. Landlocked Mali suffers from significant deficits in services, exacerbated by monopoly pricing. Although this huge country needs major investment, austerity is generally the norm. This is reflected in a balance of trade approaching equilibrium because imports are relatively low. Similarly, repatriation of profits and dividends often reaches significant levels. Deprived of monetary sovereignty, and with little access to international financial markets, Mali remains reliant on development aid. And recently some of this aid has been diverted to meet the military expenditure of countries like France in their fight against terrorism in the Sahel.

In this context, Mali's recurrent military coups are a symptom of the disconnect between the legitimate aspirations of its people and a prevailing political and economic framework that marginalises them. Endless talk of the need to return to "constitutional normality" represents a defeat of the progressive imagination, as it is precisely this "constitutional normality" that has caused breakdown of the civil constitutional order. Something more is needed: a more democratic, more inclusive framework which is impossible to reduce to elections that normally exclude a significant proportion of the population. The paradox is that transitional governments are often more inclusive and transparent in their conduct than the elected governments that alone are deemed legitimate! Like many African countries, Mali needs a democratic revolution – a restructuring of political power in favour of popular interests – and also a pan-Africanist regional integration framework.

Of course, none of this absolves NATO, the US, France and

Britain of their responsibility for Mali's descent into hell. Their destruction of Gaddafi's Libya was the immediate cause of the spread of jihadist terrorism in the Sahel.

20. Tunde Zack-Williams (2021), Alternatives to Western Prescriptions

ROAPE's Peter Dwyer speaks with the scholar-activist and long-standing member of the review, Tunde Zack-Williams. An authority on his home country Sierra Leone, for decades Zack-Williams' research and writing on economic and political reform across Africa has focused on alternatives to Western prescriptions. Here, Zack-Williams reflects on his life work, including his longstanding efforts to develop young Black scholars and how he has continually sought to combine his scholarship with direct action and engagement.

***

Comrade, can you please tell us about your early politicisation, your childhood background in Sierra Leone and your experience growing up?

I was born in Freetown, Sierra Leone and as far as I can recall there was no politician in the family though politics was always discussed. It was mainly local politics, but also international and pan-African. As a child growing up in Sierra Leone, the conflict that caught my attention was the situation in southern Africa. I just could not understand how and why the white minority imposed their brutal hegemony on the people of southern Africa. I had a deeply-felt sympathy for the people of Zambia not just for the punishment they suffered from the apartheid regime in South Africa, but also how sanctions were damaging their economy. I did not have access to books on other African countries, at least not until the Peace Corps volunteers arrived from the states as teachers and they would lend us their books. At a very young age I would take myself to the library to read, not just for peace and tranquillity but to avoid unending domestic tasks. Our generation had hoped for a radical transformation of economy and society, which has no similarity to the kleptocracies that now constitute the Sierra Leone state.

What were the experiences of coming to the UK, and then trying to establish yourself as a scholar?

Coming to Liverpool was a totally new experience, not least because everything seems larger than similar items in Freetown. I came to join my mother, who was already in Liverpool, working as a nurse. She was a loving but no-nonsense mother, who expected me to work hard to enable me to look after myself with a good job. On arrival in Liverpool, I registered for A Levels in Economics, British Economic History and Government and my tutor was a Labour and co-operative supporter, Robert (Bob) Wareing, a fascinating guy, a staunch socialist and an excellent teacher. He was very active in the Labour movement and later became a member of parliament for the Liverpool West Derby constituency. I thoroughly enjoyed his classes; he encouraged debates and always had time to answer our questions.

I think I can describe myself as a studious individual and I spent most of my spare time in libraries, which were easily reached in Liverpool prior to Tory austerity. Indeed, apart from my house, I have probably spent more time in libraries than anywhere else. I went on to study and research for a PhD. On completion of my PhD, I moved to Nigeria.

You moved to Nigeria in the late 1970s to lecture. What were your experiences of this period, and your years in Nigeria? Can you tell us something about the atmosphere at the time, and also the work you were doing?

In 1979 I went to Nigeria, where I worked initially at Bayero University in Kano, and later at the University of Jos with one of the greatest sociologists (human beings for that matter) that I have ever met, and his name was Omafume Friday Onoge. We all called him "Prof", not that he wanted it that way, rather because it exemplified the high regard we held him in. Prof had the biggest head that I ever saw on a human being and as a Sierra Leonean I was convinced his head was full of books. He was well read and well published, and despite his great achievements, he was a modest, generous and fair-minded person. He had published extensively in various sub-disciplines in sociology: literature, theory, development, deviance etc. Prof saw me as an important member of a strong staff team he was building of young radical, research oriented, excellent teachers and researchers. He spoke to me about the future shape and direction of the department, and he made it clear to me that I was at the core of his plans. I knew he respected my work and wanted me to stop thinking of returning to Britain. He wanted the University of Jos Sociology Department to be the best in the country. It was full of young dynamic scholars (men and women) from all over Nigeria and Ghana, Sierra Leone, Britain, Uganda, India, USA and Eastern Europe.

Though I was not a senior staff member at the time, Prof gave me major portfolios as Examination Officer, Admissions Officer and Departmental Seminar Organiser. These were important offices, [which] if not well-managed can damage the image and reputation of the Department. As Examination Officer, I would invite colleagues to submit examination papers to me, ensure they were ready without errors and leakages and get the same papers typed [for] each examination. The main issues were the integrity of the papers in order to avoid leaks and other malpractices. These issues never arose.

Whilst I was in Kano I had developed an interest in gender study and, by the time I got to Jos, I had written two papers on women in Africa: "Female Labour and Exploitation Within African Social Formations" and "Female Urban Employment" (1985). The first article came out of my reading of Marx and Louis Althusser and the other was an empirical study of women working in construction sites in the Jos metropolitan area.

Women in Nigeria (WIN) soon emerged as an important pressure group of women, though virtually all its members were middle class, often university-based, as well as a few university-based men who gave support to the activities of the movement. WIN became a rallying point for many middle class women, supported by socialist inclined men. However it was not long before WIN became a bête noire to many conservative husbands and boyfriends, who saw it as a source of radicalisation and domestic discontent as women, particularly northern Nigerian women were now asking awkward questions around gender equality. Nonetheless, much of the activities of WIN continued to be based in the universities and most of the participants were university people including expatriate women from Europe and North America largely from Amadu Bello University, University of Jos, University of Ibadan and University of Port Harcourt. WIN was a major tour de force for gender consciousness in Nigeria during the 1980s.

When the history of radical politics in Nigeria is written, the period of the late 1970-1985 will be seen as a period of serious political engagements and challenges. For example, the value of the Naira – the country's currency – was quite strong, stronger than the pound sterling, and as a result the universities were better resourced and academic campuses were vibrant and free from oppression.

Omafume Onoge was a real intellectual giant, a friendly and trustworthy individual. He was a Harvard graduate, but unlike the "been to" (blabbers) that one encountered from time to time, I had been working with Prof for almost three years before I knew he got his PhD from Harvard. It came as a consequence of a death threat I received from a student, who wrote an anonymous letter threatening me that I had come to Nigeria "to frustrate Nigerian students", otherwise, how can I justify the mark I gave him. This individual warned that since I had come to frustrate Nigerian students, "it is my corpse that will return to England". This note was slipped under my office door and I was aware that weak, lumpen students used this strategy to threaten young and foreign lecturers. Unfortunately for the culprit, I trusted my integrity and my sense of justice and fair play. I took the letter straight to Onoge, and I told him that I had a suspect who was lurking around my office as I came from a lecture. Onoge's face dropped and he started perspiring and apologised to me profusely for this act of a student. Next Onoge summoned the entire class and invited me to come to the meeting. Prof turned to the assembled class and said to them: "I want you to know how disappointed and ashamed I feel today to hear a Nigerian student referred to Dr Zack-Williams coming from Sierra Leone as a foreigner, who has come to destroy Nigerian students". It was at this point Prof Onoge told them: "You people do not realise how lucky you are to have Zack-Williams teaching you. I studied in Harvard under Talcott Parsons, but I never learnt any sociology". He told them that all he got from Harvard was bourgeois sociology. Finally, he told the class that he was disgusted with the fact that someone from Sierra Leone could be called a foreigner in Nigeria.

You are well known for your work on Sierra Leone and you are regarded as an authority – cutting your way through much of the academic nonsense that has been written about Africa. You have helped analyse the state in Sierra Leone and the historical circumstances that have contributed to conflict and underdevelopment, and examined the ways in which the complex political emergencies in West Africa can be grasped within a radical political economic framework. Can you explain what you were trying to do and how you kicked back against prevailing intellectual fashions?

The truth is that Sierra Leone was a development tragedy waiting to happen. Throughout history, one can hardly speak of a consensus as to how the country was to be governed as a nation – both between the colonial power and the local governing classes. From its inception, the various groups and nationalities that came together in the new formation that became Sierra Leone after 1787 did not have the ability or opportunity to impose hegemony over the rest of society, due to slave raiding and internecine wars, as well as the weakness of each section. For example, in Ghana the Asante managed to impose hegemony over less powerful groups or the Fulani in Northern Nigeria.

The Peninsula, consisting of Freetown and its environs was chosen as the home for the liberated Africans whose status differed from that of the indigenous people in the country, who unlike the freed slaves were not accorded British subject status, but were deemed as British protected people. Throughout the colonial period, the settlers now referred to as Creoles or Krios were governed by British laws and both government and mission schools were available to them from as early as 1845. It was not until 1906 that the first provincial school was opened to boys who were sons of Chiefs. This political dualism came to haunt both rulers and subjects as certain privileges (education and land) were available to one group and denied to the other.

This history had a direct impact on subsequent decolonisation, and independence. Siaka Stevens and his All People's Congress (APC) wasted no time in declaring a one-party state under his leadership in 1978, thus laying the foundation for economic and political chaos that led to the country's civil war. The one-party state led to curtailment of freedom of expression as opposition leaders and critics of the emerging kleptocracy were harassed, thrown in jail or forced into exile. Coincidentally, the rise of the one-party state was characterised by the collapse of the economy and frequent visits to the International Financial Institutions for aid, which simply exacerbated the situation.

Structural adjustment programmes and later neoliberalism brought misery and chaos to the people of Sierra Leone, whilst the political elite survived through widespread corruption by mortgaging the country's resources and by strengthening the authoritarian state. Stevens' administration tried to suppress opposition from young people who bore the brunt of the economic irresponsibility of the state but, in 1991, war broke out when a group of rebels entered from the southeast of the country near the Liberian border to challenge the APC government for state hegemony. The rebels were able to capture important posts in the country including parts of the rich diamond mines in the Kono District, near the Liberian border, which they continued to mine. The success of the rebels on the diamond field posed a major threat to the ability of the APC to raise resources to prosecute the war. As the war was being prosecuted by the already discredited APC regime, a coup was unleashed by a section of the army.

Charles Taylor, the Liberian warlord, decided to teach Sierra Leone a lesson by arming a local warlord, Foday Sankoh, whom Taylor had met in Libya when both were undergoing military training in Benghazi during the regime of Muammar Muhammad Abu Minyar al-Gaddafi. Inevitably, given the close proximity between the two countries and the cultural ties between them, the fighting in Sierra Leone spilled over to Liberia, when Economic Community of West African States forces struck Taylor's position in Liberia as his troops were about to capture the Liberian capital. Consequently, Taylor swore revenge on Sierra Leone for allowing its airport to be used to strike at his units. It took the intervention of Nigerian-led ECOWAS troops and British troops, including the Gurkhas to put an end to fighting. Taylor was subsequently charged with 11 crimes including terrorism, rape, murder and the use of child soldiers by rebel groups in Sierra Leone during the civil war of 1991-2002.

Unfortunately for the toiling masses, the DNA of the governing class is fuelled by corruption and indiscipline. These "natural causes" are simply pointing to the precarity which defines life for the ordinary citizens of this unfortunate land. Progress will not come to Sierra Leone until the governing classes realise that their raison d'être is not self-serving, but to work for and with the people for the transformation of society in order to raise the standard of living of the masses. Only popular democracy based on the will of the people will bring progress and sustainable peace to this unfortunate land. The role of the young people is crucial, if progress is to be consolidated.

You were a young scholar when Walter Rodney wrote his pioneering 1972 book, How Europe Underdeveloped Africa. *You shared much – in terms of approach and politics – with Rodney. He was also, like you, a man deeply connected to the struggles of Black people in North America and the Caribbean. Can you describe how his work and life influenced you and your research- activism?*

Throughout my undergraduate life, there were a number of books and writers that I found intriguing and which left indelible impressions in my mind. These authors include Amílcar Cabral's *Revolution in Guinea: An African People's Struggle*, Frantz Fanon's *The Wretched of the Earth* and *Black Skin, White Masks*, Stokely Carmichael (Kwame Ture) and Charles V. Hamilton's *Black Power: The Politics of Liberation in America* and of course Walter Rodney's *How Europe Underdeveloped Africa*. I also read Rodney's *The Groundings with My Brothers*. Here Rodney was able to discuss with the Rastafarians in a relaxed manner whilst drawing attention to the injustices of slavery, which left slaves and their dependents empty handed and in a state of destitution whilst compensating people like Edward Colston who had already made a fortune out of the misery of millions of Africans. Now you can appreciate the reason behind the ecstatic celebrations of the young people (black and white) who liberated the people of Bristol from the presence of such an unsavoury character. This was the young Rodney, post-PhD, full of energy, not afraid to engage the brothers in discussion on such issues as black power, black consciousness, above all about the brutality and humiliation early capitalism imposed on the African people on the continent and its diaspora.

How Europe Underdeveloped Africa was a path-breaking project, which called it out as he saw it. Rodney was able to reassure the reader that development was not an alien phenomenon to Africans. The format of the book, the style of writing, the language all point to the fact that it was not necessarily produced for academic consumption, but to raise consciousness among the toiling masses and their allies.

In Nigeria, I encountered students who were eager to read the text, listen to discussions and learn about the "counter discourses" that writers like Rodney, Fanon and Cabral produced. At this time Nigerian universities were reasonably well resourced with relatively good library facilities, regular well organised conferences and seminars, which brought together students' and staff participation. I was surprised to learn in the universities [where] I taught that prior to my arrival, they had never heard about these great black radical thinkers. By the time I left these authors and books were in the curriculum and books on these topics were available in the library and campus bookshops.

Your research and writing on economic and political reform in Africa have been important but you have also developed alternatives to western prescriptions for decades, which has helped keep alive a tradition of thought that was marginalised in the 1980s and 1990s. How have you managed to do this, what has helped sustain you politically and intellectually? I am aware of your years on ROAPE as an editor, and member of the Editorial Working Group. Has this been important to you?

It is imperative that those of us who witnessed the destructive effect of structural adjustment and neoliberalism must stand up to be counted. These two Western constructs derailed African progress and far from aiding democracy, strengthened the authoritarian state and anarchy in Africa. Leaders became disconnected from their citizens as they slashed vital budgets on health, education and food imports in order to settle crippling and mounting debts owed to donors. Democracy did not survive under these conditions, as challenges to the state lead to economic uncertainty, political upheaval and a series of military coups, which in turn impacts on economic progress. What is clear to me is this: one cannot study Africa and remain neutral to the problems African people face.

My objection to what I saw as the imposition of Western

paradigms or solutions to African states is based on one simple observation: these policies do not benefit the toiling masses of the continent. Far from aiding their struggles, they are designed to tie Africa and its governing class even deeper onto the neo-colonial umbilical cord of Western domination and to make the continent perpetually subservient to Western dictates. Indeed, this has been the fate of much of Africa, and Sierra Leone in particular: policies are dictated from Washington, London or Paris, policies which are in the interests of those who developed them, such as the Bretton Woods Institutions or the International Financial Institutions and the World Bank.

In short, after years of destructive structural adjustment programmes and neoliberal economic policies, African leaders should have ended this economic suicide imposed by the IMF and the World Bank. Prior to the imposition of structural adjustment, many African countries had nascent (infant) industries which were destroyed by these programmes forcing African countries with infant industries to compete with "mature" industries in the capitalist economies, a battle that they were incapable of winning.

For me it has not been easy given the fact that my work environment could not be described as Africanist, which meant that some of the concessions or benefits of working in Africa were not available to me. Indeed, I was recruited as a Lecturer in Social Policy, initially teaching social policy and I am sure this has influenced my perspective when it comes to issues of poverty and social inequalities. However there were other colleagues in the university who were working on Africa, such as Giles Mohan (a geographer) and Bob Milward (an economist). Indeed, Mohan and I collaborated with Milward and Ed Brown – a geographer from Loughborough University – in producing a much-acclaimed critique of structural adjustment, *Structural Adjustment: Theory, Practice and Impacts*.

I also worked with other colleagues, whilst taking the lead in producing *Africa in Crisis: New Challenges and Possibilities* with Diane Frost and Alex Thompson; and *When the State Fails: Studies on Intervention in the Sierra Leone Civil War* with a group of Sierra Leonean academics in Sierra Leone and the USA. I also edited another text in 2008 on *Sierra Leone: The Quest for Sustainable Development and Peace*. In both cases, Cyril Obi was very helpful. I want to take this opportunity to thank him for all his support. He is a fine comrade. One other work that I want to mention is that which I put together with Professor Ola Uduku of Manchester Metropolitan University, our book: *Africa Beyond the Post Colonial: Political and Socio-Cultural Identities*. For sure, I have been able to work with people committed to change in Africa.

In addition, as you have pointed out, this period coincided with the decades when Thatcherism and the New Right took centre stage in British politics, a period when the nation was told that, "there is nothing like society, only individuals". It was also a period when thousands of miners struck to protect their jobs, families and communities. I must pay tribute to comrades in *ROAPE*, a journal that I consider my intellectual home and one that has helped me and others to reflect on seemingly puzzling issues and where I have met comrades who have helped me to further develop my ideas. Though I have been mainly involved with editorial work, nonetheless I have also been involved in outreach work, including the invaluable writing workshops in Britain and in Africa working with young academics who are interested in publishing articles in journals on topics of their choice, which is then critiqued by moderators from the *ROAPE* collective. I have found this exercise quite rewarding in that it helps to improve and consolidate writing skills for many young academics in Britain and in Africa and in this way, *ROAPE* is making a difference.

What does an alternative vision for the continent look like today? How do we draw in radical social movements and protests closer towards this kind of vision?

Well, there was a time a few years ago when I would have sought comfort in a few countries such as South Africa, Nigeria or Ethiopia. Right now, these countries are all troubled with conflicts. In the case of South Africa, the jury is still out on the new regime with its millionaire leader, Cyril Ramaphosa. Nigeria, despite its enormous wealth, has still not assumed its leadership role in African governance or development. To many Nigerians, President Buhari's second coming is already a disappointment as he has not been able to deal with pressing economic, social and security problems, including widespread corruption among the unruly elite. Ethiopia, Africa's second most populous country, also occupies a highly sensitive geographical position on the continent. [It has an] economic performance that many feel deserves attention, but is now engrossed in a new war with one of its associated provinces.

The alternative vision for Africa in my view should be premised on a desire to put an end to gerontocracy and a greater involvement in national and local politics of young people, in particular women. The politics of gerontocracy is the precursor to totalitarianism; its outmoded nature renders it antithetical to progress and modernity. Not only is it impervious to alternatives but it is hostile to new ideas, seeing them as undermining its core belief: age is superior to brain. How can any progressive state justify the constitutional position that people must be at least 40 years old to stand as a candidate to lead his country, especially a state like Sierra Leone where the life expectancy was only 53 in 2017? Young people can work closely and quickly for the liberation of African women from genital mutilation and freedom from gender oppression, which has meant that society has not seen the best of the African woman.

Women would make the case for, and fight to end the school shift system, as girls would be the major beneficiaries of such policies which currently mean that half of the children in Sierra Leone, for example, go to school after the morning shift has ended and those who go to the afternoon shift are already overwhelmed with domestic chores as well as petty commodity activities – thus arriving in school already tired, and finishing school when it is dark and there is little time for studying or to complete homework. A youthful parliament will help to end silent gender oppression and girls and women could realise their full potential.

Much of your work – again for decades – has been developing young black scholars, within, of course, your specific frameworks and perspectives. You have also been active in Lancashire and Liverpool arguing for black and ethnic minority interests. Can you talk about these combined activities?

In my view, the welfare and progress of students are important if only because the future is theirs and progressives must utilise their position to aid students so that they can get the best out of them. This is true of students who come from working class backgrounds – particularly those who are the first in the family to enter higher education, who find what Nigerians call *"acada"* (university life) not just strange, but also stressful and daunting. In order to aid students' welfare, it is important to build alliances with like-minded colleagues, in other words, people committed to transform[ing] the atmosphere under which students work.

One mechanism I utilised, with colleagues, was to set up a weekly Wednesday afternoon workshop open to all students who gained entry via the access programme (those coming late to university, without many study skills) to which other students could join if they so wished. The whole point of this exercise was to demystify the academy and take the fear out of the students by finding what they found difficult to understand and to deal with it in a place that is less pressed for time than formal lectures and tutorial settings. As the programme proceeded, we noticed that students' confidence grew, questions asked were becoming more sophisticated and these were reflected in better results. We were also able to attract a few young black scholars to our graduate programmes and some are now working in Africa and others are now teaching in Britain and we are still in touch. At least one is a regular reviewer for *ROAPE* and head of department in his university.

As you pointed out, I have also been active in Liverpool and Lancashire arguing for black and ethnic minority interests. These activities have taken several forms. Firstly, following the publication of the Stephen Lawrence Inquiry and the Macpherson Report, I was invited by the then Chief Constable of Lancashire Constabulary, [Sir Paul Stephenson], to become one of their Independent Advisers. Prior to that appointment, I had been appointed an Independent Member of the Merseyside Police Authority. Indeed, by the time I left I had become the longest serving Independent Member of any police authority in the country. The inspiration for my involvement in this venture was the Stephen Lawrence Inquiry and the Macpherson Report, which gave the impression that Tony Blair's Labour Government was serious about standing up to racists and bullies. My main interests included the force's policies, programmes on race, gender, young people and gay and lesbian people.

For over a decade, I also chaired the Granby Mental Health Community Group (GMHCG). This group was set up by a group of women who were concerned with the poor state of mental health provisions in the city of Liverpool, in particular the fact that there was no centre dealing with the specificity of black mental health. The GMHCG was set up to address some of the problems of black mental health in our community and the Mary Seacole Centre was where it was situated. The centre on Upper Parliament Street is at the heart of the black community, and to locate it in any other region would have alienated our members. Though most of our members were black, we also had members from different ethnic groups and different faiths. My involvement with Mary Seacole House deepened my interest in black mental health, to the point where I co-authored a book on black mental health with a group of social workers for the Central Council of Social Work Education.

I was also involved with a dance theatre for young people on Merseyside, via Merseyside Dance Initiative as a committee member for over twelve years. Finally, I have been involved as

Governors for three schools in Liverpool: Mosspits Infants and Juniors School, Calderstones School and Kingsley Junior School. Both Mosspits and Calderstones draw their children from predominantly white catchment areas, whilst Kingsley School has children from predominantly Muslim immigrants including Arabs, Somalis, Pakistanis and a few Eastern Europeans. My involvement in schools and community groups is really to bridge that gap between what community needs are and what ruling authorities understand and are offering.

What are we without activism, and action? Idle pontificators, at best, so, yes, involvement and engagement has always been at the centre of my life.

21. Lyn Ossome (2019), Talking Back

Lyn Ossome is a Senior Research Fellow at Makerere Institute of Social Research, Makerere University in Uganda. In a wide-ranging conversation, Rama Salla Dieng and Françoise Kpeglo Moudouthe discuss her politics and activism. Ossome argues that the maintenance of a façade of stability across Africa rests on the super-exploitation, repression and violation of women and gendered bodies more broadly.

***

Can you briefly introduce yourself, Lyn?

I am a researcher and educator from Kenya, presently living and teaching at Makerere University in Uganda. My primary interest both inside and outside of the academy has been in understanding the production, nature and manifestations of inequality in society. The historical question of violence and the function it plays in societies preoccupies me a great deal. I am also interested in questions of difference. I decided quite early on that I wanted to understand these issues in a deeply theoretical sense and, because gradually this path has compelled me on to more structural critiques, this has meant at the same time making sense of them in a lived and existential sense. That path has led me into a kind of activist-scholarship which bridges my work as an educator with movements and practice beyond the academy and guided me nearly two decades ago towards feminism. I am also a daughter, sister, lover, aunt, friend and comrade.

You have written extensively on women's land rights in Africa. Why is it important to you, as a feminist political economist, to focus on this issue? What have been the contributions of African feminists to land is-

sues, and what would be your main critique of the dominant discourses on this topic?

The predominant discourses on land insist on linking it to questions of economic development (the industrialisation myth). Our critiques have on the contrary tried to show the unrealistic basis of this insistence. Most of the world is simply not going to be lifted out of poverty on the basis of access to land, and yet the peasant path remains relevant and needs to be defended today more than at any other time. For millions of people existing under capitalism's utterly immiserating conditions, access to land and the commons is the only recourse they have for survival. It is no longer even feasible to think of wage labour and petty commodity production in isolation from peasant livelihoods, as all three are intertwined and necessary for the survival of most households in the global south. In this regard, feminist agrarian scholars have focused on exposing the fallacies built into some of the women's land rights discourses that continue to hold great sway.

I want to highlight two in particular that have been extensively critiqued in the more radical feminist political economy scholarship. First is the discourse on titling as the quintessential basis for securing women's land rights. This discourse was popularised by the World Bank from the late 1980s, entrenched by prominent neoclassical economists of the north and has remained unsurprisingly influential, given the predatory and unequal funding structure of NGO-driven activism. In Uganda for instance, the World Bank literally will not fund grassroots organisations speaking against the grain of this argument. Yet empirical evidence shows us that titling is less likely to favour poor and effectively landless women, who are likely to dispose of their assets including land at the first sign of economic distress. The market orthodoxy that underlines the titling discourse needs debunking.

The second discourse is the one that continues to tie the question of women's land demands to accumulation and development. The reality is that for the majority of semi-proletarianised households with a net supply of surplus labourers (compared to the effectively employed), most of whom are land poor or effectively landless, land forms the primary basis for the social reproduction [and] is not a basis for accumulation but rather part of a cornucopia of livelihood strategies which are primarily geared toward survival. Even as agriculture's contribution to the GDP of most African countries has steadily declined, the relevance of land and landed resources, especially access to the commons, has continued to rise – but for reasons other than those justified in neoclassical economic thinking.

There has been a relatively small but significant voice of African feminist scholars countering this conservative thinking, including Dzodzi Tsikata, Marjorie Mbilinyi, Dede Amanour-Wilks, Rama Salla-Dieng, Celestine Nyamu-Musembi, Ambreena Manji among others. I am also inspired by the work of grassroots women's organisations such as the Land and Equity Movement Uganda that are magnificently challenging the dominant discourses around titling, re-engaging debates on customary tenure and, of course, paying the price for it in terms of funding opportunities. Part of our feminist strategies in support of such progressive thinking/praxis has to be imagining alternative ways of resourcing these local movements. It is their practical illustrations of possibility among local communities that strengthen and challenge the dominant discourses that are only doing the work of obscuring much of reality.

The continuous shrinking of civic space for feminist organising has been a source of increasing concern for African feminists – you recently wrote about it in an article for Buwa! *in relation to women's work. What do you think African feminists can do to adapt to or, if possible, fight to reverse the closing civic space?*

As I said in that piece, growing unrest, protest in all forms, and demands for recognition and representation are among the more immediate signs of the distress that African women are experiencing, and also reflect the fact that many feminist demands actually exceed the civic space. That civic spaces are shrinking in response is therefore not surprising. But the larger question with which we must grapple is the extent to which these spaces can address issues such as the agrarian distress and dispossession that continues to place significant strain on women's productive and reproductive labour, pushing millions of rural women out of common lands and restricting their use of communal land, compelling women into tenuous informal, low-status and low-wage work. We must also deal with the contradiction that while under neoliberal capitalism, more women than ever before have entered the labour force, their terms of entry remain highly unequal and exploitative compared to men, partly because women's participation in the labour force has failed to ease their historical burden of reproduction at the level of the family and household.

With regards to what paths of struggle are available to African women in the face of shrinking civic space, I posed a number of questions that I think we ought to consider: firstly, whether the state has been successful in its not so hidden objective of divorcing women's rights activism from the structural bases of women's oppression; secondly, whether and which alternative paths for social organising are possible in contexts where authoritarianism dominates civic space; and thirdly, whether the role of civil society organisations in mediating social change is, in fact, an exaggerated one.

I have argued in that piece and in much of my work that the separation between what is considered political and economic under neoliberal orthodoxy constrains interpretations of women's structurally defined positions in the global political economy. In this regard, the attack on civic space mirrors the purported divergence between cultural oppressions, with their basis in gender, and oppression emanating from the political economy, with their basis in class struggles. While the former is trivialised, the latter is regarded as the subject of politics proper. The effect has been to privatise and render the embodied nature of the domination and exploitation of working women invisible to law, policy and public discourse. But as is becoming apparent now with not just protest but actions being taken by women in response to the war on our bodies, these spaces shall be demanded and claimed if they are not readily available. Our personal and political resources are neither infinite nor beyond further harm, but they are powerful tools that do not always bend to the magnanimity and disciplining of civic authority.

In your 2018 book, Gender, Ethnicity and Violence in Kenya's Transitions to Democracy: States of Violence, *you state that "the prevalence of gendered and sexualised forms of violence against women observed in Kenya's democratic politics has far-reaching implications for the country's democratisation as a whole." Can you please tell us if this is specific to Kenya, or if this is relevant in other African countries?*

The link between democracy and violence is no longer a tenuous one, and is now more acknowledged in the literature – even by liberal and mainstream theorists of democracy. What, however, is less readily acknowledged is how much, historically and at present, the maintenance of a façade of stability of society has depended on the exploitation, super-exploitation, discrimination and violations of women and gendered bodies more broadly. This was as true of Europe's transition to capitalism as it was [of] its colonising mission and present-day theatre of regular political contestations (elections) that is a normative marker of democratisation. So yes, in this regard, the theoretical lens through which I examined the case of Kenya could apply just about anywhere in Africa and the colonised world including Asia and Latin America. The interpretative difference would of course emerge from the historical and structural specificities of each context, but the attachment of political violence to gendered bodies would be a common denominator across these countries. Women's experiences with the democratisation project have been remarkably similar – which places the imperative for interrogation on the liberal variant of democracy rather than on its casualties. Liberal democracy is an inherently violent mode of organising politics, not because one disagrees with liberalism's idealised notions of freedom, equality, liberty, rights and so on, but rather because our histories of slavery, colonialism and imperialism and their attendant legacies (of racism, politicised ethnicity and violence) that need to be accounted for have remain marginalised in the mainstream discourse and treated as an aberration.

In March 2019, you took part in a fascinating panel about "decolonising the university and the curricula" at the London School of Economics. What would a decolonised academia look like? And what would it take for all the talk there has been around this issue to lead to tangible change in the academic world?

That was a fascinating discussion, and of course, one whose demands are invariably determined by the contexts in which it is being held. The issues that concern young people under the common banner of decolonisation are as diverse as the contexts in which people experience the weight of the colonial academy. A number of interesting questions/comments emerged from that audience, on which I am still reflecting. There are also many views on this issue that have been made available to me in discussion with my students, colleagues and friends.

For instance, one of the things I pointed out was that the colonised curriculum has turned away from reality – obscures it – and is in fact dependent on the denial of reality. The work of decolonisation in this regard has to deal with this fact. In all of the difficult spaces we encounter within the academy, part of our commitment has to be in insisting on a version of the world that reflects our own experiences of it, that approximates our daily realities of the world. There is a reality that is constantly imposed on us but that is based on the experiences of the coloniser – be it through the disciplines, curriculum content, the world of publishing, in pedagogical approaches and in hierarchies of recognition and tenure. The colonial university is also a patriarchal, phallic structure in which the presence of particular women, queer bodies and colonised races remains very offensive to the status quo.

So the work of challenging this structure and superstructure is an exercise invariably fraught with threats, intimidation and sometimes just plain bullying as I have come to discover. Decolonisation is and will remain an exercise that goes against the grain. A question therefore that we need to seriously pose and repose as we go along is this: how much are we willing to lose? What price are we willing to pay? Furthermore, if all this talk of decolonisation remains in the ivory tower and ignores the broader social and political milieu that necessitates it then it will be for nothing.

A friend who is a creative also recently reminded me that it is in the locations where one spends most of their time that education takes place. The academy is a miniscule part of those locations. Meaning that even as we challenge the curricula within the academy, we must pay attention to the voices, practices and struggles beyond it (or cynically, marginal to it).

In your opinion, which research areas deserve more attention from feminist academics, and why?

There is actually nothing of importance that feminist academics are not already critically engaging and interrogating. So, for me, it is not as much about a lack of attention as it is about the readiness to deliberately modify our approaches as and when the conditions and circumstances (what might be termed as the problem space) demand. That said, I think that a lot of what our attention has been trained on does not emerge organically from below; as suggested above, a lot of the research questions to which we are responding travel to us from outside, from the colonising world. Whatever the questions may be that we prioritise, they need to be ones which we ourselves formulate out of our own understanding of our social and political contexts. They need to be relevant to us, and they need to take our own histories seriously. This is an additional challenge that must be posed to the issue of decolonisation.

There has been much debate recently, especially on social media, about whether African feminists should anchor their activism in feminist theory or in their personal/collective experiences. As an academic, what would you say to those who question the importance of feminist theory?

My own eventual self-recognition as a feminist, and acceptance of its centrality in my political orientation, came through a concrete engagement with feminist theory. Through it I discovered a long and consistent history of African women challenging oppression of all forms. I learnt that I was not inventing anything, and that feminism offered a vantage point to the world that was distinct and meaningful and powerful. There is something very empowering about stepping into the proverbial room full of feminists who have literally, and sometimes with very little at their disposal, changed the course of history and knowing that all one had to do was acknowledge those earlier struggles as well as learn from them and then renew them based on the present challenges. In short, feminist theory has for me also been an encounter with history, with thought, with politics, with lived realities and with the necessity to question everything. That said, I believe we must eschew the kind of intellectual narcissism that convinces us of the correctness of our positions just because we can articulate them in certain complex ways. The disarticulation between the rural, urban/elite, and grassroots elements of feminist movements across the continent is symptomatic of this. We need to understand the field as also a space of theorising.

In another interview, you stated: "activist work is dangerous when we are isolated or insular", and added that solidarity was the best protection. Can you tell me more about how feminist sisterhood has been a source of strength and protection for you personally?

The sense of community has been important for me, the knowledge that my struggles are not singular or isolated occurrences. It is, for instance, from within feminist sisterhood and networks of solidarity that I understood that every other woman I encountered in trust and friendship had also suffered some form of abuse or another. There is a lot of gaslighting when it comes to our life experiences. This is usually half the trauma, being compelled to exist in one's head. Feminist sisterhood has been for me an important place of sublation, of rejecting the constant pressure to remain silent or question or modify my reality to suit the status quo or dominant perceptions. If I have found this solidarity in obvious spaces and sometimes also in the most unexpected ones, it is precisely because of the work that solidarity does – enabling encounters with freedom as diverse as the people with shared commitments who we meet every day.

What acts of radical self-care do you practise?

Exercise – I have been faithful to yoga for a couple of years now. It taught me to breathe deeply and I am physically stronger for it. Sleep – every once in a long while I allow myself very long stretches of "death" sleep whenever my body needs it. Music has always felt healing to me, and nowadays so does cooking. I embrace silence and solitude, but also seek the company and inspiration of spirited people everywhere.

Allow me to ask you the final question I ritually ask my Eyala *guests: what is your feminist life motto?*

Stand in your power. For Black and queer women, because so much of our histories have deprived us of formal and institutionalised power, substantive power for us has taken a variety of forms that remain marginalised and devalued – spiritual, mental, emotional, corporeal, intuitive and so on. We have been taught to distrust and turn away from these sources, and those who nurture them are labelled all sorts of things. But power for me would have fared under this regime, the bureaucratic indignities they would go through and if they would have been able to build such a life and legacy in the UK, not that it was ever easy. I was also seeing how shocking and frightening deportations could be for people who had long established themselves in the country.

A friend from East Africa, who had been in England with her family since childhood, completed the wrong visa form after finishing her studies and then the criteria changed. This meant she was not earning enough for the visa renewal. She had no real connections in her home country and had to work underground in London with a relative to get some income, then try to leave the country undetected to avoid a ban on returning. The thought of someone having their whole life pulled away from them like this was incomprehensible and I hoped that one day this atrocious order would end and be seen for what it is – not as an issue on the edges of the Western liberal democratic system but something that defines it.

I had a growing interest in Africa after such an inspired period at Leeds, which transformed my ideas of the continent, and went on to do ethnographic research in Senegal, Mauritania and Spain. This incorporated life history research among migrants, those who remained and their families with a Marxist political economy understanding, ultimately identifying a regime of "unfree labour mobility" in the not-so-contradictory agendas of borders and deregulated labour markets. There was a strong element of chance in where people may end up in the "stepwise" migrations towards the Maghreb and Europe that I was looking at. In the Senegalese communities I went to, the state's fishing agreements with the EU were destroying artisanal fishing and other opportunities were closed down by the long-term effects of structural adjustment and continuing neoliberalism – factory closures, no safety net, rising food prices etc. A local women's collective, led by bereaved mothers after young people were lost at sea heading to the Canary Islands, managed to obtain visas for people to work in Spain and gained support from President Wade but, with or without visas, people ended up in precarious labour. The EU system contributes to surplus labour and controls migration movements with visas, border regimes, amnesties, deportations and managed labour markets, and this aggravates inequalities with Africa, as the great Marxist scholar and activist Samir Amin identified.

In terms of activism, I joined various protests over time – the Iraq War, defence of refugees, anti-racism etc but didn't have much of a political home beyond *ROAPE*. I joined the Labour Party and Momentum when Jeremy Corbyn was elected as leader and had local officer positions in both for a time. I also joined Jewish Voice for Labour and found the group courageous. A Jewish socialist, non-Zionist tradition was being cast out by the party and Jewishness essentialised and used against Corbyn and left critics of Israel – to the loss of anti-imperial struggle, the fight against Islamophobia and fascism, and socialist politics. I was not particularly active though – I felt conflicted as someone who was called to action by the cynical instrumentalisation of my heritage by the party's right, but for whom Judaism has not really been an active part of my life since childhood. Through this debacle, it was clear how the state machinery produces class antagonisms in the most detestable ways and prevents unity between the labouring classes, and how wider consciousness of these methods and strength against them will be essential to any transformative programme. I am also a University and College Union rep.

Your book, Migration Beyond Capitalism, *continues work you have done on global remittances, migration and labour mobility in West Africa. What were your objectives with the book?*

I wanted to intervene in the conversations about migration on the left in the UK and elsewhere because I felt they were at an impasse. A revolutionary theory, as Amílcar Cabral put it, might bring some clarity. While there were new ideas and possibilities for radical change in Corbyn's Labour, there was little to tackle the imperial division of the world and its consequences for labour on an international scale. This need also seemed to resonate with the left in Germany, the US and Canada. The overall research question was to analyse what kinds of political alliances, programmes, policies and arguments do – and do not – work in the interests of global worker solidarity and progression out of cheap labour as a mainstay of wealthy economies.

As Marx argued, and then Stephen Castles and Godula Kosack in their 1973 book on *Immigrant Workers and Class Structure in Western Europe*, humanitarian appeals against anti-migrant sentiment will not convince the workers being forced into competition while the state and capital actively divide them. And being pro-migration as opposed to anti-migration could sustain divisions between migrants and native-born workers as well as the class divide. The divisions between workers do not only allow cheap labour to continue but are also the secret of capitalism's success – and left-liberalism can also be divisive.

Further, it does not help to have largely middle-class people – who benefit from the growth of the economy – arguing for the economic benefits of migration. It is alienating to those who have been directly affected by the deregulation of labour and these native-born workers are often workers of colour. It was important to separate migrants from the regime – i.e., to recognise that it is not progressive to defend the regime and this does not dignify migrant workers.

Jeremy Corbyn, when he talked about cheap labour and undercutting, faced disapproval from his underlying movement and there seemed to be a fear that talking about these things will stir up anti-immigrant sentiment and nativism. There is truth in that because of the way immigration debates have played out and been polarised to the benefit of capital, but if the labour movement cannot deal with the concrete problems of cheap labour in its international dimensions what is it for? I thought my approach may be similarly misunderstood and not win me many friends, so the support of *ROAPE* comrades and others has meant a lot.

It has been proven in numerous workplaces around the world

that working people are perfectly capable of separating the groups they are pitted against from the regime that forces them into competition. Racism and anti-migrant sentiment are largely a top-down phenomenon of the capitalist, imperial state and exists in the middle classes at least as much as the working classes, while there are also "the traditions which haunt human minds" as Walter Rodney put it. At a time of empowerment for the left that I hadn't seen in my lifetime, I felt that we needed to stop worrying about what the right thinks or does, or what the media will say, develop our own concrete analysis and go forward with it.

You tackle the abstract and utopian thinking of liberals and leftists on the question of migration, these thinkers and commentators you argue downplay patterns of displacement and can divide working people. Can you give us some idea of these arguments and why they are important?

Rosa Luxemburg's ideas of "empty utopias", and of measuring the strength and aspiration for these utopias by speculative reason, resonated when I saw arguments being made for open borders or free movement that are contradictory and unable to address the underlying causes of border repression. Such utopianism, which Luxemburg saw in anarchic revolutionary movements, can risk contorting reality and making alliances with opportunistic and harmful forces.

On one hand, the human rights of migrants are rightly being defended; on the other, it is being argued that they are good for the economy and this is supposed to deter the nativist arguments. It is contradictory because people become such useful workers, in massively undervalued and degrading jobs, as a consequence of displacements that should worry humanitarians, whether by conflict or in capital's struggle against the natural economy.

The migration of labour is not comparable to the international travel opportunities enjoyed by the middle classes, even if there are times of success, mobility and agency for migrant workers within this apartheid-type regime. They are being treated as a resource, not people, by bourgeois economics that look at migration from a national perspective and do not adequately capture precarious and outsourced work. There is the maxim that migrant workers do the work native-born workers don't want to do and therefore should be celebrated – but this plays into divisions. Why is it acceptable for racialised "others" to do undesirable jobs, and why would it be acceptable that useful work, often known as unskilled work, should have such a low value and become so undesirable in areas like agriculture, food production, care, cleaning etc? All of this work could be more rewarding or at least less burdensome on individuals in an economy oriented to the needs of society.

Luxemburg also showed that capitalist imperialism can demolish borders, as well as create them, for the interests of capital. There was a fixation by liberals and leftists on free movement in the EU, as though defending this at the time of Brexit may naturally lead to more free movement globally. But the EU framework is racist and exclusionary, and free movement within the EU came at the expense of immigration from outside it, historically shutting down established migration channels from Africa at a time when its economies were struggling with debt and structural adjustment. The deadly EU borders and those around other wealthy countries follow a militarist logic today and this militarism is a product of capitalism for Luxemburg just as imperialism was for Lenin; thus, any strategy to prevent border repression and support the rights of migrants needs to deal with the social relations of production on an international level.

What does your use of a Marxist framework bring to our understanding of migration and alternatives?

Particularly the points made in Marx's 1870 letter on the "Irish Question" underpin the book's structure, argument and strategy and offer quite a rounded picture of the political economy of migration. He argued here that the only way to wrest power from the English ruling class was through the emancipation of Ireland,

and that this required a social revolution in England that sided with Ireland. Migration was at the centre of this strategy because colonial land evictions in Ireland forced people to migrate to England. This movement of labour lowered the position of the English working class and created antagonisms between English and Irish workers. The ruling class aggravated these antagonisms using all means possible, including through the media and entertainment, allowing it to gain even more from cheap labour than from the imported meat and wool produced on expropriated Irish land. This division of people was the secret of ruling class power in England as well as in Ireland and agitated international working-class cooperation too. By this logic, the defence of migrants' rights and of workers' rights more generally requires an internationalism shared by all workers in oppressing and oppressed countries against the domination of the ruling class in countries that both send and receive migrants.

On this basis, the book analyses the relationship between migration and imperialism today, found in capital's destruction of the natural economy and the creation of racialised patterns of labour mobility. It then examines, in turn, the relationship between borders, militarism and inequality, the nature of today's bitter labour conflicts, the ways that class antagonisms have been produced through racial ideologies and other social oppressions, the existing modes of internationalism and labour struggle and finally ideas for a socialist approach to migration.

Your final chapter imagines an emancipatory or emancipated future and the programmes and approaches the world needs to promote global worker solidarity. It seems that today, with multiple crises of capitalism, we need to exercise our creative capacities. What could the future look like, and how is this a universal project applicable to the Global South?

There is so much to learn from the thinking of Amílcar Cabral, Walter Rodney and other revolutionaries about class analysis, methodology, visions for the future and strategies to get there.

Based on the theories and praxis in the book, the chapter sketches out a future without cheap labour – where peasant uprisings and labour insurgencies in the global South as well as grassroots antiracism, working class solidarity and democratisation of the media in the global North can inform progressive politics. Work is revalued and countries have a simple and fully egalitarian entry process. The logic of borders is destroyed by the decline of corporate domination over land, resources and labour, autonomous development and the end of imposed competition between workers. My thinking was that such a sketch of states and the international system could suggest where energies might be focused and could also illuminate how brutal and senseless the current order is for the vast majority of people. It draws particularly on the work of Samir Amin and Ben Selwyn for imagining a different future.

As it stands, many Northern progressive/social-democratic strategies – even those that call themselves socialist or radical – continue to mystify how national wealth and the food, devices and other goods that are available to people appear, how they are extracted and produced and the social relations they embody. Global South countries are seen either as competitors, emerging powers or continuing paternalism is presumed. This perspective has emptied these "luxury communist", "post-capitalist", "post-work" etc. visions of meaning and ambition and leaves no hope for eradicating racism either. The logic of the Irish Question remains – upending the ruling class, and a real change in social relations requires anti-imperial struggle or the labouring classes in oppressing and oppressed countries will continue to suffer.

23. Ray Bush (2022), Justice, Equality and Struggle

Ray Bush is Emeritus Professor of African Studies at the School of Politics and International Studies at the University of Leeds. He is also a leading member of *ROAPE*'s Editorial Working Group. Reflecting on African studies, the neoliberal university, decolonisation and resistance, Ray Bush discusses in a conversation with Richard Borowski what it means to be a scholar-activist working on Africa and how his teaching and research have been informed by a commitment to the radical transformation of the continent, and the world.

***

Could you give us a brief synopsis of your academic career – when and how did you enter academia, and how did you progress to where you are now?

I suppose I am what used to be called a late developer. I left school at 16 with few qualifications, and it took me more than four years to realise that the work that I was doing after school was not what I really wanted to continue doing. So the sooner I could get some qualifications, I realised, the better. I did qualifications part-time while I worked as a civil servant in the Church Commissioners, of all places, which is the institution that pays and manages the clergy and the clergy's land, which of course is extensive. So I left school early, I didn't get very much, and went back to study part-time. I left work in the anticipation that I would finally be able to get A levels, which my mother thought was the biggest mistake of my life in that I was in work and should stay in work!

The admission tutor at Kingston Polytechnic said to me, basically, just get your A levels, he didn't set grades even, and I remain really grateful for that. I thought if only I could get into the institution, I'll try and do my best, and I did. I was the first 1st-class degree holder in social sciences at Kingston Polytechnic. The gamble paid off, the anticipation worked, and I was very lucky to have two fantastic mentors at Kingston. One was Bob Sutcliffe, who sadly passed away earlier in the year, and the other was Anne Showstack-Sassoon. Bob was an incredible Marxist scholar-activist, an engaged economist in development and the meaning and understanding of imperialism and labour studies. Anne was and remains a very important commentator on the Italian Marxist Antonio Gramsci. She was then a PhD student supervised by Ralph Miliband, who was Head of Department at Leeds.

I came to Leeds from Kingston Poly in the hope that I would be the successful applicant for the ESRC (Economic and Social Research Council) grant to do the MA in Political Sociology, which I was, and I had a formidable interview panel to get the ESRC grant which was Ralph Miliband, David Coates and Hamza Alavi. Hamza was a Pakistani Marxist – the most amazing commentator, analyst and theoretician on rural development in India and Pakistan who authored a path-breaking article on the state in postcolonial societies – and much else besides. So that's how I got to Leeds, with immense excitement and optimism, which was well, I guess 1978 – I kind of hung on in different reincarnations.

After I got the MA, I got the ESRC quota award to do a PhD in the old Department of Politics. I should be grateful to the late Justin Grossman, who also was Head of Department then, who has also just passed away – it's terrible to reflect on the number of people that you knew and are now leaving us. I researched and wrote a PhD on African Historiography of the Gold Coast from the Fourteenth Century to 1930. I also had as a supervisor, Lionel Cliffe, who as you know certainly made the biggest impression and impact on my life, as a dear close friend, comrade and mentor. So that's how I got to Leeds: as a migrant labourer from London – and I recognised that work in the semi-periphery of Yorkshire, God's own County, wasn't too bad after all.

Based on your experience, what are your key insights into teaching African studies at a UK university?

I've always thought that teaching has to be exciting. Teaching has to be engaging and you have to capture very early on the room that you're teaching in. The job is made easy by teaching political economy and politics. Political economy in general, but basically the structures and processes of African underdevelopment, is very exciting and very dramatic. I found it relatively easy capturing the engagement of students. Sustaining it, of course, is then a challenge if they come with views that are somewhat historically grounded in prejudice and the ideology of Britain being the (ex-) colonial power and a notion often brought from the UK school system of "what was wrong with colonialism anyway?" I've tried constantly in the teaching that I've done, and certainly in my writing and activist work, to try and go beyond this view of Africa as the child that needs to be cared for, or Africa as a continent of crooks that need to be policed. I have rejected this constantly and it's got me into hot water at different times with some of my colleagues.

I've rejected the nonsense of Western views of responsibility to protect and Tony Blair's idea that the conscience of the world has to be revealed by how we deal with Africa. And I've also tried to go beyond the debate about governance and neoliberal tropes about liberal democracy and assumptions that African politics and society are corrupt. I've always been absolutely emboldened by students who recognise the importance of locating Africa in world historical sociology. They do see the importance and the relevance of race and racism, slavery and of course recently Black Lives Matter and how that's located in struggles in and around Africa and different historically constructed states in Africa. There was a time in the early 1980s – at the height of Thatcherism in this country, after 1979 with Kohl in Germany and Reagan in the United States – when there was a very strong hegemonic driver for intervention in Africa. Western liberal values constructed by ideologues including people like Samuel Huntington, who was involved at the time of the Vietnam War advising the US government, or influential economists in the UK like Paul Collier, considered that there was a moral but mostly an economic duty of the West to intervene in African political economies.

During the apartheid years in South Africa the US and European states bolstered dictatorship in Zaire to hinder and frustrate national liberation in Angola and Mozambique and to inhibit the end of apartheid in South Africa. The 1980s was a decade of economic interference and disruption by Western and especially US policymakers seeking to shape development throughout Africa. Neoliberal economic intervention in Africa, the lost development decade and economic and political conditionality destroyed patterns of growth after World War II. It also shaped African opportunities for struggles against imperialism.

Some students did kick back against continued Western intervention and recognised that you needed an historical view of the continent especially when, as a lecturer, you interrogated the romanticisation of liberal frameworks. Instead, I have always highlighted how the post-colonial state was a terrain of struggle where the power of the wealthy was often aligned with Western interests but workers and peasants in Africa have constantly struggled against the drain of surplus from the continent of its capital, savings and raw materials resources.

The conundrum is of course that the West always talks about wanting to help and defend the poor against the powerful. Yet the historically constructed relationship is one that extracts the resources and the wealth of the continent to benefit the industrial North and has done so since the period of informal merchant colonialism in the 14th century. If you actually understand how the movement of resources from the continent to the North has been developed over long periods of time, and how that's been moderated by different kinds of struggles on the continent, you develop a sense of not only the constraints on development but also how underdevelopment can be and is being contested. This then enables students to explore and engage with writings of African scholar-activists like those of Kwame Nkrumah, in *Neo Colonialism, the Last Stage of Imperialism* (1965) and Frantz Fanon's *The Wretched of the Earth* (1965) to get a feel and sense of the historical struggles in Africa for genuine sovereignty and to explore the relevance of African scholar-activism today.

So, students are fascinated by contentious debates regarding the hegemonic views of food security and famine prevention driven by the international agencies and the alternative food sovereignty. Food sovereignty is the idea and practice that drives an epistemic shift from the notion that food security is only sustained by trade, rather than local food production that is driven by sustainable local patterns of food production.

A student remarked at the end of my third-year module on this area that she could never have imagined how interesting agriculture could be! This was not a surprising comment for me, as most debate about food and agriculture in Africa is discussed without any reference to farmers – the men and women and children who produce food. I highlighted in my classes that African farmers not only feed themselves (of course sometimes with great difficulty because of land hunger and poverty) and their communities, but also engage with a wide array of political, economic and social practices that link the African countryside with the urban sprawl – notwithstanding high levels of social differentiation among farmers. The issue of food and agriculture cannot be separated from broader questions of development, the role of urbanisation – but with employment, not slums, and petty commodity production, industrialisation... And if so, producing what for whom at what cost and with what kind of environmental hazard in the context of the West's refusal to entertain reparations for African economies decimated by Northern industrialisation.

The debate about food sovereignty enables students to counter the hegemonic views of green revolution technology, genetically modified seeds and continued mining of African soil by agribusiness. Students are fascinated by the counter-narrative that small farmers are fighting back and need to be supported, not undermined; that diversity in farming techniques and cropping needs to be sustained and expanded, thereby rejecting trade specialisation and monocropping; and that an analysis of the gendered dimensions to food production needs to go beyond hand-wringing over the toughness and often everyday drudgery of family farming to raise questions about why food production is often difficult – not because of poor African farming techniques but because of poor and uneven access to resources, and the absence of land reform that can ensure land to the tiller. This necessarily requires students to explore issues of modern-day land enclosure or "grabs", often by agribusiness companies producing high-value foodstuffs for export to European and US dinner tables rather than the production of food for local consumption by African farmers.

Over many years, you've been part of – and contributed to – African Studies at Leeds, in the UK and beyond. How have you seen the field develop? Which developments are you excited about, and which ones worry you?

There's lots of reasons to be excited. I was privileged last year to be the Chair of the African Studies Association UK Book Prize, which is a biennial jury, and for that prize we received 85 books from 39 publishers, many of which were published from Africa. Many of the books were really exciting, dynamic, interesting and interdisciplinary. I think what's crucial and most exciting about African Studies (whatever African Studies means, as I think that's a contentious debate because African Studies itself is a title that emerges from colonial content and foreign offices of France, the UK and elsewhere). But there's lots going on in African Studies that's exciting and vibrant, and I think that I would mention two things that I think are really important for me in relation to academic activism.

One is the publication *Agrarian South: Journal of Political Economy*, which is a journal of the Agrarian South Network, with contributors mostly from Southern activist academics. It is a journal that really pushes the envelope about local knowledge production and how it engages with struggles against imperialism. The other is www.roape.net, which I have a particular interest in, because *ROAPE*, as the website and blogging area of the journal, has really accelerated contributions from the continent rather than only from Western academics. Both these journals reflect serious engagement with African experiences of colonialism and imperialism, the importance of exploring local patterns of capital accumulation and the differential impact of the development of capitalism and what is the room for manoeuvre to transition to socialism.

I think that my anxiety is around the continued preoccupation with what has seemed to be timeless Western concerns with African governance, the promotion of liberal democracy and the study of elections – usually without any historical grounding or understanding of the countries concerned. As we've already mentioned, history is crucial in setting parameters of inquiry and the questions to ask, and the other is the worry about the generalisation of responsibility to protect – "R2P" – which is very, very strong in terms of contributors at the University of Leeds. But I always ask the question, why is it that Africans end up in the International Criminal Court and Israel doesn't for its many crimes of occupation of Palestine? Why is Africa singled out? Is it because there is more brutality in Africa than there is elsewhere in the world? Or perhaps it's because there is more Western leverage over many African states? The trope that there is more brutality in Africa needs to be quashed. I think one of the ways in which it's quashed is to recognise that R2P has become a veil for intervention. That is not to say that African elites can be allowed to go without punishment for some of their actions, but that those actions can be punished by Africans in African states themselves and by the African Union. The irony of course about the African Union – it's not an irony, it's a paradox or contradiction – is that it's funded mostly by the West, and so its agenda of action and its types of intervention are constrained by Western sources of funding.

But the worry of course is the continued spread and intervention of US militarisation and the role of AFRICOM in trying to establish US bases in Africa. A kind of a foil to that has been the role of China although it may be too soon to say whether it's a positive or a negative role. China has nevertheless provided in a sense what the former Soviet Union did until the end of the Cold War. Whether one supported the former Soviet Union or not, for states and leaders and people, workers and farmers in Africa, the presence of an alternative to the US and Western intervention, the fact that there was the Soviet presence, created the conditions for helping develop and promote alternative visions in Africa. China in Africa has a similar effect because it advances a policy of non-intervention in terms of respecting African sovereignty. And that's why Britain, the US and the EU find China so challenging. China works with states without insisting on economic and political conditionality or intervening on issues regarding human rights. But I think the debate about human rights is reified beyond an understanding of what the constraints are for existing development in states in Africa. It's not to excuse or in any way minimise the consequences of human rights violations, but it should also not be an excuse for Western intervention in Africa.

Your scholarly work has been closely linked to the Review of African Political Economy, *the journal that you helped lead for decades. How do you look back at the radical transformation that ROAPE aims to understand and enhance? What is the need and potential for further work in this area in our current era?*

The journal started in 1974 and I joined in 1979. I think the important thing about *ROAPE* is that when it started with Lionel Cliffe, Ruth First, Gavin Williams, Peter Lawrence and others, it was seen as a journal that was certainly advancing understanding and themes of liberation and solidarity with National Liberation struggles at that time in Africa. The view was always that the journal would be moved to Africa and that it would be based there. But then something happened, neoliberalism, about the time I joined, and the lost development decade which we know now has been so dramatically documented.

The struggles on the continent during the 1980s and 1990s were ones that really changed the shape of what we felt a journal could do. In a sense, what the journal did in the 1980s and the 1990s was document and chart the consequences and the dynamics of neoliberalism and understandings of imperialism from the North. In so doing, partly the journal came under pressure to simply become another academic journal and it lost a radical defining edge. I'm happy to say that in the last few years the initiatives we've taken in the journal have tried to counter the view of it just being another academic journal on Africa.

The good thing about being yet another academic journal on Africa is that it helped raise income for us to stabilise the journal and circulation and it's also enabled us to develop something that we've called the Connections Workshops. This is basically to try and reconnect with the continent: to engage with an activist audience of scholars and younger people. We had workshops in Accra in November 2017, Dar es Salaam in April 2018 and Johannesburg in November 2018. These were workshops with agendas set by activists and academics and social movements in Africa. It's a collaboration, and an agenda from the continent that has focused on popular protest, with the Nyerere Centre in Dar es Salaam, the Third World Network Africa in Accra, Centre for Social Change at the University of Johannesburg and Society, Work and Politics Institute at Wits University. These are collaborative ventures to try and show – and we hope actually to gradually move the journal to Africa again – a way that enables the process of producing a journal that is more closely aligned to struggles and activist interest in the continent directly.

So we're asking questions about how to reconnect with the continent debating politics and activism. That's somewhat been held up by Covid-19 because at the time of lockdown we were on the verge of having an activist meeting in Windhoek in Namibia, but we have postponed that for all the obvious reasons. What we've tried to do with the Connections workshops, and what we've tried to do with roape.net, is to try and reduce the distance between academics and activists, recognise that the 21st century is different from the struggles of the late 20th century and that there is now an amazing range of struggles, highlighted of course by the uprisings and revolutions in Tunisia and Egypt in 2011 that toppled dictatorships.

Yet this is also highlighted by Covid, the struggles by states to quell resistance during Covid has been so violent and so extensive that we've been busy trying to highlight that with involvement in Kenya of the Mathare Social Justice Centre, in Zimbabwe with the Zimbabwe Labour Centre and also through our Africa Editor, Yao Graham, based in Accra. The journal I think has moved on; I hope in a sense it's coming back to what it originally was founded to try and do, which was to offer much stronger activist interventions and to embed those interventions with the development of how workers and farmers and peasants can construct an alternative to post-Covid neoliberalism.

ROAPE has always had a section of the journal for briefings and debates, which Lionel Cliffe was the editor of, and which I've now taken on in my "retirement." I think it's an opportunity to seek out where struggles are taking place and to allow the social movements to have platforms and voices which they wouldn't otherwise have because they're written up only as academic discourse. The formatting of academic articles has a very set agenda which doesn't always touch the main themes that activists want to promote and engage with.

There's recently been much debate about "decolonisation", of African Studies, and of higher education more generally. What are your thoughts about this?

I think at best the debates about coloniality highlight a potential link with Marxism that looks at an analysis of people in the continents of the colonial world, how knowledge is being produced and reproduced, and by whom, and the power dynamics that underpin them. That's what decoloniality does, I think, at best. More descriptively, it's basically sought to try and problematise the so-called age of discovery and put centre stage indigenous peoples and struggles over land – and struggles over land I think are quintessential to understanding the debate in the contemporary period.

Struggles over land go to the heart of capital accumulation that takes place prior to capitalist development in Europe and which remains persistent in Africa and elsewhere in the Global South. In short, accumulation by the dispossession of land requires an analysis of commodification of and privatisation of land, the expulsion of peasants and struggles to retain access to the commons – those areas of activity that have not yet been converted to exclusive private property, usually under the rhetoric of modernisation. Some of the most violent and contentious struggles in Africa take place around attempts to erode indigenous forms of production and consumption and the ways in which farmers and the dispossessed are able to respond to accumulation by dispossession.

I also think Black Lives Matter as a social movement, despite its very disparate and heterogeneous construction, has added to the view of the importance of understanding how knowledge is produced and how colonialism was built on an epistemology of domination. A theory of knowledge that effectively creates the "other", of African peoples subordinated to other aspects of humanity. My own view is that within that debate about decolonisation I would not want to lose sight of, and what I have constantly reiterated in my own work, is an analysis that the late Samir Amin advanced. That is, the best way of understanding late capitalism is to look at how capitalism is organised around five monopolies: monopolies that control technology, financial flows, access to resources, access to media and communications and access to weapons of mass destruction.

I think what that characterisation of how capitalism is sustained and reproduced – what that view of the five monopolies directs us to – forces us to ask is how it is possible for African states to begin to construct a new auto-centred view of development. A view of development that is not dependent upon a persistent international law of value that has been constructed historically to exploit resources from the continent. That, to me, is how coloniality offers a relationship with Marxism that tries to look at different metrics of power, and I prefer, of course, to look at it through the view of those five monopolies. But what decoloniality has also done is basically to say look, there's an illusion of modernity. Modernity is constructed as a palliative, it's window dressing. This is what you could have if only you did this and you're not doing this so therefore you won't get it. It becomes a mechanism for exerting power. But it's also directed as a quite concerted effort to look at the role of labour, labour migration, dynamics of energy and extractives and environmental destruction. So as a dimension of contemporary analysis, it's important if for me it runs alongside, and is structured by a material analysis of how historical patterns of underdevelopment have been fashioned and what forms they take now.

To conclude, do you have any final thoughts, wishes or words of wisdom to your students, colleagues and comrades?

In terms of individuals working in the area of African Studies, and with students but especially of young academics, I think my view would be to try and avoid chasing money as a goal in itself. It's now interestingly spoken about as "grant capture", but effectively it is about how to sustain yourself within an organisation that is a university. But universities and higher education should themselves have agendas of research and scholarship that aren't driven only by a financial Excel spreadsheet. So colleagues must continue to think about innovative ways of navigating the neoliberal university and its commercialisation so we can continue to celebrate the important work of academic activists. As Lionel Cliffe once commented in one of the last pieces that he wrote: as academics, we need constantly to be aware of our vocation and be prepared to rebel and rebel because you make choices about your agenda and the approach that you take. The approach that you take means that you take sides, and you advance those sides because of the importance of justice, equality and international development.

24. Yusuf Serunkuma (2021), Oil, Capitalists and the Wretched of Uganda

Yusuf Serunkuma is a columnist in Uganda's newspapers, scholar and a playwright. In conversation with Leo Zeilig, he discusses his forthcoming book on oil, capitalists, and livelihoods in western Uganda, which brings together junior Ugandan scholars and activists. Serunkuma details the struggles of rural people to confront and harmonise interests with oil explorers, with environmental destruction and the limits of compensation that has turned lives upside down.

***

For ROAPE readers, can you please tell us something about your background and work?

I'm a scholar and activist based at Makerere Institute of Social Research, Makerere University. I'm an anthropologist (eyes on Somalia/Somaliland), who also studied political economy/Agrarian studies. I wrote *The Snake Farmers* (2015), a play inspired by debates on foreign aid, and endless violent conflict, and media and secondary schools in East Africa found it useful. I write a column in the Ugandan weekly newspaper, *The Observer*. I have also written for *Pambazuka*, roape.net and a host of other publications.

You are publishing a new book on oil and Uganda; can you tell us about the book and how you came to write it?

We focused on the window between discovery and actual extraction, that is, before the pipes begin to flow (exploration, calculations, displacement, resettlement, compensation, waiting, speculation, anxiety and all related aftermaths), and this is the first book-length publication on the subject that specifically speaks from the vantage of point of the displaced – and develops analyses from these voices without the noise in Kampala. Focus is given to items such as food, land, compensation itself, the environment, violence that displaced persons suffered, education as schools were closed for years, etc. Our focus is narrow but deep, and we ask questions about the extent of state involvement in the lives of ordinary folks, who tend to be "the first 'extractions' from the earth," but are simply unwanted! We prioritised the view of uneducated and poor folks (by far the majority in rural areas, even when they received handsome compensation packages), children, rural country women, etc. How do they play in the larger view of things – and how did they end absolute impoverishment?

The experience of Nigeria and the Niger Delta looms large, as do many other resource rich countries on the continent, and the manifest failure to harness wealth in the interests of development and the poor – what some academics have called the "resource curse". What transformations have the arrival of the oil industry in the country prompted? Has it brought an economic boom, as many thousands were led to believe?

From the vantage point of the persons in western Uganda (specifically, Hoima and Buliisa), ever since the discovery – even with the sumptuous compensation packages to some people – it is difficult to point to tangible transformations by the time of our fieldwork. There are new roads in the area, but those have not translated into food and water for the people, nor have they translated into improved livelihoods. Maybe it is too early to tell, but also our fieldwork does not seek to speculate on the future benefits but the state of affairs as they were then. Afterall, what sort of development would hurt people for 15 years before making lives better? Part of our contention is to highlight the plight but also make visible the accumulation of discontent, which could possibly end in the so-called oil curse. The over-accumulation of neoliberal interests in the area is one of the undercurrents of our fieldwork.

Interestingly, and extremely relevant for a publication like ROAPE, *you write powerfully about the compensation that was paid to those evicted to make way for the construction of the refinery in Hoima. Please tell us about this process and the impact this has had on communities and people in the affected areas.*

What happened is that after lengthy negotiations involving local influential elders and NGOs, such as Benon Tusingwire of NAVODA (Navigators of Development Association), and civil society activists, there are persons who actually received sumptuous compensation packages. These became our focus when, by the time of fieldwork, which took place about two years after their compensation packages arrived, [they] were considerably worse off than before. We found them disgruntled. It is easy to dismiss their disgruntlement as their own fault after they misused their monies. But that would miss the point and underplay their condition as poor, uneducated people who were turned into millionaires overnight – and this new condition simply destroyed them.

What happened was that after being displaced by the state under state-citizen paternalistic arrangement, when compensation came, the relationship turned into a market arrangement, as if these people had sold their land on a willing seller, willing buyer arrangement. By switching the relationship (from a state-paternalistic one, in which the displacement happened, to a market-oriented relationship), which was easy and cheaper, the state abandoned its duty of ensuring that the displaced rebuilt their lives. The idea is to rigorously critique the supremacy of compensation; it should never have been reduced to just money. These people were never willing sellers.

Ahead of COP26 in Glasgow, in the UK, there is an important aspect of your book that reflects on the environmental impact caused by oil and gas exploration. You write about how oil related activities have led to rivers drying up and surface and ground water becoming polluted. Please tell us about the environmental implications to the region's ecology.

I think because Uganda is in sub-Saharan Africa, there are no robust campaigns to care for the environment because people think, with the rains, the climate impacts are less visible. But by the time of fieldwork, locals told us 13 rivers had dried up in Buliisa where most exploration has happened. This had never happened before. These rivers had been reclaimed or turned into landfills and because of their smallness, they could not survive. Only three were still flowing. Flaring was also happening within a five miles radius. No one was taking stock of waste disposal. None. Bungoma Forest was being cut down by Hoima Sugar Ltd, which was established under the premise that they'll need to supply sugar to the city in the wake of the oil boom. Yet as the rains continue to fall all this gets forgotten.

Your book also brings in the question of gender and I wonder whether we can discuss this. You argue that the oil and gas industry in the country impacts on women in destructive and distinct ways – can you tell us what your research revealed?

It was a disaster for women and children. In most rural areas, women have tended to be the main breadwinners – farming on their husbands' plots! This enables most women to enter into peasant relationships selling their small surplus and earning a little income. But while compensating for these plots, only the man was considered as owner and thus beneficiary. He was the sole signatory to the money. In the end, the woman received no money and most husbands failed to buy other pieces of land. Often men, in complete disregard for their wives, spent the money marrying more women, and living lives they had seen on TV. Then, with schools closed in the refinery area, for example, without new ones built, many children were denied education because the next schools were over ten miles away, and this is a rural area, with the only means of transport being on foot. It was a disaster.

Your attention to the voices of those directly impacted by this new extractive industry in a model neoliberal country on the continent is particularly powerful. What were your hopes writing this book? What does the story of Uganda's oil and gas bonanza tell us about the continent's political economy and the continued struggles for autonomy and development?

Presently, the sector continues in a long and very secretive pause. Not much information is available to the public. Agreements remain hidden, and very little is known to the public (which is typical in neoliberal clandestine manoeuvring). In Kampala, a crude pipeline project was concluded (including Tanzania and Uganda, and Total), the Total executive Patrick Pouyanné was in Kampala and entered [into an] agreement with the government of Uganda. An airport is being constructed in western Uganda, etc, but this is not our concern, or of any use to the people of the region – for the last 15 years since the evictions happened.

Capitalist exploitation tends to conspire with states to bamboozle the poor with big infrastructural investments (frequently useless and unnecessary) while the real devil is hidden in the fine print of agreements. Our intention is to make visible and permanent the lives of the poor in the oil conversation. Many lives are continuously being wasted in this period, which sends a signal to what will happen once the oil in the pipes begin[s] to flow.

Finally, what sort of resistance organised or otherwise has there been by the communities impacted and are there any organisations helping to advocate or assist these communities?

There has been resistance and negotiations. At the peak of the conflict, residents resisted with protests in the areas but were often violently suppressed and many ended up in jail. There have also been organisations at the forefront, leading resistance, but also negotiating, and pushing for better packages. Organisations such NAVODA negotiated compensation packages, negotiated native-settler wrangles; Global Rights Alert, and the National Association of Environmentalists, who have utilised their community radio to report atrocities in record time, but also keep an eye on the wreckage to the environment.

Capitalist exploitation tends to be extremely violent, but these groups have tried to push back with limited success. You must appreciate that their capacity against the capitalist machine enabled by a Museveni secretive and comprador regime is surely miniscule. With a long pause in oil related activities, and a judicial system that takes ages, in the end people are broken and crushed. Others fall into poverty, some die, while others are bought off or imprisoned. Prominent activists such as Benon Tusingwire, Richard Oribi and journalist Robert Katemburura have received threats for being at the forefront of some of these campaigns.

25. Nombuso Mathibela (2017), Protest, Racism and Gender in South Africa

Nombuso Mathibela was involved in the student movement in South Africa in 2015-2016, and her work focuses on expanding political education for the purposes of assisting social movements in their struggles. In conversation with Leo Zeilig, Mathibela speaks about student protests, institutional racism and gender in South Africa.

***

Can you tell ROAPE a little about yourself, where you grew up, your involvement in the student struggles in South Africa in recent years?

I grew up in Durban, a coastal city in eastern South Africa's KwaZulu-Natal province, I lived there for about 13 years and then moved to Johannesburg, a landlocked city in the province of Gauteng. When the time came for me to go to university, the first choice was to get out of Johannesburg and I then decided to move to Cape Town in the Western Cape.

Having lived in three historically and culturally different cities that equally have a distinct history of struggle – I began to understand the manifestations of colonial and apartheid rule to play out quite differently. So, in Durban the tensions between the Indian communities (most came to South Africa as indentured labour and some as merchants) and Zulu communities were quite rife at a historical and interpersonal level – old wounds of internal division as a result of colonial wars and apartheid, built up a lot of stereotypes and prejudices within these communities. But at the same time, I saw a lot of solidarity, cultural co-creation amongst these groups of people specifically within the working-class communities. This solidarity took form through trading in the food markets as one example – in fact you could find many working class Indian people speaking isiZulu or dialects – in many ways also defying the spatial separation between Zulu people in the townships, informal living spaces, and Indian people who were located in Indian township areas such Phoenix and Chatsworth. I grew up eating mostly Indian foods and Zulu traditional meals and most of the people I grew up with came from these communities – the tensions were there but some sort of understanding too.

Living in Durban shaped my understanding of race, the dynamics that exist within middle and working-class communities, and I also got to witness the legacy of apartheid, specifically how it highlighted, exaggerated tribal and ethnic difference to the demise of oppressed people. This, then contextualised my experience of Cape Town, a city that reeks of dispossession and hectic spatial inequality of racial and class lines. In some ways the relationship between black and "coloured" people reminded me of my experiences in Durban and helped me adjust to the political climate that I found in the city. My early years of university were quite politically different, the traditional structural formation of party-aligned student organisations dominated quite clearly i.e., SASCO, PASMA and DASO,[30] which are student organisations that are aligned and affiliated to the ruling party the ANC and its opposition parties. Student protests in South Africa were already taking place way before the Must Fall movement[s] in 2015,

---

30 SASCO (South African National Students Congress) finds its origins in the 1924 founding of the first student organisation in the country, the National Union of South African Students. Today, it continues as the South Africans Students Congress guided by the principles of democracy, non-racialism, African leadership, and working class leadership. PASMA (Pan Africanist Movement of Azania) was a revolutionary student movement whose origins lay in the founding of the Pan Africanist Student Organisation of Azania in 1989. It was guided by a Pan Africanism rooted in the philosophy of Marxism-Leninism understood as the total liberation of all humanity through working class revolution and the establishment and construction of a classless society. DASO (Democratic Alliance Students Organisation) is the student branch of the Democratic Alliance, a South African opposition political party to the ANC.

through party aligned organisation and other student formations were also rallying under black consciousness and black feminism. But my critical involvement at a collective organised level came into being in 2015 when students formed the Rhodes Must Fall movement.

Can you discuss how you became involved in the protests in South Africa, what were the major issues and how did these develop?

My experiences in Cape Town were largely shaped by my outsider status as someone who came to study at one of the whitest universities on the continent. It took a while to actually understand Cape Town outside of the university and part of this I am indebted to the student movement, the people I met in this space and the political formations that were made on the basis of collective recognition that there is something wrong with the University of Cape Town (UCT) – with the city and quite frankly South Africa as a whole.

This collective recognition, from my understanding, was the key catalyst in the formation of what then became the Must Fall Movement[s]. People were no longer suffering in silos or agitating against power at a personal level but there was a recognition that the crisis in legal education, for instance, is a broader crisis of pedagogy and an institutional culture that exists across South Africa. It doesn't only concern the realities of knowledge production of the historically dispossessed and oppressed.

So I suppose I was one of those students who felt they did not belong in the university and the struggles of other black students were quite personal. My involvement in the student movement sort of came from that place – a place of needing to deal with historical injustice, current manifestations of anti-blackness, be it the curriculum, the financial exclusion of black students, the exploitation of outsourced workers and the patriarchal nature of the university.

Like many black student activists at UCT during the time of

Rhodes Must Fall, I was involved in supporting the struggles of the movement right through to the formation of the #feesmustfall and #endoutsourcing movements. Most of my involvement subsequently moved towards a law faculty based movement that students had formed called Decolonise UCT Law, which came out of the need to branch out; Rhodes Must Fall couldn't deal with all the demands and some could be achieved at a faculty level. Hence, we saw the formation of other faculty-based movements although not all explicitly Rhodes Must Fall aligned.

The initial outburst of the "fallist" movement was unfortunately understood as primarily an obsession to remove the statue of a European settler and coloniser Cecil John Rhodes, situated at UCT overlooking the city. But as many people have clarified, the demands were much broader and the statue was simply a symbolic catalyst for us to talk about historical justice, the Eurocentricity of curriculum, the racist and alienating institutional culture, the mentally destructive space of UCT, the financial exclusion of black students and exploitation of workers with undignified wages.

With the uprising of students around South African universities the demands began to take a national front where the main demands basically centred around free education and the end to outsourcing. These were two issues that all campuses could rally behind and in fact many people saw the reformation of the student-worker coalition as an important step towards contesting the current democratic dispensation – moving the issues outside of our individual campuses and putting forward these two issues as a national crisis.

To start with, in 2015, the protest wave at South African universities raised questions of student fee increments, but rapidly seemed to develop into a more generalised movement that targeted the nature of the 1994 settlement. Reflecting on your direct involvement in these struggles, how would you chart the rapid growth of the movement in 2015 and afterwards?

The movements' move towards critiquing the 1994 settlement began long before the Rhodes Must Fall movement or the subsequent Fees Must Fall movement, many of the student groups and political blocs that came to form these movements were already calling the 1994 settlement into question. In fact, these groups infused this critique into the 2015 movements and the response was quite organic because their articulations aligned with the sentiments that students held with regards to the current state of South Africa. The radical call for free education from some groups instead of no fee increment[s] was in fact a response to the 1994 settlement – because some of us saw this demand as a way of restructuring the nature [of] education and its institutions as a whole. That said, I think the rapid growth was largely due to the formation of the student worker coalition. The involvement of workers totally changed the dynamics of protest intervention and strikes, before then students were protesting alone; because of the precarious nature of workers' jobs most of the time the strategy revolved around students having to shut down campus and dining halls on their own – through that intervention workers would then be released. We all know that these universities cannot function without workers so the Fees Must Fall movement became much stronger through this coalition.

Students and workers realised that their temporary power was in their combined numbers and their ability to stop the functioning of the university – so there were many attempts to build this coalition, though it was harder in some campuses because of stifling trade union involvement [and] the levels of securitisation from the side of the university and the state became unbearable. Unfortunately, at a collective national level, there was no consolidated national programme. Therefore, in most cases insourcing of workers was partially won in some campuses and in some of those campuses this victory came with a lot of punishment – through the retrenchment of many workers to compensate for the so-called end to outsourcing. At the moment we still have workers who have been dismissed at the University of Stellenbosch, University of Western Cape, Cape Peninsula University of Technology and other universities across the country are having difficulties with insourcing.

As the movement grew, and drew in wider layers of students, lecturers and workers, other issues were raised. These included questions of continued colonial control of the university curriculum, the continued public symbols of the previous racist state and the failure of real and lasting transformation for the majority of black South Africans. What, today, are the major issues confronting the movement and students?

When Rhodes Must Fall formed, the movement took on a flat structure and it was known as a leaderless movement, which is complicated in itself because ultimately there were people who formed some sort of leadership structure invisible or not. So when the Fees Must Fall movements formed they sort of took on this structure but in some campuses there was a more defined leadership structure – some political party affiliated and in many ways this became one of the major issues confronting the movement. There's no consolidated national student movement but, simply, pockets of students organising under Fees Must Fall. The movement has no membership, students move in and out of it, there is no organisational structure and because of the political and personal differences it has become increasingly difficult to hold national or even regional meetings to chart a way forward or a programme of how students are going to build a mass movement for free education, get the buy-in of parents, civil organisations, workers etc. The power dynamics internally have become one of the stifling blocs for the student movement. This is merely one aspect that has really troubled quite a few of us because it has made it quite difficult to assist students – so a lot of people are sort of picking areas where they think they can assist in corners, but there is not a consolidated voice that I am aware of even though there are many people working in the background in many campuses.

How have issues of sexism within wider society and inside the movement played out during this period of activism?

Patriarchy and deep manifestations of sexism broke down Fees Must Fall's momentum, inasmuch as movements like Rhodes Must Fall initially took up intersectionality as an organising theory – the persistence of specific hyper-masculinities made it quite difficult for bodies existing outside of those masculinities to find expression. Many black women found it really difficult to organise within these movements but perhaps the groups that found it most difficult were the queer community and non-binary bodies. Many people felt that the space was extremely patriarchal and that it centred the voices and expressions of male figures. The division of labour within the movement was quite contested, who does what, when it came to speaking out in plenary session[s], who are the dominant voices, when students are in the middle of action who are the people on the ground leading the programme of action, who writes statements and sits in meetings with management and who can publicly speak about the movement – all of this was contested. And remains contested. That said, the worst aspects that made it very difficult to organise is the insidious culture of sexual violence within the student movement, this was a problem throughout the country; students at a university currently known as Rhodes, black women and non-binary people came out in full force launching a protest campaign called the #Rureferencelist, which literally revealed the rot of our university space and movements. All of this is happening in [a] country that has one of the most debilitating statistics of gender-based violence, so what is happening in our movements and the university is merely a reflection of [a] very real national crisis.

Thinking back on the Rhodes Must Fall era, a slogan that went around "Dear history / this revolution has women, gays, queers & trans people – remember that" – I think students were invoking the theory of intersectionality, that as black bodies we also exist in different spaces and hold other identities that are the cause of experiencing violence. There were attempts at the time to centre these voices and for quite some time there was a power shift and quite a solid base of black queer women and trans people exercising power within the movement – however short lived. What intersectionality did was allow "functional discomfort" within the movement and make room for people to contest the direction of the movement – its strategies and tactics and the nature of demands that were being put forward above others. I don't think Rhodes Must Fall or subsequently Fees Must Fall succeeded in dealing with patriarchy and its manifestations nor is this surprising because these movements are a manifestation and a reflection of society as it is, but some hard lessons came out of this experience for many people about organising.

What would you say, and in your experience, are the main challenges for the development of a progressive, non-sexist politics in South Africa?

I think the answer is both simple and complicated but, for me, a politics that seeks to destroy gender as an oppressive organising principle is the aspiration under different circumstances. It's quite true that many men are among the stifling factor in the quest to build a non-sexist politics because the current politics is premised on the domination of specific gendered bodies at the level of politics. The levels at which black women and non-binary people experience violence has necessitated a politics that centres gender and queer theory and practice simply because the culture of marginalisation is so rife. South Africa's history of struggle is loaded with similar issues of patriarchy, sexism and sexual violence – the collective sidelining of black women and non-binary people is not a new phenomenon nor is it particular to South African history.

That is part of the challenge, that patriarchy and manifestations of sexist behaviour have been able to mutate at different levels of struggle – the scary part is that many people want to particularise these challenges to current movements and not look outside. That in itself is a challenge. This is a big question and I think people need to come together and think about these challenges, because of the nature of capitalism and colonialism is that working class and black people in particular are impacted by different forms of oppression in a more acute way. These groups must be at the forefront of determining what way we move forward – in a sense that is a prerequisite and it's something that cannot be solved by one person, it will have to be solved by a movement.

26. David Seddon (2021), Riots, Protests and Global Adjustment

David Seddon is a researcher and political activist who has written extensively on social movements, class struggles and political transitions across the global South. Here, David Seddon reflects with Leo Zeilig and Peter Dwyer on popular struggles, politics and global adjustment in Africa and the world. Reflecting on the tenth anniversary of the North African revolutions, Seddon argues that struggle takes place when the structural contradictions and inadequacies of the prevailing economic, social and political system are starkly revealed – the current period is one of these junctures.

***

Can you tell ROAPE readers a little about yourself, your life, upbringing and early politicisation and activism?

I was born in London in 1943, during the Second World War. My parents had been married for ten years at that point, so I came as a surprise; sadly, I remained an only child, and my father died when I was eight, leaving my mother and me on our own. She remains the dominant influence on my ethics and my politics.

She came from a working-class family in Halifax (Yorkshire), left school at 13 and worked in a factory, while also going to night school to "improve" herself. She married upwards. My father, who she met on a walking holiday in the Lake District, lived near Leeds and came from a petty bourgeois background (his father, the son of a coal miner, had "bettered" himself and become a baker and shopkeeper). My father won a scholarship and went to Batley Grammar School; he then became the first in his family to go to university, at Leeds, where he gained a first-class degree in physics, then went on to get a PhD and a lectureship at Sheffield University. My father died in December 1951.

My mother had to struggle to make ends meet. She sold our house in Blackheath and we moved to a flat; she learned to drive and got a job as an administrator in the local hospital, gradually working her way up to a senior position with the Woolwich Group of Hospitals, which she retained until she retired. In my school vacations I worked in a variety of jobs, including as a hospital porter.

In the summer of 1961, having managed to get a place at Cambridge to read archaeology and anthropology, my mother arranged that I should spend a couple of months in Uganda, based at Makerere College with an old family friend from Sheffield who was Professor of Botany there. It was an extraordinary and transformative experience.

Although Uganda was still under colonial rule, there was excitement among Ugandans about the future. Uganda gained independence the next year. At Cambridge, I enjoyed the freedom of university and also the intellectual challenge of my programme of studies. But [then] I wanted to travel. In my final year, I was torn between doing a PhD in archaeology or securing a job. I applied for several jobs and was delighted to be offered a junior lectureship in the School of African Studies at the University of Cape Town. My mother was less delighted but was amazingly supportive.

Can you talk about your early research and work as a scholar-activist? You had a varied trajectory, travelling to Cape Town and to Morocco on research. How were you radicalised by a world that seemed to be rapidly radicalising and changing under your feet?

In August 1964, not long after my 21st birthday, I sailed from Southampton. Two weeks later, we docked in Cape Town. It was the start of an extraordinary and critical period of my life. Already alerted to the social divisions of a colonial society by my brief visit to Uganda, I was totally unprepared for the impact of life under apartheid. I had been largely uninterested in politics in Britain and only marginally aware of class and racial inequality and discrimination more generally. But from my first day in Cape Town to my last day flying out of Johannesburg – on the day Dr Verwoerd, the so-called architect of apartheid was stabbed to death (6 September 1966) – I was now confronted by something unavoidable.

By the time I arrived in Cape Town in late 1964, the African National Congress, the Pan-Africanist Congress and the NCL (National Committee of Liberation), later the African Resistance Movement (ARM) had all initiated various forms of armed struggle and had all been effectively repressed and crushed by the Special Branch, Bureau of State Security and other agencies of the state apparatus. Robben Island – where only a few months before (June 1964), Nelson Mandela had been incarcerated together with so many other non-white political prisoners – was directly opposite UCT as a reminder. I was all too aware, furthermore, that some of my colleagues and friends were directly affected.

On campus the main concern was the fall-out from the disintegration of the ARM and particularly the role played in that by former National Union of South African Students leader, Adrian Leftwich. Some UCT students and members of staff were involved, either directly or indirectly. Some had been arrested and detained; some had already left the country to go into exile, to study or take jobs abroad; others were soon to depart. It was the low ebb of the struggle. But even at this point there was considerable political activity at UCT and in Cape Town more generally. I was unavoidably drawn into this.

In the meanwhile, I also continued to be involved in teaching and in archaeological research. But I was beginning to consider my position and, when it came to a choice between a post as a field archaeologist or as a full lecturer at the University of the Witwatersrand in Johannesburg, I chose the latter as a way of keeping open the direction of my future career. I was veering increasingly towards social anthropology as I struggled to make sense of contemporary social and political realities.

On arrival at the London School of Economics, in September 1966, I decided to pursue research in Tanzania, as this was now an independent state with a growing reputation for progressive government policies and a centre for African political activists from South Africa and Mozambique among other countries. I started learning Swahili. I joined the Anti-Apartheid Movement and the Institute of Race Relations.

I was turned down for a visa to carry out research in Tanzania, ironically enough because I had lived for two years in South Africa. This was a major blow. While desperately exploring other possible field sites for my research, however, an opportunity arose to join a research project in Morocco that would involve social anthropological fieldwork. I applied and was accepted. I started learning Arabic at once and re-registered for a PhD with Professor Ernest Gellner, whose own thesis had been on Morocco and was about to be published as *Saints of the Atlas*, as my supervisor.

In the course of your early research, you were influenced by E.P. Thompson's The Making of the English Working Class *(1968), the writings of the French Marxist anthropologists, and the work of André Gunder Frank,* Capitalism and Underdevelopment in Latin America *(1969), and of course Walter Rodney's work. Can you describe the influence of these writers on your own work, political development and teaching?*

I had already become familiar with some of the work of the new French Marxist anthropologists, like Claude Meillassoux and Maurice Godelier, and I began to try to apply some of their thinking to my own field data but, to be honest, although it was helpful in trying to make sense of Moroccan economy and society in the pre-colonial period, as in its own way was Gellner's own distinctive approach, it seemed about as useless as the other, more traditional anthropological approaches and paradigms when tackling colonialism and the radical transformation of local economy and society during the 20th century.

It was not until I had read E. P. Thompson's *The Making of the English Working Class* and a Danish anthropologist lent me a copy of André Gunder Frank's *Capitalism and Underdevelopment in Latin America* that I was able to see how the whole study of economic and political change in the Eastern Rif of Morocco could be framed in a way that combined neo-Marxist theories of underdevelopment with a historical Marxist class analysis of agrarian change.

In the early 1970s, I translated a short work on the Berbers of Morocco by Robert Montagne (a French colonial administrator and anthropologist) which was published in 1973 and then became involved in putting together a collection of work by the French Marxist anthropologists. This led to a collaboration with French Marxist anthropologist Jean Copans (with whom I wrote a joint introduction) and with translator and Middle East anthropologist Helen Lackner (author of several excellent books on Yemen). The collection eventually was published, after inordinate delays, in 1978, as *Relations of Production: Marxist Approaches to Economic Anthropology*.

Sometime later, you moved to Development Studies at the University of East Anglia (UEA). Can you explain why development studies was an important and original (and in some hands) radical endeavour? How did your work progress through this period?

I always found the Department of Sociology and Social Anthropology at SOAS, and indeed SOAS itself, to be generally conservative – a place where even an attempt to form a branch of the Association of University Teachers was regarded by the management as threatening. One of my colleagues was nearly sacked for producing a pamphlet which analysed SOAS as a "Byzantine bureaucracy", and I personally was reprimanded by my Head of Department for wearing jeans in the senior common room because I "might have been mistaken for a student".

When I saw an advertisement for a range of posts in the School of Social Studies at the University of East Anglia in Norwich, with a view to working together to build a new School of Development Studies, it seemed very attractive.

I was much taken from the outset by the openness of UEA, which had been part of the wave of new universities set up in the 1960s. I was also impressed by the fact that the Professor who was to head the new School wore jeans and a roll-neck pullover! Several colleagues were members of the International Socialism group (IS) – later, in January 1977, to become the Socialist Workers Party (SWP). I was impressed with the personal and political commitment of these comrades to the cause and with their intellectual rigour and became in effect a kind of fellow-traveller – as I suppose I continue to be.

The first year (1972) was very exciting as we planned for a whole new interdisciplinary undergraduate degree programme in development studies, with foundation courses in natural resources and social sciences as well as development studies. Our first intake was in 1973 and a small group of us taught a radical development studies course together. Key texts included works by A. G. Frank and Walter Rodney's *How Europe Underdeveloped Africa*, which had just been published. Exciting times.

During the heady political period of the 1970s – in the UK and in Africa – many far-reaching questions were being raised about Marxist political economy. A generation in Tanzania – and elsewhere – saw the largely top-down project of transformation as signalling a possible dawn for socialist change. How did you understand what was happening in the radical movements at the time? Where did you put your activist energies?

In 1974, Harold Wilson became Labour prime minister for a second time with a radical agenda for change; he also initially appointed a cabinet minister for overseas development. It began to look as though Labour might take a more radical approach to overseas development. I joined the Labour Party and became active in local politics, eventually becoming chair of my local branch and standing (unsuccessfully) in 1979 for district council. I was also active in trade union politics within the university.

As regards our practical involvement in what was still called the Third World, the UEA had already approved the formation (in 1967) of a not-for-profit international consultancy group called the Overseas Development Group (ODG), which provided specialist advice and short-course training to governments and to non-governmental organisations, and fed the income earned into maintaining a level of staffing well above that funded by the University and into providing scholarships for students and trainees from Asia, Africa and Latin America.

During the 1970s, the ODG provided training courses for cadres from various organisations struggling for independence now but also looking to the future when they might spearhead new governments. These organisations included the Zimbabwe African National Union - Patriotic Front (ZANU-PF), South-West Africa People's Organisation and the Mozambique Liberation Front from southern Africa. From 1976 onwards, I personally developed relations with the organisation representing the Saharawis in their struggle for independence from Moroccan occupation, the Polisario Front and began to write about the Western Sahara and Morocco (including articles in the *Review of African Political Economy*). I also began to develop links with the PLO (Palestine Liberation Organisation), particularly with the PFLP (Popular Front for the Liberation of Palestine), links which would become more significant in the 1980s when I visited Israel/Palestine several times with the covert support of Oxfam and Christian Aid.

In 1973, the ODG landed a major research grant from the Ministry of Overseas Development to undertake an evaluation of the impact of road construction in Nepal where British aid was contributing to the building of the East-West Highway. The team working on developing the proposal into a viable research project was lacking a sociologist and social anthropologist, so I was drafted in to assist – although I knew nothing about Nepal and was still struggling with my PhD thesis. The differences and similarities with Morocco were fascinating and I needed more perspective on my theoretical framework.

So, in February 1974, I flew out to Nepal with one other member of the team and his family and we established our base in Pokhara, in the west central region, where several roads had been recently built or were in the process of construction. In March, our families joined us. We lived and worked in Nepal on the ODG Roads Research Project, on and off for two years. We learned Nepali, the children learned Nepali, and we walked and drove over a vast region, including mountains, hills and plains, to assess "the effects of roads in west central Nepal" (the title of our main three volume report in 1976 and our summary in 1977).

As this interview is for *ROAPE* I shall keep this section relatively short, but suffice it to say that my evolving theoretical framework for my Moroccan thesis proved very effective as an overall framework for our research project in Nepal, although the canvass was far larger and our capacity for data collection immensely greater than for my solo study. Our approach was inter-disciplinary – the team included a geographer, an economist, an agricultural economist, a sociologist and a social anthropologist – and we tried to combine different levels and modes of analysis in a mutually complementary fashion.

Our final report, with its political economy approach and its conclusion that road construction does not necessarily bring about progressive economic development, created waves in the Ministry, which had now become subordinate to the Foreign and Commonwealth Office. The promise of a radical approach to overseas development had not materialised and the Wilson government was in trouble. We were hauled before various committees, and our own ODG management, and roundly criticised. It was not until a mandarin actually commended our initiative and originality, that the row eventually subsided.

Vindicated, we felt, by this eventual outcome, and with funds from the ESRC and the OECD we took our studies in Nepal further, returning several times to the same region. We produced a number of publications as a result of our work there: *Centre and Periphery: Social and Spatial Relations of Inequality in Nepal* (1977), *The Struggle for Basic Needs in Nepal* (1979), *Peasants and Workers in Nepal* (1979), and, finally, *Nepal in Crisis: Growth and Stagnation at the Periphery* (1980). All bore the hallmark of the neo-Marxist and Marxist approach we had now adopted. *Nepal in Crisis* (which was published in India to increase its availability on the subcontinent) was banned for a decade by the government of Nepal, and the British Ambassador vowed we would never work in Nepal again.

It still gives me pride to learn from Nepali comrades that this book (which was widely smuggled into the country) inspired them in their opposition to the party-less *"panchayat"* democracy of the king of Nepal. I even have a copy signed by Baburam Bhattarai, one of the leaders of the Maoist movement which would lead a People's War in Nepal during the late 1990s and early 2000s, while he was living underground, and dedicated to his "guru", David Seddon. Amusingly, we met secretly in the garden of a hotel in Kathmandu mainly frequented by foreign development consultants!

Inspired by a workshop on modes of production that I attended in Turkey in late 1979, I spent six months in 1980 teaching at the Middle East Technical University in Ankara and carrying out research funded by the Population Council with Turkish colleagues on paths of rural transformation in Turkey. I was able to contribute to the ongoing debate on the left at the time regarding the nature of agriculture (feudal or capitalist?) and the appropriate strategy for socialists and communists as a result of my familiarity with the Indian modes of production debate (which had informed our work in Nepal) and the wider debate on these issues now taking place in many parts of the world and being published in such journals as the *Journal of Peasant Studies*.

In 1983 I went to the University of Bir Zeit in the occupied West Bank, not just to give lectures at Bir Zeit but also to secretly tour the Palestinian universities in the West Bank and Gaza with funds from Oxfam and Christian Aid to assess the potential for development under occupation. I went again, under the same auspices and as a member of the Middle East Committees of both these NGOs, in 1984, and then again in 1986. These visits led to the development of several enduring friendships with Palestinian comrades, particularly those associated with the Popular Front for the Liberation of Palestine. I continue to have a very special relationship with the Palestinian struggle for self-determination.

During the 1980s, the School of Development Studies, where you were teaching in Norwich, had appointed André Gunder Frank as Professor of Social Change. Can you talk about the experience of working [with] Gunder Frank – and discuss briefly, some of the strengths and weaknesses in his work?

André Gunder Frank's ideas on development and underdevelopment started gaining circulation and influence after Salvador Allende was elected president in 1970, though when Frank – already persona non grata in the US for his support of the Cuban revolution – arrived in 1968, Allende, then president of the senate, had to meet him at the airport to prevent him being deported. Following General Pinochet's military coup in September 1973, Frank became a political exile again. He dedicated the next two decades to analysing the global crisis and the failures of neoliberalism and Reaganomics, with posts first at the Max Planck Institute (1973-78) and then UEA (1978-83).

I had the privilege of being on the selection committee that appointed Gunder, as we called him, in 1978 to a Chair in Social Change, and of co-directing with him during the early 1980s a Master's programme in Development Studies, whose core course was on Contemporary World Development, and drew heavily on his own work, including *Crisis in the World Economy* and *Crisis in the Third World*, although the list of readings also included *Nepal in Crisis*. He tended to see the big picture – at the global world systems level – but was also prepared to see development and underdevelopment as an issue of international exploitation and was, I felt, weaker on the articulation of modes of production and associated class struggle, which is where I felt in a stronger position – having done fieldwork at the grassroots and having been involved in political action at the local level. We complemented each other well, we thought, combining neo-Marxist and Marxist perspectives.

Teaching with Gunder was an extraordinary and exciting experience, for his teaching style was unorthodox – using the daily newspapers to thread together an analysis of developments across the world in each session and demanding that the students try to make their own sense of contemporary world development using the news as a basic text rather than a range of academic works. In 1983, we jointly wrote a full description of the Contemporary World Development Course in the fourth edition of *Peace and World Order Studies: A Curriculum Guide*.

He was generous and friendly to his students, but intolerant of university bureaucracy and hierarchy, and many colleagues found him difficult. I managed to maintain a warm relationship with him and his wife and children while they lived in Norwich. His wife, Marta Fuentes, had been an influential activist in the women's movement in Chile, where they met, and had a profound influence on Frank's own political and economic thinking. They left the UEA and Norwich in 1983, after a disagreement with the University administration over his joint position at UEA and the Free University of Amsterdam, and he continued to teach, travel, lecture and write while based in Amsterdam until 1994, a year after the death of Marta his wife. Gunder died in 2005.

You also co-authored, in 1994, a pioneering book on Free Markets and Food Riots: The Politics of Global Adjustment – *that placed popular resistance at the heart of development in the Third World. Specifically, you saw how global adjustment had altered the developing world, but also triggered an explosion of protest. More recently, in the last two decades, you have worked on political movements in Africa. What was your objective and motivation in carrying out this work?*

In 1984, largely in response to economic reforms introduced as part of the increasingly pervasive influence of the IMF and the World Bank and their "structural adjustment" programmes, there were major movements of popular unrest in Morocco and Tunisia (which were widely referred to as "bread riots"); and these were followed in 1985 by a popular movement in Sudan that led to the overthrow of President Nimeiry. I spent some time following the detail[s] of these movements and started to write about them in *ROAPE*, among other publications.

This interest in popular movements became a major strand of my academic work over the next couple of decades, and eventually led to a collaboration with John Walton, a Latin American specialist, on what seemed to be a wave of popular protest – a global phenomenon – reminiscent of the wave of riots and popular protest by the "English crowd" in response to the rise of the market at the end of the 18th and beginning of the 19th centuries, so well described by E.P. Thompson and by Eric Hobsbawm and George Rudé. The book was published in 1994 at the height of the Western globalisation project.

The book started with a couple of theoretical chapters, setting out our understanding of political economy, moral economy and class struggle, and then explored the dynamics and contours of popular protest largely on a region by region basis, covering Latin America, sub-Saharan Africa, North Africa and the Middle East and South Asia, as well as a chapter on Eastern Europe and the Soviet Union/Russia, but with a special chapter written by myself and my partner, on women's protest. In Africa, between 1990 and 1994, popular protest movements and strikes had brought down more than 30 regimes and led to multi-party elections for the first time, in some cases, in a generation.

What was striking, even at the time, was the relative lack of popular protest in three main regions – the oil rich states of the Gulf and Libya, Southeast Asia and East Asia. These were, in effect, the regions most insulated against the Western project of globalisation, with its emphasis on openness to foreign investment, on privatisation and on the rule of markets. Indeed, there had been growing recognition, particularly on the left, that an alternative to the neoliberal ideology of the free market – which many referred to as state capitalism – had been effectively maintained over several decades in many of the countries of Southeast and East Asia – something that was grudgingly recognised even by the IMF and World Bank by the mid-1990s.

But this was to change with what was referred to as the Asian "meltdown" or financial crisis that started in July 1997 in Thailand and had serious repercussions throughout the region. The IMF stepped in, with its usual conditionalities, and by the end of the decade, the crisis was over and globalisation continued apace, until the banking and financial crisis of 2007-2008. This decade saw the effective consolidation of the conditions for rapid economic growth, particularly in East Asia, and notably in China. Some countries in Asia, however, and even more in sub-Saharan Africa, remained poor.

Though your focus has long been on African political economy, you never limited yourself to the continent – and you have "strayed" across the globe. As we have seen, for example, you have worked on Nepal and its astonishing movements and politics. Can you take us through this work, and your hopes – and disillusionment – with the Maoist movement?

By 2001, the People's War had expanded from a local movement based largely in the remote hill areas of Western Nepal to have a presence and an impact across the whole country; also, whereas it had been seen mainly as a law and order problem in the late 1990s, to be dealt with by the armed police, towards the end of 2001, the Royal Nepalese Army became involved and the conflict intensified. For the next four years, I was employed as a part-time conflict adviser and had good access to both civilian and military government officials, as well as to the British civilian and military advisers.

At the same time, I was also engaged with different groups on the left – both those that had remained within the mainstream of party politics – like the United Marxist-Leninist Party (UML) and the Workers and Peasants' Party, and with the Maoists – many of whom were now operating underground. I also started working closely with a UML-oriented NGO, called Rural Reconstruction Nepal (RRN) whose director was a former PhD student and now a UML civil society leader. RRN gained a reputation, during the People's War, of being one of the very few NGOs that was able to operate effectively even in Maoist-controlled areas. This was largely because of the political sophistication of the RRN's director – who was able to maintain close contact with the Maoist leadership throughout the conflict and ensure that RRN's project activities were always undertaken with the approval or at least acquiescence of the Maoists.

Through my close relationship with this individual, I was able to meet several members of the Maoist leadership including Dr Baburam Bhattarai – whose PhD thesis on development and underdevelopment in Nepal had been strongly influenced by our own work, especially *Nepal in Crisis*. His thesis was subsequently published as a book, *The Nature of Underdevelopment and Regional Structure of Nepal: A Marxist Analysis*. In 2003, the director of RRN and I published a collection of essays – *The People's War in Nepal: Left Perspectives* – which included pieces by Bhattarai and other Maoists, including the veteran leader of another Maoist faction, M.B. Singh, and various independent left intellectuals, as well as an introduction by ourselves. Later, in 2008, with another Nepali colleague, I edited a second collection of essays, this time by a combination of Nepali and foreign intellectuals, called *In Hope and in Fear: Living Through the People's War in Nepal*.

The success of the Maoists in transforming the armed conflict into a political movement was in part the result of an attempt by the king in February 2005 to concentrate all power into his own hands, engineering a coup d'état, banning all political and civil society organisations, controlling the media and taking command of the army and security forces. This prompted a strong adverse reaction from a number of influential states, including India, the US and the UK; it also led to an alliance between the main political parties in support of democracy and against the king. For a while, it was unclear how the triangular balance of forces – Maoists, monarchists and political parties – would come to rest, but the Maoists managed to persuade the political parties of their good faith and, in November 2006, a comprehensive peace agreement was signed that brought an end to the conflict and effectively ousted the king from power.

Shortly afterwards, an interim government was formed, Nepal was declared a republic and planning for elections to a Constituent Assembly began. After some difficulties, including popular unrest in parts of the country that felt left out of the highly centralised decision-making in Kathmandu, a Constituent Assembly was elected in April 2008, through a combination of first-past-the-post and proportional representation, with an unprecedented number of seats filled by women and ethnic minorities. When a government was eventually formed, it was headed by the Maoist leader Prachanda (Pushpa Kamal Dahal), with Dr Baburam Bhattarai as Minister of Finance. It seemed for a short time in 2008 that Nepal was poised for the promised revolution, under an elected Marxist-dominated government.

Sadly, it was not to be. For reasons that have yet to be fully analysed, the Maoists failed to capitalise on their extraordinary success as a political movement, and, instead, became bogged down in the petty politics of what they had always complained was typical of parliamentary democracy. Personal rivalries, venality and corruption, plain incompetence and foreign interference have all been seen as reasons for the failure to implement that economic, social and political transformation for which the Maoists and their supporters had fought and died; the difficulties associated with re-orienting a movement of military and political cadres into a democratic political party should also not be underestimated. But fail they did.

In recent years, however, particularly after I took early retirement from the School of Development Studies in 2006, I have tended to refocus my efforts on local politics in the UK, and on the relationship between popular protest, social movements and class struggle in Africa.

You have been very much involved over the years in debates regarding the relevance and pertinence of Marxism as an approach to African studies. You were forthright and original in your own response – refusing to follow fashionable formulations without careful and close study. For our readers, please explain what was going on and how you responded.

I have been involved with *ROAPE* for many years and, in the early 1990s, co-edited several issues of the journal – with Peter Lawrence on "The Price of Economic Reform" (1990), with Lionel Cliffe on "Africa in a New World Order" (1991), and with Pepe Roberts on "Fundamentalism in Africa: Religion and Politics" (1991). During the 1990s and early 2000s I was very involved with work in Nepal.

But towards the end of the decade, I began to develop a new working relationship with some of those working on sub-Saharan African politics. While still at UEA, I had supervised the PhD thesis of Peter Dwyer (one of very few students to go directly from a BA Hons to a PhD) on social movements in South Africa, and in April 2002, he and I presented a paper at the 8th International Conference on Alternative Futures and Popular Protest entitled "The New Wave: A Global Perspective on Popular Protest", which in part took up some of the themes of the *Free Markets and Food Riots* book with John Walton, and also tried to break new ground in the light of the new international anti-capitalist Social Forum movement that started in Seattle in 1999, then in Genoa in 2001.

Moving from a global perspective on popular protest to consider Africa in particular, where there were a number of Social Forum meetings in 2003 and 2004, Leo Zeilig and I published an article on "Class and Protest in Africa: New Waves" in *ROAPE*. This was followed up by chapters "Marxism, Class and Resistance in Africa" and of "The History of Class Struggle in Africa" in a book edited by Zeilig on *Class Struggle and Resistance in Africa* (2009). In the meanwhile, Zeilig and I had collaborated with left historian David Renton, to produce a book on the Congo (2006). This work put class struggle in the broadest sense at the centre of the analysis and, while recognising the structural constraints of the wider political economy, focused on grassroots social movements and popular protest.

I have always been committed to the idea that ordinary men and women can make a difference and contribute to revolutionary change. I reject the idea that there is a set and prescribed revolutionary path in which certain social actors and agencies must lead the revolution, and believe that Marx was right when he said, in effect, that "men and women make history albeit not under conditions of their own choosing". This inevitably leads to a commitment to political activism as well as to analysis.

This month as you know (January 2021) sees the anniversary of the Tunisian revolution and the start of the Egyptian one. Given that your entire work has focused on popular struggle and resistance, within a global perspective and reach, and much interest and research in particular from North Africa, can I ask you about the North African revolutions of 2011. Briefly, how can we understand the immense hope and the defeats of this revolutionary wave? What are the lessons to be learned for popular and revolutionary struggles today from this period of revolt?

What you refer to as the North African revolutions of 2011 were part of a wave of popular struggle that has become known as the Arab spring. Born out of a combination of desperation and hope for better things, this extraordinary uprising – involving everything from demonstrations to riots to armed rebellion – affected almost every country in the Arabic-speaking world. Given my long-standing interest in the region, I followed the development of this phenomenon very closely.

It began with popular protest in Tunisia following the death on 4 January of a Tunisian street vendor, Mohamed Bouazizi, who had set himself on fire in response to the harassment and humiliation inflicted on him by municipal officials. Horror and outrage at this incident turned into popular protest against the petty bureaucracy and corruption of the authoritarian regime of Zine el-Abidine Ben Ali. A month later, after 23 years in power, Ben Ali fled to Saudi Arabia, to be replaced initially by an interim government and then, after elections, by an Ennahda Islamist government.

The protests in Tunisia were widely reported in the Arabic social and mainstream media and provoked mass demonstrations across the Arab world, from the Maghreb to the Mashreq. In a number of states, the protests transformed themselves into anti-government movements. In addition to Tunisia, these movements developed in Libya, in Egypt, in Bahrain, in Yemen, in Kuwait and in Syria to the point where they achieved significant purchase and brought about real political change.

For example, in Libya, the government crackdown on protesters sparked a civil war; in Egypt, Cairo's Tahrir Square was the site of three weeks of mass protests that eventually forced President Hosni Mubarak, who had ruled for 30 years, out of office and he was replaced, after elections, by Mohamed Morsi, an Islamist affiliated with the Muslim Brotherhood. In Syria, also, popular protest drew on widespread opposition to the authoritarian regime of President Bashir al Assad and included a significant number of Islamist groups. As in Libya, this led to a civil war. In Yemen, massive protests sparked a political crisis and forced President Ali Abdullah Saleh, who had led Yemen for 33 years, to step down, eventually in 2012.

While hailing the Arab spring initially as a positive democratic development, the West was also, from the outset, concerned both at the importance of radical Islamist groups in the opposition movements and also at the risk of instability in a volatile region.

There was particular concern when Mubarak was replaced by Morsi in Egypt, when Islamic State (ISIS) emerged as one of the major groups fighting against the Assad regime in Syria, and when the government led by Saleh's former vice president, Abdrabbuh Mansur Hadi, in Yemen struggled to fend off threats both from Al-Qaeda in the Arabian Peninsula and from Houthi militants who were increasingly supported by Iran.

Early Western military intervention against the Assad regime in Syria proved increasingly problematic, given steadfast Russian support for the regime and its characterisation of most opposition groups as terrorists; but reluctant Russian acquiescence to Western military intervention in Libya and support for the opposition militias enabled the overthrow of President Gaddafi and his assassination. Both Syria and Libya descended over the next few years into chaos and civil war. There is much more to say, but this would require more time and space and perhaps another interview!

Finally, in terms of your lifelong commitment to radical social change, in the UK and in the "developing world", what prospects and hopes do you see for this type of change today? What is the role of an activist-scholar in the movements we have seen and specifically in the context of Black Lives Matter?

These are hard times, as humanity struggles against Covid-19. But, as always with crises, this struggle takes place at a turning point when the structural contradictions and inadequacies of the prevailing economic, social and political system are starkly revealed. The unacceptable inequalities that result from various forms of exploitation and repression of the many by the few are shown to be not inevitable but the result of modes of production and ways of life that must change dramatically if we are all to emerge from the pandemic and have any prospect of sustainable development in a world whose resources we have so mercilessly and recklessly exploited and degraded in our greed and lack of concern for the consequences of our actions. There must be a better way!

In this context, our role as activist-scholars, as you put it, is to combine theory and practice, recognising our own position – in my case as a white middle-class older male – in the prevailing social, economic and political context (at local, national and international levels) and to assess when, where and how best to contribute to progressive movements and organisations. Those of us with a particular historical and ongoing involvement with Africa need to make sure that we work as closely as possible with African intellectuals and political activists on the left and provide whatever appropriate input we can.

But we also need to recognise that Black Lives Matter provides us with new personal and political challenges, as well as opportunities for contributions in our own countries and specific local locations – in my case in Norfolk and South London, in England, the UK and Europe – which investigate and interrogate the complexity of both European and British imperialism and colonialism, and their heritage in Britain as well as other parts of the world, and also their contemporary features.

Part III: Militants at Work

27. Abioudun Olamosu (2017), *Looking Back to Move Forward*

Abiodun Olamosu is a leading Marxist activist in Nigeria and the Senior Researcher and Coordinator of the Centre for Social Policy and Labour Research. Here, Olamosu talks to Leo Zeilig about his early activism, the challenges for the radical left, Marxism and politics in contemporary Nigeria. As he explains,

> [R]eforms of capitalism are not a new phenomenon in our political economic history. What differentiates revolutionary socialists from reformists is that the latter believe in reform as an end in itself, and in order to avoid revolution from below. In contrast, revolutionaries see reforms as a means to an end. We believe that the only lasting reform will be achieved with socialist revolution – all other reforms are eventually clawed back.

***

Can you please tell ROAPE something about yourself, your early politicisation and activism in Nigeria?

I was born in Ikere Ekiti in the Western part of Nigeria into a middle class, polygamous family. My father was a cocoa farmer and produce buyer. He was also a politician by vocation. I started my schooling aged six and attended the Local Authority Primary School and African Church Comprehensive High School, Ikere Ekiti. I worked after leaving school, in 1977, with the then Ondo State Military Governor's Office and the newly established Federal Government agency, the Public Complaints Commission which fulfilled the role of an ombudsman.

It was at this time that I became politically conscious. I had the advantage of being able to read almost all the daily papers as I stayed with an uncle who headed the Ondo State Ministry of Justice (and was later a high court judge). He usually brought home all the day's newspapers. As the result of the delay to my high school examination – West Africa School Certificate – due to examination malpractices, I was very curious for any news related to the scam and the proceedings of the judicial commission that was instituted to investigate it. The period was also characterised by the political transition to the civilian Second Republic in 1979. All these events I followed through my readings of the papers. I hardly missed any of the political campaigns taking place at the time.

I later received admission to the Polytechnic Ibadan for a two-year diploma course in insurance from 1980 to 1982. Apart from the reputation of the school for producing professionals in various fields, the Polytechnic was also notable for its political inclination. I joined the student Marxist-Socialist Youth Movement immediately when I enrolled.

The organisation was an affiliate of the Comrade Ola Oni-led Socialist Working People's Party (SWPP) based in the town. The group had sought registration in 1979 in order to participate in the elections but was not registered despite its mass following. Ola Oni was instrumental in ridding myself of illusions in Chief Obafemi Awolowo and his welfarist oriented party. Ola Oni was very critical of this leading politician as a hurdle on the path to building a revolutionary movement.

Can you speak more broadly about the Nigerian radical left in the 1970s and your political involvement?

On finishing at the Polytechnic, I got a job in an insurance company in Ibadan and this gave me the opportunity to participate in the activities of Socialist Working People's Party beyond the campus. After three years at the company, I was sacked for unionising the company. When the SWPP got to know about my plight a discussion was held with me to persuade me to serve as the administrative officer of the organisation. I worked directly under the supervision of Comrade Ola Oni for the next two years.

I then proceeded to the University of Jos to study sociology in 1988. My decision to go as far as Jos was due to information I received from a friend that it was one of the two departments of sociology where Marxist sociology was predominant, the other was Ahmadu Bello University, Zaria. Once I arrived in Jos I found this was true as most of the lecturers were socialist inclined.

Before I left Ibadan, there had been a robust debate within the SWPP that ultimately led to the break of the organisation along two trends of Trotskyism and non-Trotskyism. In fact, it was on an earlier visit to Jos that I made my mind ultimately for Trotskyism based on my readings in the Jos City library. I worked throughout my student days at the University of Jos on the side of the Trotskyites. I therefore brought the SWPP to Jos and to the entire north while working within [the] Movement for the Advancement of African Society (MAAS).

I met the MAAS on the ground when I started as a student at the University of Jos. Jos had no revolutionary tradition of note compared to Ibadan, but MAAS later became one of the most vibrant student groups.

The organisation organised public programmes such as workshops and public lectures to raise the political consciousness of the mass of the students. Youth-Students Solidarity Against Apartheid South Africa was to serve as the public front of the organisation addressing such issues as apartheid in South Africa and other contemporary issues in Africa. Both organisations became mass organisations. The school also hosted the National Association of Nigerian Students' national secretariat in 1991.

The campaign for Academic Reform was led successfully by the Marxist students on campus. I became a victim of the struggle, like other Marxist students, except that I was the only final year student expelled at the time and my project was marked as a resit. The leaders of the movement in Jos, including myself, were also charged by a Miscellaneous Offence Tribunal for allegedly committing arson.

The Lagos Branch of the SWPP had transformed into an organisation referred to by the paper's name – Labour Militant – which was linked to the British organisation of the same name. After graduation, and on finishing a compulsory national youth service programme in May 1993, I became the full-time organiser of the organisation for the north of Nigeria for the whole of 1990s.

At another time, the workers I was organising in Coca-Cola were caught with campaign materials against the Ibrahim Babangida military junta. This regime did not want to leave office and shifted the transition timetable three times. The workers, including the union chairperson, Comrade Tukura, were taken to the air force headquarters in Makurdi, Benue State, where they were detained for weeks.

The June 12 Movement in 1993 arose from the annulment of the presidential elections on that date. This struggle was to last for seven years, during which time I worked on the platform of both Labour Militant and the National Conscience Party – including United Action for Democracy and Joint Action Committee of Nigeria (JACON) – fighting to put an end to military rule. I was arrested and detained on three occasions with some other activists and friends at different times in Kano and Ibadan.

I eventually resigned from the Executive Council of Labour Militant in 2000 and left the organisation. I became the National Administrative Secretary of the mass based National Conscience Party in 2001 and formed the Socialist League together with Comrade Femi Aborisade in the same year.

JACON was a collective of pro-democracy groups – including the NCP (National Conscience Party) – to maximise pressure on the ruling class and international community. The left faction of this organisation refused to participate in Abdulsallam Abubakar's transition after the death of the military dictator Sani Abacha. We only participated in electoral politics four years later when civilian rule was already in place. I was the national administrative secretary of the NCP during the process of registration of the party with the Independent National Electoral Commission in 2003. I also contested as the deputy governorship candidate on the platform of the party in Oyo State in the same year.

What did you do after 2003 and your campaign for the NCP?

From 2003 to 2011 I worked as an organiser, researcher and administrator in the distributive and banking unions. I ultimately held the position of deputy secretary general. I also led the Socialist League until its merger to form the Socialist Workers League and served as the editor of its paper, *Socialist Worker*.

My present work is in the area of research as I serve as the senior researcher and coordinator of the Centre for Social Policy and Labour Research. This organisation is developing a database on labour related matters and conducts research, education and training on labour rights and other labour related developmental policies. Political education is central in the work of the organisation and we organise study groups with workers and other working people in the factories, communities and schools. We have been able to carry out many research works that remain to be published.

Historically, how would you chart the development of the Nigeria labour movement?

The origin of the organised labour movement in Nigeria can be traced back to 1897 when the first reported workers' strike took place in Lagos. Trade unions did not emerge officially until the formation of [the] Civil Service Workers' Union in 1912. The left in the Nigerian labour movement first developed in the 1930s. This corresponded with the period of global economic crisis which was noted for appalling working conditions with real wages lagging behind inflation. On top of this was the racial discrimination by the colonial ruling class against black workers. Austerity measures were imposed by the government. The 1945 workers' agitation demanding a cost of living allowance was to wake up the government over the increase in inflation. Even when the home government in Britain acceded to this demand, blacks in employment were excluded while their white counterparts were paid. Their demand was only met later after the strike. Such events as this further radicalised the movement and ultimately caused a break from the existing conservative union and labour centres and this resulted in militant workers forming their own unions.

Also, the Second World War was another factor in the radicalisation of politics and the labour movement. Many black soldiers were recruited from Nigeria and this exposed them to politics overseas. This included the nationalist struggle for self-determination and socialism in other parts of the world. Some were also influenced by the socialist ideology of left oriented soldiers from Europe.

Mokwugo Okoye was a typical example. He became a moving force of the Zikist Movement on returning from the war and took the nationalist struggle to greater heights. Left politics led the decolonisation struggle in Nigeria. The way and manner in which this force subsumed itself into the National Council of Nigeria and the Cameroons led by the educated elite and nationalist politicians, cannot be dissociated from the politics of international diplomacy played by the former Soviet Union in negotiations with Britain in the course of the war.

Many labour activists in Nigeria looked up to the Soviet Union as a country to emulate. So its leaders had great influence and persuaded their supporters in Nigeria to follow the path of nationalism rather than a more revolutionary path. The tragedy of the movement could be seen later when the Socialist Party of Workers and Farmers was formed in 1963 and a split came a year later with the emergence of a Labour Party.

The 1964 general strike for an increase in the minimum wage

was led by the Joint Action Committee. This was an expression of the vibrancy of the Nigerian labour movement as the various factions of the movement came together when it mattered most to fight a common enemy. However, the military came to divide the movement along ethnic lines supporting the warring factions of the Civil War of 1967-1970.

University students became the heroes of radical politics in the 1970s and 1980s. In 1981, labour opened the decade with a general strike demanding a 120 naira per month minimum wage. Other mass protests included anti-SAP protests[31] – from 1986 – and the rage against the hike in the price of oil. Political movements for regime change and an end to military rule pervaded the 1990s. Over the last decade and a half since the end of military rule, the labour movement has been involved in trying to address the devastating effects of neoliberal policies on the working people.

The current challenges facing the labour movement and the leftists in Nigeria include the policy of privatisation and commercialisation that make it difficult to fight against retrenchment, restructuring and the downsizing of workers. This raises the issue of the proper role for working-class organisations in challenging the ruling class politically, as well as through the trade union economic struggles. The labour bureaucrats are resisting playing a leading role as they see this as a threat to their privileged positions. The era of globalisation is also noted for de-unionisation and weakening of working class solidarity.

In 2015 a new government was elected to much international fanfare. The previous military leader, now president, Muhammadu Buhari promised reforms and an anti-corruption drive. Can you describe the period?

The changes taking place in Nigeria can be understood from the perspective of the absence of working class alternatives, but those previously in power also failed and therefore totally lost out in the reckoning of the people. This explains why a new group of the

---

31 SAP here refers to the Structural Adjustment Program enforced by the IMF.

ruling class was given the opportunity to rule. Muhammadu Buhari fits perfectly well into such a vacuum, as there was an illusion [around] him – by certain sections of the Nigerian populace – for his character and anti-corruption stand. How he will be able to meet up with his promise of reforming capitalism in the face of challenges facing the people is yet to be seen. His anti-imperialist posturing is now being questioned due to his withdrawal of the oil subsidy, devaluation and support for privatisation and liberalisation of the economy.

If I can speak a little more generally and theoretically: reforms of capitalism are not a new phenomenon in our political economic history. What differentiates socialists from reformists is that the latter believe in reform as an end in itself, especially in order to avoid revolution from below. In contrast, socialists see reforms as a means to an end. We believe that the only lasting reform will be achieved with socialist revolution – all other reforms are eventually clawed back. Reforms are usually only available during periods of economic boom when enough wealth is available to carry out welfare programmes. So it might be difficult for the present government to achieve its promised reforms in a period of recession, whatever might be its intention. In a situation where the economy is in shambles and has been handed over to market forces, it would be a fantasy to expect that any kind of reform could be carried out successfully.

How would you characterise the challenges in Nigeria today for a radical political and economic alternative?

In the course of Nigeria's political and economic history, its people have been subject to exploitation and oppression by various elites. This brought many problems including corruption by the ruling elites, social inequality, debt burden, capital flight, cases of poor health and diseases including HIV/AIDS and air pollution, over-dependence on a monoculture of commodity production – oil – huge imports of unnecessary goods and services for the elite.

While the government has continued the policy of neoliberalism that emphasises cutting spending on education, health, electricity, water, transportation, agriculture and so on

The blows of neoliberalism weakened the labour movement in the course of rationalising the workforce. Trade unions [were] made voluntary by law, so workers were no longer automatically made members of a union with compulsory check-off dues. Also, we saw state interference in the affairs of the union. This reached its climax when the state dissolved the Nigerian Labour Congress, and affiliated unions, NUPENG, PENGASSAN, NUNS, NANS,[32] and terminated the appointment of Academic Staff Union of Universities presidents and other leaders for their role in their union activities. Generally, neoliberalism wildly increased poverty of working people – for this reason many turned to forms of corruption as a coping strategy rather than the revolutionary path.

Until 1999, the military dominated the political space. The failure of the system is responsible for the growth of ethnic-religious nationalism such as militant groups in the oil producing Niger Delta and Islamic groups like Boko Haram insurgents in the Northeast.

The way the country is structured and organised by capitalism is largely responsible for the attendant perennial problems that seem to defy solution – politically this has been described as "pipeline politics" by the American scholar Michael Watts. The poor are the victims of the problems highlighted above as the ruling elites are not affected, but are beneficiaries, despite their rhetoric of trying to associate with the poor. This is the very reason that the working class alternative is the solution to the ruling agenda that has failed us over the years.

There is, therefore, the need to develop a real pro-poor alternative in the arena of mainstream electoral politics, and for the

---

[32] The unions listed are as follows: Nigeria Union of Petroleum and Natural Gas Workers (NUPENG), Petroleum and Natural Gas Senior Staff Association of Nigeria (PENGASSAN), National Union of Nigerian Students (NUNS) and the National Association of Nigerian Students (NANS).

working class to mobilise even if only to measure their numerical strength. A well-organised party of the popular classes has ample chances of winning an election, as the ruling parties have shown over time their incapability to rule.

The cause of struggle and solidarity with others will go a long way to foster unity among the working people. The ongoing economic recession resulting from overproduction of oil poses a clear case of the problem of international capitalism. So the solution should be sought from this premise. This explains why we are canvassing for a system of common ownership of the means of production that will be democratically controlled and managed from below.

The history of the Nigerian left and Marxist scholarship in the country has recently been the focus of a new book in Adam Mayer's Naija Marxisms: Revolutionary Thought in Nigeria *(2016), which is an important volume in this discussion of the left. What's your assessment of the book and the history it describes?*

The book is a welcome contribution on the Nigerian left and its contribution to Marxism. It can best be described as a compendium. Nevertheless, I would have expected the author to look at the contributions of Marxists in Nigeria from the point of view of the various Marxist organisations that existed. So, for example, we have great Marxists contributions coming from various organisations, across different traditions. It is only by doing this [that we] can avoid lionising the legal Marxists as representing all Nigerian Marxists. For instance, the author singled out Nkenna Nzimiro as the only Marxist anthropologist in the country while referring to Nzimiro's PhD thesis which was devoid of class analysis. So the question to ask is where does he place Omafume Onoge, an activist and social anthropologist, whose PhD thesis was on [the] Aiyetoro communist community in the present Ondo State. As important as the book is, there are gaps that have to be noted and acknowledged.

The book also gets it wrong in putting the blame for not being revolutionary enough on some of the independent African countries that held allegiance to [the] former Soviet Union. Yet the reason for this was the Stalinist stronghold on the policies of these independent left-leaning states and its leaders. In reality, they worked as a brake on the emergence of independent working class politics in these countries – as these movements were blocked or suppressed in the former Soviet Union and Eastern Europe.

The degeneration of the former Soviet Union in the years after 1917 meant that the country did not tolerate independent socialist and revolutionary movements that would not be subservient to its dictates and could not be controlled. And this was also the very reason they tolerated both the state and labour movement, including bureaucratic Nigerian labour leaders, who betrayed the working class as long as "diplomatic interests" were being served. However, Mayer's book is a valuable and important volume that will serve to educate people on the rich and varied tradition of Nigerian Marxism.

How would you describe the weaknesses of the revolutionary and radical left in Nigeria, despite a militant working class and a rich tradition of Marxist politics? Also, can you say something about the influence of the region and the continent on left politics in Nigeria?

The reasons are complex. A great number of the revolutionary left were drawn from the universities across the country as students and teachers, some of them embraced the ideas of Marxism in their scholarship for career purposes rather than for its revolutionary politics. This was partly because Marxist scholarship had been made popular by its pioneers such as Ola Oni. Another factor was the influence of the various camps, Stalinist Russia, China, North Korea, Cuba, etc, with groups and activists receiving financial assistance from these sources and seeking their patronage.

In addition, the opportunism in the leadership of the left which did not allow for internal democracy in the conduct of the affairs of the movements and parties. Also, the tendency of trade union leaders to look to themselves – rather than the rank and file – caused serious harm to the movement. Union leaders are petty bourgeois in orientation, their connection to the state and authorities cripples our struggles, and their privileged position within the labour movement distances them from the realities of working class life and struggles.

Turning specifically to Africa, during the Nkrumah era, despite the fact that his arch enemies were the Nigerian ruling class, he garnered [a] substantial following among the revolutionary left for his pan-Africanist ideas. This had an influence on us – also in South Africa, where the support and solidarity for their struggles came from the revolutionary movement here, as I have already indicated.

Returning to the weaknesses of the left, we have to step back more than two decades. Despite the limitation of Stalinist Russia and other state-capitalist countries in the East, they were still a source of hope to many working people. So this accounts, in large part, for the collapse of left movements in Nigeria and internationally when these regimes crumbled – you'll remember that most socialists thought an end had come to the left internationally in the early 1990s. One can also mention the orientation of left parties who saw building movement from above as a solution, rather than the ones that would involve the rank and file fighting from below. From these weaknesses comes the challenges for the Nigerian left today.

28. Nnimmo Bassey (2021), Extraction-Driven Devastation

Nnimmo Bassey is a Nigerian environmental activist, author and poet. He is director of the ecological think-tank, Health of Mother Earth Foundation, based in Nigeria. In early 2021, anti-extractivist struggles won two major legal victories against Shell Oil's operations in Nigeria. These wins represent decades of community organising on the part of Niger Delta activists and residents. *ROAPE*'s Lee Wengraf talks with Bassey about oil, activism and Shell.

***

In recent weeks [March 2021], we've seen two significant legal defeats for Shell Oil. Both clearly represent victories for the farmers and fisherfolk living for decades amidst ecological destruction in the Niger Delta. In both, the question of whether a foreign-owned multinational can be held responsible for its actions in a country where it's extracting resources is important. Could you speak about the importance of these cases and what these victories represent for Niger Delta communities and the struggle against extraction?

The victories are extremely significant, especially because they almost reinforce one another. After so many years, Shell has been in denial and refused to accept responsibility for pollution that was clearly not caused by a third party [i.e., sabotage]. So it was such a big relief that the appeals court in the Netherlands found that Shell had to compensate for traumas impacted by pollution that have been caused since 2004 and 2005. And then the Supreme Court ruling in the UK is extremely significant because that clearly stated that there's no way to hide for transnational corporations like Shell. When they pollute in Nigeria, they can be held to account in the courts in their own backyard.

So that's a victory for victims in Nigeria and elsewhere because often corporations behave like they can do anything, they are extremely colonial in their approach to extractive activities. So this one brings justice to the people. It's like a breath of fresh air for the people who have been choking on fossil fuel fumes over the years. And it should also be an incentive for oil companies to behave better.

As you say, in the Dutch case, the spills go back as far as 2004. There's also been cases where the pollution stretches back decades. What has been the impact on Delta communities concretely?

The impact of the pollution across the Delta, apart from the [Nigerian civil] war, these are permanent scars on the environment. Take, for example, the spill and the destructive impact on the Ogoni communities, which is where Chief [Eric] Barizaa comes from, one of the plaintiffs in the case against Shell. That community does not really have any oil infrastructure: there's no pipeline there, no oil wells. But because of the entire nature of the creek around there, oil pollution came from somewhere else and it caught fire, and the entire community burned down. That community, the Goi community, is still largely uninhabited. There's one location that I personally visit whenever I go to Ogoniland, and I just sit there for a few minutes and remind myself that this injustice simply cannot be swept under the carpet. I see children swimming in oil-coated water, fishermen fishing in this oil-contaminated water hoping to catch something. Sometimes they do come out with one or two tilapia. The last time I was there I asked a fisherman to open the fish up and we found crude oil right in the belly. The fish they catch there are totally unfit for human consumption.

The case of Orumo is also very interesting. It was a leakage in the pipeline which may have been caused by corrosion, certainly it wasn't caused by third-party interference: it was buried in the ground, about six feet below the surface, and the leakage was on the underside of the pipe. So, the arguments have always been about ways of avoiding responsibility and having the judges in the Netherlands say that Shell has a duty of care, I believe it's a very clear signal, it's saying that environmental misbehaviour cannot be ignored, they cannot always blame sabotage where there has been no sabotage.

And the Dutch case, with Friends of the Earth, began when you were there. How did that first come about, the idea of bringing this to the courts?

Friends of the Earth International is a network of like-minded, grassroots environmental justice groups that work together on certain topics. Just before this case was instituted, this network was documenting – as much as possible – instances of pollution across the Niger Delta, in close collaboration with Friends of the Earth Netherlands [and] Milieudefensie. They visited the Niger Delta a number of times, visiting communities, documenting and generally providing support, because Shell is from their backyard. Then at a climate justice meeting in South Africa, in the early 2000s, where the idea of bringing this kind of litigation came up, discussions were followed up with Friends of the Earth Netherlands and Nigeria, and then it happened.

What are your thoughts on communities using the courts as part of an activist, anti-extractivist strategy? Of course this is not a new development, but do you see this strategy gaining traction – especially as anti-extraction movements strengthen?

I do expect that more cases should be coming up. There are several cases in the Nigerian courts with corporations having this attitude of ignoring whatever the courts say here in Nigeria. So finding that the courts in Europe and the Global North will be willing to listen to the victims from the Niger Delta should be very encouraging to people who have been ignored, who have borne the brutality of industry. I believe they are going to utilise this new opening to press for justice after so many years of being ignored as victims, as if their lives don't matter.

And the case in Britain, for example, builds on a legal victory on the part of 2,500 Zambian villagers against Konkola Copper Mine plc and its UK-based parent company Vedanta from 2019.

You cannot believe the level of desperation in these communities, where they are just ignored and they are left with the wrong end of the stick continuously. Now the case in Zambia, if you read the history of that company who went in there with nothing and then [pushed] their way into millions of dollars... These are all very encouraging signs that activism by ordinary people – they are not professional activists, these are ordinary people who are taking their destinies in their hands and finding opportunities in the courts, because where else are you going to find justice?

When you hear of companies like BP and Shell who have made pledges to rid themselves of fossil fuels, what is your response to these plans?

They just make me laugh. You know, you can fool some of the people some of the time, you can't fool all of the people all of the time. They will never fool me because, for example, the strategy that Shell has dusted off, which they have brought up before, they've said that by 2050, they [are] going to achieve net zero. Now, we all know that net zero is not zero. What we want is zero emissions, not net zero, so you cannot keep on extracting, looking for new fields, moving into deeper waters and getting more fossil fuels, and you're telling me that you're working towards net zero. No, no, no, this is sophistry. I think we cannot accept that kind of arithmetic. We have to ask for zero emissions, not net zero, and be forced to watch over carbon stocks in forests and in trees while companies like Shell keep on polluting and assuming that the trees are absorbing the equivalence of their pollution. There are so many funny things, like investing in capture and storage instead of leaving it in the ground in the first place. So I'm not impressed at all by this kind of announcement that they're making. They're just trying to buy time, to lure people and yield social capital to themselves so they can avoid the questions of how they are harming people who are living now and in future generations.

How would you characterise the role of the Nigerian government and its relationship with Shell more broadly? There seems to be an attempt by Shell to deflect some of the responsibility onto the lack of state regulation, which goes along with the sabotage issue. What do you make of the role of the Nigerian state in all of this?

I think the Nigerian Government is totally complicit in both cases because they are partners in the pollution. They're running a joint venture with Shell so when the company pollutes, the government is polluting also. Whatever shame comes on Shell, if I may use that term, when Shell is held accountable, our own judicial system should be worried that Nigerians have to go abroad to seek justice, when we have a government that should protect them, and we have a judicial system that should be respected in the country. So the government is totally complicit. Here is a colonial arrangement with transnational corporations, but that doesn't excuse the Nigerian government. But the corporations are the operators, and they have a duty of care to ensure that the pollution doesn't occur in the way that it has in the Niger Delta.

There's an argument that's been made, for example in the Zambian case, that African governments involved don't have the ability to regulate these companies. What do you make of that?

I don't think that is correct. What is correct is that the legal system does not make it possible to regulate industry. African governments have to change the mechanisms for justice, have to change the legal frameworks. The Nigerian legal framework for most of what happens in the oil sector was drawn up during the Nigerian civil war [when the oil producing region] territory was a combat zone. That is why I characterise these laws as "war laws" and these laws are patently unjust when it comes to the people and the environment. The same mentality at the centre of these laws is still complicating the processes for change in the area.

So, it's not the innate inability of African governments, it's the colonial nature of the regulatory frameworks. The legislative framework is also a media coup, a public relations coup, of the companies who are always able to deflect the blame on victims in many ways and [are] investing a lot in polishing their images, so people don't always think that these guys are responsible.

And finally, let me just say that, saying that African governments are unable to regulate oil companies is almost like saying that they are unable to regulate global bodies like the IMF and the World Bank. These are all agencies that are rigged against the African continent, and the same is true with transnational fossil fuel companies coming from outside the continent.

29. Bienvenu Matumo (2022), The Struggle for Change in the Congo

Bienvenu Matumo is a Congolese activist and member of the *Ateliers de la République*, a group of reflection and action on public policies in the Democratic Republic of the Congo and in Africa. Here, talking with Ben Radley, Matumo speaks about what led him to become an activist with Lutte pour le changement (LUCHA) and their struggle for social justice and human dignity. He argues that the killing, imprisonment, and repression of Congolese activists has continued unabated under the new presidency of Félix Tshisekedi.

***

To start us off, can you tell us something about your childhood and upbringing? How did your own background lead you to become a LUCHA activist?

I grew up in a village in Nyamilima, where my father worked as an agent of the National Intelligence Agency (NIA). I'm the son of a cop. He raised me to be politically aware and to love radio so I would follow the news, and that's how I became interested in public information and politics. He came from South Kivu and would describe the conflicts and war in the 1960s, the independence struggles and especially seeing successive Congolese presidents. I come from a modest family but my father told me that I could do better than him. He wanted me to study hard so I could find a decent job and eventually go into politics. I was still very young when he died in 2001, so to graduate from school and university I needed a lot of support from my mother and her family.

I grew up amid the conflicts rife in the province of North Kivu. I saw Congolese people dying, young people killed for belonging to one ethnic group or another. I lost friends who fell victim to these ethnic practices. Other friends joined the armed groups to seek vengeance for relatives killed in the ethnic violence, and some of those friends died. Yet none of my friends chose freely to join. As victims of that violence, it was their only option.

My path was determined in the context of these conflicts, of the injustices they generated, and of the poverty endured by Congolese families like my own that struggled to provide for their basic needs. Unfortunately, several of the issues that affected my childhood continue to afflict the civilian population today: the living conditions of those displaced by war, the Rwandan refugee problem and the Rwandan and Ugandan occupation.

I was at the University of Goma in 2008 when I met activists like Luc Nkulula, Serge Sivya and others. That led me to join the citizen movement LUCHA, then still in its infancy.

Yourself and your comrades have been imprisoned under the Kabila administration for your activism with LUCHA. Can you tell us about these experiences and their influence on you?

The NIA arrested me twice in Kinshasa for my activism – in August 2015 and again in February 2016. The first time I didn't spend long on police premises. After pressure from a number of sources – Congolese human rights organisations and DRC partner organisations – I was released without trial after four days of interrogation. But the second occasion resulted in six months in Makala, Kinshasa's biggest prison. Friends arrested with me suffered from bouts of depression as this was their first experience of prison, Victor Tesongo and Marcel Kapitene in particular. But I stayed strong, in public and in private. I was the most high-profile figure in the case and I acted as a leader. I couldn't afford to appear anxious or depressed even though imprisonment was changing the course of my life – for good and ill.

I was more worried about my mother and two sisters, who rely on me so much. I'd only just graduated and received my posting to the Ministry of Agriculture. I thought that I'd lose my job and that my family would suffer. However, our imprisonment was very significant in political and symbolic terms. We came to represent a courageous younger generation prepared to fight and challenge the dictatorship, and our jailing (and that of other LUCHA activists) made the Congolese aware of the political manipulation of the justice system.

During our six months in Makala, we achieved a great deal (the Kinshasa section of LUCHA was founded there). The authorities intended the prison to be a place of punishment and detention. Instead, it turned into an activist laboratory. It also became a university, as we managed to arrange opportunities to read, share knowledge, write, debate and learn languages like English and Italian (although we didn't make much progress). While I was in prison, with the full support of Fred Bauma, I drafted my application for the grant that enabled me first to study in France and then to pursue my doctoral research at the Paris 8 University, where I now teach in the geography department.

In short, I think prison played a big part in shaping my activism and developing my social and cultural capital. I met some fantastic prisoners who gave us vital support. With Eddy Kapend, I regularly discussed the DRC's history under Laurent Kabila's regime. I developed my first serious contacts with Congolese politics while I was in jail. In short, the effect of these arrests was to supercharge both my personal commitment and the construction of LUCHA's ideas more generally.

Can you tell us a bit more about LUCHA, its history, its vision and its objectives?

I've been a proud member of LUCHA for almost nine years. In general terms, LUCHA works for social justice and human dignity. Our aim is to raise awareness among citizens to render them capable of monitoring decision-makers and holding them to account. We want to fulfil our civic responsibility, which requires us to be politically aware and to exercise our power as citizens to secure freedom, democracy and respect for human rights in our nation and to install a form of government which permits all Congolese to live in peaceful enjoyment of our natural resources and of equality before the law. Our vision is simple: it is of the New Congo, a strong, free, united and prosperous nation, where every Congolese may live with dignity and justice. We draw our inspiration from the political ideas of Lumumba and other pan-African opponents of colonisation and slavery. LUCHA is thus open to African coalitions and committed to wider African issues.

There is a contradiction inherent in our work. How can we expect young activists from regions plagued by three decades of conflict to embrace an ethos of non-violence? The answer is simple yet complex. We argue firstly that political violence has produced damage greater than any solutions to the issues it seeks to resolve, so the option of non-violence is an invitation to use alternative methods that lead to different results. The solutions produced by non-violence are also durable, while violence leads to fragile solutions and breeds hatred and a desire for revenge. Another argument highlights the success and global reach of non-violence. We can cite the meaningful and politically significant speeches and actions of Martin Luther King Jr., Gandhi and others like them. Non-violence is essential in bringing new hope to the struggle and in countering the widespread belief that young people in eastern Congo are violent by nature. Non-violence is now firmly embedded in Congolese society, particularly in the fields of political and community activism.

LUCHA has had its highs and lows, but the history of the movement is essentially built around the ideas, beliefs, rebellion and anger of its activists, and around the illegal and arbitrary arrests they have suffered. In my view LUCHA has played a historically significant role in the struggle to ensure respect for the constitution and in the promotion of certain social and security issues. For example, LUCHA helped to ensure that Joseph Kabila obeyed the constitution and did not stand for a third term as president. LUCHA activists mobilised and demonstrated in various ways – direct action, dead city days, sit-ins, petitions, strikes, marches, protests – and at local, national, regional and international level. Together these actions forced Kabila from office.

Having grown up under Joseph Kabila's presidency, how would you describe the impact of this period of Congolese history on yourself and your political development?

Yes, I grew up under Kabila's presidency. Initially, many people found his youth attractive. At school, for example, we were proud of having the world's youngest president. But as we matured and developed firm views on government, our disenchantment grew. We can forgive his early years of shared presidency, from 2002 to 2005, even while opposing him on certain matters. From 2006, however, he squandered the chance to develop the country, which is unpardonable. His regime was one of predation, corruption, impunity, embezzlement, repression, instability and uniformity of thinking. Daily life continued to collapse, hugely affecting my education and that of my contemporaries, households and the nation as a whole. Many children had families that couldn't afford for them to study. Others finished their education but couldn't find a job due to high rates of unemployment.

My political activism was triggered when Kabila decided to defy the constitution and seek a third term of office, when living standards were falling and insecurity in the eastern provinces was killing many Congolese. Lives were being cut short, families torn apart and hopes dashed, all to complete official indifference. Nothing was done but count the dead, compile statistics. Then, shortly after military commanders like Mamadou Ndala Moustapha and General Bauma had led the struggle against the M23 rebels, they were killed in dubious circumstances, again to no interest from the Congolese state. I also abhorred the poor conditions suffered by the military, civil servants, police officers and their dependents, whose protests continue while government ministers and governors lived or live in social opulence. This unequal distribution of state revenue angered me. We must fight against the social inequalities created and perpetuated by the state.

All this happened around 2014. That's when I was radicalised and became an activist. I wanted to raise awareness among my compatriots in order to thwart the plans of Kabila and his cohort of predators. Happily, Kabila was forced from office but his practices live on. The fight continues in this respect.

Kabila left power and was replaced in January 2019 by Felix Tshisekedi. Has the new regime made it easier for citizen movements like LUCHA to grow and expand?

Far from it, repression continues and activists are now dying. Three LUCHA activists have been shot dead by the police during non-violent protests since 2019: Obadi in November 2019, Marcus in May 2020, and most recently 22-year-old Mumbere Ushindi on 24 January 2022. LUCHA activists have also been subject to arbitrary arrest, and another comrade from Beni, Kambale Lafontaine, suffered an amputation after he was shot in the leg during a demonstration. 13 of my comrades have just been thrown in jail and sentenced to twelve months' detention. LUCHA has already appealed this unjust verdict. And another comrade, King Mwamwiso, has been arrested by Goma's mayor for strongly criticising the local administration.

One thing that has changed is the reason for our arrest. Under Kabila we campaigned around issues of democracy and respect for the constitution. Now we're protesting about security issues. Our demands for an end to instability, massacres and violence are legitimate, and without doubt we're contributing to the search for peace. I should stress that we're not the only group suffering a crackdown for highlighting security issues. Local activist artists in Beni are also being targeted. I'm thinking here of Idengo who is languishing in Goma's central jail.

Politically speaking, LUCHA continues to circulate proposals and ideas on the electoral process, corruption, impunity, the handling of Covid and the tricky issue of the state of emergency. Our influence permeates the religious and political spheres. To advance our causes and agenda, we engage with political, religious, and civil society actors. If they heed what we say, the Congo will be the winner. We ensure that institutions receive copies of documents relevant to them. Our annual *Fatshimetrie* newsletter, for example, is sent to a wide range of actors telling our leaders how their actions are viewed by the citizens. We send memos and letters to the authorities when consultations and conferences are held. We've met President Tshisekedi, the Prime Minister, and other ministers to discuss our proposals on various issues in national life, but three years later there is nothing to show for it. I've realised that these people don't listen and would rather carry on regardless. The only visible reaction has been to demonise and stigmatise brave activists. LUCHA is growing and will continue to do so, and its role will be crucial in the months to come.

Do the recent events and political changes in the Congo give you hope for a better future, or are the same practices under Kabila – of predation and so on that you've mentioned – simply continuing under a different leadership?

My hopes of a bright future come from the fact that I'm standing up and fighting for it, not from past political changes and events. Tomorrow's Congo will be better than it is today but only if we assume our individual and collective responsibilities. In short, I argue that while Kabila has gone his practices remain and we must be resolute in combating them.

Finally, 2021 was the 60th anniversary of the assassination of Lumumba. Can you describe his influence in today's Congo? What does he mean to you and other political activists?

The trio of Lumumba, Okito and Mpolo are considered the

fathers of Congolese independence, while Lumumba himself is a major figure in Congolese, African and world history. To describe yourself as a Lumumbist is seen as an asset conferring political legitimacy in popular opinion. Congolese political parties continue to proclaim their adherence to Lumumba's ideas in words if not in deeds. I'm thinking, for example, of the Parti Lumumbiste Unifié whose actions are a travesty of Lumumba's political thought. His influence played a key role in my development as an activist and he continues to inspire in the DRC. A lot of young activists identify with his thought and embody many of its aspects.

30. Trevor Ngwane (2016), South Africa's Fork in the Road

Leo Zeilig talks to Trevor Ngwane about political developments in South Africa, the crisis in the ANC, and the growth of new struggles on the left in the universities and workplaces. Ngwane is a long-standing socialist activist, researcher and writer.

***

Can you please, first of all, introduce yourself and explain something about your own political developments through the 1970s, 1980s and 1990s?

I was born the same year the ANC was banned in 1960. My parents, who were both medical nurses, left the country but came back two years later. My father was enthused by his brief stay in Dar es Salaam where he had a whiff of the political ferment there, the spirit of African liberation under Nyerere. At that time this Tanzanian city was a hotbed of revolution with most African liberation movements having offices there. I remember this because when he talked about "Dar", my father's eyes would light up and he would get very excited. My aunt, Victoria Chitepo, who has very recently passed away, was married to Herbert Chitepo, the ZANU chairperson who was assassinated in Zambia in 1975. My family lived a bit in Zimbabwe, then called Rhodesia, and Tanzania, then called Tanganyika. Then we came back to live in South Africa where my father was always being visited by the Special Branch police. I think they tortured him at some point because he used to tell stories about police torture.

I remember the 1973 Durban strikes as I used to visit my aunt in Lamontville, Durban. Everyone was excited and talking about it in the township with workers going around shouting "Usuthu!"

which is a Zulu war cry. I was a high school student during the 1976 June 16 student uprising. There was a student strike at our school in Mariannhill, a Roman Catholic boarding school which Steve Biko – the black consciousness leader who was killed by apartheid police – attended in 1964. My university days at Fort Hare University were also marked by "student disturbances" as the struggle against apartheid got into gear in the country and abroad. Bheki Mlangeni, an anti-apartheid lawyer who was assassinated with earphone bombs that exploded in his ears, was a student during my time there.

In the 1980s I got drawn into the struggle when studying and then later teaching at Wits University in Johannesburg. I also became active in the township civics as I was living in Soweto, Central Western Jabavu. In 1986 I spent two weeks in detention after police swooped onto campus arresting and beating up students during the many demonstrations that took place then. Marxist lecturers dominated the humanities and there was a line of division between the nationalists and the socialists although everyone claimed to be a socialist and everyone supported national liberation. I became a Trotskyist round about 1989, joining the Socialist Workers League – which later became the Socialist Group – and I am still a member today. At that time there were a lot of socialist groups in operation despite the ban on Marxism and socialist politics. When I lost my job as a sociology junior lecturer in 1989, I coordinated the Wits Workers School – a workers' literacy project on campus – and in 1993 got a job in a COSATU union, the Transport and General Workers' Union where I was later twice expelled for opposing what I called the politics of class collaboration of the ANC, SACP and COSATU leadership.

In the township we were busy setting up civic structures, street committees and later self-defence units during the political violence of the 1990s. I also worked a bit with the ANC underground and joined the organisation when it got unbanned in 1990. I joined the SACP for six months and found their "heavy duty" Marxism mechanistic; practically they were intent on subordinating the workers' struggle to a nationalist, not socialist, programme. However, we all had to work together on the ground building civics, the ANC, unions, calling meetings, stay-aways, mobilising for an ANC victory, etc. This culminated in my becoming a public representative (ward councillor) for my area in Pimville, Soweto, where I was now living with my family.

A short time after the 1994 settlement there were voices that began to be raised about the failure, limits, that the new ANC government had imposed on any serious programme of reform. Could you explain a little of the settlement and your role in slowly emerging criticism and movements that challenged it?

I was expelled by the ANC in 1999 for opposing the privatisation of municipal services in my capacity as a local councillor. The struggle against privatisation had begun when the ANC government ditched the Reconstruction and Development Programme (RDP), a mildly redistributive policy, and adopted the decidedly neoliberal Growth, Employment and Redistribution (GEAR) programme in 1996. At the forefront of the struggle was the South African Municipal Workers Union (SAMWU), a COSATU affiliate, whose members' jobs were directly on the line. Working class communities in the townships and informal settlements – shantytowns – also began to take their fights to the street demanding better services.

The reason for the conflict with the ANC government is that, a few years after its taking over, it was becoming increasingly clear that the miracle settlement that saw the peaceful transition from apartheid to democracy had been brokered in the form of a deal that protected capital and the capitalist system in exchange for the vote for the majority and other political and social reforms. The ANC leaders, actually from day one of their arrival from exile and jail, were busy whittling down the demands of the people and talking about the unviability of a socialist path. The RDP was a transitional programme from socialist idealism to a pragmatic accommodation to capital. Indeed, it did not last long and the capitalist interest reasserted itself with a vengeance through GEAR with its various attacks on the working class, namely, lay-offs of state employees, sub-contracting, privatisation, etc. The government's budget prioritised the interests of capital and the commitment to rolling back the legacy of apartheid through vigorous delivery of services and jobs for all took a backseat. Neoliberal pro-capitalist policies, such as the removal of exchange controls and other protectionist measures, led to massive capital flight and job losses. The reintegration of the South African economy into global capitalist circuits, after the (relative) economic isolation of the apartheid regime, benefited the capitalist class at the expense of the working class, including doing tremendous damage to the developmental prospects of the country bordering on deindustrialisation.

In this guise I became active in the international anti-globalisation movement, becoming a regular attendee of the World Social Forum and active in the African Social Forum. The decline in the power of this movement saw many movements that emerged at that time implode including the Anti-Privatisation Forum.

In the early 2000s, South Africa had active radical groups, community protests and civil society organisations that in different ways were trying to challenge the governments and its commitment to neoliberalism. Can you describe some of these movements you were involved in building and the experience during this time?

As the penny began to drop, various communities took to the streets in protest challenging policies that threatened their access to services such as the user-must-pay policy, penalisation and criminalisation of those who could not afford these paid-for-services, installation of prepaid water metres, reduction of electricity amperage to the poor, etc. In Johannesburg, the union SAMWU combined with students fighting against privatisation at Wits University and communities to form a fighting front against the privatisation programme of the Johannesburg City Council. This front later became the Anti-Privatisation Forum in which I was the organiser. In Soweto we formed the Soweto Electricity Crisis Committee fighting against power cut-offs to force residents to pay the suddenly exorbitant bills. This organisation soon took up the struggle against the installation of water metres.

In Durban, the Concerned Citizens Forum was formed and led by Fatima Meer and Ashwin Desai, among others, organising in Chatsworth, a working class "Indian" area of the apartheid geography, against services payment enforcement by the municipality. The Landless People's Movement was formed to fight against land evictions in the rural areas, the Anti-Eviction Campaign fought against this in Cape Town. The Treatment Action Campaign fought for the provision of medication for people living with HIV/AIDS in the face of a president of the country, Thabo Mbeki, who flatly denied the very existence of the virus, no doubt trying to shirk responsibility due to fiscal considerations. Meanwhile, the trade unions, the SACP and ANC were blowing hot and cold in the face of the emergence of these grievances, struggles and movements. The ANC-SACP-COSATU Alliance was used to contain struggle and isolate loyalists from contamination by this spirit of struggle.

When Zuma was elected to the head of the ANC, and then in elections in 2009, there was some hope that he would speak more readily for the poor. This obviously hasn't happened. How would you characterise the years of his presidency? Though much has been made of his blunders, he has also been careful to develop a rural support base.

ANC, SACP and COSATU members, including those of the South African National Civic Organisation, a fourth member of the tripartite alliance, suffered as much as everyone else from the anti-working class policies of the government, especially those on the ground. Soon the rumblings could not be contained and the leadership, especially of the SACP which controls COSATU, in unprincipled ways sought to put the blame on Thabo Mbeki's head in an internal power struggle. A closer look shows that the whole Mbeki-Zuma debacle which saw Zuma win at the Polokwane National Conference in 2007 served two political purposes. The first one was the internal power struggle itself, the jostling inside the party for ascendancy. The second one was a deeper process of hegemony consolidation, namely, aligning the party organisation to the party inside the state. In practice the two were closely interrelated but must be separated for analysis.

Mbeki was blamed for the "1996 class project", which was said to be the neoliberal prioritisation of bosses' interests over those of the workers. In this way the opportunistic ANC-SACP-COSATU leaders used the internal struggle for power as a lightning rod to channel the real anger of the working class, including organised labour, for the socioeconomic reversals experienced under an ANC government of liberation. Zuma was falsely painted as a people's leader and champion of the working class. Mbeki was painted as aloof, intellectualist and serving bosses and imperialist interests. Zuma sang his way to winning the presidency of the ANC with his trademark struggle song "Mshini wami" which means "my machine gun." I was there at the COSATU congress in 2007 when Zuma was presented to the delegates as a born socialist whose mother had been a domestic worker. Mbeki lost the election and later was recalled from being country's president before his term ended.

The fact that the ANC went straight from jail and exile into the corridors of power created a misalignment between the ANC as government and as movement. The ANC in the party branch and in the street had to be brought into line with the ANC in government. This is why one of the war cries against Mbeki and for Zuma during the power struggle was that Mbeki was not listening to the branches, as if there were two ANCs. During Zuma's rape trial, ANC supporters took to the streets – something that had not been seen in South Africa for a long time. Zuma then symbolised the unification of the two ANCs: as government and as movement. Once this unity was achieved it was possible for the ANC to speak with one voice. Unfortunately, that voice is the voice of big capital and not of the working class. Zuma defaulted on all the promises that had been made to the working class on his behalf by the ANC, SACP and COSATU leaders. That is why soon afterwards radicals like Julius Malema, Zwelinzima Vavi and Irvin Jim, respectively the leaders of the ANC Youth League, of COSATU and of NUMSA (National Union of Metalworkers of South Africa), found themselves out in the cold. They were under pressure from their constituencies whose expectations had been raised by the Zuma campaign in which they had personally made some bombastic claims. Indeed, the chickens came home to roost and Julius Malema was expelled from the ANC and went on to form the Economic Freedom Fighters. Jim led NUMSA in its break with the tripartite alliance. And Zwelinzima Vavi was expelled as general secretary of COSATU in 2015 for opposing the subsequent expulsion of NUMSA from COSATU. All three leaders became increasingly and irreconcilably critical of the ANC government's pro-capitalist policies. This has opened a new era in South African working class politics.

During the 2000s, there have been efforts to develop a left alternative out of a range of different groups. Currently the Democratic Left Front (DLF) is one such effort. How successful have these been? What are the challenges for a radical left?

I am the National Secretary of the Democratic Left Front. This is an organisation that was formed five years ago in an attempt to regroup the left. Vishwas Satgar, an ex-SACP leader who was expelled by the party, was at the forefront of the initiative. At the time there was a feeling that the social movements and community organisations behind the numerous protests in South Africa were not addressing the question of power and a left alternative to bourgeois rule. The DLF was launched with the participation of both left groups and community organisations on an anti-capitalist platform. It has evolved into a pro-socialist stance and is supportive of the call by NUMSA to build a workers' party. It also participates in the United Front, another structure spearheaded in the course of what is called here the "NUMSA moment." The United Front unites labour, community and student/youth struggles on an anti-capitalist platform. It is starting off somewhat similar to how the DLF started but it has the muscle of NUMSA behind it. The DLF is fully behind NUMSA in its attempt to build a new left pole in South Africa including the plans to launch a new trade union federation and the Movement for Socialism initiative.

The attempt at left regroupment by the DLF has been a difficult one and is currently yielding mixed results. The challenge, in my opinion, has been getting around the demobilisation and demoralisation of the working class and of the left. The vision of a different society has been systematically trampled upon for so long and this has resulted in a loss of hope that a different future is possible and that workers by themselves can lead the struggle towards that future. There can be no socialism without working class leadership. Without knowledge of and belief in the organic capacity of the working class to effect social change, that is, the self-activity for self-emancipation, the struggle begins to lose direction. Militancy without class politics gives an illusion of movement but in reality little change takes place. The DLF was formed in a context of militant struggles in working class communities and in the workplaces but the political turmoil did not seem to have a centre of authority. There was certainly little overt connection between the various struggles taking place. There seemed to be no shared vision.

The DLF was formed upon an anti-capitalist platform in a search for alternatives. It soon became apparent that being anti-capitalist is not enough, we also needed to be pro-socialist. This move created some tensions and dissension inside the organisation because initially there had been an emphasis on pluralism – in other words, accommodating different political traditions and tendencies in the DLF. Some comrades felt that an aspect of this pluralism was being lost by this political-ideological development of the organisation. Another problem has been a fundamental one, namely to what extent the DLF could regard itself as a front in the light of the absence of mass organisations in its membership. There is only one trade union affiliate of the DLF. Some comrades felt it was more realistic to regard it as a solidarity forum whose work was to support struggles while raising the flag of socialism, of an alternative.

At the moment the DLF continues its work in a radically changed political terrain containing many possibilities and challenges. The DLF worked hard to support the strikes in the platinum mines including during the Lonmin strike that resulted in the Marikana Massacre in 2012. Some of the DLF's leading members helped form the Marikana Support Campaign which is fighting for justice for the slain miners. A documentary, *Miners Shot Down*, was put together by a leading member of the DLF, Rehad Desai, and this contributed to raising awareness about what actually happened on that mountain on 16 August 2012 when 34 miners were shot dead by the state police. The DLF formed a strike support committee during the four month long industry-wide strike in the platinum mines in South Africa in early 2014. The committee organised political and material support to the striking miners including food and clothing collections and a massive feeding operation that involved the churches, community organisations and Gift of the Givers, the non-partisan disaster relief organisation. The message was spread abroad and a solidarity fund was set up and benefited from international support. Most recently, the DLF has supported the student and worker uprisings in the universities that took place in October 2015. The students and workers were demanding the pulling down of Cecil Rhodes' statue at the University of Cape Town, scrapping of a proposed tuition fee increase and an end to outsourcing of cleaning, security and other services because it adversely affected workers.

The massacre of workers at Marikana in 2012 is regarded as a fork in the road for the ANC, the Alliance and the working class. Can you tell us how you see this moment, what it means, what it exposes and how this has played out?

The Marikana Massacre was a very painful moment in the struggle for liberation of the workers here. Everyone was stunned when the police opened fire on the miners on strike. No one expected a government of liberation to do that. All illusions in the class character of the South African state, run by the ANC, were dispelled; the ANC government was there to protect capital and profits and was prepared to shed blood doing so. This shook the architecture of class collaboration that housed the South African state to its foundations, namely, the ANC-SACP-COSATU Alliance. The first casualty was the National Union of Mineworkers, then the biggest trade union affiliate of COSATU and biggest supporter and ally of the ANC: all its general secretaries became secretary generals of the ANC political party (Cyril Ramaphosa, Kgalema Motlanthe and Gwede Mantashe). The massacre led to the NUM losing thousands of its members to a new union, the Association of Mineworkers and Construction Union. The workers left the NUM because it did not support their strike and because they saw it as "eating with the bosses."

The Marikana Massacre brought attention to the power of the working class. The workers at Lonmin, where the strike happened, organised themselves and went on strike against the wishes of their union, the NUM, and against a government of national liberation and its laws. They ignored the Labour Relations Act which governs industrial conflict; they did not declare a dispute or apply for a strike certificate, they just struck. They demanded R12, 500 [£600] a month which for many meant a fourfold increase in wages. In other words, their demands were based on their needs and not on what the bosses were prepared to give. They formed a workers' strike committee to lead the strike which was directly accountable to the strikers' assembly. And after 34 of their comrades lay dead, shot by the police, they continued with their strike for another three weeks until they won substantial increases from the company.

A spectre was born which was to haunt the South African ruling class, this is the "Spirit of Marikana." The spirit of defiance, of do-or-die, of moving forward against all odds. This is what the workers on that mountain displayed. This is what millions of workers saw. The workers were ready to lose their lives rather than continue being exploited by the mine owners. Certainly, they were prepared to lose their jobs in the process. Later, a worker who was shot nine times and survived, Mzoxolo Magidiwana, said that they were fighting to make sure that their children did not suffer as they did. A few months later the same workers joined tens of thousands of other workers from other platinum-mining companies to wage a four-month long strike demanding R12 500. The strike was long and hard but the workers vowed never to call off the strike because doing so would be a betrayal of the spirit of the dead miners on that mountain. The "Spirit of Marikana" strengthened their resolve and they eventually won a significant wage increase.

At about the same time, in 2012, a sector of some of the most oppressed and exploited workers in South Africa, the farmworkers, broke out in struggle, demanding a living wage. This struggle took place mostly in the Western Cape's winelands where wages and working conditions render workers to be no better than modern slaves. The farmworkers also did not follow any procedures, they simply took action. Police brutality and state repression of the strike was the order of the day. A union which did its best to support the workers who, like the miners, struck without their unions, the CSAAWU (Commercial, Stevedoring, Agricultural and Allied Workers Union), is still facing closure today after being slapped with a million-rand damages claim by the bosses for its involvement in the strike. Despite the attacks from the state and capital, the farmworkers won a significant wage increase.

The "Spirit of Marikana" drifted around and affected the National Union of Metalworkers of South Africa, now the biggest union in the country with 370 000 members. The so-called "NUMSA moment" was born when the union decided to break out of the ANC-SACP-COSATU Alliance in a special national congress in 2014. Delegates watched the documentary, *Miners Shot Down*, and listened to some widows of the slain miners speak. Afterwards they broke into song and individually and in groups, many in tears, went to the front with money in their hands donating over R100 000 to the dead miners' solidarity fund. Later they resolved not to vote for the ANC and to form a worker's party and fight for workers power and socialism.

Working class communities were also touched by the "Spirit of Marikana." The housing crisis and the unresolved land question in South Africa saw four settlements being set-up in different parts of the country by way of land invasions and housing occupations. These takeovers were just some among many but what is significant with these four is that they named their settlements Marikana. They took over the land with the spirit of do-or-die: "Let the state kill us as they did in Marikana but we are not moving from this piece of ground." These new Marikanas are in Cato Crest, Durban; Philippi, Cape Town; Mzimhlophe, Soweto and Tlokwe, Potshefstroom.

The student and worker rebellion in the universities in late 2015 have also been infected by the "Spirit of Marikana." The students took to the street without seeking permission from the authorities as required by the Public Gatherings Act. They marched, blocked roads, boycotted classes and generally disrupted university operations forcing the authorities to listen to and eventually accede to some of their demands. Workers, especially cleaners, went on strike in several campuses without acquiring a strike certificate. The student marches to parliament in Cape Town and to the seat of government in Pretoria in October 2015 happened because the students wanted it, not because the authorities agreed to it. They sought permission from no one, the permission came from the strength of their mobilisation. The workers won an in-principle agreement in most of the universities that outsourcing would end, and the students won their 0% increase. It was the unity of workers and students and the power of disruption that won the victories.

A recent month-long strike from March this year by municipal workers who collect garbage in the city and clean the streets has also shown aspects of the new mood among workers in the country. These workers, mostly against the wishes of their union, the South African Municipal Workers' Union, and without following strike procedures, have been on a militant strike that has included trashing the streets – that is, throwing rubbish all over town to press forward their demands. The garbage piled up in Johannesburg until the city relented and an agreement was signed with the workers winning some concessions including a no victimisation clause after the hysteria of the middle classes against the trashing of the city and accusations of strike violence directed at scabs. The weapon of the workers was again disruption of business as usual and forcing the authorities to accede to their demands.

I would say that the "NUMSA moment" has recently disappointed many people who were hoping for a stronger and bolder way forward. There is a feeling that despite the radical left turn taken by the NUMSA leadership, it will take time for them to shake off the baggage of SACP politics and habits including a top-down approach to struggle and weak belief in the organic capacity of the working class to lead its own struggle to socialism. There is also the reality that none of the COSATU unions actually left the union federation after the expulsion of NUMSA and later of Zwelinzima Vavi, the COSATU general secretary, the latter for opposing NUMSA's expulsion. The nine unions that sympathised with NUMSA have not taken any visible action in support. Hope now lies on NUMSA and Vavi's plans to launch a new union federation later this year.

The actions on the ground by workers and communities, in my assessment, are the ones that are giving new life to the flagging NUMSA moment. Workers are leading the way showing that to win you need to fight based on your needs not on what the bosses are willing to give. You need to fight with weapons that you choose and that are readily available to all workers and not those chosen by your enemy – you have to fight because you are ready to and not because the enemy has given you permission to do so. You have to disrupt operations and stop the enemy's business as usual. Solidarity in struggle is the heart of the workers movement. These are lessons that many trade union, political and community leaders can learn from; the struggles mentioned here and which they appear to have forgotten during their long, cosy residence inside the ANC-SACP-COSATU edifice of class collaboration.

Recently, in 2015, there was an extraordinary uprising of students demanding both bread and butter reforms and the removal of symbols of privilege and the racist, settler past of South Africa. Much of the language in this movement has spoken of the need for black empowerment, black consciousness, rather than of class and socialism. How do you see the development of this movement?

The student movement is very important because the youth are the future. However, the only future is a worker's future. What is important about the student movement is that it began as an ideological critique of the legacy of colonialism, capitalism, racism and patriarchy in the universities, in particular as symbolised by the statue of Cecil Rhodes at the University of Cape Town. But it soon transposed into a movement against the increase in tuition fees and even against paying for education. From very early on, it united with and took on board the struggles of the workers against outsourcing. This was remarkable and partly a result of many long years of struggle by university workers, especially cleaning and security, against the hardships of outsourcing. The heightened racial consciousness among militant students, most of whom were black, led them to see the workers as black like themselves, indeed as their mothers and fathers. This showed the interrelationship between race, class and gender in the struggle for emancipation. Many cleaning workers are women and the students found this significant. The student movement rescued black consciousness and pan-Africanism from the history books into living systems of thought relevant for day to day struggle.

An important theoretical and ideological theme in the student movement is decolonisation. There is an ideological ferment and militant dynamism in South African universities that centres around this idea. It is a powerful and radical idea that goes beyond surface appearance and the usual terms in which we talk about society. The students are talking about the need to change the very structure of society. Not to change certain parts or aspects, but to change society totally. Race is central to this vision. It is an inspired vision because, ideologically, it represents a total negation: the negation of the negation. It is an idea that says no to everything existing. The radical students are saying everything is wrong about this society. The education system is wrong, it must change. The suffering of cleaning workers is wrong. White power, white supremacy and white monopoly capital are all wrong. The racism, sexism, all of it. Black pain: there has been too much suffering, we can't take it anymore, it must all come to an end. We cannot continue this way, it must all stop.

Practically it can lead to militant action. We cannot allow so-called normality to prevail. Nothing is normal in this situation and in the way society is run. Let us disrupt everything because it is all wrong. The garbage workers trash the city saying: "let it be all dirty, let the rubbish pile up because when it looks clean it is actually hiding a lot of dirt that exist[s] underneath – the corruption of the municipal officers, the exploitation of the workers, the daily pain and suffering." Students disrupt lectures and student registration processes on the same grounds: these lectures and these processes exclude the majority from higher education, we must not allow them to continue, they must be disrupted.

This total rejection may lead one to ask: what are you going to do if we change everything? The answer is that we don't know, all we know is that things cannot continue this way. Everything must change. This approach lays the seeds of a new society. It begins with the condemnation of all that exists in order to clear the ground for the new. From this point of view, the decolonisation movement is a revolutionary movement.

The movement has won workers important concessions in their struggle against outsourcing. In principle, agreements and commitments have been made by the university authorities which means that there will be struggles ahead to ensure that these are met and in ways that benefit rather than penalise workers. It is the same with the student victory where the freeze in fee increase[s] still means that higher education must be paid for and already university administrators are implementing austerity programmes on the grounds that there is less money available. The strength of the movement will lie in keeping the connection and solidarity alive between student and worker struggles.

The difference between the June 16 1976 student uprising and this one is that the first happened in working class high schools while the 2015 uprising took place in middle class universities. Universities are factories that manufacture and vindicate class privilege and inequalities. To avoid elitism, the slogan "Free education from crèche to university" is the correct one. It is also important for the university struggles to connect with other struggles in all spheres of working class life. The commodification of higher education is not the only commodification taking place in the world. There is commodification of food, water, electricity, housing, healthcare, transport, recreation, culture, etc. The student movement cannot move forward without embracing and being embraced by other working class and popular struggles in society.

The ideological shortcomings of black consciousness and decolonisation must be faced squarely. The emphasis on race, unless qualified by a rigorous class analysis, can lead to identity essentialism. The idea that black is good and suffers while white is bad and is privileged is a counterproductive oversimplification which unfortunately is rife in the South African movement. For example, the Rhodes Must Fall meetings in the University of Cape Town are racially segregated with white students not allowed in. But the danger can be much bigger. There appears to be a marriage of black separatist nationalist ideas and the more extreme or crude ideas in post-colonial theory. For example, there is talk that Marxism must be rejected because it originates from Europe and Marx was a white man. Some versions of post-colonial theory reject Eurocentrism, modernity and the Enlightenment on the ground of complicity in historical crimes, namely, racism, slavery, colonialism, etc. European theoretical categories are said to adorn the imperialist garments of universalism, that is, claiming universal applications to the whole world, a world that is different and cannot be understood in Eurocentric terms. Vivek Chibber wrote a book in 2013 where he shows the shortcomings of subaltern studies, an important strand within post-colonial theory. This problem has to be addressed by Marxist scholars in South Africa too because in practice and in the long term it represents a retreat from class analysis and the class struggle. It opens the door to middle class leadership of the struggle and can severely weaken the movement going forward.

On the left, a new organisation – the Economic Freedom Fighters – has emerged and now seems to occupy a prominent role in opposition, speaking powerfully to the anger and injustice of contemporary South Africa. How do you see the role of the EFF and how should the radical left respond?

The Economic Freedom Fighters grabbed the imagination of the youth and sections of the working class because they speak loudly and in a straightforward way about power, wealth and struggle. They talk about how the black working class needs to take power. They talk about the need to take back the wealth, to nationalise the farms, mines, factories and banks. Nationalisation figured prominently in the platform they adopted during the 2014 national election and which won them a million votes. They are a welcome development in South African politics in the manner in which they are rattling the cage to the left of the ANC and SACP. They are also youthful and their political method includes taking to the streets to push forward their agenda. They certainly revived public interest in what goes on in the South African parliament. The overwhelming majority of the ANC in that parliament had turned it into one huge sleepy rubber stamp for neoliberal policies and occasional left posturing. The EFF has also taken its struggle into the universities running candidates in Student Representative Councils (SRC) which so far have been dominated by ANC-aligned student organisations notably the South African Students Congress and the Progressive Youth Alliance who all seem to take their orders from Luthuli House, the ANC headquarters in Johannesburg. The "fighters," as they call themselves, were in the thick of the student uprising against the fee increase even though they did not necessarily lead it. However, they will likely and deservedly benefit handsomely from this involvement in SRC elections in South Africa's 23 universities. This will be the case all the more so because the "independent" or spontaneous leadership of this movement has tended to adopt an autonomist anti-electoral and anti-party political stance. Those who support the movement will find that they can only vote for the EFF if they vote at all.

The strengths and weaknesses of the EFF can be traced to the revival of decolonisation and post-colonial politics and theories – in a word: nationalism. On the one hand Julius Malema's cry is that the ANC has failed the people, it has not implemented the Freedom Charter, a document that guided the struggle for decades and which, among other things, called for the nationalisation of the "commanding heights of the economy." This is a call for the completion of the so-called National Democratic Revolution, a theoretical and programmatic formulation of the SACP. Its essence is the two-stage theory of revolution. I think it is fair to say that historically this approach is Stalinist-inspired. The EFF's official ideology is Marxism-Leninism-Fanonism. The question is whether, in practice, this will be a combination of the best or the worst of these ideologies. The nationalist inflection of the EFF's discourse finds fertile ground in the people's disappointment with national liberation and as such is powerful as a mobilising tool. However, the downside is locking the class struggle again into the nationalist cage – a repeat of the dangers that Kwame Nkrumah, with his concept of "neo-colonialism", and Frantz Fanon with his "false decolonisation", tried to avoid and failed.

Fanon somewhere quotes Marx on how the social revolution "cannot draw its poetry from the past, but only from the future." The EFF, the student movement and the working class movement has to find a way forward without going back to nationalism as an ideology of struggle. The struggle against imperialism has to break out of the discourse of colonialism without denying this history and its legacy. It has to relook at some of the theoretical categories associated with this struggle in the course of the 20th century and identify and remove the shibboleths that bogged it down and ensured its defeat or partial victories when so much could have been won. One of these theoretical legacies is that of Stalinism. Careful and systematic theoretical work is still necessary to map out the strongest way forward. And at its heart will be proletarian internationalism rather than bourgeois nationalism.

Left reformism takes the struggle forward but is not the way forward. We saw in Greece how the parliamentary road to socialism, in the form of the road to national economic sovereignty, is bound to lead to a dead-end. Revolutionary rhetoric is not the same as a revolutionary programme. It can be a short-cut that inspires in the short-term but demoralises in the long term. The only way forward for the working class and the revolutionary left is the road of struggle, of revolutionary struggle, of the struggle to replace the capitalist system with the socialist system. Under conditions of global capitalist crisis, the system is increasingly unable to yield any concessions. This means we are entering an era of struggle. It will take many different forms in different places. Our job as revolutionary socialists, wherever we are located, in the unions, universities, communities, youth organisations, political parties and social movements, is to orient these struggles towards the revolutionary overturn of the capitalist system and the taking of political and economic power by the working class and its allies.

31. Antonater Tafadzwa Choto (2016), Resistance, Crisis and Workers in Zimbabwe

Antonater Tafadzwa Choto is a well-known labour activist, researcher and the Director of the Zimbabwe Labour Centre. Leo Zeilig talks to Choto about the ongoing economic crisis in Zimbabwe, the impact on ordinary people and some of the factors that are likely to worsen or mitigate the crisis in forthcoming years.

***

Can you please give us a few details about the history of your own activism?

I have worked for years as a social justice activist after having participated in a number of workers and social justice struggles from the mid-1990s. Initially I was involved in a feminist group that campaigned against discrimination against women, with women harassed and attacked. Later I became a socialist active in the labour struggles of the 1990s. I am currently the Director of the Zimbabwe Labour Centre. The ZLC stands for the justice for working people in the workplace and society at large. We also campaign against neoliberal policies that, we believe, have had a disastrous impact on Zimbabwe.

Zimbabwe has now been in a prolonged and terrible crisis for more than a decade, can you explain what is going on and what life is like in the country at the moment?

One story seems to represent the general picture, to me. On his birthday interview in February 2016 the President, Robert Mugabe, announced that the country had lost $15 billion revenue from the mining of diamonds in [the] Marange diamond fields in Chiadzwa. $15 billion was supposed to be channelled to the treasury to help the ailing economy but was lost through corruption. Mugabe admitted this publicly. Mugabe then announced that the government was taking over the mining of diamonds in Marange. Sounds positive, right? Sadly not. While he made this announcement, he said nothing about efforts to recover money that could go a long way to helping the country and the majority of ordinary people in poverty. Instead of bringing the culprits before the justice system he stated that the government would seek to lure other foreign investors, who will come, no doubt, to loot more money from the diamond fields.

At the same time his Minister of Finance Patrick Chinamasa and Reserve Bank Governor John Mangudya were delighted to announce that the IMF would grant Zimbabwe a loan, the first in 20 years, of $984 million in the third quarter of the year after paying off foreign lenders. This is not good news for Zimbabwe. IMF money will see more austerity and worsening of life for ordinary people in Zimbabwe. In many ways the current collapse in the economy, with its long political crisis, was triggered by the conditions attached to such loans – known across the continent as structural adjustment in the 1990s. There is little different in these new loans. Why does the government not focus on bringing back $15 billion of stolen assets from the Marange diamond fields?

The reasons are complex but essentially the government refuses, for all of its black empowerment bombast, to make any serious efforts at controlling the country's riches for itself. Zimbabwe is endowed with vast mineral wealth with only a minority, approximately 1%, enjoying access to enormous wealth in kickbacks from deals with multinational corporations. At the same time more than 90% of the population struggle to afford to send their children to school, while young girls are often forced into prostitution or early marriages and boys turn to petty stealing or drugs. The gap between the poor and the rich continues to widen. Harare, Zimbabwe's capital, has always been a city of extremes, but never more so than today. The mansions the rich build for themselves match the opulence of Constantia in Cape Town, while holidaying all over the world and sending their children to top universities in Europe and America. Even South African universities, long the preferred destination for the children of the black elite, are no longer deemed adequate.

The ruling party ZANU-PF is incredibly divided, with a recent split and a new party created. The opposition too has split, again and again. Can you explain to us what the significance of these developments is?

Divisions among the elite have been incredibly unpleasant. The cake for the 1% has been shrinking for a number of years because of the global economic crisis, the slow-down in the Chinese economy and the collapse of the rand in South Africa. Each of these factors have had a negative effect on the ailing country. The political game in Zimbabwe depends on these economies for their pay-outs. The elite both in ZANU-PF and the opposition are now greedily fighting amongst themselves, while dividing ordinary people who are forced to fight for the crumbs. With Joice Mujuru, the former Vice-President expelled from ZANU-PF in 2014, the purge in the ruling party has not abated. Next in line could see Vice-President Emmerson Mnangagwa, who had previously been seen as a replacement for Robert Mugabe.

Mujuru was joined by others who had also suffered the purge in ZANU-PF, to form the political party People First (PF) – which is essentially no different from ZANU-PF, though perhaps more intensely committed to neoliberal policies, so pitching itself to the right of ZANU-PF. The Mnangagwa faction dubbed "Lacoste" – for the emblem worn on supporters' t-shirts – seems to be losing the succession battle to the G40 (Generation 40). G40 consists mainly of young and energetic ZANU-PF members, who did not fight in the liberation struggle and are pushing for Grace Mugabe – the president's wife – to succeed her husband even though Grace continuously refutes her presidential ambitions. Jonathan Moyo, Saviour Kasukuwere and Robert Zhuwavo are the leaders of G40 and are currently mobilising for a 1 million men march in support of Mugabe who is under pressure to step down due to his advanced age in May.

The diverse opposition is suffering from a similar crisis. The Movement for Democratic Change is little better than the ruling party, as it is also marred by factionalism between the current president of the party, Morgan Tsvangirai, and the former party youth leader, Nelson Chamisa, who lost his position as spokesperson at the party's last congress. Since the MDC's formation in 1999 it has seen numerous splits, for example, MDC-N led by Welchman Ncube, [and] the disbanded MDC-99 [led] by Job Sikhala, a former student activist who returned to the party fold in 2014. Tendai Biti, the former MDC finance minister in the Government of National Unity, became the secretary-general of MDC-Renewal in 2015. In September that year MDC-Renewal launched as a distinct party, the People's Democratic Party, with Biti elected president of the new party. The MDC is in total disarray. Essentially these parties, recycling politicians and elites, compete to promote neoliberal policies with similarly anti-worker austerity policies. This is all the more astonishing if you consider the fact that many of these figures, Biti, Sikhala, Chamisa, emerged from a radical socialist politics in the 1990s.

For an example of the neoliberal venality, the MDC-T which is running the city council of Harare has targeted vendors who try to make a living hawking juice cards (telephone recharge cards), fruit and vegetables, cheap imported goods [and] called for more powers to be given to city police to prosecute the vendors. Early this year we saw the council demolishing the houses of the poor, yet the council has not built a single house for more than 20 years now.

Zimbabwe's trade union movement, its impressive working class activism in the 1990s, helped to found the main opposition party in 1999. Can you tell ROAPE something about the state of workers and trade unions in the country today and how the organised representation of workers has been weakened?

For more than a decade the country has been in crisis, workers and the poor have paid the price for the crisis created by the government and [the] rich. Figures are hard to come by, but roughly 70% of organised workers – in a relatively large and developed working class – have been retrenched since 1998. The working class, in cities and towns around Zimbabwe, has been literally declassed – tens of thousands moving to South Africa, or forced into the informal sector. So the neoliberal policies adopted by the government from the 1990s has seen thousands of workers losing their jobs through retrenchments. This has had a dramatic impact, weakening organised labour. Unions have not only lost their membership through retrenchments, but those workers who have maintained their positions have sought to distance themselves from any radical fightback fearing for their jobs. Unemployment, as we know, is a massive disincentive for strike action. This was made worse by the Nyamange vs Zuva Petroleum ruling on 17 July 2015 that upheld common law, stating an employer could terminate an employee's contract by giving three months' notice. The ruling immediately saw more than 30,000 workers laid off, by being given three months' notice. Remaining workers have either been put on casual contracts or silenced to protect their jobs. The result for the organised working class has been devastating.

Not only have the unions been weakened by low membership but also through their relationship to companies as they seek to survive. Most of the unions' financial subscriptions have collapsed making it difficult for them to operate and at times receiving their union's dues from the company late or depending on contributions from NGOs. This has created a situation with the union bureaucracy compromising with bosses and being bought off by "donations" at the expense of their membership.

In some cases, the situation is appalling. Not only are the union leaders being increasingly incorporated, or more crudely simply bought-off, but some seek to compete with chief executives of companies, living similarly luxury lifestyles, driving cars donated to them by the company and drinking and dining at the same bars and restaurants. Thus many of them have become buddies with managers, further compromising workers' rights. Frequently we see union leaders urging workers to accept short-term contracts and salary cuts or face unemployment.

This has also made worse splits in the trade union movement with numerous splinter unions being formed. The petty personal differences and disputes among trade union leaders with competing trade union federations, unable to unite. Last year, for example, after the Zuva ruling, which dealt a considerable advantage to company bosses to continue their attacks on the working class, the trade union movement failed to mount any serious or sustained action.

It is important to recall that the trade union movement, under pressure from a powerful rank and file, was at the heart of every serious political challenge to the regime for more than twenty years after independence in 1980. The current situation, viewed historically, is all the more devastating.

As the economic meltdown has rippled across Zimbabwe, can you explain how this has impacted on women?

As usual the most affected by these interlinking crises are women. Women were the majority of workers in Zimbabwe employed in the retail sector, where many still work. In the middle of this crisis women have been targeted, with the gains that working women made in the 1980s and 1990s being almost entirely eroded.

Most women no longer enjoy maternity leave with many forced to take unpaid leave for a month, compelled to return to work before they have recovered from giving birth, with childcare provision completely absent. They are then forced to work normal hours, with no provisions for breastfeeding etc. Wanting to protect their jobs, most women feel compelled to accept these circumstances since any position is preferable to staying at home with no income.

Sexism, sexual harassment and discrimination have long been a problem in Zimbabwe. But in recent years, levels of sexual harassment have increased dramatically – but again it is hard to assess exactly the extent of this increase as cases are not reported because of fear of reprisals. We have dealt with a significant increase in cases of sexual harassment at the Zimbabwe Labour Centre.

The threat of job losses casts a long, dark shadow across all aspects of Zimbabwe – but, perhaps, most worryingly on the position of women in society. So it has been made to look fashionable for a woman to have an affair with her boss, showered with gifts and special treatment at work, only to be dumped in favour of another woman. Again, this is increasingly common.

As the crisis continues to worsen with firms cutting jobs at companies like the mobile phone giant Econet, the Grain Marketing Board (GMB) etc, the only way out for many young and single mothers is to accept sexual advances from the supervisor and managers. Such scandals that have been exposed show how bosses, for example, at the state National Social Security Authority received loans from the pension scheme for their girlfriends with no action taken to recover the public money. All this does is to encourage the oppression of women in workplaces around the country.

Can you talk about the state of rank and file action in Zimbabwe? What sort of opposition is emerging in the recent strikes and actions that have taken place?

Despite the attacks we have seen, and the corruption of certain union leaders, workers are beginning to organise themselves independently. Over 300 hundred workers in 2015 from the parastatal Grain Marketing Board spent more than a month sleeping outside their company premises in the middle of the rainy season to demand the payment of salary arrears dating back to 2014. These workers received solidarity from fellow unions and progressive civil society organisations like the International Socialist Organisation, the Zimbabwe Labour Centre, and many individuals in Zimbabwe and elsewhere on the continent. They partially won and only left the companies premises after agreeing to a deal to be paid US$350 per month, until all their salary arrears were repaid. They threatened to return should the employer default.

Inspired by the example of GMB workers, National Railways of Zimbabwe workers in March this year also occupied the company premises to highlight that they do not have anywhere to live, as they have not been paid for 15 months. Their strike continues. Nurses from Mutare, a city in the east of Zimbabwe, also staged a sit-in at council offices in February this year, demanding their salary arrears be paid. Frequently, such militant and often unorganised action is the only language left for workers.

Finally, for the radical left, what are the strategies and possibilities for a progressive and socialist politics in Zimbabwe?

As the crisis continues to worsen in Zimbabwe, the divisions – you could say the cannibalism – in the ruling elite will deepen as they fight amongst each other for their own survival. These divisions and factionalism are a struggle over the control of a frail and broken economy, with a divided comprador elite involved in a vicious battle over the country's puny spoils. The struggle for socialists is to ensure that the working class, women and the poor do not become involved in these battles. These forces must resist the temptations of political parties, new and old, who are calling for further austerity against the poor. The MDC, when it was part of the Government of National Unity, from 2009 to elections in 2013, and its current economic policies offer little for Zimbabwe's poor. The recent rank and file action we have seen gives an example of how unions can be strengthened, but corrupt union leaders must be replaced by those committed to advancing their members rights. There is much to be done.

32. Yao Graham (2016), Pan-African Challenges

ROAPE's Yao Graham is the coordinator of Third World Network in Accra, and long-standing activist, editor, and advocate for social justice in Ghana and across Africa. Graham has been involved with the review for decades and has helped develop its analysis of the continent's shifting political economy. In conversation with Leo Zeilig, Graham covers radical political economy in Africa, structural transformation, and the legacy of neoliberalism.

***

So, could you first tell me briefly about who you are and your political background and development?

My name is Yao Graham, a Ghanaian by birth. I was in secondary school in St. Augustine's College, the city of Cape Coast, in the late 1960s and early 1970s, at the time when there were a number of very important things taking place globally. Some of my earliest recollections were my involvement around anti-apartheid activism in Ghana, discussions about pan-Africanism, reading books by radical African-Americans. I was profoundly affected reading Malcolm X's autobiography. The school allowed us to charge subscriptions for magazines to our bills and I ordered *Africa Journal* and *Newsweek* which provided information about many things going on at the time – the Vietnam War, national liberation struggles across Africa; there were things happening around us.

But, in terms of direct political engagement, coming in contact with a friend's uncle – a student at the University of Cape Coast who was president of the National Union of Ghana Students – was important. I was around 15 and through him a group of us met the leadership of the National Union of Ghana Students at the time. We took to spending time at the Cape Vars campus.

They were beginning to re-establish Kwame Nkrumah's legitimacy, because around that time the soldiers who had overthrown Nkrumah – and their civilian collaborators who succeeded them – sought to erase Nkrumah from history. His works, images were banned. You'd be imprisoned if you were found with Nkrumah's photo or writings. So, we spent a lot of time with these guys. We were fascinated by their activism and their ideas – that was a very profound influence. We brought some of that activism to our school, initially in the students' representative council. We began to even take part in some NUGS events. I remember three of us going to a National Assembly of Students and demanding that NUGS take on board the concerns of secondary school students. At this time we were prefects in St. Augustine's, elected by the students. We reached out to prefects in other schools in Cape Coast about the formation of a national association of secondary school students. We did not succeed.

My years at the University of Ghana was in the period of some of the most intense student activism in Ghana's postcolonial history. The military regime at the time faced a lot of student activism, initially against brutalities by soldiers, then demands for it to go as economic conditions transformed into a broad front movement against its attempts to entrench itself in power. So, university led to a deepening of my activist engagements. I studied for a law degree and did not formally study political science or philosophy but I began to read political theory and philosophy. I was very interested in these. I began to read Marx and radical literature generally, a fairly eclectic wave of books about anti-racism, anti-imperialist volumes on the Middle East, etc so a fairly eclectic intellectual formation.

By my late university years, I could say that I'd definitely become oriented towards a kind of Marxist politics. The first Marxist study cells were emerging on the campus. The embryonic foundations of what would emerge as the Marxist influenced political left which came to prominence in Ghana of the 1980s and 1990s were laid founded in the student movement of that period.

And this is the mid-1970s?

Yeah, this is mid to late 1970s. This was a very important period in my formation.

Can you talk briefly about what your first involvement in ROAPE was?

I knew about the journal. I'd been reading after I came to England as a student in 1979, but my first direct involvement with *ROAPE* was in 1984, when I was invited from Ghana to speak at a *ROAPE* conference at Keele University, a conference on the world crisis and food security in Africa. I had suspended my PhD studies at Warwick University and was in Ghana working as a full time political activist, in the Rawlings government and the New Democratic Movement (NDM). The upheavals unleashed by the Rawlings-led coup of December 31 1981 and the regime's initial anti-imperialism had attracted intense interest and I was invited to present a paper at the conference. At this time I was a leading member of the NDM, also involved in the national leadership of the Defence Committees set up by the Jerry Rawlings government. I presented my paper at the conference and subsequently wrote a piece for the journal on Ghana.

The Keele conference was a very lively experience, let me put it that way. By this time Rawlings' relationship with his closest allies on the Ghanaian left had started fracturing and a number of them who were in exile in the UK came to the *ROAPE* conference and caused an uproar about my presence. This reflected the deepening rifts within the sections of the left who had supported the PNDC regime. These ex-comrades were in the crowd when I spoke in the plenary session and generated a huge uproar. Such was the heat that the organisers put on an emergency side meeting on Ghana. This was packed out and marked by sharp debates.

And the reason for the uproar was because you were being too critical?

No, I was being denounced as a traitor for continuing to work in the Rawlings government by those who were now in exile who felt that the project of the revolution had been betrayed. This was an important point of difference within the Ghanaian left. Some of us never thought it was a revolution, rather something that offered possibilities for progressive work. So our expectations of the Rawlings regime were a lot less exaggerated. Our analysis of the twist and turns of the new government were different from those who thought it was a revolution. Such analysis is important; if you thought the coup d'état had been or ushered in a revolution then, of course, the revolution had failed. However, if you didn't think it was a revolution but a coup d'état regime which had created some space for the progressive politics to operate, then you could continue to try and do your best in that space. My paper to the *ROAPE* conference reflected this standpoint.

The invitation from *ROAPE* was important for me, also, because it forced me to put down on paper my analysis of the context of Rawlings' return to power and some of the features of the unfolding situation. In a situation of some fluidity and intensive day and night activism the pause to reflect and write the paper for the *ROAPE* conference was useful. So that was my first involvement in that way with *ROAPE*.

Brilliant, and you were obviously aware of the journal before that?

Yes, I'd been reading it as part of my work as a student at Warwick and I met some of the editors involved in it at various political events in Britain in that period.

How would you assess the role of the journal? Did you regard it as a companion in some of the struggles you were involved in?

I must confess that during the time that I was back in Ghana in the 1980s, during that seven-year period, occasionally, you came across *ROAPE* but during that time I didn't have much of an engagement with *ROAPE*, but when I came back to England in 1989 to complete my PhD thesis it was something I returned to reading.

And, looking back at the history of the journal and your direct involvement in it from 1984 and then afterwards in the UK in the 1990s, how would you assess the contribution that ROAPE has made?

The invitation to me as an activist in Ghana to come to speak at the Keele conference in 1984 points to a recognition of the importance of that kind of dialogue, bringing activists into the space that the journal was creating. For me, as an activist, it got me to work through my analysis of the context within which I was working. Subsequently, I read *ROAPE* mainly as a general analysis which offered ideas and also information about what was happening across the continent. I wouldn't say that it occupied a particular place, because I was reading a lot of things and, also during the period that I was working as an activist, I must confess that I was more in interested in reading about the experiences of people in building organisations – what happens in struggles, what people did to reform economies and so on and so forth – in a way that would help me with the work I was directly involved in. That kind of theoretical and analytical writing was very important to me at the time. Occasionally I read articles that touched on my concerns at the time. So there were those kinds of moments when I saw the value of the journal, but it was one of an array of publications that I looked at – and for a long period of the 1980s, when I was in Ghana, I didn't have access to it at all.

If you look at the origins of ROAPE from 1974 in that second wave of independence, a radical movement that came about on the back of the failure of the 1960s and 1970s – the hope of that first wave of independence. The review was borne in that period, particularly with the struggles in Angola and Mozambique. It then goes on to analyse and to critique structural adjustment in the 1980s and 1990s. How successful has that project been, in your mind, in providing, to some extent, radical analysis of the continent's political economy through that period?

I think the critique of structural adjustment and the role of those who provided the critique was an extremely important contribution in [that] period. Why? Because first of all, the discussion of the failures of the immediate postcolonial period to the crisis of the 1970s was presented in the dominant narrative as a zero sum way, that whole period was a kind of blank slate, that it was all a waste of time. And, yet, during that period, there was important support for other national liberation movements to grow on the continent. Within that period, people had some experience of what the state could do, in terms of welfare, education, health and so on.

I think a journal like *ROAPE* was very important in providing a critique of the World Bank and the IMF, providing a counterpoint to these institutions with their very large machinery of propaganda. Academia in Africa was increasingly taken over by the politics and machinery of structural adjustment and neoliberalism, so to have a minority of scholars and intellectuals who continued to offer an alternative perspective was very important indeed, in terms of keeping a view that something else was possible. And, for those of us who were engaged in struggling against structural adjustment on the ground, having the sense of that community was quite important.

Tell me how you see the challenges today for a journal of radical political economy? What are the important issues that need to be tackled? What's the orientation, the thinking that needs to take place, in a fairly limited way, so that the journal could make a contribution?

If you look at the contemporary world and the African situation, ever since the global crisis of 2008-2009, neoliberalism has been repositioning itself to maintain its dominance by absorbing critical discourses. The current one, of course, is to reduce everything to inequality, without going to the foundations in the political economy. In the African context this approach is expressed in the strength of the Africa Rising narrative, which also sees a celebration of an African middle class, the rise of a consuming class in Africa and an occasional nod to inequality. Yet it's also becoming clear that the colonial bequest of raw material export dependence continues to determine the fate of Africa and its people in the global economy. Today the continent is more entrenched in that division of labour than it was in 1974, when the global crisis began to take hold.

So, in a certain sense, the political economy of neocolonialism remains highly active. Africa remains very much locked in that, although the global configuration has changed. Today there's a new discussion about the fact that Africa needs to implement structural transformation to escape this dependence. But, within that seeming agreement, there are different ideological positions and I think it is quite important for journals like *ROAPE* to become part of that debate, because it involves an examination of the legacy and the consequences of more than thirty years of neoliberal dominance. It's an analysis of what growth represents in Africa. It's an analysis critical of the so-called Africa Rising narrative.

But the other dimension that is also really important has to do with the fact that political liberalisation in the early 1990s was significant in opening up space for popular organisation and expression. But there's a growing realisation that electoral politics, what I call the electoral carousel, is not the sum of democratic politics. Increasingly we see protests which are about people's living conditions, protests about rights, protests around the new frontiers of capital accumulation – whether it's land grabs or the growing movement to privatise services. These are the new frontiers for making money on the continent, whether it's the so-called public/private partnerships that reach into areas which, historically, everybody would have agreed were the realm of public goods, these have now all become issues of public concern and struggle. And I think, again, these are issues that *ROAPE*, as a journal, needs to connect itself with, in terms of analysis and engagement.

Because, you see, *ROAPE*'s project in the 1970s was easier, because the national liberation movement in Africa was internationalised, in terms of the support that they had. England was an important staging post for representatives of the national liberation movements. It was an important place for such movements to be located in exile. So academics, who were interested in working in Africa, in supporting African struggles, actually had a community here that they could work with and a community through which they could link quite easily with similar communities on the African Continent. So, in a certain sense, there was a community that stretched from inside Africa to outside it around certain kinds of questions. Today, that community doesn't exist in the same way.

But the point I'm making is that with the shrinking of the historic community of activists from the continent in the North, how the journal builds a community with people, the involvement of activists and scholars in Africa, is vital in ensuring that the ideals that drove the foundation of the journal continue to be pursued in different conditions. The important question is how do we work out that continuity in a new period? If we do not it can become quite easy for the journal to become just another peer-reviewed publication where an Africanist will publish papers on Africa, without really engaging in the continent beyond seeing it as a site where you collect data. But the founders of the journal were involved with the continent as a place where they were reflecting on and supporting struggles to build a certain kind of economy and society, and saw the journal as a place where certain ideals should be pursued. So Africa was a laboratory where they were participating with African people as activists for change – as opposed to a place you can simply write about us, where you interrogate the concepts through which society is analysed. This [is] the danger and the challenge for *ROAPE*.

Could you talk briefly about the relationship between academic analysis and activist engagement, and how when you came here in 1984 on an invitation from ROAPE you spoke as an activist but also as an analyst. How do we create the spaces where that can take place?

I think the business of interpretation, of course, is fundamental to being able to have a correct appraisal of reality, so as to work effectively for change. If you characterise something as a revolution, as many saw the Rawlings coup in 1981, then you have certain expectations of it and you would engage in a certain kind of political practice. Now, if you are wrong in your characterisation, your political practice is likely to be wrong and the consequences could be pretty appalling. So the analytical function is quite important but, for me, the key thing is how do we continue to create a dynamic where, as much as possible, *ROAPE*, in terms of its work, continues in analysing society but also creates a community where what is being discussed is influenced by what people are engaged in struggling around. We also need to make sure that the analytical work that is reflected in the pages of *ROAPE* is more widely available for activists to use. I think that process is quite important.

I say this, also, because on a continent where today some [of] the most influential analysts influencing the orientation of people are religious figures – Christian and Muslim – a progressive, political economy and materialist analysis, which tries to ground people in the here and now, as opposed to the afterlife, is imperative. In a climate of pretty desperate conditions for many, religion has mobilised people across the continent, so we must offer analysis and perspectives which help people to engage with their material reality as agents, who can actually make meaningful change, rather than leave human misery to some spiritual force to resolve. In Ghana, with the collapse of manufacturing, large buildings – warehouses, factories – which have been abandoned in the industrial areas of the capital Accra, have been bought up by charismatic Christian[s] and turned into huge prayer halls. Material production has been replaced by the enterprise of spiritual redemption. You can't get a more poignant symbolism than that.

Where the working class used to be gathered, where people used to work, organise and discuss as unions and discuss their material conditions, where people earned an income are now prayer halls. Today people gather in their thousands to listen to sermons about how, if you continue to be a good Christian and pay your tithes to the pastor, something good will happen to you.

What an astonishing example. On that question on the role of analysis and political activism the journal engages with in different ways – and it was a mixed bag and a very broad church when it was formed – did you see a pan-African project with socialism as a project for national governments, but also regional and continental transformation? Do you still see that as a feasible project for the continent?

Yes. This morning I got a WhatsApp from my colleague who had gone to a meeting on a continental free trade area organised by the African Union Commission and he wrote, "I'm sitting here, feeling like a dinosaur. Everybody here wants liberalisation, liberalisation and more liberalisation." I think, given the current state of forces, there's a substantial challenge of defensive action that is required against the still quite strong forces of neoliberalism on the continent. Because, whilst there are protests, their organisation and the strength of progressive forces, the organisation of alternatives across the continent is not at a stage where one can feasibly talk about socialism as a near term objective.

I think, however, in terms of the demands that people are making for an alternative, the agenda remains unchanged. But the near term challenge, the frontline challenge, must be a complete and coherent replacement of neoliberalism in Africa. I think that also retains important pan-African challenges for us, because the old arguments that were made about the smallness of African countries, as economies, as markets, the need to unite forces behind our common hurdles remains extremely valid. The work that we do in Third World Network-Africa, on trade policy, on the structures and inequities of Africa's role in the global economy, is important work for everyone across Africa, because the regional and the continental have become key sites of policy making and decision making. So it is quite important that in the context of global capitalism to see the limits of small national markets, that we accept the limits of national economies. Policymakers are also interested in expanded geographies, for investment, for selling goods and services and so on. So there is a dynamic process where the supra-national is becoming a more and more important unit for political economic activity in Africa, we have to respond to this as activists and intellectuals.

So, our response, the response of progressives...

Has to [be to] engage with the regional and the pan-African, within a global engagement.

As a final question, can you reflect on your work as Coordinator of Third World Network-Africa?

Third World Network-Africa was created by a group of us who were previously associated in Ghanaian politics. We set it up as a policy research and advocacy organisation with a pan-African remit. We are very clear about the limits of NGO[s] as a vehicle for transformative, progressive work. However, what we have done over the years is to pick issues which we think pertain to the nature of Africa's role in the global economy – trade and investment, finance, development issues – which determine the way Africa is inserted in the global economy and then try and work around those issues from the perspective of the defence of popular interests as well as pushing for alternative policies that challenge the dominance of neoliberalism. Have we been successful? To the extent that the organisation has gained a lot of credibility as contributing to a progressive African alternative perspective, influenced debates and in some cases influenced outcomes of struggles, to that extent I think we've been successful.

So, in Ghana, where it has been possible to organise and mobilise, for example around mining issues and the interests of mining affected communities, we have at least significantly transformed the debate on mining in the country. On trade policy issues, in about 20 years of working with others across Africa, around the World Trade Organisation, the EU's Economy Partnership Agreements, we have had an important influence and exerted pressures on the debates and key institutions. An NGO is not a political party, you need to find the methods that optimise the influence that such an organisational form can exert. And we're fortunate to be based in Ghana, where the laws on NGO activities are pretty liberal. We've also been lucky over the years to have been able to raise money, from like-minded organisations and also foundations, who find our work useful. Yet such dependence on other organisations for our funding is also a serious constraint on what you can do.

33. Guy Marius Sagna (2021), Decolonising a Neo-Colony

In March 2021, Senegal experienced unprecedented popular protests. Recently released from prison at the time, activist Guy Marius Sagna – founding member of the Front for an Anti-Imperialist Popular and Pan-African Revolution (Frapp-France Dégage) – argues in this interview with Florian Bobin and Maky Madiba Sylla that anti-imperialism is gaining ground in the country. While welcoming this upsurge in popular mobilisation, he warns African progressives against the "manoeuvres of imperialism and its local henchmen" and contends that a sovereign Senegal can only be achieved "within a united and sovereign Africa."

***

You have been fighting for years for a sovereign Senegal; facing the neo-colonial status quo prevailing since independence, you call for blocking the road to foreign interference through "pan-African anti-imperialism." Where does this political awareness come from?

I was lucky enough to have an uncle, Ludovic Alihonou, who was a member of a left-wing organisation [African Workers Rally - Senegal], organised within the framework of a newspaper called *Serñent* ("The Spark" in Wolof), in reference to *Iskra*.[33] So, it was these left-wing activists – Birane Gaye, Assane Samb, Fodé Roland Diagne – who took charge of my education from the age of 11-12. Later, militants like Alla Kane, Moctar Fofana Niang, Madièye Mbodj, Jo Diop, Malick Sy, Ousseynou Ndiaye, etc, were added to the group. We are the heirs of our glorious predecessors: from Lamine Ibrahima Arfang Senghor, Seydou Cissokho, Birane Gaye,

---

33   *Iskra* was the official paper of the Russian Social Democratic Labour Party.

[and] the elders Alla Kane, Dialo Diop to Cheikh Anta Diop. We can go further back in history, with Aline Sitoé Diatta, [Biram] Yacine Boubou, and even our religious resistants Mame [Cheikh Amadou] Bamba, [and] Maba Diakhou Bâ. Studying and reading people like Omar Blondin Diop will only give us the tools to better analyse history and especially the present and better guide us out of poverty and underdevelopment.

When you are raised by the left, your understanding of life is that the misfortune of the majority is made by the happiness of an overpowering minority. To understand why there is so much homelessness and poverty in France – the same France that claims to be helping us while letting its own people freeze to death – it is because there is a system called capitalism, which can only function through the oppression of the majority in the capitalist centres and the oppression of the majority in the peripheries, to speak like Samir Amin. This is the vision of life that I have inherited, a political vision that it is the people who make history and that it must be taught that no one else will come to save them.

This is why, for decades, we have been standing alongside unpaid workers, like public kindergarten teachers. My first imprisonment in 2012-2013 was part of this struggle: five days in prison in Tambacounda [in the southeast of Senegal] alongside nine teachers. We had blocked the national road to Tambacounda following months of unfruitful struggle. And since 2012, nearly a thousand kindergarten teachers have been trained and paid thanks to these struggles. So yes, freedom comes only through struggle. We have also stood by other fighting actors, like arbitrarily dismissed contractual Senelec (National Electricity Company of Senegal) workers, who were able to be recruited again. We stood by workers like those at the PCCI call centre, who went 14 months without pay. And that battle was won. In this struggle, we have been beaten, detained several times, inhaled tear gas.

When big businesses like Auchan and Carrefour were setting up in Senegal, there existed no regulation for supermarkets. We had to fight and say *"Auchan dégage"* (Auchan means get out), with, of course, content to it: we asked the state to suspend their contract and make an impact assessment of what would be the consequences. *"Auchan dégage"* was also to hold a conference on domestic trade, to see what went wrong and why Senegalese markets are the way they are: what is the share of responsibility of citizens, municipalities, retailers, the state and how to have Senegalese markets that meet the needs of its people. Because it is neither Lidl, nor Walmart, nor Leclerc, nor Auchan, nor Carrefour that will transform Senegal: they are going to come, skim off the profits and take them back abroad. Of course, many of our people will follow these benefits out of a bled-dry Africa: that is the tragedy of immigration.

Facts have only reinforced my worldview. Facts may contradict theory, but in my personal experience, this theory, this political vision of life, inherited from my worthy predecessors, has only been reinforced, refined by the tragic reality of the Senegalese people. We fight while being Gramscians, that is to say having the pessimism of analysis: we give blows to the neocolonial system, but this neocolonial system will not remain inert to our blows. It will not accept that it can be struck like that. While having the pessimism of analysis that neocolonialism is going to do everything, imperialism will be more and more ferocious – we maintain an optimism of the will. The optimism of the will is to know that whatever imperialism does, whatever the alliance between imperialism and Africans who accept to be its servants do, the peoples can be strong enough to transcend this, and ultimately win.

The popular uprising from March 2021, expressive of a generalised resentment toward the country's ruling political class, is an illustration of this power balance you describe. Throughout February and early March, dozens of Pastef-Les Patriotes opposition party activists, members of the Frapp movement [Frapp is Front for an Anti-Imperialist Popular and Pan-African Revolution] – yourself included – and various citizens were arrested and imprisoned for their political activities. What is your take on the situation in Senegal?

I think that what happened recently is an uprising, a revolt, not a revolution. Now, many uprisings, many revolts can lead to revolution. And an organisation like Frapp is trying to contribute to the advent of this revolution. What happened recently is at least two things. First, it is expressive that neocolonialism, imperialism, is afraid because there is an unprecedented situation in Senegal. Never in Senegal, since 1960, has a candidate been campaigning against the CFA franc, against the EPAs (Economic Partnership Agreements), against foreign military presences – let's say against the neocolonial system. This is the first time in Africa, in a country formerly colonised by France, at least in West Africa, that a candidate has 16% of the vote while campaigning openly against imperialism. And I think that President Macky Sall knows that if nothing is done fundamentally, the fifth President will be called Ousmane Sonko,[34] [which means] the victory of an anti-imperialist political family. They understand the danger; they know that those fighting still have a lot of room to manoeuvre and that the political parties that imperialism relies on are much more discredited. And this discredit will grow increasingly worse.

The second thing to decipher is that the awareness-raising campaign against imperialism has made great strides in Senegal. This way of going out in the street, of mobilising, is unprecedented in Senegal. And it is the result of work to which several organisations have contributed, so-called nationalist, patriotic, pan-African, anti-imperialist organisations. When we created Frapp, we said: "We want to contribute to putting questions of sovereignty – economic and monetary sovereignty, but also popular and democratic sovereignty – at the heart of the political, economic and social debate." We must radically transform the relationship between Africa and the rest of the world; Africa must stop being the rest of the world's wallet. But we must also transform the relationship between the people, the citizens and

---

34 Sonko is a leader of the Patriots of Senegal for Work, Ethics and Fraternity (PASTEF) party and an MP; his arrest on 3 March triggered a wave of youth protest that Guy Marius Sagna is referring to here.

the elites who come to power. We have states held hostage by elected officials who are not servants [of the people] because of the political system.

I believe that democracy is for the people to choose, either in the ballot box or in the street. For me, when the people of Burkina Faso ousted [Blaise] Compaoré [in October 2014], that is democracy. But for me also, if a people oust Macky Sall and elects a pan-African through the ballot box, it would prevent deaths. But everyone knows that a class as a class never abdicates. The member of a class can commit revolutionary suicide, to speak like Amílcar Cabral. But a class as a class never commits suicide. The parasitic Senegalese bureaucratic bourgeoisie, subservient to imperialism in general, will never willingly accept that Senegal enters the camp of pan-Africanism, of anti-imperialism. Imperial France will never accept that its former colonies leave its private preserve. Senegal is Françafrique's "democratic showcase"; Ivory Coast is Françafrique's "economic showcase." We are the pillars of Françafrique. If only one of these two countries leave, Françafrique collapses, the CFA franc collapses. That is what is at stake. So organisations like Pastef or the Frapp are a danger.

France, imperialism in general, sees that this private preserve is slipping away. And throughout these past years, we have heard France and its supporters in the media say: "there is an anti-French sentiment." In reality, it is not an anti-French sentiment, it is an anti-imperialist sentiment. What country does not wish to be free? Yes, we have a deep desire for freedom. Not, like France or the United States, to oppress other peoples… An anti-imperialist, a consequential pan-Africanist, wants to be free and be sovereign but not oppress others. On the contrary, to work so that they [can] be free.

Malcolm X explained that when black people start becoming conscious, the first step is to hate white people. When populations also begin to be anti-imperialist, they hate its external aspects – hence the ransacking of Auchan, Total, of French symbols. It's the same process. It's not bad, but you have to quickly raise your consciousness and understand that there are whites who are as oppressed as blacks, that it's the same system. You have to refuse division and manipulation of racial, religious, ethnic or national sentiments aimed at weakening and dividing workers and peoples in struggle. When the ordinary, conventional voices are no longer able to hold down workers and peoples, to make them accept their oppression, the oppressors – if you study [the] history of humanity – have always resorted to using division through manipulating ethnic religious and racial sentiments. So that, today, they prevent people from looking to neocolonialism, and that Peuls come and say: "you, the Wolof, are the cause of my situation"; that Sereers use Joolas as scapegoats. That's why someone like Karl Marx said to the white workers: "the white worker will never be emancipated as long as the black worker is oppressed."

Imperialism and its local henchmen – the bureaucratic bourgeoisie led by President Macky Sall – will manoeuvre. I think that, in some ways, the religious leaders saved Macky Sall. If it was not for them, he might not have spent an [extra] night in Senegal. But with the March uprising, it's the first time in a very long time that an African people from one of the countries formerly colonised by France has blocked the ruling bureaucratic bourgeoisie against an opponent. Look at what happened in Ivory Coast or Guinea. The voices of the revolution, liberation or emancipation are unfathomable. Perhaps this was the preview to a much more significant struggle to come. For me, what happened recently is a step in the very long struggle of the Senegalese people... This is the umpteenth stage. And there is reason to be hopeful with the people and the youth.

In response to the protests that rocked Senegal in March [2021], the government used live fire and marauding militias to crush the movement – recalling the single-party state's violent methods 50 years ago. In addition to the 100s injured, 14 people died in less than a week. Many accounts have also painted a chilling picture of prison conditions. What can you tell us about political repression in Senegal today?

First, I often hear people say that [Leopold Sedar] Senghor left us a state, [but he] left us a neocolonial state. And for there to be a neocolonial state with solid foundations, it was necessary to go through this repression and "reduce resistance to its simplest expression." This is what President Senghor tirelessly did. I believe he had the best profile to continue to make Senegal a "little Paris", to perpetuate the cooperation agreements, to make our Constitution the twin of the French Constitution, to leave the CFA franc untouched, to make our official language French and to continue – from the cradle – to dominate the Senegalese in their minds. France needed to leave to stay better. When we see what we are living, it gives you the impression – even if today there is social media and all that – that almost nothing has changed. We are almost in the same positions, the same contexts as in the 1950s and 1960s. In the 1950s, some said yes to independence and others no to independence or that we should remain in the French sphere. Today, there are still those who say, "France get out," "Auchan get out," that we must get out of the CFA franc and those who say that the CFA franc is a good currency.

Yes, because of our actions, our activities and our struggles, we face acts of repression that remind us of what our predecessors experienced decades ago. First, it is often very difficult to get permits to demonstrate… We have been invited by people in certain localities in Senegal, and I was surprised to hear the locality's sub-prefect say that they had to ask him for authorisation to invite me and that he gave it before I could come. It is no longer participating in a banned demonstration that gets you into police custody or prison, but the simple fact of taking a letter and going to police headquarters to inform the prefect, who then takes the liberty of banning or not.

In police stations, you are also a victim of many other things. I remember being slapped hard by prison officers there. I arrived at court, the guard who was doing the search told me: "Guy Marius, you are back again. You really are an asshole." And when I told him that he "was much more of an asshole than I was," I received a slap in the face. In one of the central police station's cells, we are sometimes dumped there and, to urinate, we are forced to use the same water bottles we drink out from. But we understand that one of the functions of defence and security forces in a neo-colony like Senegal is frightening the population. And so, subjecting demonstrators and protestors to such treatment that they no longer feel like resisting – that they surrender, that they become afraid, that their parents and their families become terrified. You regularly hear that comrades are tortured. The latest is one of the protesters arrested on February 8 and 9, 2021, they took him out of his cell at the central police station and brought him upstairs. There, they kicked him in the testicles. And then the Senegalese police threatens ... those who would accuse them of torture.

This is why even ordinary citizens who are not fighters, or are arrested in a context other than resistance, are victims of the fact that our defence and security forces are neocolonial, the heirs of colonial France. This is how we must understand that a citizen like Pape Sarr, simply accused of stealing a sheep, was tortured in the Thiaroye police station, diluent poured on him and electrocuted, before catching fire and dying like a mummy in his bandages at the hospital [in July 2018]; Seck Ndiaye found [dead] in his room, beaten by five police officers [in June 2018]; Abdoulaye Timera hit by a police car on the Allées du Centenaire [in April 2018]. And so far, for all these cases and others, no justice, no truth...

I worked at the regional hospital in Sédhiou, one of the two or three poorest regions in Senegal, and discovered the system and mechanism through which its different directors embezzled money. Since 2014, when I spoke publicly about it, I have been pushed to the sideline by the Ministry of Health. So, since 2014, I have had no office, no place to work. The Senegalese state prefers to have me in the street rather than in work, so I don't see things to denounce and they can keep me in a precarious situation, preventing me from thinking and acting optimally for the anti-imperialist and pan-Africanist struggle. But our worthy predecessors were victims of the same methods. These are the same practices inherited from the colonial past, which are, in fact, not a past but more than ever a feature of contemporary reality.

You just mentioned anti-imperialism and pan-Africanism. In line with the long history of theorising and implementing the pan-African ideal, "the United States of Africa", as Cheikh Anta Diop spoke of it, what is your vision of it in the early 2020s?

I think that today, necessarily for all African states, Senegal included, there will be no way out of underdevelopment and poverty without sovereignty. In other words, sovereignty is today a sine qua non condition, a necessary condition, so that we can get out of the situation where 64% of small and medium-sized businesses (SMBs) collapse in Senegal before their third years. How can you solve the problem of unemployment when Senegalese SMBs have such a high mortality rate? Being sovereign will also allow us to solve scandals such as four women dying every day from pregnancy or sixty children under five dying every day from minor illnesses such as acute respiratory infections, i.e. coughs, colds, diarrhoea, malaria. That's more than 25,000 children [per year]. Elsewhere, we would have spoken of genocide. Yes, the imperialist system is genocidal.

So we need to be sovereign in Senegal, in Gambia, in Mauritania, in Mali, in Burkina Faso, etc. We need to escape imperialism and have states that guarantee and ensure monetary sovereignty, commercial sovereignty, military sovereignty – all sovereignties. Even this language that we use, French, we have to escape from it. Our children – whether Wolof, Jaxanke, Bassari, Koñagi, Puular, Joola, Sereer – must be able to learn in their languages. Because a language is first and foremost a vision of life. By educating our children with a different vision of life, we make them little French people. And so, instead of wearing Ngaay shoes [leather sandals], like the ones I'm wearing, we prefer wearing Italian or French. Instead of eating fondé [millet porridge], using our millet, sorghum, corn, we will prefer eating camembert. We must therefore wrest this sovereignty.

In order to be viable and sustainable, the project of a sovereign Senegal will only be done within a united and sovereign Africa. How will 16 million Senegalese citizens be able to face 300 million Americans, a state with a billion Chinese or some 300 million of the European Union? Our micro-states cannot guarantee it in the long term. Personally, I wouldn't mind if Senegal, Gambia and Mauritania, or Senegal and Guinea, decided today to have a federal state. If it is on the scale of ECOWAS or of West Africa, it could work. We should not underestimate anything. The problem is that progressives are not at the head of these different states, and we don't know when they will be. So, we can't say, "We need 54 states to be united." That's why everyone has to fight, and if everyone wins in their state we will win everywhere.

We need a sovereign Africa, disconnected from the International Monetary Fund and the World Bank, from the World Trade Organisation, from fisheries agreements and other EPAs with the European Union, from foreign military presences – whether French or American. An African unity that can have a common policy in terms of employment, agriculture, education. A currency that serves the fight against unemployment and allows us to put enough credit in the hands of our farmers and employers – people cannot claim that "since the others have not yet left the CFA franc, we cannot leave." A policy that allows us to give markets, when possible, to Africans and not export our jobs by giving our markets to foreign companies. And even where we do not yet have the capacity, signing agreements so that, very quickly, there is a transfer of technology. But Senegal's 16 million inhabitants, Gambia's two or three million inhabitants, what weight can they have against these mastodons to impose a rapid transfer of technology?

But we must be careful with institutions like ECOWAS. I am one to think that even French Equatorial Africa and French West

Africa[35] were also a type of African unity. But African unity serving imperialism. It is not this African unity that we seek – an African Union whose headquarters are financed and whose microphones are listened to by China, whose budget, like that of ECOWAS, comes more from the European Union and the United States.

To be pan-African for me today is necessarily to be anti-imperialist. Their vision of uniting Africa is to serve imperialism, but also African bourgeoisies. For me, Afro-liberalism, with agreements like the African Continental Free Trade Area, is not pan-Africanism. Free trade is a law that allows big fish to eat small fish. It is an open boulevard to Western capitalist companies and multinational corporations in a context where we talk about companies under Senegalese law… Yet its capital and owners are not even African.

Whoever may implement free trade, it will be destructive, dramatic and tragic for the majority. Tragic as our youth dying in the Sahara desert, the Atlantic Ocean or the Mediterranean Sea, like the fact that 54% of the Senegalese population can neither read nor write, like the fact that we import 64 billion [CFA francs] of dairy products every year and export our jobs through them, maintaining our farmers, their children and their families in poverty…

To get out of this tragedy that is neo-colonialism, it is urgent today to be sovereign – a sovereign Senegal in a sovereign and united Africa.

---

35 Sagna here is referring to the French colonial division of Africa.

34. Esther Stanford-Xosei (2022), Afrika and Reparations Activism in the UK

Esther Stanford-Xosei is a decolonial pan-Afrikanist jurisconsult, reparationist, community advocate and "ourstorian" engaged in reparations policy, research and movement-building in the UK. Stanford-Xosei speaks to Ben Radley about the struggle for the total liberation and unification of Afrikan people and an indispensable and self-empowering reparatory justice. She argues that reparatory justice and pan-Afrikan liberation is central to reparations activism in Britain.

***

Can you please describe to us a little about your personal background, and what experiences or encounters had the strongest influence on your early political development?

I was born in South London and brought into this world by parents who were born in the Caribbean (Barbados and Guyana), yet who retained their genetic and cultural memory of Afrika. My activism has sought to remember the historic, geopolitical and cultural ties between diaspora communities and our ancestral motherland, Afrika. By vocation I am a jurisconsult, or legal specialist in applied jurisprudence, the science, philosophy and study of law through its actual practice. As a jurisconsult, my unique professional niche is serving as a pan-Afrikan internationalist guerrilla lawyer, a grassroots scholar-activist law practitioner. I am also in the process of completing my PhD research on the UK contingent of the International Social Movement for Afrikan Reparations.

The Anti-Apartheid Movement had a strong influence on my early political development. I recall that in 1987, at age 13, I entered a competition for young black writers, and my winning entry was a piece of creative writing under the theme "Not only equality but justice", about the abolition of apartheid featuring the role of an imagined woman protagonist who was a freedom-fighting "mother of the nation" named Mauba Sheshea. The impact of the Anti-Apartheid Movement had a strong influence on my emerging race and national consciousness as an Afrikan woman in the diaspora as well as recognition of the connections between global racism and imperialism.

Another significant encounter was my activism as an aspiring lawyer as part of a UK organisation of black lawyers, to effect and secure holistic reparatory justice – organising with fellow pan-Afrikanists who were in exile in the UK and had been involved in Afrikan liberation struggles in their home countries in Afrika. Recognising the fact that there was a political vacuum in championing the cause of pan-Afrikan reparations, these encounters led to my involvement in 2000, with fellow-Ghanaian pan-Afrikanists Kofi Mawuli Klu and Kwame Adofo Sampong, in co-founding the Pan-Afrikan Reparations Coalition in Europe.

Part of your academic work has focused on studying the history of reparations activism in the UK. How far back does this history go? Who were its earliest advocates, and did they share a similar understanding of reparations to how the issue is framed and addressed today?

The history of reparations organising in the UK goes back to the 18th century. Some of the earliest documentation of calls for reparations that influenced organising in Britain go back to a letter written by Fiaga Agaja Trudo Audati in 1726, addressed to King George of England, demanding an end to chattel enslavement and trafficking by setting up "local plantation agriculture" within Ouidah, a coastal city in the then Kingdom of Whydah (in what is now Benin). This intervention by Agaja has increased awareness about indigenous Afrikan abolitionists in Afrika and their influence on the slavery abolitionist movement within and beyond the UK. Some of the earliest documented organising to effect and secure reparatory justice can be traced to the Sons of Africa, including one of its key protagonists Attobah Kwodjo Enu aka Ottobah Cugoano (1757-1791). Cugoano was an enslaved Afrikan originally from the Fante village of Ajumako in present-day Ghana. The Sons of Africa movement was formed in London (1797) by Cugoano and Olaudah Equiano (1745-97) as a "political group led by Afrikan abolitionists who campaigned to end slavery".

However, these men were not just abolitionists, they were also reparationists. In 1787, Cugoano published the book *Thoughts and Sentiments on the Evil and Wicked Traffic of the Slavery and Commerce of the Human Species*. In the postscript to the 1791 edition, Cugoano raises "the issue of adequate reparation and restitution for the injuries enslaved persons received", making him the first published Afrikan author in English to denounce the trafficking and enslavement of Afrikans and to pronounce the Afrikan human right to resistance against enslavement, as well as to advocate in a letter to the Prince of Wales the demand for reparations including "restitution for the injuries".

What is traditionally termed "repatriation", a return to one's homeland, represents the oldest form of Afrikan reparations, dating from the fifteenth century when the first Afrikans were kidnapped and trafficked from the continent and their cultural and spiritual way of life. Cognisant of Afrikan peoples' desire to be reconnected with their homeland, in the 18th century, the British Government developed a nation-state colonial scheme which included aspects of returning Afrikans to Afrika but devoid of the true essence of reparations which is more correctly rematriation.

Rematriation describes the historical, cultural and spiritual restitution needed to repair and redress the dispossessions and other violations suffered by enslaved Afrikan people. Rematriation includes the right to return and belong to "Pan-Afrika". It encompasses the Akan Sankofa principle of returning to and renewing forms of decolonial Afrikan indigeneity to fetch one's Afrikan personality in material, cultural and spiritual terms, which are all rooted in the land and peoplehood of Afrika. In this way, rematriation contributes to repairing enduring historical and contemporary injustices by paying attention to the ongoing psychological, cultural and spiritual damage caused to the sensibilities of people of Afrikan ancestry and heritage through epistemicide and the continued existence of coloniality.

In every subsequent generation since these times, there have been efforts made to effect and secure holistic reparatory justice. In the twentieth century, the Pan-African Congresses in 1900 (London), 1921 (London, Paris, Brussels), 1923 (London, Lisbon), 1927 (New York) and, most importantly, 1945 (Manchester) consolidated a growing pan-Afrikan movement out of which contemporary movements for reparations both globally and in the UK would form.

Today, the UK contingent of the International Social Movement for Afrikan Reparations both acknowledges this history of reparations organising and builds transgenerationally from the knowledges and solidarity that it generated. Many of those twentieth century pan-Afrikanists who organised in the UK and who were involved in reparatory justice organising work are well known and have been well researched as contributing to the pan-Afrikan movement in the twentieth century, such as Marcus Garvey, Amy Ashwood Garvey, Funmilayo Ransome-Kuti, Kwame Nkrumah, Claudia Jones, Constance Cummings-John and Una Mason.

When many people hear the word "reparations" they tend to think of economic compensation, but as you have just touched on, it is about much more than this. What does the term mean to you and others involved in the struggle and how does it relate to the broader radical project of African emancipation and self-determination?

In *The Making of An African Intellectual*, Robert Hill recalls how Walter Rodney asserted that the role of Black people in institutions of higher learning was "as a part of the development of Black struggle". He used the term "guerrilla intellectual" to "come to grips with the initial imbalance of power in the context of academic learning". He strongly advocated that sincere intellectuals within European academic institutions should embrace the first and major struggle – the struggle over ideas. Like all other terms, reparations itself is contested. As such, it is important to know that the term reparations has its roots in the modern English term repair, meaning to restore to good condition, to set right, or make amends.

Influenced by the analysis of the indigenous Yaqui scholar, Rebecca Tsosie, who researches reparations for indigenous nations in the Americas, the framework for understanding the role of reparations for Afrikan people worldwide necessarily must be intergenerational and intercultural and must address indigenous Afrikan epistemologies. The Maangamizi – which is a Kiswahili and pan-Afrikan term for the intent to destroy Afrikan people in terms of everything that represents Afrikan personhood, manifesting itself in the continuum of chattel, colonial and neocolonial enslavement including crimes of ecocide and genocide – not only included the theft of the Afrikan person but also, and equally importantly, severed the captive Afrikan from the knowledges that inform the very foundation of human identity; in this case, the Afrikan personhood and personality. Accordingly, there can be no authentic reparatory justice for Afrikan people without global cognitive justice, meaning reparations must also entail restoring indigenous Afrikan knowledge systems of language, spirituality and philosophy, music, art and symbolism, as well as science and technology resulting in Afrika redefining her own knowledge systems.

As I have written elsewhere, the core objectives of pan-Afrikanism, including the attainment and securing of holistic reparatory justice and pan-Afrikan liberation and nation-building, have been central to reparations activism in Britain. This has been defined by the taking back of Afrika, restoring Afrikan sovereignty and building Afrika into an unconquerable powerful pan-Afrikan Union of

Communities known as Maatubuntuman, which is collectively governed by Afrikans on the continent of Afrika and the diaspora.

One of the unique features of Afrikan reparations organising in Britain is that it has always had a pan-Afrikan focus. Our emphasis then as Afrikan reparationists in the UK has been on relating to reparations not just as a legal case or claim and political struggle, but also as an international social movement, embodied in the International Social Movement for Afrikan Reparations. Many Afrikans organising as part of the UK contingent are in pursuit of comprehensive holistic land-based reparations. This means that pursuit of effecting and securing reparatory justice for us as Afrikans in the diaspora – and certainly those of us who identify as the Maatubuntujamaa, Afrikan Heritage Community for National Self-Determination in the UK – is umbilically connected to the liberation of Afrika, restoration of Afrikan sovereignty and the self-determination of Afrikan people worldwide. Maatubuntujamaa is a model of non-territorial autonomy premised on autonomous community institution-building, resource exchange and service-provision.

The Maatubuntujamaa in the UK has come up with a set of 10 proposals for reparations as part of a plan referred to as the Pempamsiempango. In the Pan-Afrikan Reparations Coalition in Europe, we recognise the economics of reparations but only insofar as "receiving the financial component of reparations ... serves the holistic purpose and strengthens the integral whole of our self-repair process". So, for us, the economics of Afrikan reparations relate to how Afrikan heritage communities people provide for and re-equip ourselves, as Afrikan people, with the dignity of community self-reliance, reclaiming our stewardship of Mother Earth and securing the restituted resources of Afrika and Afrikan people worldwide. This includes access to land and other tangible and intangible heritage and property, distributed and utilised within planetary boundaries and in harmony with all life forms.

Concretely, this entails first and foremost the urgent need for pan-Afrikan reparations and other global justice movements to compel the stopping of neocolonialism and its inbuilt manifestations of genocide, ecocide and extractivist plunder in Afrika and other parts of the Global South that we have re-made home. In addition, combining our collective power to ensure the redistribution of wealth and ushering in a new international political and economic order which supports transformative adaptation and is based on ecological restoration, community governance and stewardship of work and resources for the re-making of our world.

A vital mechanism in achieving this is the demand for the establishment of the UK All-Party Parliamentary Commission of Inquiry for Truth and Reparatory Justice, as part of a global process of dialogue between Afrikan people and state institutions of perpetrators of the Maangamizi, such as the British parliament, in order that Afrikan heritage communities across the world can harmonise our own self-repair plans and actions towards not only advocating for ourselves before all state bodies, but also working to guarantee the non-repetition of the Maangamizi as an aspect of reparations recognised under international law. This goes beyond mere compensation which, as Robin Kelley argues, does not challenge the terms of racial capitalism, but rather reinforces neoliberalism and capitalism including the logic of property rights and compensation without radical transformation.

You often invoke the work and legacy of the Ghanaian political revolutionary and intellectual Kwame Nkrumah when discussing and advocating for reparatory justice. Can you talk about his influence on your work and activism?

In his 23 September 1960 address to the General Assembly of the United Nations in New York, Kwame Nkrumah demonstrated continental Afrikan input to the movement for reparations when he stated:

> The great tide of history flows, and as it flows it carries to the

shores of reality the stubborn facts of life and man's relations, one with another. One cardinal fact of our time is the momentous impact of Africa's awakening upon the modern world. The flowing tide of African nationalism sweeps everything before it and constitutes a challenge to the colonial powers to make a just restitution for the years of injustice and crime committed against our continent.

This is important in the sense that Nkrumah and others felt that the struggle for the total liberation and unification of Afrikan people was a self-empowering reparatory justice process which, if enabled to develop, would then allow Afrikans to repair themselves by their own people's power. Revolutionary leaders like Nkrumah put a lot of effort into seeking to ensure that the struggle for Afrikan liberation realised this objective of self-repair. Part of this struggle was the reparatory justice conceptualisation of national liberation from the agenda of the Garveyite movement and the Pan-African Congresses. That is why the US-sponsored plots to overthrow governments, such as that of Kwame Nkrumah and the earlier assassination of Patrice Lumumba, were attacks on that state-building reparatory justice process, being spearheaded by the then resurgent pan-Afrikan movement. This is what Susan Williams, the author of *White Malice: The CIA and the Covert Recolonisation of Africa*, refers to as the struggle for Afrikan independence being strangled at birth.

Particularly from the late 1970s, when neocolonialism became the dominant form of the nation state in Afrika and the diaspora, the reparatory justice process was expunged out of emerging nation states which became cogs in the wheel of neocolonialism, devoid of any truly self-repairing substance instead of them becoming building blocks of a truly independent pan-Afrikan union of states as envisaged by Nkrumah and others. This complete divorcing of the pan-Afrikan reparatory justice process from the nation states that emerged after so-called independence compelled the pan-Afrikan movement to have a life of its own from the grassroots. My activism – especially working through structures such as the Pan-Afrikan Reparations Coalition in Europe, the Stop the Maangamizi: We Charge Genocide/Ecocide Campaign, and the Global Afrikan Peoples Parliament – is returning to that understanding of reparations as rematriation and an independent sovereign nation-building process.

In the Pan-Afrikan Reparations Coalition in Europe's approach to reparations campaigning, we are guided by the strategy and tactics for the pan-Afrikan revolution outlined by Kwame Nkrumah in his post-1966 works such as *Revolutionary Path* and *Handbook of Revolutionary Warfare*. In these works, Nkrumah recognised and advocated that indigenous Afrikan ethnicities, communities and nationalities should constitute the core base for the establishment of a repaired Afrika which frees itself from the constraints of European coloniality and the structural violence of Euro-American dominance in Afrika. Integral to this process is the shutting down of what the Stop the Maangamizi Campaign refers to as Maangamizi crimes scenes, which are those sites of extractivist plunder which prolong the criminality of neocolonialism and Afrikan peoples' dispossession and exploitation.

How do you assess the current state and strength of the struggle today?

There was a lull in the early 2000s, due to gains of the pan-Afrikan movement being eroded and many liberation movements departing from the reparatory justice essence of struggles for national and social liberation to embrace neoliberalism, and the states formed by such movements resigning themselves to neocolonialism. More recently, Afrikan reparations is winning back international recognition as the imperative of our times. A lot of focused work has been done by some of the organisational formations that I am part of to give visibility to the International Social Movement for Afrikan Reparations from below, and to also recognise the intersectional nature of the cause of Afrikan reparations.

Looking back, I would say that between 2000 and 2015 was

for us a period of regrouping and re-catalysing the International Social Movement for Afrikan Reparations. But by 2015, the Pan-Afrikan Reparations Coalition in Europe had consolidated its position as a vanguard formation around which other structures started evolving, which we have been able to intellectually influence in regards to strategy and tactics, such as the Stop the Maangamizi Campaign, Global Afrikan Peoples Parliament, the Afrikan Emancipation Day Reparations March Committee, and the International Network of Scholars and Activists for Afrikan Reparations, formed in 2017 and with its exemplary principles of participation.

In the UK, there is a contingent of the International Social Movement for Afrikan Reparations which I believe is one of the most revolutionary in the world because of its explicit pan-Afrikan focus and objectives of the restoration of Afrikan sovereignty and bringing about fundamental social and ecological transformation. From this, we see the promise of an emerging "blackprint" which remains true to the pan-Afrikan foundations of reparations movement-building.

We are seeing the growing influence of Afrikan reparationists on other movements such as environmental and climate justice movements, aided by the fact that resistance to the worldwide climate and ecological crises is radicalising forces both in the Global South and the Global North.

For instance, the Pan-Afrikan Reparations Coalition in Europe took reparations into the environmental movement here in the UK and has been strategically building affinities with movements such as Extinction Rebellion (XR) through the Stop the Maangamizi Campaign which co-founded the Extinction Rebellion Internationalist Solidarity Network soon after the inception of XR in 2018. Through the Stop the Maangamizi Campaign's influence, XR and a specific formation within it known as XR-Being the Change Affinity Network have embraced the Pan-Afrikan Reparations Coalition in Europe's advocacy of "planet repairs".

This recognition of Afrikan reparations and planet repairs

has also led to mainstream political parties in the UK such as the Green Party of England and Wales embracing planet repairs and working with the Stop the Maangamizi Campaign to co-produce the text of "Reparations and Atonement for the Transatlantic Trafficking of Enslaved Africans" motions, which have now been passed by Islington and Lambeth Council and Bristol City Council. The key purpose of these motions is to build glocal support at the local and city council level for the Stop the Maangamizi Campaign's demand for the UK parliament to establish the All-Party Parliamentary Commission of Inquiry for Truth and Reparatory Justice. It took the strength and mobilisation of support of people on the ground locally, nationally, and internationally to create the public receptivity to the passing of these motions.

Despite these advances, there are dangers in the increasing recognition and embracing of reparations, such as the ever-increasing potential of movement-capture, the NGO-isation of reparatory justice resistance, counterinsurgency and the promotion of neoliberal measures purported to be reparatory, but which reinforce global white supremacy, neocolonialism and racial capitalism.

Building on this impetus, underpinned by two decades of mobilising and organising communities, the All-Party Parliamentary Group for African Reparations (APPGAR) was launched on 20 October 2021. The significance of this parliamentary group is that it is the first space created within the state institutions of the UK for dialogue in pursuit of holistic Afrikan reparations, meaning embracing planet repairs. Since its launch, APPGAR has opened up prospects for programmes which can support Afrikan heritage communities to be drivers of policy on Afrikan reparations through community links to the group. Work has already begun in developing youth perspectives on Afrikan reparations and educational repairs. On 20 February 2022, and in association with the Maangamizi Educational Trust and the International Network of Scholars and Activists for Afrikan Reparations, I initiated the launch of the Mbuya Nehanda Afrikan Women and Reparations

Project. These focus groups will explore the rights, needs, and perspectives of women of Afrikan ancestry and heritage on holistic Afrikan reparatory justice with a view to concretising Afrikan "womanist" approaches to policy-making and other strategic interventions relevant to the work of the APPGAR.

The significance of launching this project on the 20 February 2022 is that the date falls on the 124th anniversary of the 1898 arraignment of Mbuya Nehanda Charwe Nyakasikana at the High Court of Matabeleland in the case of the (British) Queen of England vs Nehanda. Mbuya Nehanda-Charwe was a powerful spirit medium, who today can be characterised as a reparationist committed to upholding traditional Shona culture and a heroine of the 1896/7 first Chimurenga war for national liberation against British settler colonialism. Mbuya Nehanda-Charwe, along with three others, was falsely accused of murdering a brutal and terroristic British commissioner, Henry Hawkins Pollard of the British South Africa Company, and was subsequently hanged by the British settler colonial regime on the 27 April 1898 for her contributions in mobilising communities against colonial misrule and dispossession. Before Mbuya Nehanda-Charwe was hanged, her dying words of resistance were that her bones would rise again to lead a new, victorious rebellion against the British colonialists. To us as Afrikan reparationists, she is one of the greatest Afrikan sheroes who shaped and influenced the early Afrikan Liberation struggle against the Maangamizi of colonialism.

35. Femi Aborisade (2019), The Roots of the Crisis in Nigeria

A wide-ranging conversation between Tamás Gerőcs and the Nigerian Marxist Femi Aborisade. From his early days as a labour militant in the 1970s and 1980s, organising and building socialist and labour organisations, Aborisade discusses the crisis of capitalism in Nigeria today and the struggles against it.

***

Could you briefly describe your entry point into the labour movement and national politics in Nigeria?

I got involved in labour movement activities through my membership of the Marxist Socialist Youth Movement as a student in the Polytechnic Ibadan in the late 1970s. I later became the Secretary General of the Movement. The Movement's tradition was to have an orientation towards the working class. Members were always involved in supporting the struggles of organised and unorganised workers. Our publications used to be produced by a system of stencil and cyclo-styling, [and] were preoccupied with promoting the interests of workers within and outside the institution, nationally and internationally, particularly in campaigning against apartheid [in] South Africa.

During the compulsory National Youth Service (NYSC) programme for all graduates in Nigeria, in 1982, I was officially posted to work in a bank in Ondo State. But I requested that I should be deployed to work with the Nigeria Labour Congress (NLC), Ondo State Council. My request was accepted by the authorities and so I did my NYSC at the Nigeria Labour Congress in Akure, in the Southwest of Nigeria between 1982-83. At the Congress, apart from gaining experience in the strike activity organised by public sector workers against the government led by Adekunle Ajasin in 1983, I devoted myself mainly to organising trade union education programmes for affiliated unions of the NLC.

Along with another friend of mine who was deployed in one of the states in the eastern part of the country for his NYSC, I started the production of a socialist publication called *Progress*, which was being distributed free of charge to rank and file workers in Ondo State and elsewhere. Before my NYSC programme period formally came to an end, the National Headquarters of the Nigeria Labour Congress based in Lagos announced job openings for graduates. I applied for the position and I was employed as Administrative Officer in 1983. But in reality, I functioned more as an Administrative and Education Officer. The leadership of the Congress at the national level became uncomfortable with the emancipatory education programmes I was organising based on the militancy which rank and file workers who had attended my education programmes were displaying to the leaderships in individual affiliate unions. For this reason, the NLC national leadership sacked me in 1986. But I did not break my links with the rank and file workers. Along with friends, we started the publication called *Labour Militant*, which was being distributed semi-legally under the military dictatorship (the second junta between 1983 and 1998). As the public face of the publication and its editor, I was arrested and detained several times, starting from 1988.

A national organisation was consequently built in 1989 by socialists and non-socialist human rights activists to campaign for my release. The organisation, initially called the Free Femi Aborisade Campaign Committee was later changed to Committee for the Defence of Human Rights after my release, which was also based on international campaigns which the London-based Militant Tendency, led then by Ted Grant and Peter Taaffe, had built.

I later joined forces with one of the most renowned Nigerian human rights lawyer[s], the late Chief Gani Fawehinmi, to form National Conscience as a human rights body, concerned mainly with advocating socio-economic rights. The organisation transformed into a political party, the National Conscience Party in October 1994, in defiance of military decrees prohibiting the formation of political parties. The NCP was built as an anti-privatisation political party. The party played a leading role in the formation of the Joint Action Committee of Nigeria, one of the umbrella organisations that campaigned for termination of military rule in Nigeria. I was the national general secretary of JACON while Chief Gani Fawehinmi was its national chairman.

In 2003, I stood for the post of Governor of Oyo State on the platform of the NCP but lost the election. The electoral contest was used mainly to advocate and popularise socialist programmes. For example, I stood on the programme of a Governor on a worker's wage, following Lenin's own approach when he earned only the average salary of a public officer as the head of the government in the USSR.

Moving into the current period, can I ask you how the on-going crisis of capitalism in Nigeria – popularly described as neoliberalism – affects the labour movement in the country?

Paradoxically, economic hardship and material deprivations have grown to unprecedented levels even in times of relative plenty. We can measure this collapse in living standards by any governance, economic or social well-being indicators. I think there is no question about this. Even the ruling classes with their parties and media must admit this as a fact. Indeed, currently, members of the national legislature, particularly at the House of Representatives have admitted in resolutions that Nigeria is a classic example of a failed state when all indices of governance, particularly the genocide-like political, religious and ethnic killings are considered.

The federal government is incapable of ending the scourge of insurgency and other forms of insecurity. The economic programme of the capitalist APC (All Progressive Congress)-controlled federal government fuels insurgency by increasing the number of the jobless, hopeless, frustrated, hungry and angry youths. Pervasive poverty over several decades of criminal neglect of the welfare of ordinary people produces the unprecedented insecurity being witnessed today all over Nigeria. The economic programme of the APC called [the] "Economic Recovery and Growth Plan" which reflected the needs of the private sector, rather than the public sector, being the engine of economic growth is fuelling poverty and by implication, insurgency and other forms of insecurity.

Poverty is also being fuelled by the anti-poor policies of state governments. For example, Kaduna State is one of the most dangerous states in Nigeria to live, work or visit in terms of the regularity of bloodshed, kidnappings and killings by bandits and ethno-religious inspired violence. The level of insecurity in Kaduna State today is a function of unprecedented, cruel anti-workers policy of the Kaduna State government in terms of the mass lay off of about 40,000 workers in different ministries, including 22,000 teachers, 8,000 workers of MDAs [Ministries, Departments and Agencies], over 4,000 workers of local government councils, thousands of medical and health workers, 800 workers of Kaduna State Internal Revenue Service, among many others, all sacked, more or less, about the same time, simultaneously, in different Ministries of the Kaduna State government in 2017.

The uncontrolled insecurity is therefore the harvest or product of anti-labour policies. It is a phenomenon that can be explained rationally. The solution does not lie in [the] militarisation of society. If the resources being pumped into military-focused solutions were used instead for implementing poverty reduction policies in order to provide humanising and enduring jobs, social housing units, free medical care in a revamped health care system used by the President himself, free education used by the children of the ruling class, food for the hungry, a policy of minimum income for the weakest in society, care of the aged, etc, insurgency and physical insecurity would be massively undermined and reduced in ways better than any military focused solution could achieve which the successive governments in Nigeria have been pursuing over the years.

The critical question is what is the way out? If labour could provide an alternative program and platform around issues of poverty, inequality, corruption, insecurity and so on, we could win the heart of ordinary people, build a broader viable social movement, strong enough to win elections on a nationwide basis beyond local communities and state levels and with the possible benefit of a long run systemic change not only within the confines of Nigeria but one that would actively support the struggles for systemic change on an international scale.

There are good examples of such movements with specific agendas gaining much attention and popular support. Unfortunately, the tendency of the unions' top leadership appears not to have confidence in the capacity of the rank and file of the labour movement to struggle and effect fundamental changes in the system. That is why some of the key figures in the leadership of the unions tend to prefer to contest elections on the platforms of the incumbent bourgeois parties. A good number of top union leaders have won elections on the platforms of bourgeois parties based on the prominence they acquired as unionists. Unfortunately, they usually end up betraying the interests of the working class by implementing anti-worker and anti-poor people programmes and policies.

Despite the weaknesses of the labour movement and its leadership, I am convinced and optimistic that there is a huge opportunity for political intervention and electoral victory of the labour movement. Labour is strategically positioned to intervene successfully in politics, even on the national scale. The progressive wing of the ruling classes which is now in power, the party controlling the federal government, has eroded much of its legitimacy. Its woeful performance, measured in the massive collapse in living standards and unprecedented insecurity since 2015, has shown that there is no fundamental difference between the ruling All Progressives Congress and the main bourgeois opposition party, the People's Democratic Party (PDP). Both are built on a neoliberal programme of privatisation of public assets and the perspective of the private sector being the engine of economic growth.

Is the phenomenon of trade unionists contesting on the platform of bourgeois parties an institutional decision or individual decisions?

It is not an institutional question. The decisions are usually taken by the individuals and not the collective decision of the union. In fact, the union is usually not consulted. It is therefore a reflection of individual motivation and ambition. Indeed, the individual unionists who decide to contest on bourgeois platforms hardly have any meaningful influence or control over the workers or the union, once they take such decisions. The weight of the harsh economic realities tends to be overwhelming so that mass struggles are difficult to suppress even with the presence of a former leading trade unionist in government. Though this does not mean there is an absence of efforts to use their influence to weaken workers' struggles.

What is therefore required to get out of the political quagmire and bring about decisive political intervention is for the rank and file in the trade union movement to build social movement networks with pro-labour forces, pro-labour political parties, pro-labour intellectuals, community activists, rights activists and other mass organisations that are organising around other wider social issues. If social networking were strongly pursued, even informally, the unions would be better able to take strategic collective decisions on political participation. But the activities of such networking would have to be based on giving support to the practical struggles of different segments of the masses in their day-to-day strivings to defend and improve their living and working conditions. When the masses receive support from such a network of fighting organisations, the labour movement would begin to record more effective electoral participation and electoral victories. However, in the long run, the working masses would inevitably draw the conclusion that their interests cannot be guaranteed or sustained on the basis of capitalism and that there is a need to bring about system change. For tactical reasons, however, the masses should exhaust the electoral opportunities offered by the capitalist system before they are compelled to draw the conclusion that it cannot guarantee their interests on a long-term and sustainable basis.

These are interesting ideas, Femi, can you explain what this networking looks like in practice?

Social networking is conceptualised as a civic movement to intervene politically or campaign around social issues from the experiences of the workers and other subordinated groups. These networks could form broader social movements and launch political campaigns as it occurred during the anti-fuel price hike mass protests in January 2012. Political platforms could co-exist simultaneously with the trade unions. While unions are used primarily to advance economic interests of the workers, the political platforms and networks would be used to mobilise wider sections of the oppressed classes to give political support to the industrial struggles of the trade unions. Similarly, when wider social issues arise such as an increase in the prices of fuel, which affects workers and the poor generally, trade unions could declare strikes to support agitations by the political platforms and networks. This is the concept for the Labour and Civil Society Coalition (LASCO) which is an umbrella organisation for Nigerian Labour Congress, the Trade Union Congress (TUC) and the Joint Action Front. I would call it a platform for pro-democracy and pro-labour groups where civil society activists and workers can meet, discuss and take practical actions together on the most burning current issues concerning the plight of the masses.

The key weakness of LASCO is that it is more of a coalition between top leaderships of the central labour centres and pro-labour activists; it does not include rank and file workers. The effect is that in any mass action, as it occurred in [the] January 2012 general strike in Nigeria, pro-labour activists have little input in deciding when to call off a strike action. If rank and file workers were involved, it would have been required that resolutions are taken at various levels of the unions and communities, outside the unions, to terminate or continue a mass action. In that way, the national leaderships of the trade union centres alone would not have the power to call or call off mass strike actions without the inputs of rank and file union branches and several other individual communities in action.

Can I now ask you about unity in the labour movement, or what have been some of the historical (and recent) dividing lines?

The division within the trade union movement is usually created artificially at the top level of the Nigeria Labour Congress leadership. The NLC has been the umbrella organisation for all the Nigerian trade unions since the 1950s and confronted the military regime strongly (many members were jailed during the dictatorship). The central labour organisation, NLC, has gone through various divisions since then. The current division and the emergence of the United Labour Congress (ULC) is traceable to the stalemated March 2015 Congress based on the leadership-induced election crisis rather than ideological differences. This gave rise to several affiliates forming a new centre called the United Labour Congress in December 2016. The ULC is currently led by Joe Ajaero while the NLC is led by Ayuba Wabba.

There have been many attempts to reunite the labour movement because history has shown that the unity of the labour movement is the key to confront the ruling classes, check the excesses of their governments and curtail attacks on workers' rights. Although the movement has not been reunited, the two centres tend to form joint action committees for collective fightbacks on critical social issues whenever necessary. Apart from the NLC, which is the central labour organisation, predominantly for junior staff unions, there is the Trade Union Congress for senior staff associations. Both the NLC and the TUC have a robust history of joint activities, rallies and protests over wider socio-economic issues affecting the poor generally in the country.

You mentioned the privatisation scheme. How do you see the question of property relations in Nigeria?

Besides the question of inequality and poverty, or the low quality of public services, there is a need for raising the issue of property relations. However, campaigning on changing property relations seems only possible in the public sector and in respect to public enterprises. This is because the two big ruling parties, the APC and PDP, both have a programme to privatise the state owned Nigerian National Petroleum Corporation (NNPC), among other public enterprises despite the opposition by some trade unions. In fact, in the last election, the presidential candidate of the PDP openly declared that "even if they will kill me, I would sell off NNPC." But sale of public assets is actually the policy of the incumbent APC-controlled federal government, as enunciated in its economic programme.

The labour unions, to a large extent, oppose privatisation plans and instead favour public ownership. In some past privatisation, particularly in the electricity sector, unions were allocated a percentage of the shares. However, in the context of privatisation and mass layoffs of workers, the allocated shares became meaningless. In one particular instance, a former General Secretary who resigned from the Nigeria Union of Pensioners went ahead to form an Incorporated Trustee and channelled the money there although it was originally meant to be allocated for the union collective. Workers did not benefit a penny from this privatisation in the end.

From this experience, it is clear that unions should not support any form of privatisation. The minimum policy the trade union movement should advocate is public ownership based on democratic management and control of the working people, including elected community representatives in the case of the oil industry. Workers should not advocate a policy of co-ownership with private capital.

I like your description of Nigerian elections as a renewed inter-capitalist struggle. Could you elaborate on that comrade?

What we have encountered in the most recent elections was a heated struggle for the control of resources amongst various capitalist parties. International capital with its comprador allies seeks to maintain control over Nigeria's economic resources, especially in the oil and gas industry. The incumbent APC-controlled government sought to use allocation of licences over oil blocs to maintain its hold on power in its negotiations with international capital and the local comprador bourgeoisie. Such negotiations are therefore not in the interest of workers and the poor but in the interest of national oligarchic capitalist groups and international capital. The President Muhammadu Buhari-APC regime thus threatens not to renew the oil bloc licences once they expire so they can be allocated to capitalists (local and international) who gave political support to the APC/Muhammadu Buhari's presidential re-election. His contender, Abubakar Atiku from PDP, was supported by local and international capitalist groups with a view to having access to those licences.

It is interesting to note, however, that Buhari enjoyed the support of international capital in the previous election in 2015 but due to failures of governance coupled with unprecedented insecurity, he lost this support and international capital appeared to favour another candidate. This was the environment in which Abubakar Atiku could capitalise on the legitimacy deficit, and the subsequent political vacuum. He didn't succeed, because in these dire economic conditions, the struggle between the capitalist fractions intensified and could not get easily settled. The thing to remember is that the national bourgeoisie is relatively weak in Nigeria, in fact it has no productive basis upon which it could independently grow. The social reproduction of this bunch of oligarchs heavily relies on state patronage. Most of them own no factories or no industries, but they are either subsidised by the state or the state outsources functions of the government with allocated funds into the hands of these oligarchs. This is how they can make their fortunes. This could be termed a form of outsourcing public services into private hands. These oligarchic groups are also strongly connected and interlinked. We see this network around Buhari now, and this is one reason why he won the election despite the widespread disillusionment and the inter-capitalist struggles. One good example for such a politico-oligarchic national capitalist is Aliko Dangote, the richest man in the continent who specialised and profited in these outsourced and allocated functions. He is a state-fed, state-created multi-billionaire oligarch, the biggest amongst the national oligarchic capitalist class in Nigeria.

We must understand that what has been allocated to him and his company group are public companies or economic opportunities the government should have maintain[ed] control over through massive investments. But instead they have been outsourced to individuals, which is the typical rent-seeking behaviour of those state-fed oligarchic capitalists. Dangote could however create a productive base with the cement industry which was sold to him. The other important example is that Dangote is willing to build a new coastal refinery which is much needed in West Africa. The state should have been responsible for that, but due to its failure – or maybe even intentionally – this has become another opportunity for the oligarchy. There is a dialectical relationship as well: Dangote must still rely on the state and his business is dependent on the domestic infrastructure, but his business also weakens the state on the other hand. There is a strange interdependence which is characteristic in this global dependency with the dominance of the comprador capitalists, but it is a close enough circle as well for these oligarchic groups to remain both in power and in business. The oligarchy actually controls Buhari but they also depend on his government. These sorts of complexities need to be understood by those seeking to analyse the state and capital in Africa.

For example, one telling moment was when Buhari's wife, Aisha Buhari, expressed this openly in public when she spoke to the media of how a few "cabals" control her husband and his government, which must have been a very shameful but honest moment for Buhari. I would say the build-up of this system is the hotbed for the rent-seeking behaviour prone so much to corruption. What needs to be added is that this system is very fragile, the political oligarchy is tactically behind Buhari at the moment but they can switch loyalty anytime if they feel threatened – and this is exactly what they do.

Another lesson for us is that it is not enough to fight corrupt figures, but we must go down to the systemic roots of this problem, otherwise it will always be reproduced at the expense of the majority of the people. And we will have to do this job sooner or later, because for labour there is just no benefit in the inter-capitalist struggle. The compradors and the national oligarchs are all the same, they pay the same wage and exploit the workers with the same tactics. We must look at their intra-class struggle as a moment of opportunity to intervene on behalf of the people. And not only in the name of the labour movement but, as I have highlighted already to you with the example of the umbrella organisations, we need other political activists, civilians and ordinary people to organise, [to] provide an alternative to change this corrupt system.

What does the future hold for Nigeria, what is the way out of the recent crisis?

Many new parties and movements have been recently formed by young people as a response to the intensification of the social crisis. This is also the result of the political crisis and the political vacuum. The two large parties are clearly not helping the people but enriching themselves and their oligarchic circles. The problem is that both of the two large parties seem so desperate to stay in power that they do not hesitate to deploy violence. This explains the rising tension, especially during times of election. The level of killings and bloodshed and the escalation of violence before the February elections were unprecedented and clearly show the de-democratisation process or how democratic institutions have been hollowed out. Ruling classes have also mobilised enormous electoral money to induce the electorate, to make sure they either displace the incumbents or maintain their hold on power. Ordinary people, in large numbers, were simply excluded from the election. So the smaller or newer parties had not much chance to challenge this system with little or no means at their disposal. By these explicitly undemocratic methods, the big parties of the establishment managed to stay in power but by doing so they have also deepened the contradictions of the legitimacy crisis.

In terms of what the future can bring, let me recall what Antonio Gramsci referred to as the "pessimism of the intellect, optimism of the will." As for the former, within this systemic trap into which Nigeria has been pushed into, no solution seems to arise to tackle this multifaceted crisis, including the social, political crises imminent in this system. It has already produced enormous suffering and social tension in the form of ethnic or religious violence at different levels of the state, and we can anticipate that as the contradiction grows further, the tension will escalate accordingly. To illustrate the extent of the scale of the crisis of political representation, we need to refer to the undemocratic constitutional amendments which members of the two main parties in the national assembly made. For example, they have secretly amended the constitution to the effect that small or new parties that are unable to win seats or certain minimum percentage of votes in elections would be deregistered. This amendment is to preserve the political interest of the incumbent parties of the establishment. The secret constitutional amendments actually show how the old establishment parties feel threatened by the emergence of new political platforms and they are ready to use any means to protect the status quo. This is partly why the repression, authoritarian rule, political corruption and the subsequent organised and spontaneous ethnic violence have been on the rise. I expect the crisis of representation to escalate in the coming years.

Finally, can I ask you what is beyond the confines of politics in Nigeria – where do you see geopolitical constraints?

Nigeria is highly dependent on the export of oil and the price movements have very strong and direct effect[s] on the economy as well as on the state budget. There is always this fear of a new price collapse which could push the economy into severe recession as it had happened several times in the past few decades. My concern, though, is that whether prices go up or down, the majority of the people still suffer from the same or even worse conditions. The crisis in reality has nothing to do with the price movements, and people tend to misunderstand it when they link Nigeria's structural crisis to the question of oil. This is just the surface of the problem, but the origin of the crisis is deeply rooted in the global system of dependency.

Obviously, dependence on oil export is a very negative economic legacy whether prices are up or down. One thing that people encounter in this respect is that the oligarchic ruling classes use oil revenues, and even more the ideology of the oil economy, to justify their misconduct and repressive governance. The Nigerian state uses oil revenues to please the excessive greed of the ruling classes. This is the channel through which they are most closely linked to international capital. So the way they integrate themselves into the global economy and the way it is linked and translated into the local political dynamics is all organised around the oil industry and embedded in the question of NNPC privatisation. In terms of the ideological package, the state and the associated ruling classes only use the oil crisis as an excuse to pass the cost and pressure of this very bad legacy onto ordinary working people.

International capital and the national oligarchic ruling class are in an absolute agreement on how to push the burden of the crisis on the working class. This is not just the oil industry, but international financial capital is actively involved. Christine Lagarde, the managing director of the IMF, came to Nigeria early this year to argue for cutting fuel subsidies in a country of large oil reserves where people face difficulties to make their living when prices are high. Nigeria has been in the shadow of international finance capital which is one of the most absurd things. Nigeria is not a poor country. Ordinary people are poor because of the theft and waste of wealth by greedy oligarchs. A massive debt is accumulated from time to time to satisfy the greed of the ruinous ruling class and this gives financial capital leverage over Nigerian politics. For example, in the crisis they wanted to cut subsidies and divest from social infrastructure but they asked the government to bail out the so-called failed banks. International capital is also behind the privatisation scheme especially in the oil industry.

Despite their disagreement and sometimes struggle with domestic oligarchs, international capital and the national capitalist class are in alliance to exploit this country and their people for their own benefit – even though they sometimes fight over the share and distribution of this prey. This is exactly where the roots of the systemic crisis come from. They use what I would call the "imaginary economic crisis" to encourage the government into a debt-spiral which allows them to impose ever stricter conditionality of external financing. Unless we do something about it, the contradictions will worsen and the violent nature of the crisis both the political and the economic can go nowhere but escalate further. I believe that there is just no way for Nigeria to improve while remaining a slave to global capitalism. It can only systematically end up trapped in the systemic crisis which we have been experiencing since independence. This is not only our history but

The Roots of the Crisis in Nigeria 451

also the result of the working of global capitalism.

I have already mentioned the Gramscian framework. This was the pessimistic view stemming from our analysis. But on the other hand, I also have the "optimism of the will" as well. We want to use the moment of the crisis to organise labour and if we do this organisational work correctly, there is a chance that we can change the course of events and intervene in politics for the benefit of the ordinary working people. Yet it is critical to build up the labour movement's own capacities because the crisis will deepen further and we don't have much time to resist effectively.

36. Irene Asuwa and Cidi Otieno (2022), Imperialism and GMOs in Kenya

Pan-Africanist filmmaker, scholar and social justice activist Noosim Naimasiah speaks with Irene Asuwa and Cidi Otieno about food sovereignty, ecologically appropriate production, distribution and consumption, social-economic justice and local food systems in Kenya. They also discuss the role of social movements in raising popular consciousness and defending the rights of Kenya's popular classes. Asuwa is a social justice feminist activist and member of the Revolutionary Socialist League. Otieno is secretary general for the Kenya Peasants League (KPL) and a peasant farmer who advocates for food sovereignty.

***

If you have been watching TV or reading the newspapers in the last year in Kenya, you see that the government has been actively donating genetically modified (GM) seeds to farmers. This comes in the wake of the still existing moratorium on GM seeds that was installed by the Kenyan government in November 2012 against the importation and planting of any genetically modified organisms (GMO) product. I want to place our discussion in the context of the global debate on the viability of GM seeds. With this in mind, we can begin the conversation by understanding firstly what precisely we mean by GMOs. What does the acronym stand for and what exactly are they?

Cidi Otieno: Thank you comrade, for organising this timely and important meeting today. In simple terms, GMO[s] are actually those crops that have been genetically engineered. Genetical engineering is basically altering the DNA of a particular organism or of a particular crop, and we have seen that scientists have been arguing that genetic modification is not new and has been taking place naturally. Through natural selection we have seen organic genetic engineering taking place. But what is happening in the labs is that different foreign components are being added into an organism's DNA, motivated by the potential for massive profits for transnational corporations and basically having a potential of artificially altering an entire population.

Why is this genetic engineering a big issue, because – as they say – if we are going to get a better variety of a crop, resistant to certain pests, increasing the yield, reducing the maturation period of the crop, why would we be against it?

CO: Firstly, if GMOs are coming to solve the problem of hunger and accessibility to food, why do we have a country like South Africa, despite their long-held adaptation of GM, having the problems of hunger? Secondly, you find that some of these GM crops are highly dependent on chemicals pesticides and herbicides like Roundup that has been sued for its carcinogenic effects. Thirdly, as the KPL, we focus on indigenous seeds, and we tell farmers to bank seeds which can be replanted after every season and shared among members without altering their nutritional benefit. However, with GMOs, you have to keep buying them every season and not only is this very expensive, but it makes farmers very dependent.

When you are a farmer, you have land, and you don't own the seeds, then you cannot attain food sovereignty and that's why we say that food sovereignty starts with seed sovereignty. This means the farmers owning the seeds, the farmers owning the land, the farmers owning the water systems, the farmers owning the food production system. Seed is very important in ensuring the availability of food and once our farmers are left in the hands of multinational corporations like Monsanto Syngenta, Bayer and One Acre Fund, then we lose that aspect of seeds sovereignty.

If you look at Migori County in western Kenya where we have members, we saw farmers protesting that there are no seeds in the agrovets [a supply store for farmers], but our members had the seeds. During this corona[virus] period we have seen increased demand for seeds from us because there is [a] shortage of seeds. So the whole premise for the need for GMOs is false because we are not hungry because there is no food, we are hungry because of distribution. We are hungry because of the failure of the food production system.

Irene Asuwa: I remember doing research with an organisation in Siaya county in western Kenya and there were these millet seeds that a big company had distributed. The people told me how that had interfered with the whole chain of production from the pollinators to their ability to accurately predict weather patterns and to tell the health of the soil because some of the birds that ate the millet were dead, and the bees disappeared. As for the sunflowers, the birds were not coming anymore because that sunflower was alien. And you realise that when that chain in the ecosystem is broken there is a huge problem for farmers and for nature.

Also, as you might know, most of the chemical fertilisers and pesticides that we use are contraband. They have been banned in other markets in Europe but we still use them. So we are using carcinogenic things that put other people['s] health at risk in the name of providing more food. So if you are providing food and people go to the hospital after eating that food, then what's that?

It is very enlightening – especially for people who have done research on the ground and understand the material implications of what actually is happening. There is now, in the continent, a general trend towards unbanning GM, installing trials and legalising their importation and production and it is pertinent for us to understand the political and social factors that are facilitating this new wave. Comrade Cidi, could you share your thoughts on this?

CO: In 2012 in Kenya, the then Minister of Public Health Beth Mugo established a taskforce to review and evaluate information on the safety of GMOs. And on 15 November 2013, the taskforce released a report, noting that the government was right in banning [the] import of GMOs. The taskforce came to a conclusion that the safety of GM foods had not been conclusively demonstrated to allow for the lifting of the ban. It gave some recommendations which included a need to develop guidelines for testing of GMOs, the priority of safety with regard to human health and the need to develop capacity for the determination of the safety of GMOs on a case-by-case basis through the national regulator – National Biosafety Authority. Fundamentally, the committee noted that there was [a] need to develop adequate infrastructure for carrying out and – where necessary – replicating long term trials by Kenyan scientists funded solely by the Kenyan government.

However, we see that some of these authorities are being funded by the same transnational corporations that are promoting GMOs so their independence actually is in question. Because I am part of the ad hoc technical committee [of the] expert group for the Food and Agriculture Organisation (FAO) as part of La Via Campesina, I know based on the FAO reports that small scale farmers globally contribute over 70% of food on the table. We know right now that the in-house trials of GM maize done by scientists from the Jomo Kenyatta University in Kiboko and Kibwezi and the reports generated, no small-scale farmers were consulted, even after we raised this issue with [the] KARLO (Kenya Agricultural and Livestock Research Organisation several times. Instead, the government should be doing farm-based research because the farms are large laboratories. Farmers have been conducting research from time immemorial using natural selection and saving seeds. What we are saying is that it is high time the government started investing in farm-based research, supporting small scale farmers and peasant farmers, livestock keepers, fisher folk communities who are actually the ones who are contributing to the food on the table.

Right now, if you look at the Big Four agenda of the current government, we are seeing a very big push for GM foods. For example, if you look at the food security pillar, it states that the government will accelerate the introduction of GM-insect resistant crops. As we know, food security does not distinguish where food comes from or the conditions under which it is produced and distributed. National food security targets are often met by sourcing food produced under environmentally destructive and exploitative conditions, and supported by subsidies and policies that destroy local food producers but benefit agribusiness corporations. That's why the government is saying [it wants] to revive manufacturing companies like Rivatex, Kitui County Textile Center and Kisumu Cotton Mills with Bt cotton. But we know what has happened in Burkina Faso, we know what has happened in India with GM cotton – farmers have committed suicide in those countries because they were expecting to earn money and instead they are plunged into debt.

Specifically, we know the Deputy President has been pushing a lot in terms of lifting the ban. People have been asking why the Kibaki government banned GMOs and the Jubilee government is pushing for lifting the ban. If you look at the debt equation between the two governments, Kibaki, Kenya's second president, left the country with about 1.2 trillion Kenyan shillings debt [about US$10.5 billion]. Today we are 7 trillion in debt. These debts come with conditions like imposing GM seeds, pushing for the legal lifting of these bans and pushing for chemical herbicides. It is the IMF and World Bank that dictate that since you are borrowing from them, you can only spend on certain sectors and they only choose sectors where they have interests.

IA: I also wanted to add to Cidi's answer that, even in [rural] society, there is a class and race component. For example, I know farmers who specifically grow organic foods for the Indian market in Kenya which is only available in certain supermarkets and spaces.

In terms of class, you can clearly see the intent to alienate farmers from their land. Because when farmers are fully dependent on GM seeds, and they can't afford them anymore, then who is going to grow the food? The corporations are going to grow the food and they are going to do it on a large scale, in monoculture, and damage our land so we will be at the mercy of companies to grow food for us. There is also segregation in the sense that what you will find in Naivas supermarket in Kasarani (a high-density neighbourhood) is not what you will find in Naivas Lavington (a middle-class neighbourhood). So there is also a class question in that.

Now, in terms of democracy, how do we deal with the sudden imposition of GM foods without public participation? Is taking the matter up in the law courts a possibility? It is important to know that both the current government and the unofficial opposition (led by Deputy President William Ruto) all endorse GM seeds. We know that Kenya was one of the first countries to sign the Cartagena protocol that advocates for the protection of biological diversity from the adverse effects of GMOs. We also have the Kenya Biosafety Act which was signed into law in 2009. Kenya is also a signatory to the Africa Model Law which was put in place by the Organisation of African Unity (now the African Union (AU)) in the year 2000 and it provides for the protection of the rights of local communities, farmers, breeders and for the regulation of access to biological resources. Can these laws provide any sort of protection?

CO: There is what is called debt colonisation. The structured Aspen programs reorient the food production systems towards export-oriented food production and promote large scale cash crop food production. And also, some of these IMF conditionalities of liberalisation also come with conditions that attach themselves to GMOs.

You mentioned the Cartagena protocol which was adopted in 2000 and it entered into force in 2003. Kenya has ratified this protocol, but this depends on the goodwill of the politicians. However, we are already seeing Bt cotton coming into Kenya despite the fact that the government has ratified this protocol. The farmers were not given any information. Meeting government ministers in hotels does not constitute meeting farmers.

You also mentioned the Kenya Biosafety Act that was signed into law in 2009. Section 18 of the Act prohibits the conducting of any activity involving GMOs without written approval of the authority. The authority, however, is not the farmers. If you look at the composition of the authority, there are no farmer representatives. If you look at Section 19, it prohibits the introduction into the environment of a GMO without authority. Section 20 prohibits importation into Kenya of a GMO without approval of the authority. 21 prohibits placing on the market any GMO without approval of the authority.

Who are these authorities? How are they appointed? As I said earlier, some of these authorities are funded by the same organisations/institutions that are supporting GMOs. Despite the fact that we have good laws, or the 2010 Constitution, the real issue is if we have the political goodwill of those in authority to be able to implement them?

Sadly, our government has been privatised. It has been captured by the forces of capitalism, so whenever the president who is captured appoints the chairman of the authority the chairman is also captured and therefore that's why we are seeing these approvals taking place. That's why we as KPL are encouraging farmers to disobey and not wait for so-called good laws. We are already banking seeds and sharing them. We are already ensuring when the farmers who need the seeds can get them. That's where we can start. When we have consumers saying we are not going to eat GMs, we are going to start eating indigenous crops, our farmers will get a market for their non-GM produce.

It was very sad during Covid to hear the Cabinet Secretary of Agriculture say that they are going to import maize, yet we have farmers with maize in Kenya. That's because it's one of the conditions that the World Bank gave Kenya [for] a Covid-19 loan. Now Kenya has to import maize from somewhere in Mexico and yet we have farmers from Kitale, Migori and many other counties who have maize but who don't have a market to sell the maize. This is totally irrational. The only way we can get the market is through a boycott of GM crops while creating a food distribution system to link farmers directly to customers – that's the only way our farmers are going to get their income and continue to plant indigenous seeds. These laws are not going to help. We have to come up with our own laws! We can't wait for them to make laws for us that are then not implemented.

Thank you, comrade, for bringing up this issue of debt colonisation. It is important for people to understand how legislation comes into being because we use legislation many times as our defence, as our recourse to justice, but a lot of times this legislation can be enacted and abolished and banned at political will or just ignored essentially. Our recourse, then, is to plant our own seeds.

IA: We are also party to the Paris Agreement, but we have violated the agreement despite the fact that we were one of the first countries to sign it. Kenya ratifies everything. The Paris Agreement also has sections that say that we recognise indigenous people, vulnerable people and their rights and commitment to guard indigenous knowledge which includes indigenous seeds, indigenous ways of farming, indigenous methods of predicting and managing climate change and adapting to climate change. As Cidi says, it is one thing to sign and ratify these things into law and it's another thing to implement them. On the suggestion of going the legal way, sometimes it gives small wins but it can be very draining. I was part of the decolonise campaign during the time that we had the court battle and it is not a very nice experience because you are in and out of courts for years before getting the judgement which might not even be in your favour. And there are a lot of interrogations, judges not showing up for the bench intentionally, they don't communicate, or changing of court venues. It's just a back and forth and people are likely to lose momentum. We can get a court order, but the government will not obey the order!

I would now like us to discuss the role of multinational corporations. To present the lay of the land, we can begin with Monsanto. Monsanto has been the largest agri-tech GM Company in the world. It was acquired recently by Bayer which was the largest German pharmaceutical company, even though now the merger is falling apart because there are so many lawsuits against Monsanto. So many people have lodged lawsuits going into tens of millions in US dollars. There is also the Dow and Dupont merger and ChemChina acquiring Syngenta which presents a huge shift in the agri-tech industry in the way of creating monopolies that globally dominate the food industry.

There are very serious implications of these mergers on our food systems. The history of these companies is telling. A company like Bayer was responsible for the production of aspirin. It was the first company to legally sell and commercialise heroin before it was removed from the market. It was heavily involved in the Holocaust, using techniques tested in concentration camps for medical experiments and of course many of them died as you can imagine.

Monsanto itself assisted in the development of the first nuclear weapons. It started as a chemical company in the US, and it has introduced very harmful chemical pesticides like DDT and PCB. They also produced Agent Orange which was used in the Vietnam war as a chemical weapon.

Then there is the African Agricultural Technical Foundation and you see that it is involved in so many organisations like AU, New Partnership for Africa's Development, with the national biosafety authorities in the continent and you would imagine that it is an African company, same with the Alliance for Green Revolution in Africa. But these are just subsidiary organisations for the Rockefeller Foundation which is in partnership with the Bill and Melinda Gates Foundation as well as USAID. They are essentially the brokers between biotech companies and the African state scientific council to facilitate research on GM crops. They lobby for laws and patent rights for these companies.

So the main thing that these multinationals really advocate for is the privatisation of land and seeds by introducing property rights over plant varieties and criminalising farmers who plant their own varieties. They are doing all these things by carrying out training for media to present GM seeds; they hold workshops and lobby government officials to change biosafety regulations and patent their GM seeds. So they patent life itself. If you can patent a seed, it means you can patent life. And owning life for profit seems to be the long-term game. They laid the ground for neoliberalism with the structural adjustment programmes in Africa that ushered in privatisation, liberalisation and deregulation of public institutions. What are your thoughts on these multinational corporations?

CO: Recently, we had an online virtual meeting of the Ad Hoc Technical Expert Group on Farmers' Rights and again we saw how transnational corporations like Monsanto, Syngenta are lobbying for the patenting of seeds. If you look UPOV 91 (Union for the Protection of Plant Varieties) has worked exclusively to privatise seeds around the world by imposing intellectual property rights on plant varieties as fundamental parts of bilateral trade agreements. The Kenyan Seeds and Plants Varieties Act is a copy and paste of UPOV. Look at the draft East African Seeds and Plants Varieties Bill that is being developed, again, it is a copy and paste of the Kenyan Seeds and Plants Varieties Act.

Kenya is at the forefront of the neoliberal offensive in this region. So, with the African Free Trade Agreement, it is Kenya that is pushing it. You find that Kenya is now the country that is being used to promote the neoliberal policies in the region. The question we are asking is why are countries like Kenya so quick to implement bad laws yet slow to implement laws like Article 9 of the International Plan Treaty or Article 19 of the Peasants Rights Declaration? The answer is the influence of transnational corporations.

If you go to Siaya County today, a region in western Kenya, you will find that Syngenta or One Acre Fund are giving farmers seeds and forcing them to get mobile phones and television sets on credit, which a farmer has to pay back for over 21 months and when they don't pay then their produce is taken. The government is silent about all this. If you look at the regional governments, they are allocating funds to buy seeds from agrovets using taxpayers' money. Yet we know that [the] government should allocate money to buy these indigenous seeds from farmers to distribute.

We also know that in addition to controlling the production of seeds, these multinational corporations are also producing herbicides. The most infamous one, Glyphosate, commonly known by its trade name, Roundup, produced by Bayer has been subject to numerous studies that have argued that it is carcinogenic, increasing weed resistance and environmental hazards. A recent study done by Kenyatta University researchers on tomato farmers in Kenya, especially in Kirinyaga county who are the largest producers (50,000 tonnes at the Mwea Irrigation scheme annually) have found that the use of WHO class II pesticides whose residue is likely to remain in the crop has linked effects of its consumption to cancer, malformation of the foetus and damage to the immune system. The reason given is that farmers are ignorant of its effects.

Further still, a research report by Route to Food Initiative in 2019 revealed that many pesticides that are actually registered by the government's Pest Control Products Board (PCPB) have the potential to cause serious health and environmental problems. The Kenya Organic Agriculture Network did a study on the pesticides actually used by farmers, 30% of whom did not use personal protection equipment while spraying, and found that 48% have an effect on human reproductive systems, 70% on fish and 41% on bees.

We know that Europe banned the planting of GMO and 34% of the active ingredients of the pesticides registered in Kenya are either withdrawn or heavily restricted by the European market, which ironically is the second highest exporter of pesticides to Kenya. It is claimed that the reason farmers continue to use toxic amounts of pesticides is because farmers have not been trained on pesticide use and they rely on their untrained neighbours for information. Why have these issues not been flagged by the PCPB or the Kenya Drug and Poisons Board and why were they registered in the first place?

CO: Recently, the Kenya Peasant League in collaboration with a professor from the University of Graz in Austria, War on Want in Britain, and a movement from Turkana (a region in Northern Kenya), were talking about having field tests for organic pesticides in response to the locusts. The professor from the University of Graz has actually developed an organic pesticide. When we went to the pest control board, the requirements that they made – well, it's only people like Monsanto who can manage this level of bureaucracy. You find that these pests boards are public institutions that have effectively been privatised. They are public by name but private by funding. Together with War on Want we are working on a campaign to expose this information.

If you look at some of these pesticides [there is] clearly written "POISON, KEEP AWAY FROM CHILDREN", so you wonder why something that you cannot use without protection is safe. Some of these pesticides are not target specific, they kill all other organisms in the soil. There are some soil microorganisms that are very essential for the life of soil and for soil development. When there is surface runoff for example, some of these pesticides are flushed into the rivers and they kill fish. We have heard farmers complaining of several diseases, but the problem is most farmers take such diseases as common sicknesses so they don't report them. If someone is at the PCPB and he or she is allowing a pesticide that has been banned in Europe to come to Kenya to kill people, then that person must be held responsible for manslaughter or murder. It's depopulation, it is genocide!

The health impact has been catastrophic. In this continent we have seen the escalation of cancer related deaths by at least 45% since the year 2000. By now, all of us know someone – maybe a friend, a very close family member or neighbour – who is suffering from or has died because of cancer, a disease hitherto unheard of in our childhood. It's killing more than 500,000 people each year. Women are being very adversely affected because breast and cervical cancer are the most prevalent of the cancers in the continent.

They say that over a third of all cancer deaths in women are in South Saharan Africa even though we are only 14% of the total female population in the world. So you can imagine what that means. Globally cancer has caused more deaths compared to HIV, TB and malaria combined. In Kenya, it's the third highest cause of morbidity after infectious diseases and cardiovascular diseases. A lot of documentaries have exposed how families are increasingly devastated when a member has cancer, selling all their property in order to access treatment.

I want to cite just a few studies that were done linking GMOs to cancer. There's the most famous one, the Seralini study in France that led to the banning in Kenya. Unlike most scientists funded by these multinational corporations who carry out research for 90 days, this one was research conducted over two years. Seralini scientists found that there are severe impacts on kidney and liver functioning after four months because when they did the study on rats fed on GM maize, they developed cancerous tumours.

This is just to show the extent of the problems. All of us know that a lot of people in our lives are now suffering from not just cancer but also reproductive health problems. All these health issues that we had never heard of are now becoming an everyday discussion. In India, buffalos which were consuming GM cotton suffered from infertility, miscarriages, prolapsed uteruses and a lot of them died. It is important to point out that all the mentioned studies have been done by independent researchers. It is critical to know who is funding a particular study so that results are measured against the potential bias because many pro-GMO multinational corporations and international organisations fund a lot of the studies that show their "benefits".

Lastly, comrades, what are you doing in your prospective movements to collectively promote food sovereignty?

IA: We are linking already existing youth groups that have environmental departments with each other and with [the] RSL. We have a number of social justice centres as well that have environmental pillars. They have activities of rehabilitating spaces, having small ecological gardens and some of them have also started banking indigenous seeds, propagating them and sharing the seedlings. We have very thankfully received indigenous seeds from KPL. We are working on a biweekly political education class with specific regard to ecological justice.

CO: During the Covid pandemic, KPL has seen an increased demand for seeds from farmers who are not even members. Right now, we are working with support from the Agroecology Fund to enhance seed banking and distribution – linking farmers who want seeds with farmers who have the seeds.

As the KPL, we push for food sovereignty and food sovereignty is basically the total control of the food system from the seeds to the land, water, natural resources and the food distribution networks. We do this by linking farmers directly to consumers, we have seed exchange festivals annually. Right now, we are documenting all the seeds that our farmers have so that we have a chance at an equable and just system.

37. Habib Ayeb (2018), *Food Sovereignty and the Environment*

Radical geographer Habib Ayeb is a founding member of the NGO Observatory of Food Sovereignty and Environment (OSAE) and a professor of geography at Université Paris 8. As well as being a researcher, teacher and writer, Ayeb is also a celebrated documentary filmmaker. His most recent films are *Om-Layoun* (2021) on water issues, and *Couscous: The Seeds of Dignity* (2017) on food sovereignty. Here, he speaks with Max Ajl about food sovereignty, filmmaking and peasant struggle in North Africa.

***

Habib, you have made many films and written at length about food sovereignty in Tunisia and in Egypt. Can you start by telling us how you see the conversation around food sovereignty in this part of the world?

In recent years, the issue of food sovereignty has begun to appear in academic and non-academic debates and in research as well – although more tentatively – in all the countries of the region. That said, the issue of food and thus agriculture has always been important – both in academic research and public debate as well as the academy, political institutions and elsewhere. During the 1970s and 1980s, in Tunisia and throughout what was called the Third World, we spoke mainly of food self-sufficiency. This was, in a way, and at that time, a watchword of the left – a left that was modernist, developmentalist and statist.

If I'm not mistaken, I believe that the concept of food self-sufficiency dates from the late 1940s with the wave of decolonisation which began after the Second World War and probably also dates to the great famines which claimed millions of lives in India and other areas of the South. Furthermore, many states, particularly those governed by the state-socialist regimes that had acquired political independence during the 1950s and 1960s, had initiated Green Revolution policies. These had the aim of achieving food self-sufficiency to strengthen political independence, in a cold war context wherein food was already used as a weapon and a means of pressure in the context of the confrontation between the USSR and the Western bloc. It is in this context that the experiences of agrarian reforms and agricultural co-operatives in Tunisia (from 1962), in Egypt (from 1953) and in many other countries had proliferated. But almost all of these experiments ended in failure or were aborted by liberal counter-reforms, which were adopted everywhere beginning in the 1980s amidst the victory of liberalism, the USSR's disappearance, the development of a global food regime and its corollary: the global market for agricultural products and particularly cereals.

It is at this point that the concept of food security, based on the idea of comparative advantage, began to gradually dominate. It would appear for the first time in the official Tunisian texts in the sixth Five Year Plan of the early 1980s, in which the formula of food self-sufficiency would give way to that of food security. From then on, agricultural policies would favour agricultural export products with a high added value whose revenues would then underwrite the import of basic food products.

Paradoxically, agricultural issues, food issues and rural issues writ large would gradually disappear from academic agendas. There was a sharp reduction in funding for research on the rural world, and instead it went first to the urban research profile but also to examine civil society and political organisations. It was not until 2007/2008 and the great food crisis that agricultural and food issues, and furthermore the peasant question with its sociological dimension, would reappear in public debates focused on these matters. It was during the same period that the concept of food sovereignty, proposed by Via Campesina in 1996, would appear in Arab countries and to a much lesser extent in research. Even today, many use the food sovereignty frame to talk about food security even while the two concepts are radically opposed – even incompatible.

In Egypt, I participated in many discussions on issues of food security and sovereignty. We were, with some other friends and colleagues, including the anthropologist Reem Saad, responsible for helping to initiate the first discussions around the specific theme of food sovereignty. We organised workshops, research seminars and other activities, too, more oriented towards civil society and the media. We also organised two seminars in Damascus, in Syria, in 2008 and some others in Tunisia between 2007 and 2011. Concerning Syria, it should be noted that it is one of the very few countries in the South that did not suffer from the food crisis of 2007 and 2008, because the Syrian state has always thought – amidst a particularly hostile and explosive geopolitical context – that the food issue was part of its national defence strategy. Thus, agricultural policies before 2011 (and even after, with the difficulties that we can imagine) always aimed at a level of cereal production sufficient to cover basic needs. The lesson of the embargo imposed on Saddam Hussein's Iraq after the war of Kuwait was well learnt by Damascus.

From 2011 on, spaces and opportunities for debate would greatly expand – touching upon a multitude of topics and diverse themes, even if the rural world, and more specifically, agricultural and food topics, remain relatively marginalised, or often forgotten. Nevertheless, the issue of food sovereignty has seen some fairly significant actions and initiatives. In Egypt, the principle of food sovereignty was enshrined in the first post-Mubarak constitution (2012). In Beirut, there was an attempt to form an Arab Network for Food Sovereignty. In Gaza, food sovereignty is a strong demand to which the Israeli embargo gives shape and consistency. And then in North Africa, public discussions and various activities around food sovereignty began in 2012-2013. It must be noted that, throughout the region, there is still a kind of confusion around concepts, slogans and even demands and claims. If the notion of food sovereignty begins to spread there is then a risk of trivialisation and misuse of the expression which may occur – it has happened with other concepts, including that of sustainable development which has been totally emptied of any real meaning.

One puzzle I have come across while doing my research on food sovereignty – and I mean the narrow meaning, or the specific use of the term, as it has become linked to Via Campesina – is that there are very few regional social movements that are tied to Via Campesina. There is one in Morocco, there is one in Tunisia. And there is the Union of Agricultural Work Committees, which is the regional coordinator, and has been a part of Via Campesina, I think since 2003, since the second Intifada. This is the part of the world where Via Campesina has entered least – or has the fewest links. Why do you think this might be the case?

It is difficult to explain. Without being categorical, it seems to me that this is largely due to the paradoxical absence of direct relations between the city and the countryside which go beyond the marketing of agricultural products, an exchange which does not necessarily bring the two areas into continuous contact. Between the countryside, especially the peasants and agricultural workers who live and/or work there, and the city, including the ordinary inhabitants, the intellectuals, the activists and the trade unionists, communication and exchanges are relatively limited. The former does not necessarily have access to the city, whose codes they do not know, and the latter do not understand the countryside, and stigmatise its inhabitants. In the city, the word *fellah* (peasant) has become an insult.

When the Egyptian government carried out its agrarian counter-reform in 1992 by adopting the so-called 96/92 law which completely liberalised the land market, and which resulted in a massive rise in the price of agricultural land, overnight about a million peasant families, former tenants, found themselves without land to work and therefore without income. In response to an attempt at resistance, the government reacted with great brutality from its police – leaving about 150 dead, not counting the dozens of wounded and imprisoned. Astonishingly, these events in the Egyptian campaign did not provoke any rush of solidarity from urban political and intellectual elites, with the exception of a few activists and NGOs, already more or less engaged in the peasant milieu, who tried to organise some demonstrations and support activities. Today, I tend to think that these isolated and repressed peasant movements of the mid-1990s were the first fruits of the revolutionary processes that ended the Mubarak regime in early 2011.

Few people in the area know about Via Campesina. Even those people who, by a kind of mimicry, use the expression food sovereignty, often know nothing about Via Campesina and the history of this concept. In itself, this is a real political problem that further aggravates the invisibility of rural and peasant populations and widens the rift between the city and the countryside, thereby limiting relations to exchanges of products and services through closed circuits.

I wonder if some of the separation you talk about between the city and the countryside is also because, speaking generally here, with exceptions such as Yemen, it's been a very modernising left. Whereas in Asia you had Maoism, and in Latin America you had liberation theology, Christian-based communities, and you had all these ideologies and forms of organising that were much more centred on the world and the culture of the countryside. Whereas in North Africa it's generally been, or rather there has been, an embrace of a modern/traditional dichotomy.

Yes, sure. Compared to North Africa specifically, I think not only does the city not know the countryside, but additionally, the urban lefts subjugated by modernity have developed a sort of disregard for the peasantry, which they consider as a brake and an obstacle to development. We know that this is not new. Already Marx, in his day, had little regard for the peasant world which, surprisingly, he had never tried to understand.

Generally, the Maghreb left – excepting a few generally

unorganised intellectuals – reject the idea of rural social classes. I have the impression that this rejection is more a reflection of the contempt towards the peasantry than the output of a serious work of reflection and conceptualisation. But this is an issue that deserves a real dispassionate debate.

Let's take the example of the considerable difference between the history as it has been constructed and told – storytelling – of Mohamed Bouazizi[36] and the real story, which is much more interesting, because it is linked to the stories of many peasants in Sidi Bouzid, and their sense of being robbed, dispossessed, marginalised and impoverished. We know today that Mohamed Bouazizi, whom almost nobody knew outside his immediate circles, was not an unemployed graduate as had been claimed, and that he had not been slapped by the policewoman. Yet this false story had been disseminated and used to mobilise as much as possible against the Ben Ali regime. We understand the reasons and the political objectives of this invented history and we can even accede to such a use. For, in any case, no one can deny its formidable effectiveness since it allowed Tunisians to bring down a true dictatorship, while the real story probably could not have done so.

However, I continue to think that despite its undeniable effectiveness and its historical importance, Bouazizi's constructed history has dispossessed the peasants of Sidi Bouzid and the rest of the country of their stories of struggles and resistance, stories with which the real history of Bouazizi fits perfectly. The popular understanding of the Tunisian revolution stems from a false history, and constitutes in fact a denial of truth and a marked contempt – albeit unconscious – for peasants, their functions, their roles and finally their resistance. It is in fact a blatant expression of the opposition of the urban middle class and in particular the Tunisian left to any idea of rural social classes. The debate on rural social classes, opened a good 30 years ago, deserves to be

---

36   Mohammed Bouazizi was the Tunisian street vendor whose immolation in Sidi Bouzid, a city in Tunisia's Center-West, has often been heralded as the spark that lit the Arab spring.

revived and enriched. I have already published on the relationship between the peasants of Sidi Bouzid, Bouazizi and the revolution.

I also wonder if somehow there is a link between the fact that in Tunisia you have actually an incredibly rich tradition of Marxist intellectuals in the academy that wrote about the countryside. So, like Hafedh Sethom, Slaheddine el-Amami, to some extent Azzam Mahjoub, Habib Attia, who all, of course, wrote under the dictatorships. Some of them helped with the planning process in the 1970s, but they could not possibly be linked to any form of left that was actually organising otherwise they would lose their job and livelihood. So this made it harder to have a convergence between an activist left and the academic left, especially on this question of the countryside.

Yeah, definitely, at least in Tunisia. I don't know about Morocco or Algeria. Have you encountered attempts to converge between the Marxist researchers of the time, such as the ones you just mentioned, and the left-wing activists of the time? I do not know any. I must admit that it would have been extremely dangerous for anyone at the time of Bourguiba or Ben Ali, which must be a part of the explanation for the absence of convergences. One could imagine a birth of peasant or pro-peasant unions. But knowing a little about the political context of postcolonial Tunisia, characterised by a dictatorship that has closed all political spaces and the suffocating hegemony of organisations, such as the Tunisian Union of Agriculture and Fishery and the Tunisian General Labour Union, related through a system of alliances to the existing political power structure and its single party, it is very difficult to imagine political initiatives to create independent organisations.

In fact, it would be unfair to reproach Marxist scholars under dictatorship for not engaging politically. They did a great deal of observation, documentation and analysis in an extremely difficult context. They have left us with materials that have proven to be rich and indispensable for understanding current agricultural and food policies and the evolution of these policies during the last decades. Anyone who does not know the work of Amami, Sethom, or others cannot understand current agricultural issues and their ecological, economic, social and political dimensions. Those who ignore these valuable materials produced and accumulated during this relatively long period cannot understand what happened between December 17 2010 and January 14 2011. It is extremely important to recall these facts especially since very few contemporary academics could present a record as rich and politically useful as their predecessors.

Even when they proposed it, it was often just a proposal – they might write in their work that a specific programme "rests on the activity of the peasants" but this was a dead letter. Imagine someone going to the countryside and trying to organise the peasants! For all we know there were such attempts, but we don't know what happened to the people who tried to do these things. Even to take Brazil, which is supposedly a democracy, it's known that the Brazilian Landless Workers' Movement militants are assassinated all the time by the landowners.

And it's still the case in many other countries.

And this has been in the post-democratic period in Brazil. So, imagine in Tunisia...

Something like this also happened in Egypt, where the pro-peasant activist Salah Hussein – who was the husband of Shahenda Maklad, also a great pro-peasant activist who died in June 2016 — was murdered in 1966 in Kamshish, his village, which was located in the Nile Delta. He was killed because with Shahenda and the small peasants he had won a political battle against the big landowners of the Delta who were trying to avoid the agrarian reform initiated in the early 1950s by Nasser.

In Tunisia, Ahmed Ben Salah would never have allowed anyone to resist his policies. He would have used every means to prevent any resistance. This is the main explanation for the absence of trade unions and farmers' organisations before 2011 and even since the end of the dictatorship. This also explains why committed researchers did not get involved directly on the ground with the farmers.

If we can shift gears a little bit. How do you see your cultural work, your films, contributing to the Tunisian debate or collective discourse around food sovereignty? How do you see the contributions of all the films? Because you make a lot of films – Green Mirage, Fellahin, *Gabès* Labess, *and most recently* Couscous *which was shown at the ROAPE workshop in Accra in 2017.*

When I first began making films I did not plan to work on food sovereignty, it came much later. I had in mind work on questions of access to resources – land rights, water rights, environmental rights.

The first film, *On the Banks of the Nile: Sharing Water*, was made in 2003, at a time when, after 15 or 20 years of work on water, I realised that the real problem was not water but farmers and other water-users' access to water resources. It was conditions of access that could, at least partially, explain complex social and political situations. Access to water is a precondition for biological life. But it is also social and therefore political.

So, as I often say, [I] came out of the water to see the peasants, to understand the different mechanisms and questions they face, including those related to water access. The main objective was to contribute to the ongoing discussion, and to bear witness to the peasants' difficulties as well as their social conditions.

Of course, all this was not by chance. I did not find myself accidentally lost along Egypt's Nile Valley. I have done nothing, so to speak, by chance, during my career. My research activities have always focused on subjects which I considered, at the moment of my engagement, as causes to be defended. It's my way of engaging. I am not in any political party or movement. I am somewhere in the radical left and that suffices for me as an affiliation.

As far as filmmaking was concerned, I had felt the need to get out of my role as a researcher publishing for a relatively limited number of more or less specialised publications and readers, and to address those who are not necessarily in academia or the university environment. Documentary films seemed to me an excellent tool of communication and interchange with a public which was very broad compared to academia. Watching a documentary takes an incomparably shorter time than reading a book, or even a scholarly article.

I take advantage of what I believe I know to provoke debate. Water was my specialty. Rural issues too. This knowledge and experience allowed me to have special and close relations with the agricultural world, including peasants and all manner of farmers, and therefore with their living spaces and/or work. These relationships have allowed me to observe the rural space, the activities which go on there, their living and working conditions, the changes underway, as well as ways of organising rural and agricultural populations. It is, moreover, the privilege of social scientists who choose to be physically and intellectually close to their objects of research and their interlocutors in the field. That's what has always interested me. In any case that's what inspired me in my film *Green Mirages* that I made in 2012 with my friend, the Egyptian director Nadia Kamel. Basically, I try to do what I can do using available and accessible means and by mobilising the three or four things that I think I know and understand.

I tried to film in Tunisia in 2007 but I quickly realised that the camera represented for the Ben Ali regime a weapon of mass destruction and, in a sense, I agree with this idea. It's terrible what you can do with a camera. In any case, I quickly gave up the idea and I did not take out my camera again until much later for *Green Mirages* which I shot almost entirely in my village, Demmer, in the country's southeast, where there is no visible police presence.

You were a little protected.

I have a kind of protection that comes from my family's history, and a bit from my current status as an academic. People have their own perceptions. They do not necessarily see you as you are in reality, but as they want to see you.

In any case, we were able to make the film without too much difficulty. The film criticises dominant development models, by showing how they are complicit in the destruction and disappearance of an extremely rich local ensemble of know-how, of techniques and technologies, developed over time, through generation after generation, by local populations to adapt to local conditions and/or protect themselves against the various hazards of natural or non-natural origins. Demmer is a rocky village perched above the arid mountains of the southeast of the country. It is an open-air museum exhibiting hydraulic skills composed of both physical management of the water through hydraulic engineering (harvest, storage, dikes, earthworks…) and social water management, composed of an extremely rich and complex ensemble of mechanisms for conflict resolution between resource users. Thanks to these riches, Demmer has been able to withstand for centuries the worst conditions, whether permanent or contingent, but could not resist the modern models of development that dispossess people of their last tools of defence and survival.

Okay so you were able to show it in Tunis, as well?

Yes, especially in protected areas like universities. I remember a screening at the University in Tunis in front of dozens of viewers, both teachers and students. The ensuing discussion was one of the richest and most rewarding that I have had since I started making documentaries. The film only lasts 45 minutes, but the whole session lasted more than four hours. It is there that I understood that engaged films always find their publics, and systematically incite debate. That's exactly what I'm looking for.

Before we talk a little bit about Gabès Labess, *can you give a little more sense of what the reaction to* Green Mirages *was like from the students?*

The questions and comments of the students who were present at the screening that I was just talking about went beyond the bounds of a strictly academic context. They intervened as citizens who ask questions of substance concerning the choice of agricultural policies, the location of hydraulics and the immediate or long-term consequences of these policies on the environment. Some commented on the film in technical and artistic terms. Some questions related to my career, my choices and my commitments. An academic who makes movies was something relatively unusual for them and intrigued them. But the most important questions and comments were about development models and their actual or potential consequences. Some questioned me on the substance of my speech and asked me the question that I often heard then and I still hear today, "But sir, you want us to live like our grandparents?" In fact, I really like this question because it opposes, or juxtaposes, a certain representation of what is modern and what is old or traditional and forces us to re-pose the recurring question: what is modernity?

During the same discussion, there was another recurring question: "How to develop the country so as to resist global competition, without technological modernisation?" I answered with a series of questions, as I often do: "Why this race? Running forever behind development? Why don't we think more about the very notion of developing? For whom, for what? For growth rates? What is development? What does it mean to develop a country by increasing the number of poor people?" It is interesting to ask these questions, because people had not considered them.

I told them that Sidi Bouzid was the region that received the most investment between 1990 and 2011. The leading region. It is a region that had an extensive semi-pastoral farming system, and it became in less than 30 years the premier agricultural region of the country. At the same time Sidi Bouzid had been a "moderately poor" region, in a sense, and I put that in quotation marks, and it is now the fourth poorest region in the country. This is the development which people desire. Regueb, which is part of Sidi Bouzid, looks like California. Regueb is a perfect technical success, an exemplar of the Californian model. The problem is that the local population does not benefit. These are people from Sfax and the Sahel who get rich in Sidi Bouzid, not the people of Sidi Bouzid. Hence the link with the story of Mohamed Bouazizi.

Moving onto Egypt, there was a larger opening for freedom of expression in Egypt relative to Tunisia. For example, I was shocked when I heard in Egypt there was a Center for Socialist Studies.

I worked there for a few years. I did interviews in the Egyptian media, including on TV, where I spoke exactly as I speak to you now and in Egyptian, and on national channels. I did an interview about an hour long, about my book *Water in the Middle East* (published in Arabic in Egypt). In Tunisia it would have been just impossible!

But I think that if I did something in all my militant and professional life, which had a totally unexpected effect, it was my documentary Gabès Labess, made in 2014. It's a bit crazy. Something has happened, which is largely related more to the new political context than to the film itself. I really like this movie. For once, for the first time, there was a film addressing the issue of the environment by placing that issue alongside the dominant development models. I think that Gabès Labess favoured forms of mobilisation that did not exist before.

And you showed Gabes Labess *in Gabès many times?*

Yes, the first screening was in Gabès. In the Cultural Center of Chenini. The Oasis of Chenini, which is a part of Gabès. The first screening was just incredible. I was really very surprised. Over 200 people came. That means there were people waiting – not for my film itself, exactly, because nobody knew me, but they wanted something about the environment. There was demand on the environment, on the environmental issue.

The screening took place as part of a small festival, Lights and Colour of the Oasis which is still held in February. It is useful for people to know that I received death threats just before this first screening. I imagine it came from people in the factories – bosses or perhaps people who were naturally afraid for their livelihoods. However, I think that it must have been bosses and businessmen – that seems to me more likely.

It seems that since 2014 people are really beginning to reject the type of environmentally damaging development model, even though there isn't yet an articulated alternative.

Now people are really debating the question of development models. Sometimes the debate is very rich, and sometimes it's more of a provocation or challenge. Today, the debate is unquestionably touching on fundamental questions: "What do we do with water?", "What do we do with the earth?", "What do we do with our natural resources?", "What do we do with oil?", "What do we do with phosphate?"... The demonstrations in El Kamour, the strikes around the phosphate in Kasserine, Redeyef and so forth; the movements around the environment in Gabès, Sfax and Kerkennah; closing chemical plants, shutting down the road, stopping the oil pipeline – these are actions. But what is behind them? I think there we find the debate on the development model. When the people of El Kamour say "We want our share of oil revenues", they are speaking of development models.

I've been in Tunis while you have been distributing and showing Couscous, *which touches on food sovereignty. Even if it does not explicitly put forth a different development model, it nevertheless centres a different form of development as something people need to look at. Do you think this is part of why people are so receptive?*

Yes, that explains at least part of the good reception of *Couscous*. The film does not directly address the issue of development models, but it says that there is something that does not work in the current system. The peasants who appear in the film say so clearly, and they go further by explaining the causes of the various difficulties they encounter. By giving the floor to female and male peasants who express themselves with great clarity and precision and exhibit a real political awareness of the complex mechanisms which explain their difficulties, the film speaks directly to people, beyond their educations, opinions, social backgrounds and trades. This is why they are very receptive both to the film and to the central idea it conveys, the idea of food sovereignty as a political alternative and as a fundamental requirement.

The advantage for the movie *Couscous* has been that the debate had already been opened. The movie came as an additional document to enrich the debate and cast upon it a specific kind of light. There were already people sitting around the table, discussing, and I brought them something new. What surprised me most has been the overall positive reaction to the film. The debate is constantly revived, as it expands, as new people of diverse social origins engage for the first time. Recently, a journalist I interviewed said, "What, for you, is a *fellah*? How is it useful to society?" These two questions can be considered extremely simple, or even simplistic. Their significance stems from the fact that many people thought they had already been bypassed, considering farmers part of the past, and that their contemporary usefulness is almost nil. The film says the opposite and it's always productive to shake up frozen ideas.

Politically, people have started to know me since 2014. They know that I make movies. Some subscribe to my blog, which has about 4,000 subscribers, of whom more than 90% are probably Tunisian. Of course, my name attracts people, and I am very happy. But I also think that those who already knew my other films came to see *Couscous* with a fairly positive preconception. That, in part, explains why the movie *Couscous* received a much wider reception than the other films.

The film is not yet available online. People have seen it in theatres during the Carthage Film Days: three screenings, three different rooms, three full rooms. One must note that Tunis's theatres average around 400 seats. During that event there was also radio, TV, the press and of course social networks and electronic newspapers which, in fact, offered coverage to *Couscous*, whereas the other films had not benefited from such visibility. It makes a fundamental difference.

Obviously, the movie *Couscous* did not initiate the debates on food sovereignty. There have already been many other events and actions around this broad issue whether they have occurred under the concept of food sovereignty or not. But it seems to me that the film has given some visibility and some new impetus to these discussions. It's the magic of cinema that escapes the director completely.

I know you've shown the film to not just general audiences but also agricultural schools in certain places. Can you talk a little bit about the Q&A sessions, the reception to the film both in general but also especially how the agricultural and agronomy students have reacted to it?

It is exciting to discuss food sovereignty and agricultural policies with agronomy students. Some students say to me, "But, sir, how would we be useful, with the training we have, if the current model is not good?" These are young people who are in the process of obtaining their engineering degrees and who have a fairly solid technical background. They are generally even more challenged when I provoke them deliberately by suggesting that a large portion of the problems we are debating is due to the work of the experts who design the policies which are adopted, and who know nothing outside their specialties.

If you ask experts what to do to solve the problem of lack of water somewhere, they are likely to answer that it is necessary to build a dam or dig a borehole. A technical answer to a political problem. This is what students learn in Tunisian agricultural schools. Therefore, their reactions to my provocation are related to their current and future social status and their schooling. But as I went through these schools, too, from high school to engineering school, I could talk to agronomy students, using their languages and their tools.

So, to answer their questions about their future and their roles after school, when they have the engineering degree in their pocket, I tell them a bit about my state of mind at the end of my studies, where they are today. I tell them that if, when I left engineering school, I was given the keys to the Ministry of Agriculture, I would have erased everything old to create something beautiful, modern, impressive with big modern machinery, chemical fertilisers, pesticides. I would have installed a new California on Tunisian soil. It is this dream of technical modernity that I learned at school without any perspective and without any analytical ability to think otherwise. In these schools, the social sciences were totally absent – and this is obviously not a coincidence. The function of these schools in Tunisia is to train technicians, not citizens. Unfortunately, this model is becoming widespread and affecting the entire education system, including in many countries of the North with specialisations increasingly narrow and closed to any other knowledge. So I say to these future technicians that the problem comes from our training and that we must question not only our individual training, but the whole system that trains future decision-makers. I tell them that I had to re-educate myself to free myself from the training that the engineering school had imposed on me.

Do you discuss agro-ecology with them?

Yes of course. When I went to these schools – and I have done three so far – I initially went with the idea of not addressing technical issues because they know more than me and that would prevent productive discussion. I just wanted to tell them this: "Listen! You have been deprived of tools for reflection, you have been deprived of social sciences, political science, history, debates on the model of development, debates on liberalism, and basic knowledge about the major currents of thoughts: What is capitalism? What is Marxism? What is right?" This is knowledge that is needed in order to have the foundation to better analyse and appreciate the situations that they will inevitably encounter in their professional life and, if necessary, bring the right answers. My challenge was to tell them that we cannot answer the big questions and the big current challenges concerning development and ecological problems by having a strictly technical approach and without calling on other knowledges and especially the social sciences.

Have any of these students, that you know of, returned to the debates from the 1980s? I know the Arab world in general and Tunisia especially had an exceptionally rich debate about alternative technologies, particularly in the agricultural sector, which were less energy intensive and less polluting – has this happened, or perhaps it is something that will develop in the future?

These debates, which you mention, date from the 1970s and 1980s at a time when rural studies were still relatively important and where the discussion focused on the choices between the development of agriculture or the orientation towards what was called industrialising industry, the economic liberalisation which occurred from the mid-1980s contributed to the extinction of these debates. As a result, rural research gradually gave way to urban research. The debate simply changed. But I have seen the return of these debates since the food crisis of 2007-2008.

I recently received a letter from a young student who is about to finish her studies as an agricultural engineer at a Tunisian school. She wants to undertake a doctoral thesis on the evolution of agricultural technologies and their perceptions by small Tunisian farmers. Roughly, she is posing the question of whether and how small Tunisian farmers adapt to new agricultural technologies and to what extent they adopt them. This specific question was asked by another student during the debate we had in their school. I remember answering that a small farmer can die if – to replace a plough he has just broken – he does not find the right plough suited to his terrain and his own material and social conditions. He can disappear simply because without the good plough, he cannot work his land. I added that the issue of adaptability and adaptation is a complex issue that does not just answer financial or technical criteria.

Another question that often comes up, and not only in agronomy schools, is "Can small farmers feed humanity?" This is a very serious question that cannot be answered with a simple "Yes." The world's population has reached 7-8 billion people. Can small farmers feed them? Obviously my answer is yes. But for that the peasants must be able to control the market and production. In other words, it will be necessary to leave the current dominant model. It will be necessary to change everything that now exists and move to a peasant agricultural model whose objective is to feed humanity instead of the enrichment of some. In short, we must take our leave from this liberal and capitalist agriculture to return to peasant agriculture. Today the peasantry no longer lives exclusively from the land, their work and their functions are devalued and they are increasingly marginalised and progressively excluded from the agricultural sector. In these circumstances, no one can say that the peasants alone can ensure the sufficient food for all humanity. It's just not possible.

And it is almost impossible to imagine a neoliberal or even state-capitalist regime to be interested in devolving power to the poorest people in society.

Or even feeding people. They don't care.

They care about neither. Technically it is possible to shift the existing system, but we can't see it. So maybe this leads to the last question.

Habib, now you have an organisation, the Observatory of Food Sovereignty and Environment, what kind of work is it doing, how do you see it contributing to the debate around food sovereignty, and how do you see it moving forward?

I was at the founding of the Observatory of Food Sovereignty and Environment, but I am not alone since we are four founding members (Nada Trigui, Amine Slem, Adnen Ben Haj and myself) and therefore accountable for the association. I think that the debates since 2011 have been too political, and do not usually rely on accurate and verifiable knowledge and data.

In addition, social science research on issues such as food sovereignty, peasant issues and the environment are very limited and poor. The few researchers working on these subjects publish in foreign languages and rarely in Arabic and even less in local dialects. As a result, they are seldom read and discussed since people do not know them, and they do not know their work, which is almost never discussed publicly outside research environments and associated spaces. But important debates need a certain amount of knowledge and analysis based on research. Otherwise we are no longer in a real debate, but immersed in sterile and unproductive chatter. If you do not do research, people cannot know things. And if they cannot know, they cannot debate from a solid foundation.

Our idea, and it is, perhaps, the novelty of OSAE, is to be a structure that aims at debate and proposals based on research, and verifiable and verified information. Secondly, perhaps advocacy activities and support for peasants and those engaged in the struggle against the destruction of the environment, nature and natural resources. But that will be a second stage.

We want to start by forming a solid research nucleus, which examines these current issues of food sovereignty in relation to law, justice, the environment and social conditions. So OSAE is primarily a committed civic research organisation. Therein lies its contribution. As far as I know, it is alone in working on the rural world and aims to put forth a new reading of its situation and its problems, and to advocate new discourses based on the research and analysis produced by members of OSAE or by others who wish to collaborate with us. Research at first, training of researchers, information and invitations to debate are our agenda for the current and future moments. In a second step, once we are more settled, we will intervene on the ground with actions more directly engaged with farmers, consumers, young people and, of course, civil society.

There is also a question of sovereignty here. There is a real problem which we have not as yet discussed. The majority of those who contribute to and set the boundaries of political debates around food sovereignty, including in the social sciences, are composed of foreign or foreignised actors. People who are from here, but totally disconnected from realities and local communities. They live elsewhere. They work elsewhere. They think elsewhere. Some do excellent work but from the North and with questions, problems, analytical tools and readings from the North. My dream for OSAE is to initiate a research programme which thinks from here, without, of course, cutting itself off from those who think from their own fields, specialties and problematics.

38. Marjorie Mbilinyi (2017), Gender and Politics in Africa

As a teacher, analyst and organiser, Marjorie Mbilinyi has inspired a generation to question patriarchy and to set up groups to study and fight against it collectively, and to do so in tandem with struggles against class oppression, neoliberalism and imperialism. Here, in conversation with *ROAPE*'s Janet Bujra, Mbilinyi offers a powerful and critical account of 50 years of campaigning against patriarchal oppression on many fronts in Tanzania, in which Mbilinyi has herself been at the forefront. She traces the legitimisation of feminism as a means to understand and a way to organise for and with women. In this growing movement she identifies and describes resistance not only from men in power but also from those who position themselves on the radical left.

***

Your life in Tanzania has been one of gender and left activism and you have made major contributions, working collectively with others. What motivated you initially towards such objectives? As someone born in the USA, did your politics precede your move to Tanzania or were they generated by events and conditions in Tanzania?

I would say both: my politics preceded my move to Tanzania in a general sense, but events – both personal and public – galvanised my activism. From adolescent years I was committed to challenging inequality and injustice, propelled in part by personal struggles at family level. Later, exposure to the women's movement literature of the 1960s provided me with the tools to understand and name patriarchal structures of oppression in the family.

As a member of the 60s generation, I was actively engaged in the civil rights movement in the early 1960s in and out of Cornell

University where I did my first degree. Participation in the voter registration drive in Fayette County, Tennessee, in 1964 as part of a Cornell University students group was a landmark, providing me with first hand exposure to community led activism and the intricacies of "outsider" participation.

Arriving in Tanzania at the end of 1966 to join my husband-to-be, Simon Mbilinyi, after completing my MA in Education Psychology at Stanford University, I was caught up in the excitement of the debates over socialism and self reliance on and off campus. As a young wife/mother, and academic at University of Dar es Salaam (UDSM) I was forced to confront the challenges and struggles of patriarchy in the family and on campus, as well as in the general community, while also actively engaged with others in efforts to implement socialist principles, transformative pedagogy and participatory action research. My position, as an American born European/white female married to a Tanzanian, complicated these struggles.

In 1967 I made a conscious decision to become a Tanzanian citizen. Our family adopted Kiswahili as the family language and sought in every way possible to provide our children with a local Tanzanian upbringing, feeling at home and belonging in their father's culture, community and extended family, and building strong bonds with their grandmother, aunts, uncles, cousins and non-kin family friends. Fluency in Kiswahili was also a must for anyone seeking to participate in the social transformations taking place at that time.

Why do I dwell at length on language and culture issues? We had observed the harm caused by identity issues among a few Tanzanian friends of mixed racial heritage, who were born in the colonial period – usually of European/white fathers and African mothers. Some were separated from their mothers and maternal community, and sent to boarding schools for African children of middle-class aspiring parents. The mixed children had their own dormitory room, clothing and food to eat, and were taught "proper" European manners and table etiquette, and they wore shoes!

My husband Simon and I have been fortunate to have four remarkable children, three girls and one boy: NnaliTausi, AninaMlelwa, LyungaiFilela and Mhelema Michael. We lost Mhelema at the tender age of one year and three months, following one of several bouts of severe high temperature and infection during his lifetime. At the same time, we have been blessed by the birth of four grandchildren who are our hope and inspiration.

Within two months of Nnali's birth, I was employed on a full-time basis in the university's Department of Education and had to find an ayah/nanny to help take care of my child. On 1 January 1968, Mwamvua Saidi entered our household and family and remains part of us to this day, as mama *mlezi*. Mwamvua, or Mama Shija, played a major part in helping to socialise our children – and me — and ground us in Tanzanian culture. She also freed me to be able to devote time to my work as a university lecturer and researcher, to my PhD studies at UDSM from 1968 through 1972, and increasingly, to my engagement in the women's/feminist movement. Mwamvua was also balancing work and being a wife, mother, family. She had five children, four boys and one girl, spaced very closely to our own children. Soon she and her family were able to move into our compound, and our children grew up together, becoming part of our extended family.

The famous feminist slogan, the personal is political, had special resonance for me as a young wife/mother and academic/activist, trying to cope with the often conflicting demands of patriarchal society and at the same time belong to my new community. Friendship with like minded women and the sisterhood we developed as part of a feminist movement for change became a major source of inspiration, hope and support, as well as the overall progressive group of scholars and their families both on and off university campus. My family became another, and the two worlds often coalesced in joint activities – Sundays at the beach with children and friends, drop in visits, rotating dinner and dance parties in one another's homes.

These were also formative years for the university at many

different levels: a shift from largely expatriate and European staff to Tanzanian and African; struggles over ideology between the dominant imperial bourgeois position, a pan-Africanist Marxist vision, and transformative feminism which challenged both; struggles over structures and ways of decision making between the inherited top-down bureaucratic structure and alternative democratic systems; and conflicts over the relationship between the university, the state and the people. Women/gender struggles were situated within each of these struggles and also helped to shape them.

Can you describe the heady political atmosphere at the university in the early 1970s? What kind of debates took place and between whom? What part did you play in university politics?

The university was an exciting place to be in the late 1960s and early 1970s. There were debates on the role of the university in building socialism and self-reliance, involving lecturers and students as well as participants from town. This included advocacy of curriculum reform and structural transformation of the university itself, enhancing the voice and power of lecturers and students vis a vis the administration. The common courses (East African Society and Environment and Development Studies) were designed to expose all students, regardless of their subject specialisation and career choice, to an understanding of Tanzanian/socialist ideology, history and political economy. In the Department of Education, we created a joint foundation first year course [Psychology and Sociology of Education] to enable future teachers, researchers, [and] school administrators to better understand and engage with the challenges of implementing the state's Education for Self-Reliance policy at school/college and classroom level. My particular interest was in the promotion and practice of transformative pedagogy at university as well as in other education institutions, in order to promote creativity, critical thinking, problem posing and democracy in the classroom.

Efforts to democratise the university led to periodic confrontations with the university administration. I was involved with fellow lecturers in mobilising support for students' autonomy and defending the student organisation leader at that time, Simon Akivaga, when he was seized by police forces and eventually expelled to Kenya, his home country. I also joined forces with other women lecturers and administrators in challenging sex discrimination at the university, and in society as a whole.

UDSM had a rich seminar culture; nearly every arts, humanities and social science department organised weekly seminars involving both lecturers and students (undergraduate and graduate) in often heated debates on academic and political issues combined. Through these fora, scholars launched preliminary research reports and research proposals for discussion and feedback. Some succeeded in drawing a substantial number of town[s]people as well, providing space for a cross-exchange of views with government and political leaders, intellectuals and increasingly civil society activists. Most of my writing was presented in one of these seminars, and several became controversial. The progressive left at the university was dominated by dogmatic Marxists who had no conception of, nor tolerance for, the notion of (class/gender/race) intersectionality. They demanded a purist static class analysis that could not grapple with the grey areas of structural change and power relations/struggles in postcolonial Tanzania. My critical analyses of race and gender were labelled diversionary in studies of colonial education and agriculture policies. My painstaking study of different forms of peasant differentiation in contemporary Tanzania, using Lenin's methodology in his study of rural capitalism in Russia to examine the results of numerous empirical studies, was also denounced as "petty bourgeois thought".

The seminars were exciting, but the discourse was brutal, personalised and macho. Participants focused on finding weaknesses in a paper and were only satisfied when they could thrash it to pieces. I remember the day in the mid-1970s when Deborah

Bryceson and I presented our seminal paper on women's involvement in peasant production and reproduction in Tanzania! A notable historian denounced the analysis, saying "you are dividing the masses!" In my experience, the greatest resistance to gender/feminist analysis came from the Marxists – or from the right, from bourgeois nationalists who talked about how good things were "back home in the village where my mother is very happy". Until today, many land rights activists repeat the same Marxist line, blind to the way in which social relations in peasant economies are constructed by gender, age and class relations, and women bear the brunt of government anti-peasant policies and lead the popular resistance against local plunder by mining, agriculture and tourist corporations.

In contrast to the university macho culture, I adopted an alternative style of discourse in my postgraduate seminars whereby participants were expected to identify positive aspects and strengths of research proposals and essays first, and then provide constructive criticism of weaknesses and gaps. The focus was on the text or narrative in question, and not the person. The women's studies groups and feminist organisations I have been associated with have adopted a similar position, creating an alternative safe space and style of discourse, in order to encourage women, youth and other marginalised people to share their work and to learn to welcome helpful constructive criticism.

To what extent was there gender awareness and politics on the campus at that time? What was the gender composition of the student body and staff? Compared to the lives of women beyond the campus, did women students enjoy a degree of gender equality?

The university was organised according to male bias principles, with blatant sex discrimination in terms of service for staff, and in practices of their recruitment, employment and promotion, as shared in my article, "Gender Struggles at the University of Dar es Salaam: A Personal Herstory". Women lecturers and administration staff, including myself, organised ourselves informally to fight against sex discrimination in the early 1970s, galvanised by a blatant case of discrimination. Thus began my involvement in collective struggles for women's rights.

The composition of university staff became increasingly Tanzanian and/or East African during the 1970s and 1980s. Many of us participated in campus activism which centred around the struggle for socialism and against capitalism and imperialism in general, and colonialism and apartheid which remained in several neighbouring countries and in the south. We also joined together as members and leaders of the University of Dar es Salaam Academic Staff Assembly (UDASA) in the 1980s to struggle for more democracy at the hill [as the university is known], with more voice from academics in making basic decisions, as well as for more substantive change in curriculum. Immediately however, the issue of sex discrimination at the university emerged as a problem and eventually a source of division. The major struggle emerged over efforts by women staff to organise ourselves through UDASA to denounce sex discrimination in employment, promotions, recruitment, etc and to demand change.

Nearly all women academics joined the women's caucus within UDASA, and collectively carried out a quick survey to establish the number of women and men at different levels of employment within the university; the gender breakdowns in terms of student enrolment at undergraduate, MA and PhD level; and in leadership posts as heads of departments, deans and directors and the top administration. We also investigated staff views about the causes of the problems and what to do about it. People documented the extent of sexual harassment of women staff and students, for example, and the lack of any serious strategy to deal with it.

A joint report was prepared collectively and presented at a special meeting of UDASA in Nkrumah Hall and aroused a major and intense debate. What was alarming and bitter for me was that the most furious rejection of the paper and of our demands for gender equity and equality came from progressive leftists! They took the position that the women's caucus was dividing academic staff unity in the struggle against university bureaucracy and for academic rights, and that sex discrimination was a secondary contradiction!

Nevertheless, this organising activity helped to catalyse the setting up of a Gender Sensitisation unit [now Gender Studies] under the Chief Administrative Officer. The unit develops and implements gender sensitisation sessions for students and top management on an annual basis.

Another major area of discrimination which women faced, and which led to male biassed research and a deformed curriculum for all students, was gender stereotyping in curriculum and research. There were no formal courses on women's studies or gender studies let alone feminist studies in those days, with the welcome early exception of a second year option course in Development Studies on women's liberation..[37] Gender mainstreaming was carried out by many women and men staff to insert gender/women's issues into course syllabi. Moreover, in Fine Arts, lecturers and drama groups created positive and active imagery of women who acted on their own behalf and were not simply victims. Students were also encouraged to research on gender issues in undergraduate and postgraduate essays as well as independent research and MA and PhD dissertations.

One way to validate gender/feminist studies was to compile an annotated bibliography of all the research reports and analytical essays written about women and/or gender issues in Tanzania, especially those written by Tanzanians themselves. Ophelia Mascarenhas and I prepared a bibliography on women and development for the African Centre for Research on Women at [the] United Nations Economic Commission for Africa, [at] Addis Ababa in the late 1970s. We shared the first cyclostyled version of this bibliography with participants in the Bureau of

---

37   Marjorie Mbilinyi noted that "An informal group of staff and non-staff feminists, including myself, developed and taught the course syllabus, and compiled appropriate readings, largely from unpublished papers."

Resource Assessment and Land Use Planning workshop on Women and Development in 1979 as part of a process of celebration, validation and knowledge generation. Many of the authors cited in this work were participants; the workshop represented a major contribution towards the recognition of women and gender studies as a valid area of analysis and research. Ophelia and I later expanded the number of items in the bibliography with more in-depth annotations, and wrote a substantive essay which focused specifically on the resistances and struggles of Tanzanian women against patriarchy and capitalism during the precolonial, colonial and postcolonial period. *Women in Tanzania* (1983) deliberately challenged the usual western feminist view of African women as being powerless victims, or the bourgeois nationalist view that the concept of gender equity was a foreign importation, or the Marxist view that it was possible to separate gender and class struggles in the world of marginalised women.

Eventually and largely through the struggles of women academics and students, specific gender courses were established in many social science related [curricula] during the 1980s and 1990s. A good example is the MA optional course on Gender Issues and Socio-economic Development which we created in the Institute of Development Studies, and which I coordinated and taught until my retirement in 2003. This led later to a full-fledged master's degree programme on gender and development.

As with other feminist initiatives, these efforts faced immediate resistance and backlash from fellow lecturers. Postgraduate students were told that women/gender-related dissertation themes were "not academic"; fellow lecturers were told that their research reports were irrelevant to Tanzanian realities and were influenced by foreign ideology. Vocal women students and lecturers who challenged the status quo faced a backlash. Many women, including myself, decided to organise ourselves in groups so as to provide solidarity and moral support, and enhance our power and capacity to make changes at curriculum and institutional level. Most notable for me were the Institute of Development Studies

- Women Study Group (IDS-WSG), which later gave birth to the Women Research and Documentation Project (WRDP) and the Tanzania Gender Network Programme (TGNP).

Please tell me more about how you engaged with gender/class issues in research and analysis on and off the University of Dar es Salaam campus. In your research and activism, you use the concept of "animation" – can you describe what this meant in practice and what kind of issues it was used to address?

My focus of research and analysis has been on gender and agrarian issues, beginning with studies of education in rural areas in the 1960s and 1970s; through analyses of changing gender and class relations in the rural economy based on participatory research in West Bagamoyo District (1980) and Rungwe District (1985-1990); rural food security in the context of the policy shift from public support for small family producers during the 1970s and early 1980s to free market policies with a growing emphasis on large-scale production in 1980s to the present. At the same time, I have been actively involved in creating advocacy and activist organisations, again on and off campus.

My initial terrain of engagement was in the field of education, and specifically teacher training at the UDSM. My first research experience at UDSM was survey research on parental decision-making about enrolment of girls and boys to primary school, based on field work in Tanga and Mwanza rural districts. This study helped to challenge stereotyped notions about "coastal" and Islamic bias against girls' education, and highlighted the significance of household income differentials in determining girls' chances of going to school compared to boys. This led to the publication of my first book entitled *The Education of Girls in Tanzania* (1969) and my PhD, "The Decision to Educate in Rural Tanzania". It was also the first and last time I relied entirely on research assistants for field research. I have been actively involved in participatory action research ever since, usually as part of research teams.

While in the Education Department I coordinated and participated in the Secondary School Research Project during the 1970s, using participatory research methods and partnering student[s], teachers and myself with role model teachers to observe each other's teaching methods and classroom interaction, with a focus on gender relations. A joint report on our findings was presented to teachers in participating secondary schools and widely endorsed, and included the teachers' recommendation that they be allowed to organise themselves in an independent teachers' union. Although the Ministry of Education closed down the project in retaliation, the Tanzanian Teachers Association was formed not long afterwards.

Linking academic work and activism, several researchers outside as well as within the university embraced and further strengthened the concept of participatory action research, or *animation*, in the late 1970s, and eventually formed the Tanzanian Participatory Research Network, a forerunner of the African Participatory Research Network. Animation is predicated on the understanding that women and men who are exploited and oppressed are active knowers of the situation and many of its causes. Animators or facilitators use a variety of participatory methods, including codification pictures, case studies and drama, to provoke the oppressed to assess their/our situation, analyse the major causes and act to make change happen.

Animation creates a creative and dynamic space in which the class, ethnic, gender differences between researchers and/or middle-class activists and members of the marginalised exploited class of – in this case – women are recognised and challenged. Illiterate working women become teachers, and together we create new knowledge and plan strategies of action. In the case of "real" participatory action research, the activist researchers participate in and/or follow up the action of their grassroots partners. The results of the knowledge so produced are immediately shared with participants in the animation research and others in the community, including village government leaders, and later, district leaders, and so on (or it could be with teachers and school heads; factory management, etc), in order to receive critical feedback and plan together how to move forward. Creative use is made of alternative forms of communications and media, especially local forms of song, dance, poetry, drama and artwork, as well as interactive videos.

In the late 1970s and early 1980s, I was actively involved in two off-campus participatory action research programmes which became milestones for animation in Tanzania, the Christian Council of Tanzania's Vocational Education Project and the Jipemoyo Research programme. Jipemoyo was hosted by the Tanzanian Government's Ministry of Culture with Finnish support, with two co-directors, the late Odhiambo Anacleti and Prof Marja Lisa Swantz during the late 1970s and 1980s. Based in West Bagamoyo District, Jipemoyo worked with pastoralists (*Waparakuyu*) and cultivators (*Wakwere*) in *ujamaa* (socialist) villages near Lugoba trading centre; I participated in regular meetings to reflect on the varied research experiences, and carried out field research for a short time in a very poor village called Diozile, following on the heels of another researcher (Asseny Muro). We both focused our respective studies on changing gender relations at household and community level in the cultivating community. I remember being struck by the high level of political awareness among village women and youth, who actively challenged corrupt village government leaders and demanded change. I also learned more about the changing but still empowering aspects of matrilineal society and the intricacies of polygamous life.

Regional and district authorities in West Bagamoyo were unsettled by the way in which community activists organised themselves, provided articulate and informed critique of dysfunctional policies and corrupt leadership, and won the attention of a broad audience beyond the local level. This led to a backlash, but the lessons learned by the Jipemoyo experience informed later participatory action research and organising activities.

Animation work has provided me with invaluable learning

experiences, helped to ground me locally, and strengthened my understanding and knowledge about the interlinkage between patriarchy and neoliberal globalisation. In the world of a peasant woman, there is no question that gender, class and imperialism are integrally linked together; she confronts and resists these relationships on a daily basis. In the same vein, providing students in a secondary school – and their teachers – with the opportunity to reflect on their different realities and design alternative ways of learning not only produces new knowledge, it also contributes to immediate change in and out of the classroom.

Personal life histories became one avenue to explore changes and struggles through the subjective life experience of individual women (and men). In 1985 I devoted a sabbatical to analysing changes that took place in class, race and gender relations in Rungwe during the colonial and immediate post-colonial period. In the 1940s and 1950s, more than one fourth of young Nyakyusa men worked as migrant labourers in the Copperbelt of then Northern Rhodesia or the gold mines of South Africa – I wanted to find out what happened to the women. In-depth interviews were carried out with several elderly women and men in Rungwe, as well as archival research at the Rungwe mission at Tukuyu, Rhodes House, Oxford University, the National Archives of the UK at Kew, and Tanzanian National Archives. It was exciting to discover all the fuss caused by rebellious "runaway wives" in Rungwe, according to reports by male district commissioners, the Native Affairs Commissioner, managers of copper mines and "native chiefs" in the archives and then to go find out what older women and men had to say about it. Oral history confirmed the fact that large numbers of Rungwe women ran away from forced marriages and joined their "brothers" in the migration to the Copperbelt. Alliances were formed between colonial officers, mining management and local "chiefs" to bring the unruly women home! These and other stories confirmed the fact that the personal is political; and that custom and tradition were inventions of the colonisers and their local male allies.

In colonial Rungwe, the Moravian Church provided an emancipatory space for many women who struggled to overcome the patriarchal oppression and discrimination they experienced at home. Women could become elders, and travel from one village to another for days on end with their male colleagues. Yet both the Moravian and the Lutheran church practised racist and sexist policies in the colonial days and refused to ordain African ministers for many years. Discriminatory wage structures were found in mission schools, hospitals as well as the church, with different wages for African and Europeans, and within each racial category, women were paid the least – if they were paid at all.

An elderly woman named Rebeka Kalindile became my teacher, mentor, mother and partner in countless debates over patriarchy and colonialism at this time. Together we compiled her life story in an animation process, focusing on those events and happenings which Rebeka believed were most significant. Rebeka forced me to interrogate my own strategies of resistance; one of her favourite slogans was "you have to be clever" ("*lazima uwe mjanja*"), imbibing classical conceptions of resistance by slaves as well as women.[38]

I presented the results of my Rungwe studies in my professorial lecture of 1985, later published as *Big Slavery, Agribusiness and the Crisis in Women's Employment in Tanzania* (1991). *Big Slavery* explores the interaction between patriarchy and capitalism through the histories of women's resistances in the private and public domain during the colonial and post-colonial period.

In 1998, a group of four university researchers – Bertha Koda, Claude Mung'ongo, Timothy Nyoni and myself – began the Rural Food Security Policy and Development Group, otherwise known as KIHACHA, which was situated within IDS (Institute

---

38 Marjorie Mbilinyi "I'd have been a Man! Politics and the Labour Process in producing Personal Narratives" in *Personal Narratives Group* (eds) Interpreting Women's Lives (Indiana University Press, 1989) and Marjorie Mbilinyi and Rebeka Kalindile "Grassroot Struggles for Women's Advancement: the story of RebekaKalindile" in Bertha Koda and Magdalena Ngaizae's *The Unsung Heroines* (Dar es Salaam, DUP for WRDP Publications 1991).

of Development Studies) and guided by a national advisory committee consisting of leaders from four activist civil society organisations. During 1998 through 2002 we carried out intensive animation work in Ngorongoro, Shinyanga and later Njombe Rural Districts, inviting peasant women and men to assess the situation of food security in their local context, analyse the basic causes and decide on concrete actions to improve if not radically transform the situation. Feedback sessions were held at village, district and national level where village activists helped to explain the findings to government officials and NGO leaders, and argued on behalf of the recommendations and demands which they had generated in the animation process.

KIHACHA participants agreed on one core campaign slogan, *"haki ya chakula, ardhi na demokrasia"* ("the right to food, land and democracy") through intensive discussion in each of the nine participating villages. KIHACHA produced a powerful set of campaign messages using colourful popular leaflets, posters, t-shirts, song and a drama – the last two items produced by one of our most accomplished theatre groups, Parapanda, in close consultation with the research team. E & D Limited, the only woman-owned publishing house in Tanzania, designed and co-published all of our leaflets, posters and publications, including *Food is Politics* (2002). HakiElimu leaders helped desin the cartoons used and supervised the work of the artists. In other words, KIHACHA pulled together and depended upon the creative talent, expertise and commitment of a wide array of individuals and organisations.

An informal loose coalition was also created almost spontaneously around 2000 called the KIHACHA Network, consisting of more than 30 grassroots groups and national NGOs. The network helped plan the KIHACHA campaign, which was launched to the wide public in 2002, and voluntarily disseminated the campaign materials throughout the country, using their own partners at local level. Working closely with the media, videos capturing the images and voices of women and men grassroots activists were shown on national news, denouncing the devastating impact of

As a scholar activist, your contribution to the establishment and support of collective organising in civil society is well known. Which organisations have, in your experience, made a substantial impact, even if short lived, in the struggle to enhance equity and social justice? Who was involved and what was your role in them?

I have been actively involved in several exciting advocacy groups, including Kuleana in Mwanza, HakiElimu, Institute of Development Studies Women Study Group, Women's Research and Documentation Project and TGNP Mtandao [formerly known as Tanzania Gender Networking Programme]. With other organisations, TGNP Mtandao also created and hosted the Feminist Activist Coalition. Let me focus on IDSWSG, WRDP and TGNP Mtandao.

As shown above, the university was a hostile place for any woman who was critical about sexism and wanted to change things. Some of us were desperate to learn more about what causes such intense patriarchal structures and attitudes and behaviour, so as to change them. Out of that desire for space to learn more together, came the seeds of what became the IDS Women Study Group. A small group of women (Tanzanian and non-Tanzanian) began to meet together informally in our homes as a study group in 1978. We read top feminist literature from Europe, North America and Asia and began to concentrate on writings by African feminists. By 1980 our group had expanded and we decided to seek a base in IDS, becoming one of the first IDS study groups, along with two others on rural development and workers.

IDS-WSG grew rapidly to 30 members and met on a weekly basis, with no funding of any kind. The majority were not working at the university, a very important point in our later struggles, and many were not academics; two thirds were Tanzanian. From the start, we worked collectively, with an elected leadership structure; I was elected as the first Convenor. We decided to carry out our own research on the "women's question", and began to prepare proposals for fundraising, working collectively according to themes such as women peasants, women in the media, women and education. The separate research proposals were compiled into one organisational proposal, to which we added basic costs to facilitate the development of a documentation centre – as well as a four wheel drive vehicle to support the research work. We successfully negotiated for a grant from [the] Ford Foundation. Just as we were about to receive the money and the car in 1982, the all-male IDS management team intervened and claimed that all such resources belonged to the institute! They directed that the research funds go to the Institute's Research and Publications Committee which would decide how to allocate them!

A clear case of male domination, oppression and appropriation, this was exactly what happened to the women cooperatives which we had studied in *ujamaa* villages, and now it was happening to us! The group members refused to accept the hijacking of their proposal, and asked the funder to retain the funds until we could access them ourselves. The original IDS-WSG members moved out of the institute and formed an entirely new organisation which was registered independently as the Women's Research and Documentation Project (WRDP) in 1983. WRDP members went on to conduct research, organise a series of workshops with government and civil society leaders to share the results of their analysis, and established the Women's Research and Documentation Centre on the ground floor of the university library, one of the top collections on gender/feminist issues in the nation at that time. For many years WRDP was a leading critical voice on behalf of women's issues and helped to lead Tanzanian women NGOs to the Women's World Forum in Nairobi in 1985.

During the 1980s and 1990s several other women focused organisations were set up at the university, focusing on science and technology and on education. The scientists succeeded to get a change in university student recruitment; with affirmative action to provide pre-first year courses in sciences and mathematics for young women, initiatives later institutionalised within and by the university.

The Kikundi cha Akina Mama Mlimani[39] (KAMM) was an entirely different kind of group which concentrated on improving the welfare of women, children and their families at the university in a practical way. Begun in 1989, one of their major achievements was the setting up of a community library at the UDASA club on the hill which had a strong children's collection. KAMM also organised other children's activities for the campus community, such as film shows, sports and art lessons. Numbering some 20 women, the members of the group lived at the hill; they were not all staff. This provides a creative example of alternative ways of organising.[40]

In 1992 and 1993, a group of about ten women and men came together with me as coordinator to facilitate a triple-A process of reflection and planning for the leaders of top women/gender civil society organisations, in preparation for their participation in the Women's Decade meeting in Beijing in 1995. With the support of the Royal Netherlands Embassy and the NGO SNV (Netherlands Development Organisation), more than 30 women activists shared their experiences and strategies of organising for the promotion of women's rights and gender equity at the national and district levels in three workshops, and planned concrete strategies of action for the future. The combination of rigorous feminist theory and animation methodology led to a high level of analysis and participation, and fostered enthusiastic networking among ourselves and with East African organisations who participated in the 1993 regional preparatory meeting in Kampala.

The results of this analysis and planning were edited by TGNP and published as the first *Gender Profile of Tanzania* in 1993. More important, however, was the demand by participating

---

39 This translates to Women at University Campus.

40 See Marjorie Mbilinyi's chapter, "Transformative Education and the Strengthening of Civil Society" in Haroub Othman (ed) *Reflections on Leadership in Africa* (Dar es Salaam, IDS/UDSM, 2000).

NGOs that a new networking organisation be established by the facilitation committee. In 1993 the Tanzania Gender Networking Programme was established as a membership organisation by the original committee members. We moved into our own office in town, and I became the first Executive Director (then called Coordinator), on leave from the University for three years.

From the start, we were committed to a struggle against patriarchy and neoliberal globalisation which focused on gender, class and imperial/race relationships and their transformation. Eventually we named this transformative feminism. We also were committed to retaining and strengthening a collective process and culture of decision making, drawing on the experience several of us had had in WRDP which was based on group centred leadership rather than the usual leader centred group. The continued reliance on animation and collective decision-making enabled TGNP to sustain itself and grow in spite of many challenges. We adopted concrete activist strategies from the start, along with gender mainstreaming, which enabled TGNP and its partners in the Feminist Activist Coalition to reach out to the wider public on many issues and have our views noted, and in some cases, acted upon. This provided members and staff with a support group and a base for feminist activist work which helped to keep us grounded locally while acting at all levels.[41]

TGNP Mtandao adopted multiple strategies, including training and consciousness-raising using animation approaches; knowledge generation, dissemination and information through participatory action research, multimedia platforms and policy analysis; advocacy work on strategic issues with strategic government sectors/departments, local government authorities and members of Parliament; and media engagement at all levels. Of particular importance is the Intensive Movement Building Cycle, combining participatory action research, support for local knowledge centres and linkages with investigative journalists.

---

41 See Marjorie Mbilinyi, Mary Rusimbi, Chachage S L Chachage & Demere Kitunga (eds) *Activist Voices: Feminist Struggles for an Alternative World* (Dar es Salaam, TGNP & E&D Limited, 2003).

Community activists have succeeded to raise gender/class issues with government and non-government leaders, including the commercial private sector, and through wide media coverage, their demands have been met in many cases. In the process, women and youth leaders in particular have strengthened their negotiation and advocacy skills, as well as their understanding of macro-economic policy, structures and systems.[42]

I remained an active member of TGNP Mtandao after returning to my employment at the University of Dar es Salaam. In 2003, I retired from academia and became the Principal Policy Analyst at TGNP for ten years, devoting much of my time to mentoring younger scholar activists in policy and budget analysis and participatory action research. During its now 24 years of activism, TGNP Mtandao has become one of the most outspoken and visible advocates for gender equity, social justice and women's empowerment in Tanzania and Africa, challenging both patriarchy and capitalist globalisation.

---

42 See Marjorie Mbilinyi "Transformative Feminism in Tanzania: Animation and Grassroots Women's Struggles For Land and Livelihoods" in *Oxford Handbook of Transnational Feminist Movements: Knowledge, Power and Social Change*, ed Rawwida Baksh and Wendy Harcourt, New York: Oxford University Press (2015) and Marjorie Mbilinyi and Gloria Shechambo "Experiences in Transformative Feminist Movement Building at the Grassroots Level in Tanzania" in Akosua Adomako Ampofo, Cheryl R Rodriguez & Dzodzi Tsikata eds *Transatlantic Feminisms: Women and Gender Studies in Africa and the African Diaspora* (Lexington, 2015).

Glossary of Acronyms

AFRC – Armed Forces Revolutionary Council

AMR – Alliance marxiste révolutionnaire

ANC – African National Congress

APC – All People's Congress

APC – All Progressive Congress

APPGAR – All–Party Parliamentary Group for African Reparations

ARM – African Resistance Movement

AU – African Union

CAWDIG – Campaign Against Waste Dumping in Guyana

CNS – Conférence Nationale Souveraine

CODESRIA – African Council of Social Sciences and Development

COSATU – Congress of South African Trade Unions

CPP – Convention People's Party

CSAAWU – Commercial, Stevedoring, Agricultural and Allied Workers Union

CSOs – Civil society organisations

DLF – Democratic Left Front

DRC – Democratic Republic of the Congo

EFF – Economic Freedom Fighters

EHESS – École des hautes études en sciences sociale

EPA – Economic Partnership Agreement

ESRC – Economic and Social Research Council

FAO – Food and Agriculture Organisation

FLN – Front de libération nationale

Frapp – Front for an Anti–Imperialist Popular and Pan–African Revolution

FRELIMO – Mozambique Liberation Front

G40 – Generation 40

GCMHP – Gaza Community Mental Health Programme

GM – Genetically Modified

GMB – Grain Marketing Board

GMHCG – Granby Mental Health Community Group

GMO – Genetically Modified Organism

GND – Green New Deal

IDS – Institute of Development Studies

IDS–WSG – Institute of Development Studies – Women Study Group

IS – International Socialism Group

ISIS – Islamic State

ISSA – Information Centre on Southern Africa

IUS – International Union of Students

JACON – Joint Action Committee of Nigeria

JC – Jeunesse communiste

KAMM – Kikundi cha Akina Mama Mlimani

KARLO – Kenya Agricultural and Livestock Research Organisation

KNRG – Kwame Nkrumah Revolutionary Guards

KOAN – Kenya Organic Agriculture Network

KPL – Kenyan Peasants League

LASCO – Labour and Civil Society Coalition

LUCHA – Lutte pour le changement

MAAS – Movement for the Advancement of African Society

MDC – Movement for Democratic Change

MONAS – Movement on National Affairs

MPLA – Popular Movement for the Liberation of Angola

NANS – National Association of Nigerian Students

NAVODA – Navigators of Development Association

NCL – National Committee of Liberation

NCP – National Conscience Party

NIA – National Intelligence Agency DRC

NLC – National Liberation Council

NLC – Nigerian Labour Congress

NNPC – Nigerian National Petroleum Corporation

NPP – New Patriotic Party

NUGS – National Union of Ghana Students

NUMSA – National Union of Metalworkers of South Africa

NUNS – National Union of Nigerian Students

NUPENG – Nigeria Union of Petroleum and Natural Gas Workers

NYSC – National Youth Service

OAU – Organisation of African Unity

ODG – Overseas Development Group

OSAE – Observatory of Food Sovereignty and Environment

PAC – Pan–Africanist Congress

PAI – Parti africain de l'indépendance

PAIGC – Partido Africano para a Independência da Guiné e Cabo Verde

PCP – Portuguese Communist

Party
PCPB – Pest Control Products Board
PDP – People's Democratic Party
PENGASSAN – Petroleum and Natural Gas Senior Staff Association of Nigeria
PF – People First
PFLP – Popular Front for the Liberation of Palestine
PIDE – Polícia Internacional e de Defesa do Estado
PLO – Palestine Liberation Organisation
PNC – People's National Congress
PNDC – Provisional National Defence Council
PP – Progress Party
PPP – People's Progressive Party
RASD – Arab Democratic Republic
RDP – Reconstruction and Development Programme
ROAPE – *Review of African Political Economy*
RRN – Rural Reconstruction Nepal
RSL – Revolutionary Socialist League
SACP – South African Communist Party
SAMWU – South African Municipal Workers Union
SAPs – Structural Adjustment Programs
SASO – South African Students' Organisation
SDS – Sozialistische Deutsche Studentenbund
Senelec – National Electricity Company of Senegal
SMAU – Students Movement for African Unity
SMBs – Small and medium-sized businesses
SNV – Netherlands Development Organisation
SRC – Student Representative Councils
SWAPO – South West Africa People's Organisation
SWP – Socialist Workers' Party
SWPP – Socialist Working People's Party
TANU – Tanganyika African National Union
TCLPAC – Toronto Committee for the Liberation of Portugal's African Colonies
TCLSAC – Toronto Committee for the Liberation of Southern Africa
TGNP – Tanzania Gender Network Programme
TUC – Trade Union Congress
TWR – *Third World Review*
UCT – University of Cape Town
UDASA – University of Dar es Salaam Academic Staff Assembly
UDF – United Democratic Front
UDPS – Union for Democracy

and Social Progress

UDSM – University of Dar es Salaam

UEA – University of East Anglia

UEC – Union des étudiants communistes

ULC – United Labour Congress

UML – United Marxist–Leninist Party

UNEF – Union nationale des étudiants de France

UP – United Party

UPOV – Union for the Protection of Plant Varieties

WIN – Women in Nigeria

WPA – Working People's Alliance

WRDP – Women Research and Documentation Project

XR – Extinction Rebellion

ZANLA – Zimbabwe African National Liberation Army

ZANU – Zimbabwe African National Union

ZIPRA – Zimbabwe People's Revolutionary Army

Index

A

AIDS 16, 354, 377

Algeria ii, 41, 181-182, 184, 185, 189-190, 193, 206, 472

Amin, Samir 21, 171-172, 176, 184, 194, 201, 221, 251, 253-255, 292, 297, 308, 414

ANC, African National Congress iii, 6-10, 13, 14, 18, 41, 42, 43, 46, 48, 123, 160, 161, 164, 166, 167, 318, 373, 374, 375, 377, 378, 379, 382, 384, 386, 390, 507

Angola ii-iv, 15, 17, 40-46, 51, 107, 125, 131-133, 136, 142, 205-206, 301, 405

Anti-capitalism i, vi, 2, 5, 12, 14, 204, 207, 233, 239, 241-242, 246, 251, 341, 379, 380

Anti-colonialism 27-29, 31-34, 83, 126, 208, 245

Apartheid 2, 5, 7-8, 10, 13, 15-18, 24, 43-44, 46, 54, 64, 120, 127, 160-162, 166, 168, 198, 265, 294, 301, 317-318, 328, 349, 374-377, 401, 425, 436, 493

APC, All Progressive Congress 438, 439, 444-445

B

Biko v, 160-165, 168, 374

Black Lives Matter 130, 187, 223, 300, 308, 344-345

Black Power 61, 70-71, 86, 272

Britain 7, 26, 28, 29, 31, 32, 42, 50, 76, 81, 83-84, 86, 88-92, 95, 97, 99, 121, 156-157, 159, 207, 222, 241, 264, 266-267, 275, 277, 291-292, 300-301, 303, 305, 313, 328, 331, 340-341, 344-345, 352, 359, 362, 403-405, 424-430, 433-434, 463, 499

Burkina Faso 42, 107, 141, 155, 262, 417, 421, 456

C

Cabral, Amílcar iii-vi 4, 30, 58, 107, 114-116, 126, 129, 130-140, 227, 272-273, 292, 296, 417

Canada 2-4, 15-20, 23-24, 54, 102, 208, 293

Cape Verde 107, 116, 131, 133, 136, 140, 206

Capitalism i, vi, 2, 4- 6, 10-12, 14, 18, 21-22, 32, 55, 63, 77, 79, 80, 158-159, 162, 166, 170-171, 173-174, 194, 202-208, 210-214, 216-223, 226-227, 230, 233-234, 239-242, 245-246, 248, 251, 254, 262, 272, 274, 281, 283-284, 293, 294-297, 304, 308-309, 316, 325, 334, 338, 341, 347, 354-356, 358, 375-376, 379-380, 386, 391-392, 411, 414, 423, 430, 434, 436, 438, 442, 445-447, 450-451, 458, 483-484, 491, 493, 495, 500, 506

Césaire, Aimé 30, 137

China 15, 30, 35, 46-47, 113, 138, 188, 203-204, 206-207, 211, 217, 221-222, 244, 261, 305, 338, 357, 423

Class struggle i, iv, 11-12, 24, 160, 193, 229, 233, 336-337, 341-342, 389, 391, 447

CNS, Conférence Nationale Souveraine 102-105, 108, 113

Colonialism iii, 4, 24, 29, 32, 34, 41, 63-64, 80, 110, 114, 116, 122, 124-125, 127, 130, 132, 134-135, 138-139, 149, 158, 185-187, 224, 285, 300-301, 304, 308, 325, 329, 345, 386, 389, 391, 423, 435, 493, 500

Communism 26, 29-30

Communist International 29, 30-32, 34, 157

COSATU, Congress of South African Trade Unions 7-8, 14, 374-375, 377-379, 382, 384-386

Covid-19 68, 75-76, 82, 236, 261, 307, 344, 371, 458, 465

CPP, Convention People's Party 146, 150, 158

Cuba 35, 42, 45-46, 64, 138, 193, 204-205, 221-222, 357

D

Decolonial 61, 65, 68-69, 71, 424, 426

Decolonisation 72, 114, 126, 164, 186, 270, 285-287, 298, 307-308, 352, 387-388, 390-391, 466

Delinking 21, 212-213, 226-227, 256

Diaspora 26, 29-30, 56, 61, 110, 506

DRC, Democratic Republic of the Congo 25, 104-105, 110, 114, 117, 366-367, 372

E

EFF, Economic Freedom Fighters 164-167, 389-391

Egypt ii, 201-202, 206, 214, 307, 343-344, 466-468, 473-474, 478

EHESS, École des hautes études en sciences sociale 192, 195, 197, 198, 199

Environment 237, 466, 485, 490, 508

ESRC, Economic and Social Research Council 299, 333, 507

Ethiopia 33-34, 42, 275-276

European Union 145, 241, 291-292, 295, 305, 412, 422-423

F

Fanon, Frantz iii, 4, 30, 69, 74, 100, 114-116, 140, 161, 171, 180-187, 232, 236, 272-273, 302, 391

Feminism 165, 232, 280, 287, 319, 487, 490, 505

Front de libération nationale FLN 183-184, 190

Fourth International 189-190

France 31, 40-41, 48, 50, 69, 79, 107, 111-112, 114-115, 117, 121, 137, 139-140, 145, 180-184, 188-189, 190-199, 202, 206-207, 211, 251, 255-256, 261-263, 303, 329-330, 367, 413-414, 416-423, 464

Frapp, Front for an Anti–Imperialist Popular and Pan–African Revolution 413, 415-417

G

G40, Generation 40 395-396, 507

Gaddafi, Muammar 264, 271, 344

Gambia 421-422

Gender 5, 11, 15, 22, 127, 132, 165, 232, 251, 267-268, 276-278, 283, 314, 317, 323-324, 386, 487, 490-499, 503-506

Genocide 118, 120, 127-128, 421, 428, 430, 438, 463

Germany 118, 120-121, 123-124, 128, 293, 300

Ghana ii, v, 42, 107, 146-152, 155-158, 159, 161, 192, 267, 270, 401-405, 409, 412, 426

Globalisation 207-208, 213-214, 337-338, 353, 376, 499, 502, 505, 506

Green New Deal, GND 239, 241, 248

Guinea ii, 33, 61, 193, 272, 418, 422

Guinea-Bissau iii, 107, 129,

131-134, 136-137, 140, 142

Guyana 59, 61, 66-67, 69-71, 81-84, 86-99, 424

I

IMF, International Monetary Fund 132, 146, 157, 274, 337-338, 353, 364, 394, 406, 450, 456-457

Imperialism vi, 2, 5, 28, 31-32, 46-47, 55, 58, 115, 142, 145, 148, 155, 195, 213, 226-227, 237, 239, 302, 354, 378, 389, 402, 416-418, 420-421, 423, 452

Independence ii-iii, 4, 41, 44-45, 52, 56, 81-83, 107-111, 113, 121, 123-124, 126, 129, 131, 134-135, 138, 140, 147, 149, 161, 170, 173, 181, 183, 190, 198, 205-206, 208, 227, 246, 257, 261, 263, 270, 327, 332, 365, 372, 398, 405, 413, 419, 431, 450, 455, 467

ISSA, Information Centre on Southern Africa 120, 122-124

J

JACON, Joint Action Committee of Nigeria 350, 438, 508

K

Kenya vi, 41, 55-56, 58-59, 106, 177, 192, 197, 232-233, 236, 280, 284, 307, 452-459, 461-464, 491

KPL, Kenyan Peasants League 452-453, 458, 465

L

Lenin, VI 32, 55, 58, 138-139, 217, 295, 438, 491

Libya 264, 271, 337, 343-344

Lumumba, Patrice 100, 105-109, 113, 115-116, 368, 371-372, 431

M

Mali 106, 147, 202, 206, 261-264, 421

Marx, Karl 10, 58, 79, 112, 115, 169, 177, 207, 214, 216-217, 220, 229, 254, 267, 293, 295, 342, 389, 391, 402, 418, 470

Marxism iii, 30, 42, 54-55, 59, 61, 64-65, 68, 71, 83, 108, 137, 143, 147, 161, 164-165, 172, 176-177, 191, 193-195, 197-199, 201, 207, 210, 216-218, 220-221, 225, 228-229, 253, 291-292, 295, 299, 308-309, 318, 329-331, 334, 336, 339, 340-342, 347-349, 356-357, 374, 389-390, 402, 436, 472, 483 490, 492, 495

Mauritania 291, 421-422

MDC, Movement for Democratic Change 15, 396, 400, 508

Morocco 41, 107, 327, 329-330, 332-333, 337, 469, 472

Mozambique ii-iii, 2-4, 15, 22, 41, 46, 107, 124-125, 136, 142, 191, 198, 205-206, 301, 329, 332, 405

MPLA, Popular Movement for the Liberation of Angola 41, 45, 47, 52

N

Namibia 5, 15, 17, 44-45, 47, 118, 120, 122-128, 307

Nationalism 8, 67, 92, 105, 115, 126-127, 129, 131-132, 135-136, 149, 181, 183, 193, 214, 219, 225, 352, 375, 389, 391, 416, 495

NATO, North Atlantic Treaty Organization 17, 207-208, 263

NAVODA, Navigators of Development Association 313, 316, 508

NCP, National Conscience Party 350-351, 438

Neocolonialism 67, 80, 262, 407, 415-416, 418, 430- 432, 434

Neoliberalism 6, 20, 43, 124, 144, 150-151, 160, 162-163, 218-220, 223, 226, 253, 256, 262-263, 273-274, 283, 291, 298, 300, 306-307, 310, 312, 315, 335, 338, 353, 355, 375-376, 378, 390, 393, 395-397, 401, 406-407, 410-411, 430, 432, 434, 438, 441, 461, 484, 487, 499, 502, 505

Nigeria v-vi, 110-111, 147, 192, 196, 266-270, 273, 275-276, 312, 347, 350-361, 436-440, 443-450,

Nkrumah, Kwame ii, 28-30, 58, 107, 131, 137, 142, 146-152, 157, 302, 358, 391, 402, 427, 430-432, 493

NUGS, National Union of Ghana Students 147-148, 153, 402

NUMSA, National Union of Metalworkers of South Africa 379-380, 384-385

Nyerere, Julius ii, 47-48, 67, 161, 170-171, 173, 224-225, 306, 373

O

OSAE, Observatory of Food Sovereignty and Environment 466, 485-486

P

PAC, Pan-Africanist Congress

160-161

222

Padmore, George 30-31, 34, 97

PAIGC, Partido Africano para a Independência da Guiné e Cabo Verde 133-134, 138-139

Palestine 43, 48-51, 243, 304, 332, 335

Pan-Africanism 26, 29-30, 57, 61, 65, 69, 137, 147, 149, 151, 157, 401, 413, 415, 427, 431

Patriarchy 165, 233-234, 236, 324, 386, 487-488, 495, 499-500, 502, 505-506

PCF, Communist Party of France 189, 191, 195-196

PDP, People's Democratic Party 440, 444-445

Peasantry 45, 64, 186, 192, 213, 216-220, 226, 254, 281, 297, 314, 452, 455, 466-467, 469-473, 484-485, 491-492, 499, 501

PNC, People's National Congress 83, 87-88, 90, 92, 94-99

PNDC, Provisional National Defence Council 147, 152-154, 159, 403

Portugal 16-17, 65, 116, 119, 129-130, 136-138, 140, 198, 206,

Poverty 6, 46-47, 66, 75, 79, 162, 258, 274, 281, 302, 316, 355, 366, 394, 414, 421, 423, 439, 440, 444

PPP, People's Progressive Party 82-83, 87, 90, 92, 98

Protests i, v, 9-10, 50, 59, 69, 77-78, 82, 91, 110, 130, 141, 160-161, 164-165, 187, 196, 245, 257, 259-260, 275, 282, 284, 292, 306, 315, 317-321, 323, 336-337, 341-343, 353, 369-370, 376, 379, 407, 410, 413, 416, 418, 442, 444

R

Rawlings, Jerry 42, 146-148, 150-157, 403, 404, 409

Reagan, Ronald 18, 44, 54, 300

Rhodes Must Fall 145, 319-324, 389

ROAPE, Review of African Political Economy i, iii-iv, 2, 26, 35-36, 44, 50, 60, 67, 81, 100, 105, 109, 121, 141, 160, 169, 173, 176, 188, 198, 204-205, 216, 230, 237, 240, 251, 255, 265, 273, 275, 277, 290, 292-293, 298, 304-305, 307, 311, 313, 317, 326, 333, 337, 341-342, 347, 359, 396, 401, 403-409, 474, 487

Rodney, Walter v, 53, 56-64, 66-78, 81, 84-86, 90-99, 130, 171, 272-273, 294, 296, 329, 331, 427

Russia 204, 217, 221, 261, 337, 357-358, 491

Russian Revolution 33, 61, 63, 201, 225

S

SACP, South African Communist Party iii, 7-8, 14, 374, 377-379, 382, 384-386, 390

Sankara, Thomas 47-48, 107, 155, 253

Senegal i, v-vi, 141-142, 144-145, 188-189, 192-194, 198, 251-253, 256-262, 291, 413-423

Senghor, Leopold Sedar 137, 142-144, 195, 256-257, 413, 419

Sierra Leone 29, 265-267, 269-271, 274-276

Slavery 426, 500

Socialism ii-iv, 2-3, 4, 6, 11-12, 19-23, 29, 31, 81, 86, 89, 93, 125, 146, 148, 150-151, 156, 161, 171, 173-174, 190-191, 193-194, 198, 201-207, 209-210, 212-214, 216-219, 221-223, 225-226, 230, 232-234, 239, 241, 246-249, 255-256, 266, 268, 292, 296-297, 304, 331, 347, 349, 352, 354, 357, 373-375, 378, 380-381, 384-386, 391, 393, 396, 400, 410, 436-438, 467, 488, 490, 493, 498

South Africa i, iv, 2, 5-6, 8-10, 12-15, 18, 24, 31, 40- 42, 44-47, 52, 64, 69, 107, 122-123, 125, 160-162, 164, 168, 198-199, 206, 222, 227-228, 265, 275-276, 301, 317-319, 321, 324, 329, 341, 349, 358, 361, 373, 376, 378-381, 383-384, 386, 389-390, 395, 397, 435-436, 453, 499

Spain 41, 49, 291

Stalinism 8, 161, 177, 191, 193, 195, 210, 357, 358, 390-391

SWAPO, South West Africa People's Organisation 41, 45-46, 123, 125, 127

T

Tanzania ii, iv-vi, 2-4, 21, 61, 66, 68, 85, 161, 169-171, 173, 175, 198, 206, 224, 226, 315, 329, 331, 373, 487-488, 491-492, 494-496, 498, 500-502, 504-506

TGNP, Tanzania Gender Network Programme 496, 502, 504-506

Thatcher, Margaret 18, 44

Tunisia 180-185, 242, 307, 337,

343, 466-469, 471-473, 475, 478, 482-483

TWR, *Third World Review* 42-43, 48

U

UCT, University of Cape Town 319-320, 328

UDSM, University of Dar es Salaam 488-489, 491, 496, 504

UEA, University of East Anglia 330-332, 335-336, 341

Uganda 42, 109, 177, 206, 267, 280-282, 311-312, 314-315, 327-328

UK, see Britain

United States 25, 28-29, 32, 38-40, 42, 44-46, 49-50, 53, 64, 70-71, 75-79, 97, 100-102, 104, 110, 114, 117-118, 121, 130, 139, 187-190, 195, 208, 211-213, 232, 237, 239, 241, 246, 248, 263, 293, 300-301, 303, 305, 335, 340, 417, 423, 431, 460

V

Vietnam 4, 38-41, 46, 51, 64, 76, 78, 118-119, 142, 160, 204-205, 221, 244, 301, 401, 460

W

Wallace-Johnson, Isaac 28-30

Women 161, 165, 232, 235-236, 268, 276, 284, 398, 434, 463, 490, 492, 494-496, 500, 502-504, 506

World Bank 119, 146, 157, 212-213, 274, 281, 337-338, 364, 406, 422, 456, 458

WPA, Working People's Alliance 81, 86-97, 99

WRDP, Women Research and Documentation Project 496, 500, 502-503, 505

Z

Zambia 101, 121, 265, 362, 373

ZANU, Zimbabwe African National Union 15, 46, 332, 373, 395

Zimbabwe vi, 5, 15, 46, 67, 98, 121-122, 124-125, 222, 307, 332, 373, 393-400

Printed in the USA
CPSIA information can be obtained
at www.ICGtesting.com
CBHW011615220324
5718CB00010B/114